GREAT CHRISTIAN THINKERS

EDITOR: PETER VARDY

GW00570395

Fount

An Imprint of HarperCollins*Publishers*

Fount is an Imprint of
HarperCollins*Religious*
Part of HarperCollins*Publishers*
77–85 Fulham Palace Road, London W6 8JB

This edition first published in Great Britain in 1999
by Fount Paperbacks

Individual titles originally published in the
Fount Christian Thinkers Series as follows:
Augustine by Richard Price first published in 1996
by Fount Paperbacks, copyright © 1996 Richard Price
Francis & Bonaventure by Paul Rout first published in 1996
by Fount Paperbacks, copyright © 1996 Paul Rout
John of the Cross by Wilfrid McGreal first published in 1996
by Fount Paperbacks, copyright © 1996 Wilfrid McGreal
Thomas More by Anne Murphy first published in 1996
by Fount Paperbacks, copyright © 1996 Anne Murphy
Luther by Hans-Peter Grosshans first published in 1997
by Fount Paperbacks, copyright © 1997 Hans-Peter Grosshans
Introduction copyright © 1999 Peter Vardy

1 3 5 7 9 10 8 6 4 2

A catalogue record for this book is
available from the British Library

ISBN 0 00 628134 6

Printed and bound in Great Britain by
Caledonian International Book Manufacturing Ltd, Glasgow

Contents

DR PETER VARDY

The editor, Dr Peter Vardy, lectures in
Philosophy of Religion at Heythrop College,
University of London. He is Course Director
of the University of London's External BD
programme and a former Chair of the
Theology Faculty Board. Other books by Dr
Vardy published by Fount Paperbacks are
The Puzzle of God, *The Puzzle of Evil*, *The
Puzzle of Ethics*, *The Puzzle of the Gospels* and
The Puzzle of Sex.

Introduction

For two millennia, great thinkers in the Christian tradition have wrestled with issues of theology, morality, politics, warfare and spirituality. Writing under various political and Church regimes and responding to the situations in which they found themselves, they sought to show the relevance of the Christian tradition to all aspects of life. Never superficial, these thinkers were amongst the finest minds in Europe. In this book, six of the most influential figures have been brought together. They do not deal with the same issues, but they share a single Christian commitment and vision, albeit one that is expressed in different ways.

It is a matter for regret that none of these six thinkers are women. The sad fact is that the most influential thinkers up until recently have been male. This is not a cause for pride and, indeed, represents a regrettable failure on the part of the Christian tradition. However, the aim of this volume is to bring together some of the most significant writers and the six included here have been chosen irrespective of gender.

St Augustine, Bishop of Hippo, wrote at a turning point in Western history. The Roman Empire under Constantine had recently become Christian and, instead of being a persecuted minority, Christians suddenly found themselves part of the official religion of the Empire. Augustine had to wrestle with many views which he did not consider to be orthodox – the Pelagians, the Manichaeans, the Donatists and others all put forward views which are echoed by modern writers today. Richard Price concisely sets out Augustine's responses in the context of his whole theology. Augustine's ideas, which were generally accepted by the Church, became the benchmarks for what was orthodox and what was heretical. This was not always a happy situation – Augustine's views on women and sexuality have cast a long and unhelpful shadow over the Christian tradition.

St Francis of Assisi is generally regarded by many as the single individual who came closest to living as Jesus might have done and has had a profound impact on succeeding generations. However, Francis himself was not an academic, and St Bonaventure, one of the first Generals of the Franciscan order, was the person who expressed the distinctive Franciscan approach to theology more clearly than anyone else. There were two great Professors at the University of Paris at the same time – one was St Thomas Aquinas, a Dominican, and the other was Bonaventure. Aquinas looked to the Greek philosopher, Aristotle, for his inspiration whereas Bonaventure's theology started with the Trinity. Although the Church eventually sided with the Dominicans against the Franciscans, some now hold that this was one of the greatest mistakes in Church history. A Franciscan approach might have given a very different flavour to modern understandings of morality and theology. Paul Rout, a leading Franciscan theologian, succinctly captures the distinctiveness of the Franciscan and Bonaventurian tradition.

Christianity has been a religion that has always valued the role of reason and hence of philosophy – but it has also prized the spiritual dimension of life and towering figures such as St John of the Cross, a Carmelite, have expressed this clearly. John of the Cross was a remarkable man who was persecuted and imprisoned by his own Order, who saw him as a threat. He was a poet and was inspired partly by his close friendship with Teresa of Avila. Too few today, however, understand the background against which he was writing or the radical nature of his poetry and imagery. A modern Carmelite, Wilfrid McGreal, explains his significance not just for the time in which he was writing but also for today.

St Thomas More was an unlikely man to be a saint. He was a Christian humanist (although that term had a specific meaning which is rather different from the way it is used today). He loved life, was a family man and a politician. He was driven to martyrdom by a King who was his friend and whom he wished to serve faithfully. He was a close friend of Erasmus and stood for a particularly broad and liberal understanding of Christianity – a Christianity that was fully engaged with the world. However, he provides us with an example of someone wrestling with the thorny issue of individual conscience and how this is validated in the face of the demands of wife, family, community and secular powers. He was willing to go to his death on an issue of principle, but much more than this, he stood for a vision of humanity which his conscience did not allow him to gainsay. Anne Murphy sensitively chronicles not only More's dispute with King Henry VIII but also sets this dispute in the wider context without which it cannot properly be understood.

More and Erasmus stand at one pole of European Christian thought; Martin Luther stands at another. He, also, was a man for whom individual conscience reigned supreme, but he was led in a different direction. No other single figure has had such a decisive influence on the Reformation and the rejection of much of the scholastic theology that had arisen in the Middle Ages. Luther called people to faithful adherence to the Bible and rejected celibacy, indulgences and many perceived abuses in the Church. He was radical and yet humble and his legacy is widely recognized. Hans-Peter Grosshans charts the influences on Luther and his whole understanding of Christianity, which represented such a radical break with many of these ideas which had become accepted and set in stone.

These figures have helped to shape our intellectual heritage and our present culture. Their relevance is not just for their own time but also for today.

Dr Peter Vardy
Heythrop College
University of London

AUGUSTINE

Richard Price

Augustine

RICHARD PRICE

Dr Richard M. Price is Head of the Department of Church History at Heythrop College, University of London. His previous publications include editions of Greek monastic texts and articles on a broad range of topics in Early Church History. As a priest in the Diocese of Westminster he has wide experience of modern catechetical and pastoral problems.

Contents

Abbreviations

Date Chart

Life of Augustine		General Events
	258	Death of Cyprian of Carthage
	270	Death of Plotinus
	277	Death of Mani
	312	Start of the Donatist Schism
	312	Conversion of the emperor Constantine
354 Birth at Thagaste in Africa		
	356	Death of Antony of Egypt
373 Read's Cicero's *Hortensius*; becomes a Manichaean 'hearer'		
	374–97	Ambrose Bishop of Milan
384 Goes to Milan		
386 Conversion		
387 Baptized by Ambrose		
387 Death of Monica		
388 Returns to Africa		
391 Ordained priest at Hippo		
395 Consecrated bishop		

Introduction

A short book on Augustine is likely to be superficial and will certainly not be comprehensive. The range of his writing covered the whole field of theology, and much philosophy as well. Its sheer bulk is daunting: more of Augustine survives than of any other ancient writer. Nor have his works slept on the shelves through the centuries in dusty repose, for no western theologian has had so strong and wide an influence: he was considered the greatest of the Church Fathers in the Middle Ages and was hugely respected by the Protestant Reformers as well. Attention to his thought has been one of the constant threads in western intellectual history. On a whole range of issues, from the most sublime (the doctrine of the Trinity) to the most earthy (sex and marriage), present-day theologians may disagree with Augustine but cannot ignore him. Disagree they often do. Thomas Allin wrote, back in 1911, 'This great man's influence extended for evil, as his writings show, over practically the whole field of human activity, social and political no less than religious' (*The Augustinian Revolution in Theology*). Such negative judgements, though generally not so sweeping, have recurred throughout this century. At least they serve to keep Augustinian studies alive. Whether or not one likes the ideas of Augustine, everyone with a serious interest in Christian thought has sooner or later to come to grips with them.

Fortunately, Augustine is not only an important writer: he is also a very engaging one, with a style that is both clear and persuasive. No theologian in the history of the Church has been less academic in the bad sense of the word: he was a pastoral bishop who related theological reflections to practical needs, and at the same time a passionate and restless individual, who wrote with a depth and intensity that speak to us directly. A good number of his chief works have been excellently translated into English, and are easier to read than many modern books about him.

Despite the range of his ideas and the breadth of his influence there is a limited repertoire of quotations from Augustine likely at any time to crop up in preaching or popular writing. The two most familiar both come from the *Confessions*, his famous intellectual autobiography; they are worth discussing, since both can be deceptive. Augustine tells us in this work that in his adolescence he used to pray, 'Lord, make me chaste, but not yet' (co 8.7.17). Very soon he set up house with a mistress with whom he lived for over twelve years. All this can give an impression of an unhealthy personality with an overcharged sex drive, but we need to learn from the historians, who tell us that in Augustine's time living with a mistress was normal and acceptable for a young man on the make, who needed to postpone marriage till he had attained the top of the professional ladder and could marry an heiress (for, as the saying goes, 'don't marry money, but marry where money is'). Less revealing than Augustine's having a mistress is the way he remained faithful to her throughout their relationship. By the standards of the end of the twentieth century the sexual life of the young Augustine was quite unremarkable.

The other all too familiar quotation from the *Confessions* comes on the very first page, where Augustine says to God, 'You have made us for yourself, and our heart is restless until it rests in you.' When a preacher starts off with the words, 'As St Augustine says', in nine cases out of ten this quotation duly follows, as the congregation either purrs or groans. This passage on its own is misleading: it calls up a picture of a sweetly pious Augustine basking in the consolations of religion. But he was at all times an earnest and unquiet spirit; a perpetual seeker, he constantly raised difficult questions and expected no peace till the grave. He also stressed the need to pray at all times and never presume that our salvation is sure.

Those, and they are many, for whom spiritual reflection is primarily an exercise in conjuring up consoling and reassuring fantasies, should be warned off Augustine; but those who appreciate profound and often disturbing reflection on human nature, the workings of God, Christian community, and a host of other vital topics, may be advised to turn to him. I can assure them that they will find much to inspire them and much to infuriate them, and all of it should stimulate them to reflect more deeply on the content of Christian truth and the nature of Christian commitment.

The Path to the Truth

The Conversions of Augustine

Augustine was born in AD 354 in a small town, Thagaste (modern Souk Ahras, in eastern Algeria, forty miles from the sea), in the Roman province of Africa (Tunisia with parts of Algeria and Libya), at a time when the Roman control of the lands round the Mediterranean, and northwards up to Hadrian's Wall and the natural frontiers of the Rhine and the Danube, was still secure. Augustine writes of his parents in terms that reveal a certain coldness towards his father, Patricius, and a close bond with his mother, the pious and possessive Monica. The family was not well off, but the help of a rich neighbour enabled Augustine to proceed, at the age of seventeen, from the usual schooling to the University of Carthage. There he studied the standard subject of Roman higher education, rhetoric – the art of how to speak and write correct and eloquent Latin, on the basis of a careful study of the best literary models. The subject was immensely practical for members of the governing class of the empire and those who hoped to rise into its ranks, since the courtesy and persuasiveness of good Latin prose were essential tools in public life. Augustine did so well at these studies that he went on to teach them himself, holding a series of important chairs of rhetoric at Carthage, Rome, and finally Milan (384–86), which happened at this time to be the seat of the imperial government of Italy and Africa. As the teacher of the sons of the nobility, he could make all the right contacts, and by 386 a provincial governorship and advantageous marriage were pleasantly within reach.

But let us turn from his career to his religious development. His mother was a devout Christian, and enrolled him at his birth as a 'catechumen' in the Church. This meant, strictly, someone enrolled for eventual baptism; but the decision was made to postpone the boy's baptism till he was past the dangerous years of adolescence. Augustine the bishop came to deplore this delay, as implying a lack of faith in the power of the sacrament, but since baptism was understood as not merely a rite of entry into the Church but a solemn undertaking to live a virtuous life, the postponement was certainly prudent. As it was, he grew up connected to the Church by a sort of ethnic loyalty but without committing himself personally.

It was in 373 that he had his first religious crisis, sparked off (oddly perhaps) by one of his set books at university, Cicero's *Hortensius* (written in 45 BC), a call to people to renounce 'the vices and errors of mankind' and devote themselves to the philosopher's quest for truth. The young Augustine did not feel up to self-renunciation – the delights of the flesh and of a growing reputation as a brilliant student were too attractive – but his intellectual interests now took a serious turn. Being a Christian, he first turned to the Bible, which, like many Christians in any age, he had never opened. On finding the contents obscure, contradictory and at times repulsive, he fell easy prey to a semi-Christian sect he happened to meet at just this time, the sect of the Manichees, founded by one Mani in Persia a century before. At no stage of his religious wanderings was Augustine prepared to abandon belief in Christ, but the Manichees professed to be Christians and took a keen interest in the epistles of St Paul (as often, a dangerous sign). Their religion, however, was unlike that of either the Bible or the Church: it taught a radical dualism, or division, between not merely right and wrong, saints and sinners, but between two cosmic principles, of light and of darkness, that eternally confront each other. The teaching of the sect offered an account of the origin, nature and destiny of human beings which expressed rather movingly a sense of alienation in a seemingly oppressive universe. Unfortunately it also suffered from an over-complexity reminiscent of science fiction at its worst.

How could such a system appeal to the young Augustine, and indeed retain his loyalty for a decade? One reason was the sexual renunciation of many members of the sect, which seemed unique to them, since monasticism had not yet reached the province of Africa. Like many young men, he experienced feelings of compulsion and guilt in his own sexual life, and was deeply impressed by chastity. It was a major bonus that, while fully initiated members of the sect had to renounce sex and the world, second-class membership was available to the so-called 'hearers', who admired and assisted the renunciation of the few without having to imitate it; Augustine became one of these, and so was able to continue his career and keep his mistress. Another element in the appeal of Manichaeism was the effectiveness of its attacks on the Church for accepting the whole of the Bible as the Word of God. How could the Old Testament, with its primitive picture of God and shocking stories of debauchery, be part of divine revelation? And the Church defended it not by answering the problems but by claiming a unique authority given by God that excluded rational inquiry. In contrast, the Manichees promised to justify their teachings by reason alone, and their bold and plausible criticisms of the Old Testament seemed a promising start.

As, however, Augustine gradually explored the positive teaching of the sect, doubts set in. When for a time he studied astrology (which, by the way, didn't impress him), he discovered that the astronomical data with which the Manichaean myths were larded were often wildly inaccurate. It was mortifying to discover that Manichaean myths were just as open to criticism as the biblical ones he had rejected in their favour. For a few years (382 to 386) he was in the painful position of having lost faith in Manichaeism without finding faith in any other system.

Fortunately, on arriving in Milan (in 384) he became acquainted with a group of intellectuals who had developed a sophisticated variety of Christianity that combined membership of the Church with a non-literal understanding of the Bible that evaded the criticisms of the literal meaning advanced by the Manichees. This Milanese group interpreted the myths of the Old Testament in the light of Neoplatonism, a development at the hands of Plotinus (third century AD) of the speculations of Plato (fourth century BC) that by Augustine's time had become the dominant form of Greek philosophy. Augustine became a member of this group; for the next few years we may call him a Christian Platonist.

His immediate debt to Platonism was that it cured him of Manichaean dualism. In the Manichaean system good and evil are viewed as two cosmic substances or powers, greater than man, locked in indecisive combat. One effect of this combat is that the 'good soul' within each one of us finds itself imprisoned in a 'Realm of Darkness' that has invaded the 'Realm of Light'. Manichaeism promised that the good soul would eventually be set free and reunited to its heavenly source. The young Augustine, oppressed by a sense of his own wickedness, was pleasantly reassured by a doctrine that attributed moral weakness not to the fault of the individual but to the presence within him of an evil power beyond his control. 'It still seemed to me that it is not we who sin but some other nature sins in us; in my pride it was a great joy to be free of guilt' (Co 5.10.18). But reassurance was bought at a heavy price: if the good is so passive and helpless before the forces of evil, how can one be confident that it will ever be set free?

It was therefore a joy to Augustine to discover the metaphysics of Neoplatonism. This system thought evil not a power or substance on the same level as the good (as in Manichaeism), but something without concrete existence. Whatever is, is good, and 'evil' is simply the absence of good; it can be defined as a deprivation or deficiency, in a being that has become corrupted. Evil is weakness and decay, and we can define it only in terms of the order and harmony from which it is a falling away; it is not some independent power, pitted against goodness in some battle between opposites, as dualism falsely supposes. This notion of deprivation, of evil as loss, appealed strongly to Augustine because it fitted in with his deepest instincts about the nature of moral evil: in choosing the wrong, we are not gaining something positive, that God is rather mean to deny us, but losing sight of real fulfilment, as we become entrapped in compulsive behaviour which cramps and diminishes us as human beings.

In embracing Manichaeism the young Augustine had not thought of himself as giving up Christianity: he had always viewed Manichaeism as a form of Christianity rather than a different religion. And his adoption of Platonism as an answer to Manichaeism does not mean that he now thought Christianity an optional extra: Platonism never claimed to be a self-sufficient system that made religion unnecessary. In the fourth century the choice lay between Christianity and paganism, and paganism had never for a moment attracted him. The decision he made when he finally broke with Manichaeism was to become a member of the Church and embrace the religion of his mother (who had come to Italy to live with him). He made this choice a public commitment by applying for baptism, and receiving the sacrament from Bishop Ambrose of Milan in the following spring (Easter 387).

Baptism meant far more to him than simply joining the Church: he resigned his chair of rhetoric at the same time and gave up his plans to get married. Augustine and the members of his circle felt that the commitment they made to Christ in baptism made it necessary for them to renounce sex and marriage. It is tempting to see this as a lingering inheritance from Manichaeism, but Augustine accepted mainstream Christian teaching on the dignity of marriage. He shared, however, the conviction common to many earnest Christians of the time that baptism means a total commitment to the law of God, a commitment that cannot be fulfilled by those who remain in the midst of the pleasures and distractions of this world. It was this moral earnestness that produced the monastic movement of the fourth century, with its call to give up marriage and property and withdraw from the world; the *Confessions* tell us of the huge impact on Augustine of what he heard at exactly this time of Antony of Egypt and other monastic heroes. In 386 he was converted not to Christianity (he had never ceased to be Christian), and not merely to the faith of the Church, but to a special form of Christian life, based on saying goodbye to marriage and a worldly career.

Set free from worldly responsibilities, he could now devote himself to what he had come to see as his real vocation – the pursuit of Christian philosophy. By this he meant the use of rational argument and concepts drawn from the great philosophers, such as Plato and Cicero, to draw out the Christian sense of human nature as made for union with God. This would be a life's work, and it is to this work that he wished to dedicate himself. There was now no point in remaining in Italy, and by the end of 388 he had returned to Africa. There in his home town, Thagaste, together with friends who had accompanied him to Italy and back, he set up a quasi-monastic community – based on celibacy and a sharing of property, and devoted to prayer, study and discussion. Here, left to himself, he would have spent the rest of his days.

However, with his growing reputation, his literary skills, and his contacts with the imperial court at Milan, he was a prime candidate for a bishopric. People of Augustine's class and background were not supposed to seek office in the Church, but were expected to accept the burden when it was laid upon them. In 391 Augustine visited the port of Hippo (modern Annaba), some forty miles to the north, when looking for a new recruit to his monastery, and was promptly seized and forced to accept ordination – to the priesthood, since the town had a bishop. He put up some resistance, which was expected of someone in this situation. But there is no doubt that he was genuinely overawed at the thought of pastoral office. He was later to speak eloquently of the terrible burden of a pastor, who would have to answer at the Last Judgement not only for his own sins but for those of his flock as well.

The point of making him a priest of the diocese of Hippo was to line him up as the heir apparent of its elderly bishop (one Valerius) before another diocese pinched him. In 395 he was made auxiliary bishop, and on Valerius' death in the following year succeeded to the see. From now until his death in 430 he was tied to pastoral duties in this diocese. We must remember that outside a few great sees bishops were not (as they are today) administrators who delegate the chores of pastoral care to their priests; the priests did not do the bishop's work for him but formed a council to assist him. The bishop remained the father of his flock; he was expected to know them individually, to administer the sacraments (baptism, eucharist, penance), and preach at the Sunday liturgy. He had to attend also to the worldly needs of his flock, representing them in dealings with the state and acting as adjudicator in their civil disputes. One must always remember that Augustine's life was dominated by pastoral duties.

His acute sense of his pastoral responsibilities led him to redirect his intellectual gifts. A few years later (409), and in the not far distant province of Cyrenaica (north-eastern Libya), one Synesius agreed in a similar way to leave the quiet life of a philosopher for the duties of a bishop. He announced in a public letter that he had no intention of abandoning Neoplatonism or of subjecting it to Christian censorship: he would be happy, he said, to preach myths from the pulpit, if he were allowed to pursue truth in his study. Augustine's attitude was quite different. As soon as he became a priest, he abandoned his dreams of a life devoted to philosophy, and immersed himself in the Scriptures. He never shed the basic tenets about God and human nature which he had learnt from philosophy, but from now on he was primarily a biblical theologian, concerned not only to satisfy his own intellect but to serve the Church.

It was this concern for the good of the Church that generated the huge literary production that continued to his dying day: it was to help his flock that he developed his thoughts on Christian teaching, and composed the sermons that form an important part of his literary legacy; it was for the benefit of the faithful, in Africa and beyond, that he produced a huge body of writing to defend the Church against pagans and heretics. We may say that he was primarily a polemical writer responding to the critics of the Church, rather than an academic theologian following his own nose. It is fortunate that he lived in a period when Christian theology was concerned with questions of great practical relevance, and had not degenerated, as it did at times in later centuries, into an academic exercise intended primarily to maintain the status of theologians.

Reason and Authority

It was soon after becoming Bishop of Hippo that Augustine wrote, in the late 390s, the most famous of all his works and the main sources for the earlier part of this chapter – the intellectual autobiography called the *Confessions*. Anyone who has dipped into this work knows that it is much more than an autobiography. Augustine did not write it as a nostalgic exercise in the remembrance of things past, or to satisfy the curiosity of his friends. He saw in his own history a model case of how God humbles and recovers lost sheep; in the course of telling his story he discusses a whole host of theological topics – the powers and defects of the human mind, the need to centre our lives on God, the way to read the Bible, the authority of the Church. Augustine wrote the work as a bishop with a bishop's priorities. The outlook of the book is that of the bishop of Hippo in 397 rather than that of the professor of rhetoric in Carthage and Italy, or of the convert to Christian Platonism of 386.

A case in point is the treatment of Platonism in Book Seven, which treats his intellectual development in the crucial year 386, when Neoplatonism rescued him from the Manichees. Although the creators of Neoplatonism had been pagans, it was quite possible to reconcile it with Christian belief, as many Christian Platonists had already done. As Augustine wrote in the same year:

I am determined never in any way to depart from the authority of Christ, for I have found no stronger one. But as to that which has to be examined by subtle use of the reason – for I long not simply to believe what is true but also to understand it – I feel sure that I shall find it with the Platonists, and that it will not contradict our sacred mysteries. (Ag 3.20.43)

But Book Seven of the *Confessions* is altogether sharper in tone. It uses Neoplatonic ideas to refute Manichaeism, but it pays Neoplatonism no compliments. Instead, it goes on and on about the dangers of intellectual arrogance, by which Augustine means paying more attention to philosophy than the Bible. At the time of his conversion in 386 he viewed Christianity and Platonism, revelation and philosophy, as two parallel sources of wisdom, working together in natural harmony. But by the time he wrote the *Confessions*, eleven years later, he was a Christian bishop who viewed philosophy as useless for the great mass of mankind, who haven't the time or grounding to pursue it, and potentially dangerous for the learned few, who might prefer it to revelation.

Christian heresy too, including the Manichaeism that had entrapped him for so long, was a cautionary tale of what happens when the human intellect neglects the Word of God and sets itself up as an autonomous judge of truth. It was the claim to teach nothing that could not be rationally proved that had first drawn the young Augustine, back in 373, away from the Church to the Manichees:

What drove me to disown the religion which my parents had instilled in me from a child and to be a follower and devoted hearer of those men for almost nine years? It was their claim that we are overawed by superstition and told to put faith before reason while they impose faith on no one without prior discussion to discover what is true.

This passage is taken from *The Usefulness of Belief* (U 1.2), a defence of Christian faith that Augustine wrote immediately after his ordination to the priesthood in 391. The book argues that the basis of knowledge about God is not experience or reasoning but belief in the teaching authority of the Church. The immediate target of the book is the criticism of church authority put forward by the Manichees; but his arguments also apply to claims by philosophers that belief is mere opinion and cannot lead us to real knowledge. Against this Augustine insists on the necessity of belief for the attainment of knowledge. In the words of one of his favourite biblical texts, 'If you do not believe, you will not understand' (ISAIAH 7:9, LATIN VERSION).

How in this work does Augustine defend the claims of authority and belief, against the rival claim that each individual has the right, and indeed the duty, to work out his own answers to the questions of life? He points out that few people have the education or ability to think philosophically about the existence and nature of God: are we to deny religion to everyone else? In fact, there is a whole range of things we all believe without proof. We trust our friends and colleagues without proof that they are trustworthy. We honour and obey our parents, yet we know that they *are* our parents only on the testimony of others. Indeed, we rely on the authority of others – that is, trustworthy testimony – for our knowledge about most things.

But why should we trust the Church? Because of 'numbers, unanimity, antiquity' (14:31). Unlike the various sects, the Church can claim a consistent teaching tradition going back to the original apostles of Christ, maintained by an unbroken succession of bishops throughout the world, and now upheld by the overwhelming majority of believers. This is not to prefer the mediocrity of the many to the wisdom of the few, since the Church can boast generations of holy men and women, virgins, ascetics and martyrs, who prove that the Church is the place where the grace of God is active.

We may allow that this appeal to tradition has a certain force. Augustine was right to feel that in 373 he had been too quick to abandon mainstream Christianity, before he knew much about it, and the same could be said of people nowadays who jettison the faith of their fathers not for solid intellectual reasons but almost casually. Nor can we criticize him for teaching an infantile Christianity, in which the faithful are called to respect the wisdom of their elders and betters for ever and a day, without ever exerting their critical powers: for he held that simple faith is but a first step, and that Christians must aim at developing both their experience and their reasoning powers, in such a way as finally to *know* and *understand* what at first they simply *believe*.

Even so, it is startling to find the size and antiquity of the Church already stressed in the fourth century, at a time when pagans were still as numerous as Christians, and still attacked Christianity as a dangerous novelty. Christian missionaries in the second and third centuries had stressed the rationality of Christianity, against the superstition of paganism, in just the same way that Manichees in the fourth century contrasted their offering of rational proof to the Church's stress on authority. Manichaeism had been fiercely attacked as destructive of tradition by the staunchly pagan emperor Diocletian (284–305), who persecuted Christianity for precisely the same reason. That Christianity cannot defend itself by claiming antiquity was appreciated as late as the 380s by Bishop Ambrose of Milan, who defended Christianity as a new faith that illustrates the law of progress in history.

Augustine's stress on the need to respect authority and recognize the limits of reason was based on more than traditionalism, however: it arose from his faith in Jesus Christ. Now Jesus is a historical figure, who walked the fields of Palestine centuries ago; the life and teaching of the earthly Jesus remain the essential revelation about him even for those who claim spiritual contact with the risen Jesus here and now. We cannot reach Christ through the use of pure reason, since reason cannot uncover the past. Christianity offers not some pure philosophy of timeless truths, but a history of the creation and fall of man, and of the various steps, leading up to the Incarnation, by which God has sought to rescue him. Truths about the past can only be known through authoritative testimony. A Christian has the Bible, but he depends on the teaching of the Church for his knowledge of which writings to regard as inspired Scripture. Of course, such teaching has to be tested on the grounds of its weight and coherence, but in recognizing its authority we are acknowledging the limits of our own experience. The very nature of the Incarnation is a lesson for us: God, in emptying himself to take on human form, above all in undergoing the agony and humiliation of the cross, gives us a powerful lesson in the need for humility.

> *Certain philosophers of this world ... have looked for the Creator in his creation, because he can be found there ... They saw the goal to be reached; but ungrateful to the one who had enabled them to see it, they attributed this vision to their own power. Becoming proud, they failed to attain what they had seen ... They rejected the lowliness of Christ, which would have enabled them, as in a safe vessel, to reach that which they saw from a distance. The cross of Christ appeared sordid to them ... He was crucified for your sake, to teach you humility.* (JG 2.4)

A Manichee, or a pagan philosopher, with his head partly in learned tomes and partly in the clouds, will miss the presence and revelation of God in the dust of Palestine and the empty tomb. We all have a sense of our sinfulness and of our need to be healed if we are to succeed in our quest for God. Philosophers can expand on this with learning and insight, and make us more vividly aware of our spiritual needs. But only the facts of salvation history, accepted on the authority of Scripture and the teaching of the Church, can provide an actual remedy, and point us the way.

> *It is one thing from a wooded peak to catch a glimpse of the homeland of peace and yet not find the way to it and get hopelessly lost, while hosts of deserters from God, under their leader the Lion and the Dragon [the Devil], hem us in and lie in wait for us; and quite another to keep to the path that leads there, under the protection of our heavenly Ruler [Christ].* (Co 7.21.27)

Augustine's intellectual pilgrimage had taught him humility, and this lesson fitted in well with the claims for church authority that came to him naturally once he was a Christian bishop. When as a new convert he had set out to develop a Christian philosophy, he had shown more intellectual openness. His new position as an official apologist for the Church made him more narrowly orthodox, even though his ideas continued to develop. The humility of the convert who accepts authority can begin to look like arrogance and dogmatism, once he comes to serve that authority as its mouthpiece. Augustine the bishop and teacher can easily appear a less attractive figure than the young Augustine seeking the truth. But the energy and urgency of his writing, and its influence on future thought, gained immensely from the fact that he had now to address not the problems he had set himself as an amateur philosopher, but great issues that gripped the Church at large and were to shape the development of Christianity for centuries to come.

Holy Church and Sinful Members

The creed recited every Sunday in most churches throughout the world affirms belief in 'one holy catholic and apostolic Church'. The choice of adjectives should raise an eyebrow or two. In view of the number of Christian denominations, in what sense is the Church 'one'? Not all churches that reject the authority of the see of Rome are happy to call themselves 'catholic'. 'Apostolic' we can let pass, even though biblical scholars have made it much harder to claim that Christianity as we know it is the same as the religion of the Apostles. But 'holy' is the most problematic adjective of them all: if the Church is a community of saints, what are you and I doing in it? It won't do to say that the Church is holy not in its members but in its doctrines and sacraments, since 'holy Church' means 'the Church of the saints' or 'the holy people'. Christians form a holy people not primarily because of their personal holiness but because they are the people chosen by God, the Holy One; but the phrase is vacuous unless those who make up this people live holy lives.

The Early Church

In fact the early Christians felt no embarrassment in making claims to personal holiness rarely equalled in history. In the words of a text of the early second century,

Christians have the commandments of the Lord Jesus Christ himself engraved upon their hearts, and they observe them ... They do not

commit adultery or fornication; they do not bear false witness or covet the possessions of others; they honour their father and mother, and love their neighbours; they judge justly, and they never do to others what they would not wish others to do to them. (ARISTIDES, APOLOGY 15)

So now you know. If you see a Christian misbehaving, what should you make of it? In the words of Justin Martyr (mid-second century), 'Those who are not found to be living as Christ taught should be regarded as not Christians at all, even if they profess with their lips the precepts of Christ' (FIRST APOLOGY 16). Such passages were propaganda written to impress non-Christians, but they had a theological basis all the same. The Church taught that through baptism and commitment to Christ believers receive into their hearts the Spirit of God, the divine power that makes saints out of sinners. It was hard to see how a Christian who sincerely wanted this grace could fail to receive it. Sanctity, for a Christian, seemed well within reach.

On comparing themselves to their pagan neighbours in the world around them the early Christians enjoyed a very pleasant sense of moral superiority. Although it would be silly to picture the pagan world as a continuous orgy of lust and cruelty, Christians did better than their neighbours in those areas where they developed distinctive standards, notably sex and helping the poor. And they were confident of a huge built-in advantage when it came to religion. Nowadays we tend to think that we have duties towards each other but are free to choose whatever religion we like. In the ancient world, however, everyone – Christians, Jews and pagans alike – believed that justice includes giving God his due, which means worshipping him in the way *he* likes. Christians were sure that only they performed this duty, since the pagans were immersed in polytheism, the worship of false gods, while the Jews, with their curious customs and taboos, were sunk in superstition. Every Christian could say, 'I give alms (sometimes), I make some effort to be chaste, and at least I worship the right God in the right way.' Every Christian could feel that this less than heroic degree of virtue placed him way above his pagan neighbours and earned him the special favour of God.

As a result, early Christians were confident that God listened to their prayers and to theirs alone, and that at the end of time (which they imagined would be soon) Christ would return in glory to reward Christians with the bliss of heaven, and damn everyone else, however virtuous by the world's standards, to the everlasting torments of hell. Some Christians, such as St Paul, were spurred by this thought to feats of missionary heroism, but the great majority found the dreadful fate awaiting their pagan neighbours comforting rather than distressing. The early Christians, perhaps, were not very nice people.

The Church's confidence in the holiness of its members received a rude shock in the middle of the third century, under the pressure of an unprecedented edict issued in 250 by the emperor Decius, which ordered everyone to sacrifice to the pagan gods, and set up bureaucratic machinery to enforce the order. Though many Christians managed to lie low, and a fair number died as martyrs, a very large number conformed to the edict, and later returned to the Church. As a result, the Church's claim to holiness was now somewhat tarnished. The notion of the Church as a community of saints was not abandoned, but the emphasis shifted away from the sanctity of the laity to the need for holiness in the clergy, as the celebrants of the sacraments of baptism and the eucharist. Hitherto the rules for priestly purity in the Old Testament had been taken to express in symbolic form a call to moral perfection addressed to all Christians, the 'priestly' people of God. There were now reinterpreted as referring directly and in their full rigour only to the minister who baptizes, absolves sins, and celebrates the eucharist; it is he who is the 'priest', and the heir of the priests of the Old Covenant.

One of the main participants in the debates of this time of crisis was Bishop Cyprian of Carthage (d. 258), whose writings were regarded in the Africa of Augustine's time as supremely authoritative, second only to the Bible itself. Cyprian held that a bishop or priest who has committed some grave offence can no longer officiate: his sin has deprived him of the Holy Spirit, so how can he give a share in the Spirit to others? The holiness of the laity is necessary for the well-being but not for the existence of the Church; in contrast, the holiness of the minister is essential for the very validity of those sacraments that make the Christian community the Church of Christ.

The Donatist Controversy

More than a century later, Augustine praised Cyprian rather condescendingly as a wise but at times misguided spirit, whose greatest virtue was a readiness to admit he could be wrong (which one wouldn't guess from his writings). His teaching had come to the fore again as a result of a disastrous schism that occurred in the African Church early in the fourth century.

In 312 one Caecilian, who had made enemies by trying to undermine the reverence paid to martyrs, got himself hastily consecrated bishop of Carthage (and therefore the chief bishop of Roman Africa) before his opponents had time to assemble. They responded by contesting his election on the grounds that one of the bishops who had taken part was a *tradidor* ('hander over'), that is, had compromised himself in time of persecution by handing over copies of the Scriptures to the pagan authorities – an offence that counted as apostasy (betraying the faith). They therefore set up as rival bishop the deacon Majorinus, who on his death soon afterwards was succeeded by Donatus. Soon all Africa was divided into supporters of Caecilian and supporters of Donatus.

Caecilian had been consecrated first, and the argument against the validity of his consecration was doubtful both on point of fact and on point of law; as a result he gained the recognition of all the churches outside Africa. This enabled him to claim the title of

'Catholic' bishop, while his opponents were merely 'Donatists'. (Note, by the way, that when I use the word 'Catholic' in this book it will normally follow this ancient usage, where 'Catholic' does not mean 'Roman Catholic', as opposed to 'Orthodox' or 'Reformed', but refers to the universal Church of the early centuries, from which all modern Christian denominations derive, and excludes only such small schismatic groups as the Donatists.)

The Donatists retaliated by condemning the churches that accepted Caecilian: by this act they had condoned the sin of *traditio* ('handing over') and therefore shared in its guilt; this excluded them from the true Church of Christ, which was now reduced to the Donatists themselves. Like the fond parents watching a military parade who exclaimed, 'Only our Johnny is marching in step', the Donatists refused to be browbeaten by a mere number count, and indeed within Africa itself they remained strong, perhaps even outnumbering their opponents; by the time of Augustine every town in the province had rival Catholic and Donatist bishops. Clumsy and sporadic attempts to suppress Donatism on the part of the state authorities served only to reinforce Donatist self-identity as the church of martyrs, opposed to the church of *traditores*, dependent on the powers of this world. The first three centuries, when Christians were a despised and persecuted minority, had left their mark: even Augustine in the early fifth century instinctively viewed the Church as a holy remnant that would always be liable to harassment.

But Augustine's own allegiance to the Catholic Church was never in doubt: after his years in Italy Donatism appeared insufferably provincial, and its claim to be the one true Church of Christ merely silly. Already as a priest in Hippo (where Donatists at first outnumbered Catholics) and then as the chief propagandist for all Catholic Africa, he produced over a period of thirty years a whole series of works reiterating patiently, if monotonously, the great lines of the anti-Donatist cause. Like so many who take part in public controversy, he had limited freedom to choose his ground:

the debate had been defined, the battle lines drawn up, decades back. After years as a professor of rhetoric he was well able to argue the case, indeed almost any case, with confidence.

Since the writings of the Donatists themselves are lost, it is all too easy to accept his arguments uncritically. If the Donatists had survived down to the modern age (in fact they disappear from history with the Muslim conquest of Africa at the end of the seventh century), ecumenical courtesy would make us try to grasp their point of view. As it is, the great majority of modern commentators take it for granted they they had not a leg to stand on. This makes it seem that Augustine was labouring the obvious. It is worth making the effort to understand his opponents in order to make the debate interesting again. I should warn my reader at this point that the dispute was highly involved and the arguments often devious; if you have no taste for the niceties of theological debate, I would advise you to skip on ahead to the next section, 'Mixture in the Church'.

One of the points in the debate was the problem of rebaptism. What is the status of schismatic baptism, that is, baptism performed by groups like the Donatists who have separated themselves from the main body of believers and are therefore guilty of the sin of 'schism' (splitting the Church)? Are their baptisms valid, or should schismatics received into the Church be baptized again? By Augustine's time all western Catholics accepted the validity of schismatic baptism, including the baptisms performed by the Donatists; but the Donatists themselves imposed rebaptism on those Catholics (schismatics in their eyes) who came over to them. Augustine tells us that this Donatist practice, while criticized by many as fanatical, caused agonies to the scrupulous, and tempted some Catholics to receive Donatist baptism, since everyone recognized it, and then return to the Catholic fold. This gave pastoral urgency to his arguments on behalf of schismatic baptism. (Note the irony of the situation: Augustine defended schismatic baptism not out of a wish to be nice to schismatics but in order to defend Catholic baptism against schismatic attack.)

The rite of baptism is regarded by most Christians today as a ceremony of thanksgiving to God and of admission into the Church. But the early Christians had a much more dramatic view of baptism: they saw it as a radical transformation, by which the candidate is freed from the Devil, receives the Holy Spirit into his soul, is united to Christ as a member of his 'body', and adopted as a child of the Father. The Church is the community of those who are sanctified by the Spirit and made members of the holy people of God. This raises the question: is it possible to receive the grace of baptism outside the one true Church? Is schismatic baptism valid? The debate first flared up in the middle of the third century when, in the wake of persecution, a significant number of Christians were baptized in schism and then sought readmission into the Church. Were they, or were they not, to be baptized again? Cyprian was certain that they were, and argued the case cogently. The whole teaching of the New Testament presumes that the Church is a united, harmonious community. As the 'body of Christ' – the community sanctified and inspired by the risen Christ – it cannot lose the unity it possesses in him. Schism cannot split the Church: it merely separates schismatics from the Church. Since the fruit of the Spirit is love and peace, those who have rejected their fellow Christians by going into schism have rejected the Spirit; as a result they can neither bestow nor receive the Spirit.

Pope Stephen of Rome (d. 257), however, rejected Cyprian's arguments. Treating the two parts of the rite of baptism (the pouring of water and the anointing with oil) as two separate sacraments, he argued that the anointing confers the Holy Spirit, while the washing of baptism is merely for the forgiveness of sins: unlike the anointing it does not confer the Spirit and therefore it can be validly performed outside the Church. The argument was hopelessly askew, since the notion of a valid forgiveness of sins without the gift of the Holy Spirit is theological nonsense: St Paul clearly links forgiveness of sins to union with Christ, and union with Christ to receiving the Spirit. It is ironic that the whole

31

subsequent practice of western Christendom, where each denomination recognizes the baptism of the others, derives from this unsatisfactory ruling of Stephen's.

By the time of Augustine the Catholics in Africa had adopted the Roman position, while the Donatists remained faithful to that of Cyprian. Augustine, fortunately, did not repeat the arguments of Stephen. Instead, he introduced a rather contrived distinction between validity and effectiveness: baptism can be validly performed outside the Church, but it only begins to take effect and to benefit the recipient when he returns to the Catholic fold. Baptism outside the Church does not produce a single one of its fruits; nevertheless, it is valid and unrepeatable.

But what of the argument that baptism outside the Church cannot be valid since the Holy Spirit cannot be bestowed by one who, as a schismatic, has cut himself off from the Spirit? This brings us to the central issue in the Donatist controversy: can the sacraments of baptism and the eucharist be validly performed by a minister in a state of 'mortal' sin – that is, by a priest who has sinned so gravely as to expel the Spirit he received in baptism and cause the 'death' of his own soul? The whole basis of the Donatist schism was that the Catholic bishops throughout the world, having once condoned *traditio*, had been deprived of the Spirit, and therefore had nothing to bestow on either their flock or their successors in the episcopal office. The notion of guilt by association has never, perhaps, been exploited so absurdly. The Catholics in response not only defended the worthiness of their own bishops but also attacked the theological tenet fundamental to their opponents' case – the invalidity of sacraments performed by unworthy ministers. Against this they made a claim that must have made Cyprian turn in his grave: the state of grace of the minister is entirely irrelevant for both the validity and the effectiveness of the sacrament. This was the position that Augustine set out to defend in the most important of his anti-Donatist treatises – *Baptism: Against the Donatists*, written in 400–1.

Augustine makes great play of the presence within the Church of people who are Christians 'in words rather than actions', and no more in a state of grace than the schismatics; yet no one doubts their ability to give, as to receive, baptism. If the validity of a sacrament were made to depend on the spiritual state of the celebrant, we could never be certain that we had been validly baptized or validly absolved from our sins; the sacramental system set up by Christ must have a surer foundation. But does Augustine's conclusion follow? Consider, for example, the case of a celebrant who makes a serious mistake in reading out the set prayers. The standard principle is that the sacrament is nevertheless valid, since 'the Lord supplies'. But this doesn't mean that the validity of the sacrament has nothing to do with using the right words. Similarly, why not say that the normal working of a sacrament requires a worthy minister, but that the Lord supplies when the minister is unworthy? This would surely be better than to say with Augustine that the worthiness of the minister is wholly irrelevant, and that the Holy Spirit works not through the heart and mind of the celebrant but merely through his outward words and gestures.

In the mainstream churches today it is generally held that all that is necessary for the validity of a sacrament, apart from the correct ritual, is a right intention on the part of the minister – that is, he must intend to perform the sacrament. But Augustine is reluctant to admit even this: after all, in the case of an unworthy minister who has no part in the Holy Spirit, it is difficult to be confident of the rightness of his intentions. This drives Augustine to the extreme position that the correct words and gestures may possibly be adequate even when there is no intention to perform the sacrament at all. He raises as a genuine problem the validity or otherwise of a baptism performed 'in jest, as in a comedy', when neither baptizer nor baptized has serious intentions or even the faith (BAPTISM 7.53.101). Despairing of finding a theological answer, he comes up with the astonishing proposal that the only way to solve this baffling puzzle, as he sees it, is to pray for a special revelation from heaven. A theology of the sacraments that produces a 'problem' such as this stands self-condemned. How could validity depend on correct ritual alone and not at all on the intentions of those taking part? This would reduce the whole sacramental system to a form of magic.

Mixture in the Church

If there was no more to Augustine's contribution to the Donatist controversy than this, it would not deserve a chapter, but fortunately he developed a further argument that is far stronger and of much greater interest.

As we have seen, the Church of the first three centuries saw itself as a community of saints. Historians used to think that all this, and much else besides, went out of the window at the conversion to Christianity of the emperor Constantine in 312, as a result of which floods of dubious converts poured into the Church and corrupted it. But this picture is rejected by scholars today. In fact the conversion of the Roman world was a gradual process, and the Church was careful not to lower its standards; the penances imposed, for example, on grave sinners remained long and severe.

Donatism has often been described as a puritanical movement that wanted to exclude sinners from the Church. This reflects Augustine's own rhetoric rather than the facts of the case. Donatists had the same attitude as Catholics to the failings of the laity; they did not imitate the rigorist Novatianist sect which, in the time of Cyprian, had declared that those who committed grave sins after baptism had to be excluded from holy communion for life. Instead, as we have seen, the Donatists, as the heirs of Cyprian, concentrated on the need for holiness in the ministry. In practice this was not specially demanding, since it consisted of little more than the furious condemnation of a sin of *traditio* committed in unrepeatable circumstances decades before. But at least the Donatists preserved the self-identity of earlier Christians, with their stress on the purity of the Church, as an 'enclosed garden' set apart from the corruption of the world.

It was this traditional stereotype, preserved so rigidly by the Donatists, that Augustine set out to destroy. He quoted with relish the numerous passages in the writings of Cyprian on the deplorable state of the Church at the time of Decius' persecution (250), and used them as evidence that the Church is not a community of saints. Cyprian himself would not have liked his rhetoric being taken so literally; but complaints of the lukewarmness of Christians, and their failure to live up to their baptismal promises, were just as common in the early centuries as in later ones – a fact ignored by those church historians, both ancient and modern, who romanticize the primitive Church. Augustine built on this fact to make the strong claim that the Church is and always has been full of the spiritually dead, who have no share in the Holy Spirit; indeed, these, according to Augustine, are 'the many', while the righteous are 'the few'.

Again we meet the notion of the holy remnant, but he does not identify it with the Church, nor with a particular section of the Church: we shall not know till the Day of Judgement who for certain are the righteous and who the unrighteous, who (to use the biblical imagery) are the wheat and who the chaff. All we know is that both are to be found within the Church. This state of affairs is actually, Augustine argues, part of God's plan for the good of the Church, since it enables the righteous to develop the virtues of humility and tolerance. What is strikingly absent in this and similar passages is any anxiety about contamination, any fear that the presence of so many sinners might deprive the Church of its very identity; and yet this fear had been strong in the primitive Church, with its concern to maintain a clear boundary between holy Church and wicked world.

Equally notable is the stress Augustine places on an intermediate class of believers – those who are still in their sins but with God's grace are gradually advancing towards holiness. It is not even necessary for them to reach this state in the present life: on condition that they are moving in the right direction, they will be saved. For many individuals, as for the Church as a whole, the path through this world is a pilgrim state of slow, often imperceptible, progress in which backsliding and renewed repentance are a constant fact of life.

What, then, do we mean when we call the Church 'holy'? Augustine's favourite answer is to distinguish between the church community as a social entity on earth and the holy Church of those destined by God to join the communion of saints in heaven: it is possible to say that sinners only *appear* to be members of the holy Church. Does this mean that there are really two Churches – the visible Church with its hierarchy and sacraments and an invisible Church of saints? This was how many of the sixteenth-century Reformers understood Augustine; but it is not what he meant. In his view the public sacraments of the Church, performed by the clergy, do not indeed convey salvation to everyone who receives them, but there is no salvation without them; we cannot turn our backs on the visible Church and claim to belong to an invisible one. Cyprian had written, 'You cannot have God for your Father if you do not have the Church for your mother' (THE UNITY OF THE CATHOLIC CHURCH 6). For Cyprian as for Augustine the Church is the visible Church, despite the presence within it of unworthy members who will not accompany the saints into heaven.

But Augustine came to yet a deeper understanding of the presence of sinners in the Church – the 'mixture' of saints and sinners, as he liked to call it. He came to see that this mixture is not just an unfortunate accident, due to human failings, but belongs to the very essence of the Church, as the community of men and women who have been called to holiness but are still sinners. Those in the Church who are destined for salvation are indeed God's 'elect' (chosen ones), but none of them is free from sin in this age. A common need to recognize their sins unites all members of the Church, sinners and 'saints' alike.

The whole Church says, 'Forgive us our trespasses.' This means it has stains and wrinkles. By confession the wrinkle is smoothed out, by confession the stain is washed away. The Church stands in prayer in order to be cleansed by confession; and as long as it lives in this world it stands like that. And whenever somebody departs from the body, all his sins are forgiven, at least those capable of being forgiven, through the daily prayer of the Church. And then he departs cleansed, and the Church is stored up in the Lord's treasury as pure gold. This is how the Church enters the Lord's treasury without stain or wrinkle. (S 181.5.7)

So it is all the members of the visible Church, including the elect, who need day by day to pray for forgiveness. And when God forgives the sins of his elect, it is in response to the prayers not just of the elect themselves but of the whole Church. Furthermore, just as the elect depend on the prayers of all, so they depend on the sacraments and the preaching performed by all the ministers of the Church, worthy and unworthy alike. The Church remains holy in that it is the ark of salvation, whose prayers and sacraments are the channels of divine grace; but the holiness is not the scrupulous purity of fastidious souls who shun the company of sinners.

Even Christ, the only sinless man (in Augustine's view) who has walked this earth, took on himself the burden of the sins of the world; in the startling words of Scripture, he 'was made sin for our sake' (2 CORINTHIANS 5:21). Christ's cry of despair from the cross, 'My God, my God, why have you abandoned me?' (MARK 15:34), is interpreted by Augustine as the anguish of a sinful world, that Christ takes upon himself. There is, then, a deep solidarity that binds Christ to sinners in this age; in Christ's own words, he came to call 'not the righteous but sinners' (MATTHEW 9:13). We may even say that a 'perfect' Church would not be the Church that Christ died to found.

*The Church has strong members, and it also has weak ones. It can't do
without its strong members, and it can't do without its weak ones ...
because without both of them there is no Church.* (S 76.3.4)

In all, Augustine was calling on the Church to develop a new
identity: the Church's traditional view of itself as the holy
remnant in the midst of a sinful world had to be abandoned. In
issuing this call, he was pressing for a change that was in fact
achieved through a gradual evolution – the slow process by which,
over many centuries, the Christian community ceased to be the
small, self-righteous sect it had been in the age of the Apostles, and
grew into the Church of the Middle Ages and of modern Europe,
keen to embrace all men and women who at least recognize Christian values, and realistic in the demands it makes upon them.

In calling for this change, Augustine was not merely saying
that Christians ought to stop giving themselves airs; nor did he
point out, as a modern historian would, that in the conditions of a
Christian empire the character of Christianity was bound to
change. The heart of his picture of the Church lies instead in
profound theological reflection on the incarnation of Christ. In
'emptying' himself to become a human being in this fallen world,
and in 'humbling' himself to accept death, even death on a cross
(PHILIPPIANS 2:6–8), Christ gave an example of solidarity with
sinners that must be imitated even in the holy Church of God: if
Christ bore the sins of the world, we too must 'bear' (tolerate)
sinners. If the Church were to seek to exclude them, it would not
secure but lose its holiness, because it would have ceased to follow
its divine Lord. As in Augustine's arguments against pagans and
Manichees, so at the heart of his case against the Donatists lies the
paradox of the humility and humiliation of the incarnate and
crucified God.

Church and World

If the Church itself is a mixed body, this is bound to affect its attitude to the society around it. In political terms this is the problem of the relationship between Church and state. This is another area where Augustine's influence down the centuries has been enormous. His thoughts on the matter were developed in response to some of the most dramatic events in the whole of European history. In his youth the Roman empire, stretching from Britain to the Sahara, from the Atlantic to Mesopotamia, seemed as secure as ever. The emperors were Christians, and by the end of the fourth century had prohibited pagan worship. It was natural for Christians to suppose that under the protection of the one true God the empire would now go from strength to strength. But Augustine lived to see Britain, Gaul and Spain overrun by barbarian invaders, and as he lay dying in 430 his own city of Hippo was under siege by the Vandals.

Augustine and the Sack of Rome

The most traumatic moment in this sudden collapse of Roman power in western Europe was the sack of Rome by the Goths in 410. This was not in itself the fall of the empire: the Goths soon left Italy for Gaul; and Rome, though still officially the capital of the empire, had long ceased to be the centre of government. But the sack came as a terrible shock to all who still looked at the city as the symbol of Roman power and Roman civilization. Refugees, fleeing before the Goths, circulated their tales of woe round the whole empire. The reactions of many were eloquently expressed by Jerome, the great translator and commentator of the Bible: 'Oh horror! The world is collapsing in ruins. The renowned city, the capital of the Roman empire, is destroyed in one tremendous fire, and there is no part of the earth where there are not Roman exiles' (LETTER 128:4). 'If Rome can perish, what can be safe?' (123.17).

But a Christian's feelings towards the city of Rome were likely to be very mixed. On the one hand, it was the capital of an empire that no one wished to see collapse in chaos. But on the other hand its great days of glory had been as pagan Rome, the persecutor of the Church, glutted with the blood of the martyrs. The conversion of the empire (or at least the emperors) to Christianity had put an end to persecution, but injustice and corruption were just as prevalent as before.

The traditional attitude of Christians to the Roman state had been critical but nuanced. The books of the New Testament vary enormously in the attitude they express towards Roman power. At one end of the spectrum we have St Paul insisting that the state authorities are established by God and are his 'agents working for your good' (ROMANS 13:4); at the other, we have the Revelation of John, with its tirades against Rome the New Babylon, the whore drunk with the blood of the saints. The same range of attitudes continued in Christian writing till the time of Constantine (d. 337), the first Christian emperor: on the one hand, the empire was welcomed as a gift from God that secured peace round the Mediterranean and so helped the spread of the gospel; on the other hand, in pursuing its own godless aims and demanding the obedience of its subjects, it looked like a satanic parody of the true empire, the kingdom of Christ. Although in any one Christian writer of this early period one of these views is likely to be dominant, it is misleading to treat them as mutually exclusive. In fact, they were really two sides of the same coin. Yes, God had given world power to the Romans, for the benefit of the Church. But at the same time the Romans worshipped the pagan gods – in the Christian view, real but demonic spirits who set the state against the Church. The reaction of Christians was to maintain an attitude of cautious reserve. The state had its uses, and was better than anarchy. But its value was only provisional: the eyes of faith were set on the return of Christ in glory, when the true kingdom would come and Roman power, indeed all worldly authority, vanish away, like dew at the rising of the sun.

At the end of the second century the African writer Tertullian wrote, 'The emperors too would have become Christians, if either the world had not needed emperors, or Christians could have become emperors' (*APOLOGETICUM* 21.24). But in the fourth century the incredible happened: the emperors became Christian, from Constantine onwards. This did not immediately make Christianity the 'state religion', but it transformed its prospects. Most of the emperors keenly promoted the power and status of the Church, while imposing increasing restrictions on pagan worship. By the time of Augustine's death the Greek-speaking half of the empire (Greece and the Near East) had developed a new nationalism, based on belief that the true God and the Christian empire were the closest of allies: if the empire maintained the true faith against the enemies of God, pagans and heretics, God in his turn would give the empire victory over its enemies.

The attitude of Christians in the western, Latin-speaking half of the empire was more reserved. The Church was very conscious of the benefits it now received from the state, and its members had no desire to be swamped by barbarian hordes. But older attitudes of disapproval and distrust died hard. There were a number of reasons for this. Paganism remained stronger than in the east, and prevented a sense of identification between the Christian community and society at large. Moreover, patriotism was generally weaker in the west than in the east: no one welcomed the barbarian invasions, but no one was ready, either, to pay for an army adequate to drive them back. There was no patriotic wave of opinion to swing the Church away from its traditional attitude of cautious reserve towards the state. As a result this attitude was modified but not abandoned.

We have seen how Jerome was deeply shocked by the sack of Rome by the Goths in 410. Augustine's reaction was more nuanced. He had none of the sentimental attachment to the 'eternal city' of those who venerated its past, but on the other hand he felt pity for the victims of the sack and was sensitive to the distress the news caused his flock in Africa. As the leading apologist for the Christian cause, he had to refute the arguments of the pagans: it seemed to them, and to weak Christians too, that the cause of the disaster was the prohibition of pagan cult; the pagan gods had protected Rome in the past and were now punishing it for its apostasy. There was also puzzlement among pious Christians at the occurrence of such a disaster in 'these Christian times': why was God not looking after the empire, now that it was no longer the enemy but the friend of the Church?

Of course there had been similar disasters in the past, and similar debates. In the middle of the third century the empire had been devastated by a combination of plague, bad harvests and barbarian invasions. Pagans accused Christians of causing these disasters by their refusal to worship the gods. Cyprian of Carthage (d. 258) reacted with a defence little calculated to appease the opposition:

> No one should suppose that the Christians are not proved right by the events taking place because they suffer from them just as much as everyone else. World catastrophes feel like a punishment to people who find happiness and glory only in the world ... But the disasters of the present time do not upset those whose hope lies rather in the good things to come. Misfortunes do not overwhelm us or break us or distress us, nor do we moan over any turn of events or state of bodies. Living by the spirit rather than by the flesh, we overcome weakness of body by firmness of soul. We are utterly confident that the very things that torment and try us prove and strengthen us. (TO DEMETRIANUS 4)

Augustine now put forward similar arguments. Surely, he urged, it is short-sighted and unspiritual to whine about earthly misfortunes. Loss of property, even of life itself, should not distress immortal souls: the only secure and lasting goods are moral integrity and the reward that awaits it in heaven. All misfortunes pale before eternal damnation, the fate in store for the enemies of God.

In this reaction traditional Christian narrow-mindedness was reinforced by philosophical clap-trap about the indifference of the wise man to the misfortunes of the body. We can scarcely blame Augustine, with his late Roman and early Christian background, for falling back on these inadequate platitudes: we all grasp at straws when disaster strikes. But he was a man of broader sympathies than Cyprian, and in the predominantly Christian society of late-Roman Africa it was not possible for Christians to pretend that they were a sect set apart, for whom national disasters were of no concern. Augustine realized that the crisis of the empire had opened up the whole question of the attitude of Christians towards state and society, towards the pagan heritage of Rome, towards the distinctive interpretation of history inherited from the Bible. To cope with all these questions, he embarked in 413 on what, by the time he completed it in 426, had become the longest and richest of all his works (more than 1,000 pages in a modern edition) – the *City of God*.

The Two Cities

The work could have been called (to anticipate Charles Dickens) *A Tale of Two Cities*. It contrasts at length the history and destiny of the 'city of God' and the 'earthly city'. The use of the word 'city' derives from scriptural texts such as Hebrews 13:14, 'Here we have no lasting city, but we seek the city which is to come.' The city of God, or 'heavenly city', is made up not only of the saints in heaven but also of all those human beings on earth who are true members of the people of God. The basic distinction between the two cities lies in the difference in the objects of their love.

> *The two cities were created by two kinds of love: the earthly city was created by self-love leading to contempt for God, the heavenly city by the love of God leading to contempt of self. In fact, the former glories in itself, the latter glories in the Lord. The former seeks glory from men, the latter finds its highest glory in God, the witness of a pure conscience. In the former the lust for power dominates over both its rulers and the nations it subjugates; in the latter both serve one another in love, the rulers by their guidance, the subjects by obedience. The former loves its own strength shown in its powerful men; the latter says to its God, 'I will love you, Lord, my strength.'* (C 14.28)

In other words, the citizens of the heavenly city live as exiles and pilgrims upon earth with their sights set on the world to come. In contrast, the earthly city is built up by ambitious men whose aim is to dominate their fellows. Its citizens make self-gratification their goal in life, the more gifted pursuing power and fame, the majority pleasure and wealth.

Careful scholars have pointed out that the distinction between the city of God and the earthly city is not the same as that between 'Church' and 'state'. The distinction between the two cities is a distinction not between two organizations but between two states of mind. Augustine traces the distinction to before the Church appeared on the scene, indeed all the way back to Cain and Abel (the sons of Adam and Eve in biblical mythology): the murderer Cain was the founder of the earthly city, while righteous Abel was the first citizen of the heavenly one. Moreover, the concept of the 'state' familiar to us is a development of the later Middle Ages, centuries after Augustine. When we think of the 'state', we think of an autonomous secular sphere with its own place in the natural, God-given scheme of things; it is necessarily distinct from the Church, since it is not run by church officials and has different goals. But Augustine is not thinking of administrative structure, and he does not acknowledge the existence of a secular sphere that has a right to develop secular values distinct from the law of God. The earthly city is, simply, mankind in rebellion against God.

Once we are clear that Augustine is not discussing the relation between Church and state as understood in later political theory, it is safe to admit that the two pairs of terms, though distinct in meaning, tend in practice to coincide. In the final section of the preceding chapter we saw how Augustine had no wish to draw a sharp distinction between the institutional Church and a spiritual Church of the saints. It is true that within the Church a distinction exists between its true members and false brethren, but the two cannot be told apart in this life, and are intimately linked together by the bonds of Christian fellowship. The fact that the Church on earth is a mixed society of saints and sinners does not prevent it from 'being even now the kingdom of Christ and the kingdom of heaven' (C 20.9). Similarly, when Augustine writes of the earthly city, he is usually thinking of the Roman empire, except when he is discussing the pre-Roman past. In all, in Augustine's own world the distinction between the city of God and the earthly city effectively coincided with that between the Church and the Roman state.

The *City of God* offers an interpretation of Roman history indebted to the pagan historians (notably Sallust, first century BC) who had been critical of Roman imperialism, but gives it a new theological slant. Augustine's account runs as follows. Back in the early days of the Roman Republic, God decided to give world power to the Romans, that is 'to those men who sought honour, praise and glory in serving their country, did not hesitate to put their country's safety above their own, and who suppressed greed for money and many other vices in favour of that one vice of theirs, the love of praise' (C 5.13). Thirst for glory gave birth to 'lust for power' (a phrase Augustine took from Sallust), and the Roman empire expanded steadily, until at the time of Christ's birth it included the whole Mediterranean world. By that time the lack of a serious external threat had long sapped the sinews of the Roman spirit, and moral corruption had infected the whole of society. The ruling class wallowed in luxurious living and political infighting; the mass of the population was kept quiet by the amusements of the theatre and amphitheatre, whose sex and sadism pandered to its lowest instincts. Having rejected God's law, the Romans had no defence against the demons, who are the true objects of pagan worship and relish human wickedness. Polytheism and moral corruption marked the earthly city as clearly as worship of the one true God and obedience to his law marked, and mark, the heavenly one.

The fourth century had seen the arrival on the scene of Christian emperors and the destruction of the power of paganism. Did this mean the situation had radically changed? Was there reason to hope that in a Christian empire the state would cease to embody the earthly city and become instead the political organ of the city of God? Augustine was wisely sceptical. For one thing, it was too early in the early fifth century to be confident that the triumph of the Church would be permanent; persecution might return. But there was a more fundamental objection: the triumph of the Church did not mean the sanctification of the human race. Life was still to be lived in a fallen world among fallen human beings.

Augustine did not expect this to change. This was because, following biblical teaching and early Christian tradition, he accepted that the righteous will always be a small remnant in the world. The Fall has corrupted human nature, and divine grace rescues only a few. The righteous are a minority even in the Church, though thanks to them the Church continues to promote Christian values; but in the world at large they will never be able to dominate society. Human society as a whole, and the political states that administer it, will continue to form part of the earthly city, dominated by love of self and contempt for God.

Christians in the World

If, then, the state is irredeemable, what attitude should Christians have towards it? Should they detach themselves and avoid direct involvement? In the Church before Augustine's time Christians had been strongly discouraged from volunteering for public service, whether in government or the army. What place can gospel values have there? It might appear that in the world of public action Christians will always be out of place, like fish out of water.

But in Augustine's world Christians did not form a separate group. They had to take part in the life of the broader society. How could the Church, itself a mixed body of saints and sinners, look with contempt on the earthly city? In so far as the earthly city is the Roman commonwealth, all the members of Augustine's flock belonged to it; in its stricter definition as the world in rebellion against God, the unrighteous in the Church are its secret members. Mixture within the Church itself contributes to the subtle bond between the two cities. 'In fact', as Augustine wrote, 'these two cities are mixed up and entangled with each other in this age, and will only be separated at the Last Judgement' (C 1.35).

What makes up civil society? As Augustine points out, Cicero in his political treatise *The Republic* (written in the 50s BC) had defined it as 'the association of a multitude of rational beings united by a common agreement on the objects of their love'. Do members of the city of God on earth have any aims in common with members of the earthly city? Augustine replies that they do: we all equally want 'peace', that is, friendly and mutually helpful relations with our fellow men and women. This common interest enables practical co-operation, although, of course, differences remain.

The household of human beings who do not live by faith aims at an earthly peace based on the good things of this temporal life; but the household of human beings who live by faith does not let itself be distracted by these things from its journey towards God, but treats them as supports with which to endure and keep within check the burdens of 'the corruptible body which weighs down the soul [WISDOM 9:15]. In this way both kinds of human beings and both households share the use of the things we need in this mortal life, but each has its own very different end in using them. So too the earthly city aims at an earthly peace, and establishes an agreement between its citizens as regards authority and obedience, in order to achieve a certain harmony of human wills as regards the things of this mortal life. But the heavenly city, or rather that part of it which is on pilgrimage in this perishable world, is also obliged to make use of this peace, until the passing away of the perishable world for which this kind of peace is essential. And therefore it does not hesitate to obey the laws of the earthly city which regulate those things which help to sustain mortal life. (C 19.17 ABRIDGED)

Augustine's argument that Christians should collaborate with the broader society is hard to fault; less welcome is his teaching that they should conform to the laws and customs of that society. He had no sense that Christians should have their own distinctive set of political and social values. He was saddened by the harsher aspects of life in the Roman empire – external and civil wars, the regular use of torture in criminal trials, the institution of slavery. He looked forward to their disappearance in the world to come, but he could not imagine life in this world without them. In a fallen world full of vicious human beings he saw no alternative to a hierarchical society that uses violence both to repel its enemies and to impose obedience on its members.

How could this be squared with Christ's Sermon on the Mount, with its rejection of the use of force even in self-defence? 'I order you not to resist the wicked; but if anyone strikes you on the right cheek, turn to him the other also' (MATTHEW 5:39). Augustine argued that this text is concerned not with acts but attitudes: human beings often have to discipline the weak and foolish, punish the wicked and repel their enemies, but this they must do in a spirit not of brutality or revenge but of concern for the common good. It is not even necessary for the servant of the state to convince himself that each recourse to force is necessary: since the maintenance of state authority is necessary for the general good, he is right to obey orders as they stand, and leave it to his superiors to answer for them before God. He has a duty to disobey only those orders that are directly contrary to religion.

It would be unfair to say that Augustine was complacent about the harshness and cruelty of the late Roman state: he placed it high among the trials and tribulations that make us despair of happiness in this life and yearn for the life to come. But he did not think that this created any real problem of conscience for the earnest Christian engaged in government service.

The Christians of the first three centuries had tended to steer clear of involvement in public life. This was mainly due to the difficulties in serving a pagan state, but also to the Christian ideal of detachment from the sordid affairs of this passing world, as we saw illustrated in Cyprian. This misplaced otherworldliness survived the coming of Christian emperors: the popes of Augustine's time included state service as among the dangerous professions forbidden to those who were doing penance for their sins or who had already done penance. This negative attitude to state service, surprising in a now Christian empire, received a fresh impetus from the monastic movement of the fourth century: many able men who would previously have gone into public life left society for the desert, or at least the service of the Church; Augustine himself was of their number. This makes his encouragement of Christian lay people to serve society and promote peace in the world much more than the platitude it may sound to us today; here again, as in his teaching on the Church as a mixed society, he was moving it away from its sectarian origins and towards a proper understanding of its role in society. This is the positive side of his social and political teaching. The negative side, as we have seen, is an excessive political conformism. But this is a fault that can be charged against the overwhelming majority of Christians throughout history. In pressing the charge we must be careful not to blame Augustine for conforming to the ideas of his own day while we are equally uncritical of the ideas of our own.

Coercion of Heretics

As we have seen, Augustine did not suppose that the arrival of Christian emperors meant the advent of the kingdom of God. But he did recognize that it helped the Church. Not only were the centuries of persecution at an end (at least temporarily), but state law was now available for the promotion of true religion. By the end of the fourth century the emperors had destroyed the power of pagans to molest the Church. Why not complete the good work by crushing enemies who were still more dangerous – schismatics and heretics, who used the name of Christ to draw Christians away from the true fold? This leads us on to a notorious topic where Augustine was criticized in his own day and has been widely condemned since – his defence of state coercion of heretics.

Here again he was responding to events and did not choose his ground. In a series of edicts, dating principally to 405 and 412, the Roman state, at the request of the African bishops, tried to force the Donatists to give up their schism and submit to the established Church: their churches were confiscated, their services were banned, their clergy were threatened with exile, and their laity with heavy financial penalties, if they did not return to the Catholic fold.

When coercive measures were first proposed, Augustine had opposed their introduction: he did not think that error had any rights, but he was afraid that the Church would be unable to absorb a flood of reluctant converts. But he now changed his tune, partly because as an official apologist for the Church he had no option, and partly because the converts turned out better than he had expected.

My original opinion was that no one should be forced into the unity of Christ: there should be attack in word, battle in argument and victory through reason, lest those we had known as open heretics should be landed on us as insincere Catholics. But this opinion of mine was overcome, not by the arguments of opponents but by factual proofs. What proved me wrong above all was the example of my own city, which, though formerly entirely in the Donatist party, was converted through fear of the imperial laws to Catholic unity ... People were so helped by the terror of these laws that some now say, 'We already knew this to be the truth, but we were held back by some habit or other; thanks be to God, who has broken our chains and transferred us to the bond of peace.' Others say, 'We did not know this to be the truth and were not ready to learn it, but we have become keen to learn it out of the fear of losing temporal goods without gaining eternal ones; thanks be to God, who used terror to dispel our negligence and to make us seek out anxiously what in time of security we never wanted to know.' Others say, 'We were deterred from entering by reports whose falsity we only learnt on entering, and we needed coercion to make us enter; thanks be to God who used this whip to teach us how false and empty were the lies people told about his Church.' Others say, 'We thought it did not matter where we practised Christianity; but thanks be to God who rescued us from schism and showed us that the one God is to be worshipped in unity.' (L 93.4.17–18)

Augustine found support for the use of coercion in Scripture itself. God had constantly driven the Israelites to repentance by punishing them. The conversion of St Paul, overwhelmed by a heavenly vision on the road to Damascus, was a still better example of how God acts: he does not wait humbly on the sidelines and *ask* human beings whether they want to be converted. So in the case of heretics it is quite inadequate to say that people must be left to find their own way to the truth: they may in their present situation lack both the opportunity to encounter the truth and the ability to recognize it when they do. Of course it would be better for them to discover the truth on their own initiative, but often this is not possible. Their freedom is adequately respected if, after being forced to assent to the truth, they come to believe in it genuinely; their belated consent makes up for the initial use of coercion.

In the parable of the Great Banquet (LUKE 14:16–24) God is compared to a host who sends out his servant to the highways and hedges to *compel* people to come in. As Augustine commented,

> *They stick in the hedges, they don't want to be compelled. 'Let us enter,' they say, 'of our own will.' This was not what the Lord ordered: 'Compel them', he said, 'to come in.' Let necessity be experienced from without, and consent is born within.* (S 112.7.8)

These passages represent Augustine at his best and at his worst. His defence of a policy of state oppression which drove many Donatists to suicide borders on the obscene. Moreover, his argument has thoroughly unpleasant implications: once you start persecuting erroneous views, where do you draw the line? In the later Middle Ages and the time of the Reformation his arguments were eagerly exploited by pious fanatics who wished to impose their own version of Christianity by means of state law. At the same time, however, his defence of the coercion of heretics shows real psychological insight: in our permissive society we are all too well aware that untrammelled 'freedom of choice' can enslave people to social or psychological pressures where no choice worthy of the name is actually exercised.

It is painful to read that his arguments were later used to defend such horrors as the Inquisition. But this should not blind us to the sheer logicality of a policy of coercion, once it is assumed, as most Christians did assume as late as the eighteenth century, that everyone who dies in heresy or schism goes straight to hell. We do not respect freedom of choice when it leads to drug-taking or drunken driving, yet schism in Christian eyes is far more destructive than either. If salvation is through faith in Christ and if Christ founded the one true Church as the ark of salvation, what ground do Christians have for tolerating other religions or for allowing a plurality of denominations? The arguments for religious coercion can appear perfectly, indeed horribly, logical.

It was not till the Second Vatican Council (1962–65) that the Roman Catholic Church attempted the difficult task of reconciling modern ideas of religious freedom with its traditional claim to be the one true Church. The *Declaration on Religious Liberty*, one of the most impressive of the council documents, argues that the service of God is only possible where there is freedom from coercion, since 'the practice of religion of its very nature consists primarily of those voluntary and free acts by which a human being directs himself to God' (1.3). Augustine would have said that this teaching is far too abstract and ignores the concrete situation – the lack of human freedom as a result of original sin and social pressures. It is to his teaching on original sin, and on the work of divine grace to restore freedom of the will, that I shall now turn.

Freedom and Grace

Pelagius

I would imagine that for at least a century every student of theology, at some stage in his or her course, has written an essay on why Pelagius was a heretic. And yet almost none of these students actually read Pelagius: after all, his surviving writings have only recently been translated. Nevertheless, they were expected to condemn him without a hearing; not even the Inquisition was so unjust. In a broader context Pelagius often used to be mentioned as the typical Briton – a staunch active Christian, indifferent to such theological subtleties as the notion of divine grace, little given to the passive religiosity of depending on God, but confident in the strength nature has given him, and keen to realize the pious maxim, 'God helps those who help themselves'.

But first some facts of biography. Pelagius was born in Britain at around the time of Augustine's birth (354); Jerome could later describe him as having 'wits addled with Scotch porridge'. He settled in Rome in the early 380s. There he became a leader of the new ascetic, or monastic, movement. This movement primarily attracted noble ladies, widows and virgins. Though some of them gave their wealth to the poor (to the protests of their relatives), most held on to it and used it for good works, such as building up around them communities dedicated to prayer and Scripture study. In contrast to the ostentatious consumption and mild debauchery of many Roman aristocrats (so brilliantly satirized by

Jerome), they formed a very self-conscious élite. Pelagius became the spiritual director of many of these ladies, and wrote in beautiful Latin how right they were and how wicked was the life they had renounced. Just before the sack of Rome by the Goths in 410 he and several of his followers fled to Africa. Within a year he had moved on to Palestine, but his disciple Caelestius sparked a rumpus in Carthage when he tried to spread the views of his master.

Following Pelagius, Caelestius denied that the Fall of Adam had radically altered the human condition. In effect he denied what came to be called 'original sin', a doctrine particularly loved by the African church. According to this doctrine, mankind as a whole has inherited from Adam the terrible consequences of his sin – the inability to do right, and mortality experienced as not a mere fact of nature but a punishment. Since baptism, in the view of the African church, is the remedy for original sin, this teaching seemed to deny the need for baptism; in this case, the whole debate with the Donatists over when and where baptism is valid and effective had been a total waste of time. Such subversive teaching could not of course be tolerated: the African church duly condemned Caelestius as a heretic.

The matter was taken up in Palestine, where Pelagius was now staying, and there in 415 a council at Diospolis, without looking deeply into the matter, gave him the benefit of the doubt and declared him free of heresy. The African church renewed its anathemas, and Pope Zosimus (417–18) was obliged to adjudicate; sadly he disgraced the Roman see first by acquitting Pelagius and Caelestius, and then by reversing this verdict under political pressure, when the African bishops successfully lobbied the imperial court. Pelagius himself now disappears from history, but the debate rumbled on, right up to Augustine's death (430) and beyond.

The term 'Pelagian' means someone who thinks that human beings can obey God's law without the help of his grace. Was Pelagius a Pelagian? He was certainly no theologian, merely a fine preacher and an effective spiritual director; his mauling by Augustine is like a butterfly being broken on a wheel. But his views represent an interesting stage in the developing idealism of the ascetic movement of the fourth century. The core of his message is that Christians are called to perfection and are capable of attaining it. It is unfair to say that he thought unaided human nature sufficient. He acknowledged the truth of a theme found also in Augustine: bad teaching and worse example over countless generations have corrupted human society, creating a habit of sin that has become second nature. We need the law of God and the example of Christ to teach us the way; we need the free forgiveness of past sins bestowed in baptism to fire us with confidence and gratitude.

But Pelagius firmly rejected the view that the Fall of Man has left us with a weakened and corrupt nature that no effort of the human will can restore, even guided by the law of God. He saw no merit in the notion that freedom from sin requires an additional, inner grace, a change of heart and will that only God can bring about. Such views seemed to him to subvert moral effort; salvation consists not in piously twiddling one's thumbs waiting for an extraordinary gift of grace, but in an active and generous response to the call of the gospel.

In many respects the teaching of Pelagius was a genuine continuation of early Christian teaching, with its stress on the free commitment to a pure and holy life that a Christian takes on at baptism. But his insistence that perfection is possible and therefore obligatory goes well beyond the less exacting standards of the Church of the first three centuries, which was satisfied if converts avoided the grossest sins such as idolatry and adultery. His demand that we obey the whole law of God reflects the moral earnestness of the ascetic movement of the fourth century. In his own conversion back in 386, Augustine had embraced the same ideals; but after years of fighting the Donatists he had come to accept a mixture of saints and sinners in the Church and had no time for spiritual élitism.

Augustine on Grace

The Donatist controversy had established Augustine as the principal propagandist of the African church, and as early as 412 he was called upon to attack the new enemy. Pelagius' final defeat in 418 did not close the debate, which continued right down to Augustine's death in 430. It was increasingly fed by Augustine himself, as he drew out more and more the logic of his anti-Pelagian position and developed an extreme stance that shocked many of his former allies.

We saw how in the Donatist debate Augustine inherited the main lines of controversy and had limited freedom of manoeuvre. In contrast, the challenge of Pelagius was one he would have been happy to dream up: the field was new, and the topic one that had been of deep concern to him long before he had even heard of Pelagius. It had been at the centre of his thought since 396, when at one of the turning points of his intellectual development he finally saw the full force of St Paul's Letter to the Romans: 'Wretched man that I am, who will set me free from the body of this death? The grace of God through Jesus Christ our Lord' (ROMANS 7:24–25, LATIN VERSION).

The *Confessions* (written in the late 390s) have plenty to say about the limitations of human freedom and the need for divine grace; 'Give what you command, and command what you will', is a leading theme of Book Ten, and implies already that the law itself, which Pelagius thought the main instrument of grace, is inadequate to change hearts. In contrast to Pelagius' insistence on the power of the human will, Augustine's account of his conversion brings out the impotence of the will, which only attains freedom when liberated by divine grace:

You, Lord, are good and merciful. You turned your gaze on me, sunk in death, and with your right hand drew out the pit of corruption at the bottom of my heart. As a result I ceased to want what I had wanted before and came to want only what you wanted. Where had my free will been for so many years? Out of what deep hiding-place was it suddenly called forth? (Co 9.1.1.)

Pelagius thought this rhetorical and perverse. There seemed nothing in Augustine's conversion that his own theology could not explain. Corrupt culture and sensual indulgence create a habit of sin that is hard to break; but this habit can be broken by a free and spontaneous decision of the will when the soul is fired by the word of God – in Augustine's case the reading of the Letters of St Paul in the months immediately preceding his conversion. But Augustine saw in his long enslavement to sex and ambition not mere habit but the power of original sin – that radical corruption of human nature which we all experience and can trace back to our common ancestors, the first human pair, Adam and Eve.

The story of the sin of Adam and Eve that led to their expulsion from Paradise (the 'Fall of Man', as it came to be called) is a multi-layered myth that has a variety of meanings even in the original text of Genesis, to say nothing of the wealth of interpretation it received in the early Church. Augustine's interpretation of the story has dominated western reading of it ever since, to the extent that it needs a careful study of the text to realize how many other interpretations are equally possible.

According to Augustine, Adam and Eve before the Fall enjoyed privileges scarcely believable in human beings. They were free of complexes and irrational drives; they possessed a deep knowledge, and exercised a control, of the natural world; they enjoyed a relationship with God as close as that of the angels. They were far more exalted beings than the virtuous cavemen in whom conservative Christians of our own day believe, in a rather comical attempt to reconcile Genesis with modern views of the prehistory of the human race. But all these wonderful privileges were forfeited as a result of the Fall, when man lost not only the delights of Paradise but also the original harmony of his being. Fallen man has a natural love of self, not of God; and he is full of irrational drives, specially of sex and aggression, that prevent him from pursuing the good. He still possesses freedom of the will, in that he makes conscious choices; but in practice he is only able to choose evil. Augustine refused to be impressed by the moral heroes of pagan antiquity: their apparent virtues were merely 'magnificent vices', for they were not motivated by a love of God.

In view of the total depravity of fallen man, the remedies of divine grace, as described by Pelagius, seemed woefully inadequate. The Law of God and the example of Christ may possibly fire us with a desire to do good, but in fallen men this desire need not lead to action at all, still less to a consistent life of virtue. As Augustine had learnt from earlier experience, you can long to change your life without having the strength to do so. Divine grace in the Augustinian scheme, like a doctor using every drug in his bag, has to make simultaneous use of a variety of remedies. With those who are particularly resistant, there is no alternative to the major surgery of a divine miracle that shifts and redirects the deepest drives of the will – as in the case of the conversion of St Paul on the road to Damascus, who set out as a rabid persecutor of Christians and was then literally stunned by an act of God. Once there is some spark in us able to respond to God, grace has to fan that spark into life by bringing the right external influences to bear and enabling us to respond to them.

'The free choice of the will is very powerful', you say, but what power does it have in the case of those sold under sin? ... We are ordered to believe, so that by receiving the gift of the Holy Spirit we can do right actions out of love. But who can believe unless he is moved by some call, that is, by some kind of evidence? Who has it in his power to ensure that his mind attains just the right perception to move his will to faith? Who can respond enthusiastically to something that does not delight him? Who has it in his power to ensure either that he will meet what can delight him or that it will delight him when he meets it? (Si 1.2.21)

Even when the will is strongly drawn to right action, it meets the resistance of contrary drives and habits. God has to complete his 'operation' that inspires the will by his 'co-operation' that gives the will the power to progress from desire to effective action.

> *He who wishes to keep God's commandments but is unable to do so already possesses a good will, but as yet a small and weak one ... And who was it who gave Peter the first small portion of the gift of love but he who both prepares the human will and perfects by his co-operation what he initiates by his operation? He begins by operating in us to give us the will, and completes it by co-operating with us when we have the will.* (G 17.33)

God is not merely a skilful physician of souls: he is a master of his own creation, and nothing can frustrate his will. His will to save includes the 'gift of perseverance', that is, a special grace to ensure that those chosen by God do not fall away from him. No one can achieve this of his own will: it comes from God as pure gift. Augustine's final position, as set out in *The Gift of Perseverance* (written in 429), is that our contribution to our own salvation consists of praying for this gift, and of nothing more: everything else is the work of God. As Augustine insisted again and again, human beings are totally dependent on God and stand before him as the humble recipients of his grace, not as the moral heroes who have achieved their own salvation and can look God firmly in the eye.

Augustine's critics accused him of treating human beings as passive pawns and denying the freedom of the will. But the whole point he was trying to make is that freedom of the will is itself the gift of God, who restores to human beings both the ability to choose the good and the power to achieve it. The texts I have quoted illustrate Augustine's acute perception of how the human will actually operates. God's grace does not compel the will to obey him automatically, like a cog in a machine; instead, it elicits a spontaneous response by means of an inspiration given to man as a conscious and rational being.

Predestination

Against the Manichees, Augustine had insisted that human beings are not the helpless playthings of embattled cosmic powers: evil has no real existence, and man possesses free will. The Pelagians claimed that in his attacks on them he had gone back on this. Certainly he stressed different aspects of the truth in different contexts, but he had a coherent position none the less.

It can be summed up as follows. Man in his fallen state is only capable of evil, but God is able to rescue him, not by overriding his free will but precisely by empowering it. Evil is not something concrete and positive, but a mere deficiency, an absence of the good. Every created being in virtue of his mere existence has some share of the good; every conscious and rational being has some potential to respond to the grace of God. In fallen man this potential is so weakened as to be wholly dormant. But divine grace is able to bring this potential to realization, to reawaken and re-animate the natural powers within the soul of every human being; this it does by acting through both external stimuli and inner assistance within the will itself. As beings endowed with free will, we could choose to resist the healing action of God; but God can so work on us that we have not the faintest inclination to exercise this freedom. The salvation of the whole human race is something easily within the capacity of the divine will. Grace (if it choose) is irresistible.

Does this mean that every single human being will be saved? Such 'universalism', as it is called, seems to have been held by Origen of Alexandria (d. 254), the greatest Christian thinker before Augustine, and appeals, of course, to many Christians today. It could surely draw powerful reinforcement from Augustine's doctrine of the irresistibility of grace. But in fact Augustine is the very last theologian universalists think of appealing to, and for a very good reason. Augustine thought universalism quite impossible, whatever one's theology of grace. For him it was ruled out by one simple fact – what happens at baptism. The early Church proclaimed, following the gospel (JOHN 3:5), that only the baptized could be saved. It is a simple fact that not all are baptized. It followed necessarily that not all are saved; hell and damnation are the destiny of a large part, indeed the greater part, of the human race.

This conclusion is so unattractive to us today that it needs to be explained in greater detail. The stress on the absolute necessity of baptism, while very understandable in the wake of the Donatist dispute, would generally be rejected today, and was questioned by some of Augustine's contemporaries. They tried to exploit the traditional idea of 'baptism of desire', that is, a love of God equivalent to the commitment entered into at baptism: those who have this desire and yet (through no fault of their own) fail to be baptized will still be saved. Augustine resisted this line of escape; he came to recognize only baptism by blood, that is, a martyr's death, as an adequate substitute for baptism in water.

This was arguably too restrictive, but there is good biblical support for insisting not perhaps on baptism but at least on the gift of God associated with baptism – the gift of faith. The New Testament insists again and again that faith in Christ is essential for salvation; it does not hold out salvation for those (the majority of the human race) who do not commit themselves to Christ. Admittedly, this stress on the need for a conscious commitment to Christ goes against Augustine's own stress on the unconscious springs of the will, which are deeper than our choices; and Augustine was well aware that a 'conscious commitment' does not necessarily indicate a real consent of the heart. But he was sufficiently loyal to church tradition to steer clear of any suggestion that there might be a Christianity of the heart without conscious Christian belief.

A further problem for universalism lies in the biblical theme of the holy remnant, chosen by grace (e.g. ROMANS 11:5). A constant theme of the Bible is that most of mankind, even of God's own people, wander off after false gods, leaving behind only a tiny body of faithful. Those invited to the wedding feast scorn the invitation, for many are called but few are chosen (MATTHEW 22:2–14). The notion of 'grace' in early Christian thought was linked to notions of 'favour' and 'privilege'; it was contrasted to the concept of the 'natural' good that all human beings possess in virtue of their creation.

In Augustine's own day universalism was not an issue at all. All Christians agreed that only members of the one true Church could be saved, and that not even all of them would be saved: God 'elects' (chooses) the recipients of his mercy and makes them members of the Church, where they mix with fellow Christians who are called into the Church but not chosen for salvation. The only question was the relationship between human choice and divine election. Does God choose his 'elect' in virtue of their merits, already existent or foreseen? Or is election a wholly unmerited gift? Is the saving grace of God irresistible and only bestowed on a few, or is it offered to all and rejected by most?

Augustine's opponents liked citing the saying of St Paul, 'God our Saviour wants everyone to be saved and come to know the truth' (1 TIMOTHY 2:4). They rejected Augustine's argument that, if salvation was offered to all, God's mercy would be displayed but not his justice. For God's justice has been fully satisfied by the death of Christ: in the words of St Paul, 'one has died for all and therefore all have died' (2 CORINTHIANS 5:14). In other words, Christ took on himself the penalty for our sins, and we no longer have to pay it ourselves. Instead, all human beings are offered sufficient grace for salvation. The gospel is offered to all; its truth is clear from the wisdom of its teaching, its spread throughout the world, and the miracles and personal holiness that have attended it. All have the opportunity to respond to the gospel; if nevertheless they fail to attain salvation, this is not God's will but their own choice.

Augustine attacked this position as contrary to his deepest convictions about both God and human beings. Many who reject the gospel, or who fail to live up to it, never possessed the perception and the self-control necessary to make it a real option for them. To say that God wants to save everyone but can't achieve it is to deny his power and resourcefulness: how could any creature resist a creator determined to use every means to ensure his salvation? The fact that human beings have free will means that divine grace has to operate in a particular way; it does not make that grace ineffective. The verse from the First Letter to Timothy is certainly awkward, but it simply cannot mean what is seems to mean. Any fool can quote a verse of Scripture; only a wise man can interpret it. The fact that Christ paid the penalty for sin enables God to be merciful to those he chooses, but does not oblige him to show mercy to all.

A special problem arose from the fate of infants who died before baptism: it seemed unjust to send them to hell when they hadn't had the chance to be baptized. A popular solution was to suppose that God foresaw that if they had been baptized they would have failed to live up to the grace of baptism, and therefore killed them off before they disgraced both themselves and the sacrament; but their foreseen misdeeds remained adequate to justify their damnation. This argument received from Augustine the scorn it deserved. It is an affront to justice, he argued, to suggest that unbaptized infants are condemned for sins they never had the chance to commit. Their damnation can only be explained as the penalty for the sin they were born with – the guilt that each one of us inherits from Adam: he left us not only a corrupt and tainted nature but also a heavy burden of guilt, which we call 'original sin'.

Augustine claimed that all human beings in some sense 'sinned in Adam' and share in his guilt; they therefore deserve damnation even if, like unbaptized infants, they have committed no sins of their own. This argument builds on the notion of a natural solidarity between descendants and ancestors, or more generally between human beings linked by history. None of us exists apart, limited to the little world of our own personal choices; apart from the life of individuals, there is the sharing of individuals in a common life, where we must accept responsibility for the sins of the society of which we are members. As a rebuttal of the extreme claims of modern individualism this belief of Augustine's in human solidarity has much to be said for it. But whether this solidarity is sufficient to justify eternal damnation for those who die without committing sins of their own is, of course, another question. It is one where Augustine's position is particularly hard to defend.

It was not only the problem of unbaptized infants, however, that made Augustine stress original sin. Since he was sure that God is able to save whomever he pleases, and yet believed that not all are saved, he concluded that God does not wish to save everyone. How is this compatible with the Christian conviction that God is love? Augustine argued that because of the guilt of original sin everyone deserves eternal damnation. The amazing thing is not that many are damned but that any at all are saved. While damnation of the many is required by the justice of God, the salvation of the few is proof of the depths of his mercy. God does not choose to damn anyone: in the case of the majority he simply allows the effect of sin to take its natural course. Meanwhile, he shows his love by rescuing the few; he uses all the resources of his grace to ensure their salvation, despite the effects of original sin.

God's decisions are never reactive but creative. He chose his elect before they were born, indeed before the world was made, and it is this original choice that we call 'predestination'. The long course of human history is the working out of that original design; in the words of St Paul 'those whom he predestined he also called, and those whom he called he also justified, and those whom he justified he also glorified' (ROMANS 8:30).

What guides God in his selection of the predestined? Does he choose those who, he foresees, will prove themselves worthy? This answer was, of course, quite impossible for Augustine; for all are equally unworthy, and the virtues we see in some of our Christian brothers and sisters are not the *cause* of God's choice but its *fruit*. We seem reduced to saying that God's choice is simply arbitrary. In fact Augustine draws back from this unattractive conclusion. He plays with the unhappy idea that divine justice may be different from, and superior to, human ideas of justice. He insists that God must have good reasons for making the selection he does, even if these reasons are for us an inscrutable mystery, hidden in the secret abyss of divine wisdom. All this is theological gobbledy-gook for 'I haven't a clue'. Augustine's inability to answer this crucial question is yet another weakness in his theory. The doctrine of predestination, after all his efforts, turns out to be incoherent as well as repulsive.

A Dubious Legacy

Augustine's doctrine of original sin built on the work of certain of his predecessors, notably Tertullian of Carthage (*c*.AD 200), who had introduced the idea that the sinfulness of Adam is passed on to his descendants not merely by bad upbringing and social influences but by the very act of procreation. It is this view of original sin that demands the historicity of Adam as the common ancestor of the whole human race; in contrast, most early Christian interpretation of the Adam story treated him as primarily a symbol of the human race as a whole. Augustine not only adopted Tertullian's picture but developed its blackest traits: the notion of inherited guilt sufficient to justify eternal damnation was the happy invention of Augustine himself. The very term 'original sin' was probably coined by him, and it was through his influence that a strong doctrine of original sin became part of the common inheritance of western Christendom.

The idea of strict predestination was also an innovation of Augustine's. It upset many of his contemporaries and has remained highly contentious ever since; no part of his legacy has been more fiercely attacked. The claim that God wills the salvation of only a few of the members of the Church threatens his own doctrine of the solidarity between saints and sinners (see chapter 2 above), even though he tried to evade this by stressing our ignorance of who is, and who is not, among the elect. The notion of predestination, in a loose sense, as an expression of our confidence in God's power to save, was traditional and uncontroversial, but as developed by Augustine in the context of a strong doctrine of original sin and our dependence on grace it became virtually a new doctrine. In the later Catholic tradition Augustine was honoured as the 'theologian of grace' but his teaching on predestination was watered down or simply ignored. It was the reformer Calvin in the sixteenth century, and then the Catholic Jansen in the seventeenth, who revived the full Augustinian doctrine and brought it back to the centre of theological debate. The Roman Church condemned Jansen, and tried hard to pretend that this left Augustine himself unscathed.

The philosophers of the eighteenth-century Enlightenment could be more frank. Voltaire, in the article 'Original Sin' in the 1767 edition of his *Philosophical Dictionary*, described the doctrine as 'the wild and fantastic invention of an African both debauched and repentant, Manichee and Christian, tolerant and a persecutor, who spent his life contradicting himself'. Voltaire reacted strongly against the Augustinian inheritance; he rejected the whole set of notions that Augustine had spent his best years defending. Original sin, predestination, eternal damnation – all these went out of the window. For Voltaire, human beings are born with a pure and untainted nature:

> *Gather together all the children in the world, and you will find nothing in them but innocence, sweetness and modesty. If they were born wicked, criminal, and cruel, they would show some sign of it, just as baby serpents try to bite and baby tigers to tear. But nature, having created man, like pigeons and rabbits, without weapons of attack, has not implanted in him any destructive instincts.* (PHILOSOPHICAL DICTIONARY, 'WICKEDNESS')

It is only bad education and corrupt social influences that produce vice and crime. And just as human beings are naturally loving and lovable, so God himself is pure benevolence, and loves all mankind equally. There is no distinction between the order of grace and the order of nature: God bestows his love on all his creatures, not on some special class of the elect. Baptism does not bestow special privileges on the baptized but celebrates the universal gift of birth.

It is because the 'heresy' of Voltaire has become the orthodoxy of liberal Christianity, or virtually so, that strong doctrines of original sin and predestination appear so monstrous to modern believers. Most theologians would like to jettison the more negative aspects of Augustine's position while preserving many of his insights on the human will and the workings of grace. A tart judgement would be that in his writings on grace he is good on how the will operates but poor on the purposes of God – in other words, that he was a better psychologist than he was a theologian. His doctrine of original sin is repulsive to those who assert the goodness of human nature as created and sustained by God; but after all the murders and assaults we read of every day in our newspapers, let alone the death camps of Hitler and Stalin and the other horrors of twentieth-century history, we must surely concede that Augustine was more realistic than Voltaire about human nature.

To return to Augustine's own context, let us note how his reaction to Pelagianism was in many ways an extension of his battle against Donatism. Both Pelagians and Donatists proclaimed a Church 'without spot or wrinkle', a holy remnant uncontaminated by the world. Augustine did not abandon the notion of a holy remnant, but he reduced its impact by stressing the weakness of all human beings, even the elect, and their dependence on divine grace at every stage of their existence. The gift of perseverance gives no ground for feelings of superiority, since no one can tell till he dies whether or not he has received it.

The Christian apologists of the first three centuries had stressed our freedom to embrace the gospel and commit ourselves to Christ with confidence: once baptism has freed us from the sin and blindness of our former life, we possess the power to remain true to that commitment. Augustine too was a firm believer in the power of baptism, but not because it conquers sin in one fell swoop: rather, it starts us on a long and painful pilgrimage, and gives us the grace we shall need every step of the way. The Church is less the haven of the reborn, radiant with spiritual health, than a hospital where the best we can do is submit to treatment.

There are people, ungrateful towards grace, who attribute much to our poor and wounded nature. It is true that man when he was created was given great strength of will, but by sinning he lost it. He fell into death. The robbers left him on the road half-dead. A passing Samaritan lifted him onto his beast of burden. He is still undergoing treatment. 'But sufficient for me,' someone says, 'is what I received in baptism – forgiveness of all sins.' But surely the destruction of wickedness does not mean the end of weakness? ... You will remember, beloved, the man half-dead who was wounded by robbers on the road, how he is consoled, receiving oil and wine for his wounds [the Parable of the Good Samaritan, LUKE 10:30–37]. His sins, it is true, were already forgiven; and yet his sickness is cured in the inn. The inn, if you can recognize it, is the Church. While in the inn let us submit to treatment; let us not boast of health while we are still weak ... Say to your soul, say this: you are still in this life, the flesh is still weak; even after complete forgiveness you were prescribed prayer as a remedy; you still have to say, until your sickness is cured, 'Forgive us our trespasses'. (S 131.6.6)

Sex and Marriage

Augustine's teaching on original sin, discussed in the last chapter, had a particular influence on his view of sex and marriage. This subject relates as well to another key theme of this book – the holiness of the people of God. Obviously a concern with holiness makes people morally scrupulous. But there was more to it than that: the ideas connected to holiness in the early Church produced a particular form of sexual morality, new in the ancient world.

Early Christians and Sex

The early Christians prided themselves on being the holy people of God; they claimed a unique relationship with God in heaven as members of his holy Church. This gave them an inner sense of unique status in the unseen world. Inevitably this contrasted strongly with the visible reality of everyday life, where Christians had many of the same concerns as their pagan neighbours and didn't seem so very unusual, apart from their strange religion. The problem became: how were Christians to embody their inner holiness in their outward lives? How best could they express their sense of a special identity? The Church very soon came to concentrate on one area of conduct which seemed to give special scope – sexual behaviour. In the words of the brilliant contemporary historian Peter Brown,

On the surface the Christians practised an austere sexual moral-ity, easily recognizable and acclaimed by outsiders: total sexual

renunciation by the few; marital concord between spouses ... strong
disapproval of remarriage. This surface was presented openly to out-
siders. Lacking the clear ritual boundaries provided in Judaism by cir-
cumcision and dietary laws, Christians tended to make their
exceptional sexual discipline bear the full burden of expressing the dif-
ference between themselves and the pagan world. (A HISTORY OF
PRIVATE LIFE, P. ARIÈS AND G. DUBY, EDS, 1.263)

To modern Christians this stress on sexual purity seems unbal-
anced, even unhealthy, and they will wish that the first Christians
had made a different choice. But their choice is easy to understand
if we look at their social setting and ideology. For one thing it gave
equal scope to all: not everyone has the means to give alms, not
everyone has a job where he can prove his honesty and public
spirit, but everyone has to cope with his or her sexuality.

But there were solid theological reasons as well. On the level of
ideology, there was the language in the Bible about spiritual
rebirth. 'In baptism you have been raised with Christ through
faith in the working of God who raised him from the dead'
(COLOSSIANS 2:12). This spiritual entry into heaven, this gift of new
life, is bestowed not through physical procreation but through the
new birth of baptism. Even in this age Christians share in the gifts
of the age to come: what could be more appropriate than to anticipate that age by renouncing marriage, or at least remarriage,
here and now? In the words of the gospel, 'The sons of this age
marry and are given in marriage, but those deemed worthy to
attain that life and the resurrection from the dead neither marry
nor are given in marriage' (LUKE 20:34–35).

On a deeper level than that of ideology, the attitude of Christians
towards the body was strongly influenced by their feelings about
the Church. Social anthropologists have taught us how closely
attitudes to the physical body reflect attitudes towards society, the
social 'body'. The early Christians wanted to maintain a clear
boundary between themselves and the pagan world around them;

they were concerned to preserve the purity of the Church as the 'body of Christ'. It was natural that this concern should spill over into an anxiety about the purity of their own bodies. Early Christians felt a need to express and preserve the purity of the Church through the bodily purity of its members. To maintain itself as a heavenly society in exile upon earth, the Church needed members whose own bodies stood apart from the blurring and contamination brought about by easy sexual relations. This did not necessarily mean rejecting marriage: it did mean a new stress on sexual morality, and a stiffening of the rules.

These various motives in favour of a strict sexual morality cut little ice with Augustine: as we saw in the *City of God*, he was realistic about our need to accept the conditions of life on earth and the intimate links between Church and world. But there was a third motive that appealed to him powerfully – the ideal of single-mindedness. Many of Jesus' parables, such as the parables of the people who sell all they have in order to buy the pearl of great value or the field with treasure in it (MATTHEW 13:44–46), have as their message the ideal of single-mindedness or purity of heart. St Paul used this ideal to encourage celibacy: 'The unmarried man cares about the affairs of the Lord, how to please the Lord; but the married man cares about the affairs of the world, how to please his wife, and he is split in two' (1 CORINTHIANS 7:32–34).

In early Christianity (as in the Platonism which influenced Augustine so strongly in his youth) moral evil was seen as loss of unity, through the loss of rational control over man's instinctive drives, particularly those of sex and aggression. Self-control could be compared, as in Plato's *Republic*, to the political control exercised by the state: the edicts of rulers receive the rational obedience of their subjects. But in man the irrational drives (or 'passions') are, by definition, incapable of rational obedience. Some early Christian moralists, such as Clement of Alexandria, urged Christians to stamp out the passions altogether. Others recommend what we today would call sublimation – preserving the energy of sexual desire but channelling it into love for God. But the standard teaching of the Church was more realistic: the sexual drives are to be contained within marriage.

What is the essential purpose of marriage? Jewish and Greek thinkers alike said it was procreation. One suspects that the great majority of Christian lay people thought the same. But the small élite who wrote books and built up the tradition of the Church had a different view: procreation has lost its purpose in a world that is drawing towards its close and is already fully populated; we should concentrate all our efforts on a new form of procreation – Christian evangelization, as the spiritual procreation of new sons and daughters of God. Even Augustine repeated the quaint theme, often repeated in the early centuries, that sexual abstinence not only pointed to the age to come, where 'they neither marry nor are given in marriage' (MATTHEW 22:30), but would hasten its coming.

This denigration of physical procreation led many early Christians to renounce marriage; it certainly meant that a different justification had to be found for it. St Paul gave the answer: those who cannot exercise self-control should marry, since it is better to marry than to burn with passion (1 CORINTHIANS 7:9). To renounce sex altogether is the ideal, but it is beyond the power of most people. What they must do is keep sex within marriage; only within marriage can they satisfy the sexual urge without sin. This rather negative justification of marriage had the effect of putting sexual desire right at the centre of the stage.

Concupiscence

To sum up, early Christian teaching, going back to Jesus himself, promoted the ideal of single-mindedness, of the love of God as the only proper motive for action. This led Christians to be negative towards those instinctive bodily drives, particularly sex and aggression, that do not arise from a love of God, and pull the will in contrary directions. This traditional teaching was reinforced for Augustine by his doctrine of original sin. We saw in the last chapter how he gave a new emphasis to this doctrine in order to bring out our total dependence on divine grace. We shall now see how he developed the doctrine further by making original sin the cause of the sexual drive in fallen man.

Augustine observed the tragic contrast between the ideal of single-mindedness and the situation in which we human beings now find ourselves. Before the Fall man possessed self-mastery – complete control over his mind and body. In rebelling against God, he set up a rebellion within himself, a corruption of his nature that we call 'original sin'. A man's will is now the uneasy president of a republic in anarchy; equivalent to disobedient subjects in a state are the instinctive drives within the body. These drives do not arise from the desires of the soul or indeed from any rational choice whatsoever. Some of our natural drives, for instance towards self-preservation, are obviously useful. But many of them not only arise independently of the will but cannot be controlled by it. They frustrate our desire to shape our lives according to our ideals; they drive us into wrong acts. Augustine's term for these negative drives in man, not sinful in themselves but the cause of sin, is *concupiscence.*

In Augustine's view the supreme example of concupiscence is the sexual drive in fallen man. Not only is the sexual urge extremely strong and a frequent cause of wrongdoing, but the very facts of physiology have a lesson to tell. A whole tradition of bawdy poetry had celebrated the fact that males get erections when they don't want them, and can equally fail to get them when they do. The theme had been treated by pagan poets as an object of smutty humour; it was now picked by Augustine (who need not, of course, have read the poetry) as a vivid example of the way in which concupiscence resists the will. It was also an excellent illustration, or so it appeared, of the truth of his teaching about original sin. The facts of sexual physiology have nothing to do with the sins of the individual: they are part of our inheritance from Adam. Meanwhile, the female equivalent to the lack of genital control in the male is the agony of childbirth – something which had been treated as a penalty for the Fall of Man already in the Book of Genesis (3:16). Women experience appalling labour pains, and sometimes expire in giving birth.

If the behaviour of our sexual organs results from original sin, it follows that it must have been very different before the Fall and, were it not for original sin, would be very different now. According to the Bible, Adam and Eve did not have intercourse before the Fall (GENESIS 4:1); and since human mortality is a penalty of the Fall, it was the Fall that made procreation necessary for the survival of the race. As a result, many theologians in the early Church argued that, had it not been for the Fall, there would have been no procreation and no sexual intercourse. Augustine, on the contrary, held that God's commandment to the first human beings, 'Increase and multiply' (GENESIS 1:2), applied even before the Fall. Even though in fact the Fall took place before Adam and Eve had got round to procreating, they would have had children if they had stayed in paradise. But their experience of procreation would have been different from that of fallen humanity: women would have given birth without danger or labour pains, and the sexual organs would have been as obedient to the will as are our arms and legs.

Here Augustine has been accused of fantasizing, but he was able to argue that the possibility of total control over the sexual organs is supported by observed physiological fact. For even now some people possess an amazing control over their bodies:

> There are some people who can even move their ears, either one at a time or both together. There are others who, without moving their heads, can shift their whole scalp of hair down to the forehead and back again at will. There are some who can swallow an incredible number of various articles and then by gently pressing their stomachs can produce, as if out of a bag, any article they please, in perfect

condition. There are others who imitate the sounds of birds and animals or of other men so closely that one could not tell the difference without seeing them. Some people produce at will such musical sounds from their bottoms (without making a smell) that they seem to be singing from that part of their bodies. (C 14.24)

In fallen man, however, the sexual organs resist this degree of control. This makes human sexuality, as we experience it, a prime example of the effects of original sin. But its link to original sin is closer still: it is through sexual intercourse as tainted by concupiscence that original sin is passed down from generation to generation. In the very act of procreation, however worthy the motives of the couple, the sexual organs go their own wicked way. The very mode of intercourse both expresses and passes on the impotence of the human will and the power of concupiscence. As Augustine claims with a skilful use of a difficult biblical story, it is precisely because Jesus, according to the gospels, was born of a virgin without sexual intercourse that he, alone of the human race, was free of original sin.

The whole argument was for the Pelagians, with their rejection of original sin, as a red rag to a bull. Augustine's claim that the physiology of sexual intercourse and childbirth had been perverted by the Fall seemed particularly implausible. The greatest of his Pelagian opponents, Julian of Eclanum (d. after 440), argued that sexual desire is necessary for procreation and is therefore natural and healthy; he was ready to attribute it even to Christ himself. Julian argued that labour pains are not a penalty for original sin but, like sexual desire, a necessary part of the natural order. The same is true, he added, of all kinds of physical misfortunes, including death itself: man was mortal from his creation, and the 'death' that is the penalty of sin is not physical death but the death of the soul. This contrasted sharply with the position of Augustine, who understood the biblical account of the Fall (GENESIS 3:16–19) to imply that before it human beings were not subject to disease or death.

On this question – whether the physical ills of life are natural or the penalty of original sin – a modern critic is likely to side with Julian, but one can see the appeal of Augustine's position. It is inadequate as an answer to the problem of physical evil to say that it is part of the natural order, and life would be unimaginable without it; in face of the sorrows and tragedies of life such an argument is cold comfort indeed. A theologian who wishes to reconcile our experience of life to our belief that God made the world has to offer something more satisfying.

But to return to sexual desire, the contrast between the Pelagian claim that it is natural and Augustine's insistence that it results from original sin makes Augustine, if you like, more negative about sexuality than the Pelagians; it does not imply that his rules for the use of our sexuality were more restrictive. Julian claimed that sexual desire can, and should, be controlled by the will. In contrast, Augustine conceded to human weakness that men and women, without a very special gift of grace, cannot suppress their sexual drives; they need to exercise them, and this they do without sin if they restrict sex to marriage. Ideally, all sex ought to be for the purpose of procreation. But such is the strength of the sexual drive that married couples are likely to have intercourse for the purpose of satisfying and assuaging their sexual urges. This is, of course, a sin; but if they only have sex within marriage and do not exclude procreation, their sin is only a minor one, easily forgiven. And a spouse who has sex to satisfy not merely his own desire but that of his partner is paying the 'debt' he owes his partner, which is an act of justice as well as a kindness: 'Married persons are granted as a concession the right to demand from each other the payment of the conjugal debt even if they make an uncontrolled use of it' (Go 11.12).

Writing on marital sex, Augustine seems to imply that sex within marriage always involves lust; this arises from simple physiological fact, as well as from the mixed motives of even the most virtuous of couples. As a result, marital sex almost always contains an element of sin. Augustine's Pelagian opponents rejected this firmly, and accused him of an hostility to the body deriving from his Manichaean phase. But this misses the point: his concern was not to make people renounce sex but to allow them to practise it. The ideal may indeed be sexual renunciation, but this does not mean that sex even within marriage stands condemned; for life on earth cannot be wholly guided by ideals. This position is typical of Augustine's sober realism on all matters of morality.

Theologians today criticize him more strongly still. Sexual intercourse, they claim, is not only good on the physical plain but even has spiritual value: it expresses and promotes marital love – that love which shares in God's love for us. The present writer remembers from his school days a preacher who claimed that marital sex, being both loving and creative, was, of all human activities, the one where we are closest to God. In theory this may be true, but let's be more realistic about human motives: it would be fatuous to suppose that in actual fact most Christian couples engage in sex with the prime intention of expressing spiritual ideals. Augustine allows sexuality to be what it is – something instinctive and earthy.

The Indissolubility of Marriage

Although, as we have seen, Jesus' teaching on single-mindedness had implications for sexuality, his teaching directly relating to marriage lies elsewhere, in his prohibition of divorce and re-marriage: 'Everyone who divorces his wife and marries another is an adulterer; and he who marries a woman divorced from her husband commits adultery' (LUKE 16:18, probably the original form of the saying recorded slightly differently in MATTHEW 5:32 and MARK 10:11–12). The disciples, we are told, reacted with shock, not to say disbelief: 'If that is the problem between a man and his wife, it is surely better not to marry' (MATTHEW 19:10). But, as is shown by the history of the interpretation of this saying of

Jesus', the problem is less its apparent severity than its evident obscurity. The saying clearly states that divorce is a deplorable thing; no one who believes in marriage is likely to disagree. But the precise meaning of the saying was far from obvious to the Christians of the early centuries: it was not obvious that the prohibition was absolute and unconditional, it was unclear in what sense Jesus called remarriage 'adultery', and it was open to question whether the same rules should apply to both men and women.

A variety of answers to these questions is already implied in the New Testament passages that record or reflect this saying, and they tend to interpret it in a way that reduces its severity. The Gospel of Matthew allows a husband to divorce an adulterous spouse and marry again (5:32;19:9), as also, by implication, does St Paul (1 CORINTHIANS 7:11). But these texts do not allow a wife to do likewise; lifelong fidelity to a single spouse was seen as a virtue incumbent on women rather than men. The so-called 'double standard' – a strict rule for women and a lenient one for men – was enshrined, in different ways, in both Jewish and in Roman law, and most early Christians took it for granted.

Although this double standard appears to have been the most common form of marriage discipline in the early Christian communities, there was, as we might expect, considerable variation. We find evidence of a stricter rule, excluding all divorce and remarriage, and evidence too of a more lenient one, allowing women to remarry as well as men. Civil law in both Jewish and Graeco-Roman society allowed easy divorce and had no problems over remarriage; the churches appear to have concentrated on discouraging divorce on inadequate grounds, rather than attempting to prevent remarriage, particularly for men.

From the fourth century there was a gradual parting of ways between eastern and western Christendom in their rules over marriage. In the east the churches increased the possibility of divorce and remarriage by extending the grounds for divorce, and allowing wives as well as husbands to divorce their spouses. But, in the west, development was in the opposite direction: Augustine and a number of his contemporaries started a new campaign to prohibit remarriage even after divorce on good grounds, and to impose on men the same restrictions that applied to women. So both east and west came to reject the double standard, but while the east did so in the interests of leniency the west did so in the interests of rigorism.

Such rigorism was not entirely new, but the argumentation was. Earlier rigorists had simply stated, in the main, that remarriage had been forbidden by Christ. Augustine and his allies argued that so-called second marriages are not merely forbidden but impossible: a first marriage cannot be dissolved, even by separation and legal divorce; as long as both spouses in the first marriage remain alive, a 'second marriage' is a case of 'bigamy' (an attempt to have two spouses) and therefore invalid. The claim widely accepted by Christians since the time of the Gospel of Matthew, that adultery justifies divorce and remarriage, was ruled out of court: remarriage, so far from being justified by adultery, is itself a form of adultery. The marriage bond not only should not but cannot be dissolved, by any cause other than the death of one of the spouses.

This doctrine of the indissolubility of marriage was Augustine's own creation. Since the teaching was new it was naturally controversial, and debate continued for centuries. As late as AD 826 a Roman pope and council gave permission for the husband of an adulterous wife to divorce and remarry. But from the eleventh century the western Church was unanimous in upholding Augustine's teaching on the indissolubility of marriage, and this remains the teaching of the Roman Catholic Church even today. The churches of the Protestant Reform have generally returned to the Gospel of Matthew in allowing divorce and remarriage after adultery by one's spouse, while excluding the double standard of the early centuries that had restricted this concession to men.

That Augustine on this subject was a rigorist, even at a time when most of the Church was not, may come as a surprise, in view of his deep understanding of human weakness, as shown in his doctrine of original sin. But in his eyes it was one thing to stress original sin and quite another to ignore Christ's explicit teaching on marriage. Sinners are to be tolerated within the Church, but this did not mean that adultery can now count as marriage. Augustine the pastor will have seen the attraction of the lenient stance of the Gospel of Matthew, but Augustine the scriptural scholar argued that we cannot take it as the teaching of Christ: it is only found in Matthew, and the double standard on which it depends is unacceptable in a Christian Church where 'there is neither male nor female, but you are all one person in Christ Jesus' (GALATIANS 3:28).

Augustine's interpretation of Christ's teaching on divorce remains open to question. In calling remarriage 'adultery' Christ is more likely to have been giving a broad interpretation to the Sixth Commandment ('You shall not commit adultery') than pronouncing on validity. His resonant saying, 'What God has yoked together let not man divide' (MATTHEW 19:6), ought strictly to mean that a marriage *can* but *should not* be dissolved, since there is no point in forbidding the impossible. But this is to interpret Christ's words too strictly. Only one point is clear: he forbade divorce and remarriage. Augustine's interpretation has at least the merit of making sense of this prohibition.

It is also easy to criticize him for losing touch with reality. In Roman law common life and mutual affection constituted marriage; once a couple had separated, the marriage was at an end. His insistence that even after separation the marriage still continues may remind us of the Cheshire Cat in Lewis Carroll's *Alice in Wonderland*, which was able to vanish while leaving its grin behind. The doctrine of indissolubility implies that the essence of marriage is not common life or mutual affection; instead, it is some invisible bond, independent of observable reality.

What is this bond supposed to be? Augustine had no clear answer. But he was able to illustrate the power of the bond from the understanding of the Christian sacraments that he had developed during the Donatist controversy. The bond of baptism unites a Christian to the Church even if his life provides no evidence of real commitment; the holy few who are faithful to the norms of the Church are not the only members of the Church. Likewise, those couples who remain together are not the only couples joined in marriage:

> *Just as the sacrament of regeneration remains in someone who has been excommunicated for a crime, and he does not lose this sacrament even if he is never reconciled with God, so also the bond of the marital compact remains in a wife who has been divorced on the ground of fornication, and she does not lose this bond even if she is never reconciled with her husband.* (Ad 2.4)

Augustine's teaching of the indissolubility of marriage, like that of the Roman Catholic Church today, can sound negative and restrictive. But what he was actually doing was attributing to Christian marriage a new dignity. Despite his bleak view of marital sex, discussed above, he recognized in marriage what he called 'a sacramental element', arising from its indissolubility. Fidelity in marriage was obedience to a commandment of Christ's, but it was more than that: it was the acknowledgement of a bond real though unseen, akin to the grace bestowed at baptism and confirmed in the eucharist. This kinship, as Augustine pointed out, adds force to the teaching of St Paul that marital love should imitate Christ's love for his Church (EPHESIANS 5:25): can we not say that Christian marriage is a sign and symbol of this love?

The medieval Church, developing this insight further, came to recognize marriage as itself a sacrament. The new churches of the Reformation rejected this: they reserved the word 'sacrament' to the two great sacraments (baptism and the eucharist) introduced by Christ himself. But is this more than a dispute over words? Catholics and Protestants alike recognize the spiritual character of Christian marriage. Marriage is a natural phenomenon, not a specifically Christian one, but within the Church it takes on a new meaning. The greatest mystery of the Christian religion is its message that God has 'elected' (chosen) us unconditionally to be his sons and daughters; sin can deprive us of the benefits of our election but can never cancel it. This love between God and his chosen people, between Christ and his Church, would seem so extraordinary as to beggar belief, were it not for the continuing expression of this bond in Christian marriage. Here husband and wife give themselves to each other unconditionally and for life, in imitation of the unconditional love of God.

How much of this is in Augustine? Certainly he proclaimed the indissolubility of marriage, and linked it to the role of marriage in symbolizing the love of God. He thereby laid the foundations for the high evaluation of marriage developed after his time into one of the glories of the Christian tradition. This was a major contribution to Christian thought.

However, he is open to criticism in one respect: he says too much about the indissolubility of marriage even after divorce, and not enough about the value of the bond of love that unites husband and wife in a successful marriage: surely the latter is the clearer symbol of the reality of Christ's love for his Church? One has to admit that Augustine has little to say about the companionate side of marriage – the intimate fellowship and mutual support between husband and wife in a lifelong union. This was partly because of his concern to argue that marriage survives the breakdown of such a union, but there was another reason as well: he did not see this aspect of marriage as its distinguishing feature. Lifelong bonds of love are found within marriage but also in many other human relationships – in friendship, and in community life at its best. It is Augustine's teaching on friendship and community that will be the subject of my next and final chapter.

Friendship and Community

Augustine's conception of the Church and its place in the world has been one of the main themes of this book. Augustine takes for granted that the Church is an institution with its own organs of government, rules and procedures, but what interests him as a theologian is the Church as community, and community conceived in terms not of rights and obligations but of human relationships. This chapter will explore how he developed a concept of community in the Church that built on his own strong feelings of attachment towards individuals.

Love of Persons

A recurrent theme in the *Confessions* is friendship, or the love between persons. At least until he went to Hippo, Augustine was always in a circle of close friends, with whom he shared without inhibition or reserve every detail of his personal life and each development of his thoughts.

> *All kinds of things absorbed my mind in their company – to make conversation, share a joke, do each other acts of kindness; read pleasant books together, pass from making jokes to talk of the deepest things and back again; disagree without ill feeling, as a man might debate with himself, and find our harmony all the sweeter for the occasional disagreement; teach one another and learn from one another; long*

> *with impatience for the return of the absent, and welcome them back*
> *with joy. These and other signs came from the very heart as we gave*
> *and received affection. Produced by the face, the tongue, the eyes and a*
> *thousand pleasant gestures, they acted as fuel to set our minds on fire*
> *and out of many make us one.* (Co 4.8.13)

Augustine picked up, by experience illuminated by his reading of
Cicero, the ancient view of friendship as the greatest of human
blessings. The very strength of his feelings set him a problem
when as a Christian theologian he came to address the question of
the relation between the love of one's friends, the love of one's fellow men in general, and the love of God. How are these related to
each other, and what is the priority between them?

In a work called *Christian Teaching*, begun at the same time
as the *Confessions*, Augustine introduced a distinction between
enjoyment of God – a union with him in which we find complete
fulfilment – and the *use* we make of created beings, including our
fellow men, in our quest for God. Since created goods cannot
satisfy us, we cannot make them our final goal, and we cannot
properly be said to *enjoy* them for themselves. It was, of course, a
traditional theme that it is foolish to be attached to material things
for their own sake. Augustine has been criticized for treating love
of other human beings in the same way, as if we should exploit
them for our own spiritual benefit, without becoming too
attached to them, much as we make use of things. But he was well
aware of the distinction between the love of things and the love of
persons: as he wrote in another context, 'We should obviously not
love human beings as things to be consumed. Friendship is a kind
of benevolence, leading us to do things for the benefit of those we
love' (J 8.5). Augustine did not mean that we should moderate our
love for our fellow human beings and concentrate exclusively on
the love of God. The point he is making is simply that we must
avoid attributing to anything other than God a value in and of
itself, independent of God; instead, we should love our fellows 'in'

God. What did he mean by this? At this point the argument becomes intricate but also highly rewarding.

Augustine pointed out that even in loving ourselves we look to a goal that lies beyond ourselves, namely the love of God. This is because the love of God is necessary for our happiness but cannot be exploited as the means to an end: we find our happiness not as a *result* of loving God, but *in* loving him. Happiness is to be found not in self-absorption but in the contemplation of God, as an object of love for his own sake. If we attain this, self-love is satisfied in a way it would never be if we placed our final goal in ourselves and not in God.

In this way self-love, properly informed, fulfils the first of the great commandments: 'You are to love the Lord your God with all your heart, and with all your soul, and with all your mind' (MATTHEW 22:37). But there is also the second great commandment: 'You are to love your neighbour as yourself' (MATTHEW 22:39). Now if self-love points us to the love of God and we are to love our neighbour as ourselves, it follows that we should love him not in himself or for himself, but 'in God' or 'for the sake of God'. This is not to impose a restriction on love of neighbour – as if it is a good thing only is so far as it helps our love of God. No, the point being made is this: love of my neighbour means wanting him or her to share in my own aspiration towards God as the final goal.

> *Whatever else enters the mind as an object of love is to be swept along in the direction in which the whole current of our affections flows [the love of God]. Whoever has a proper love for his neighbour ought to act towards him in such a way that he too comes to love God with his whole heart and soul and mind. For in this way, loving his neighbour as himself, a man pours all his love both of himself and of his neighbour into the love of God which allows no streams to be diverted away from itself.* (CT 1.22.21)

Augustine rightly perceives that true love for a fellow human being does not consist in adoration of that person as he or she is, in a form of aesthetic contemplation. Human beings are beings in movement towards God their goal, and to love your neighbour is to want him to attain that goal. To love someone as he is, in the sense of making him an object of adoration (whether in hero worship or romantic love), is to close one's eyes to the actual reality of a human being who, so far from being satisfied with himself as he is, aspires towards a perfection he has not yet attained. True love involves true sympathy, in which the lover perceives that aspiration and makes it his own as well; to love your neighbour as yourself is to want both him and you to achieve your common goal. Augustine argues this convincingly. Having started with a confusing distinction between objects of enjoyment and objects of use, he achieves a correct conception of love of persons, a love distinct both from the desire to possess and the impulse to adore.

Apart from the relation between love of God and love of neighbour, there is also the problem of the relation of universal love to particular loves: we have a call to love all our fellow human beings; we also recognize a particular obligation to help our families and friends. How are these two related? Is there conflict between them? Pagan moralists, such as Cicero, had deplored wronging one's fellow citizens to help one's nearest and dearest, or wronging foreigners to help one's fellow citizens. But the problem becomes particularly acute for a Christian, because Christ's commandment to love one's neighbour as oneself seems to mean that one should treat even strangers as if they were friends.

Augustine understood Christ to mean that we must love all people equally. 'But since', he added, 'you cannot do good to all, you are to pay special attention to those with whom you enjoy closer contact because of the dictates of place, time and other circumstances' (CT 1.28.29). Yes, we are right to give priority to our nearest and dearest: 'A man has responsibility above all towards his own people. Obviously, both in the order of nature and in that of human society he has better access to them and a greater opportunity to attend to their needs' (C 19.14). 'Better access' is pretty weak as an explanation of the special duties each one of us has towards the members of his or her own family, but at least Augustine is trying give these duties a place in a Christian ethic of love of neighbour.

He came up with a better answer through further reflection on the nature of Christian love. Such love shares in the love of God towards his creatures, a love in which there is pure giving and no thought of getting anything in return, since God in the perfection of his being is in need of nothing. But since human beings share lacks and needs, love between human beings involves 'bearing one another's burdens' (GALATIANS 6:2 – a favourite text of Augustine's). Ideally, all human beings should help one another, and in the world to come we may look forward to a union of all the saints in knowledge and love of each other; but in the conditions of this present world this is simply not possible, and in most of our relationships there is a lack of full mutuality. Growth in Christian love requires each of us to build his own circle of friends, who love one another as themselves and help one another to grow in the love of God. This ideal of friendship gave Augustine a special interest in the development of religious community; here more than anywhere he hoped that true Christian fellowship could be realized on earth.

The Ideal of Community Life

Even before his conversion at Milan in 386 (treated in the opening section of my first chapter) Augustine was attracted by the idea of setting up a community where he and his closest friends could devote themselves to study and reflection. An initial scheme envisaged around ten companions coming together and pooling all their resources to create a common fund; but some of those hoping to join were married, and their wives rejected the scheme. But soon afterwards Augustine was bowled off his feet when he learnt about the monastic movement, started by Antony of Egypt. After a fierce inward struggle, he decided to give up his career and prospects of marriage, and devote himself to a life of chastity, prayer and reflection, out of a wish, to use his own quaint phrase, 'to become like God in a life of retirement' (L 10.2).

Accompanied by his little band of friends and followers, Augustine returned to Africa in 388 in order to start a monastic community in his native town of Thagaste, the first in the province of Africa. It was on a visit to Hippo in 391 to see a potential recruit that he was forced to accept ordination to the priesthood. This did not mean the end of his monastery: it simply joined him in Hippo. When a few years later (in 396) he became bishop of the see, he set up a parallel community for his clergy: distinguished from the lay monastery by their active ministry, they too had to renounce personal property.

Augustine wrote a rule for the lay monastery. Subsequently, both in the Middle Ages and in modern times, this rule was adopted by many orders and communities; it is at present followed by more priests, monks and nuns than the better-known Rule of St Benedict. This document, together with a number of letters and sermons, presents a clear picture of Augustine's ideal of community life. What were its essential features?

Augustine's favourite biblical text on this theme was the brief account in the Acts of the Apostles of the life of the primitive Christian community at Jerusalem: 'Now the multitude of those who believed had one heart and soul, and no one said that any of the things he possessed was his own, but they had everything in common' (ACTS 4:32). Modern commentators tell us that this common ownership was not a form of primitive communism but simply generous contributions from the wealthier members of the community to a fund for its poor members. But in the new monastic communities of the fourth century, with their strict rules of communal ownership, this text was taken more literally and often quoted. No one made fuller use of it than Augustine.

He insisted in the communities he founded that all the members should renounce personal ownership. Those who possessed property were to hand it over to their relations or give it to the community. Even clothes were to be possessed in common: they were to be regularly returned to a common store for redistribution. Private property, he knew, is divisive and a fertile source of quarrels; it is necessary in the outside world where people have families and dependants to support, but it has no place in a religious community.

Even more important in Augustine's eyes than the sharing of material goods was the sharing of thoughts, concerns and feelings. He pointed out that spiritual, or mental, goods – joy, wisdom, the love of God, and so on – are vastly superior to material ones in two ways: first, they will continue into the life to come, while material goods will pass away; secondly, they can be shared in a way material goods cannot. When a number of people divide up among themselves material goods such as money or clothing, each receives only a portion, and the greater the number of people taking part, the smaller the share received by each one. In contrast,

> *someone's possession of goodness is in no way diminished by the arrival, or the continuance, of a sharer in it; indeed, goodness is a possession enjoyed more widely if those who possess it are united in harmonious fellowship. In fact, anyone who refuses to share this possession with others will not enjoy it at all; and he will find that his possession of it will be in precise proportion to his readiness to love his partner in it.* (C 15.5)

So spiritual goods, unlike material ones, are not diminished by being more widely distributed: they are actually increased.

Feelings such as joy or love are intensified when shared with others. Even where there is perfect mutual sympathy and concern for the needs of others the fact remains that human beings are in competition when it comes to material comforts. It is only mental and spiritual riches – rejoicing with those who rejoice, sharing ideas and enthusiasms with one's fellows – that really bind communities together. It is only when spiritual goods are treasured, and material goods put into second place, that fellowship free of envy and rivalry can develop.

But it is not only material things that cause division: personal ties of kinship can do the same. As Augustine wrote to a monk who was tempted to leave his monastery to look after his mother,

> The rule that everyone is to renounce all his possessions involves hating one's father and mother, wife and children, brothers and sisters, and even one's own life too [CF. LUKE 14:26]. For all these things are personal possessions, which generally get in the way of attaining not indeed those personal possessions that will pass away with time but those lasting and eternal goods that we shall possess in common. Having a particular woman as your mother is something you cannot share with me; and accordingly it is temporary and will pass away ... But having a sister in Christ is something that can be shared by both of us, and by all who are promised in the same union of love the one heavenly inheritance with God as our Father and Christ as our brother. This is eternal and will never be eroded by the passing of time; this we may hope to retain all the more firmly, the more we declare it is to be possessed not privately but in common ... Each person is to think the same about his own soul. Let each man hate to have a feeling he cannot share with others, for such a feeling must belong to what passes away; let each man love in his soul that communion and sharing of which it is written, 'They had towards God one soul and one heart' [CF. ACTS 4:32]. So your soul is not your own, but belongs to all the brethren; and their souls are yours. Or rather, your soul and theirs make up not many souls but one soul – the single mind of Christ. (L 243)

92

Augustine rejects an individualism that sees thoughts and feelings as the property of separate and independent minds; he insists instead that they are developed through contact with others and are naturally shared with them. The happiness of the saints in heaven consists in a common enjoyment of union with God, where souls will be perfectly open to each other and share the same spiritual life. Augustine has a similar vision of happiness on earth. Perfect knowledge and love of one another cannot, it is true, be attained in this life, because of our selfishness and our imperfect understanding even of ourselves, let alone of other people; but the approach to such a marriage of true minds remains the greatest happiness attainable on earth.

What Augustine has done is to apply in a new context the concept of friendship traditional in pagan literature – with its talk of friends having a single soul, through complete harmony in pursuits, aims and convictions. Pagan society thought this ideal realizable only between a man and a tiny circle of his closest friends. Augustine applies this ideal of friendship to the new context of Christian fellowship, where all members of the Church are united by a common goal and need the assistance of one another to attain it. Christianity stimulates joint action where the whole company of believers is united by a common aspiration that inspires the actions of each one. Actions cease to express the individual will of the agent and to be his responsibility alone: instead, they become the realization of choices that the agent shares with his fellows.

This ideal of shared will and thought and action had been powerfully developed by Aristotle (fourth century BC) in the context of personal friendships between members of the Athenian upper class (see A. W. Price, *Love and Friendship in Plato and Aristotle*, Chapter 4). What Augustine did was to enrich this ideal with the biblical theme of life in Christ, and apply it to the Christian community. Since in practice the members of the Christian Church are divided by social barriers and those clashes of interest that are inevitable in the secular world, this fellowship is best realized in small communities, where the members know each other intimately, share the same aspirations, and work together to achieve them for all. This creates a life of common loyalties, feelings, hopes and goals, where all the members imitate Christ and become, through union with him, one heart and one soul.

Augustine's Originality

How original was Augustine's ideal of community life? Friendship certainly had a part to play in the new monastic movement, which developed in the Greek east in the early fourth century and spread to the Latin west in Augustine's lifetime. This monastic movement was inspired by a wish to escape from the social pressures of secular life in order to develop the inner life of self-knowledge and openness to God. But this does not mean that monks aimed at total self-sufficiency or sacrificed all social ties to the quest for mystical communion with God. The literature of eastern monasticism reveals anxiety over wrong forms of friendship, leading to possessiveness or mutual admiration societies, and is more concerned to stress the negative virtues of patience and tolerance than to promote positive ideals of friendship. Nevertheless close relations between monks are taken for granted, and numerous sayings and anecdotes illustrate how helpful a true friend can be.

Once the monastic movement began to attract educated recruits who knew the classical ideal of friendship, we would anticipate a richer development of this theme. But this occurred more slowly than we might expect. Basil of Caesarea (d. 379), who had received a full secular education and whose writings enjoy a unique status in Orthodox monasticism, wrote eloquently of the need for community if monks are to learn from each other and practise the active virtues. Particularly interesting is his claim that 'many commandments are easily performed by a number living together but not by someone living on his own' (*LONGER RULES*

7): this implies that in a community each member shares responsibility for the actions of his fellows. This insight is similar to Augustine's but is not developed.

Augustine's western contemporary John Cassian (d. around 435), spent, or claimed to have spent, many years in monastic communities in Egypt and Palestine, and later wrote a great series of *Conferences* to apply the insights of eastern monasticism to the needs of the Latin west. His *Conference 16*, on friendship, emphasizes the need to be ready to sacrifice one's personal interests and even opinions in order to keep one's friends. He is more precise, and arguably more realistic, than Augustine about the difficulties of maintaining trust and harmony within a community. But this does not change the fact that, like Basil, he falls far short of Augustine's vision.

In all, the early monastic tradition in both east and west was emphatic on the value of friendship even for contemplative monks living apart from the world, but Augustine was original in seeing beyond the simple notion of harmony between the brethren, and developing the ideal of a shared mental life of common aspirations, thoughts and feelings. It is typical of him that he explained the very word 'monk' (whose root, the Greek word *monos*, means 'alone') as deriving from the emphasis in Acts 4:32 on oneness of heart and soul. For Augustine true happiness consists in overcoming the separation between distinct human minds and creating a spiritual life developed and enjoyed by a number of friends together. In this way life on earth can imitate, however imperfectly, the communion of saints in heaven.

The theme that monastic life imitates and anticipates the life of heaven was already a traditional one in Augustine's time. It was linked to ideals of sinlessness, emotional stability, and the vision of God. It was Augustine who played down these ascetic and mystical elements in favour of the ideal of a life of shared mental experience, of an overcoming of the separateness of human souls through a common raising of heart and mind to God.

The climax of the *Confessions* is arguably the so-called 'Vision at Ostia' (9.10.23–26) – a mystical experience, momentary but unforgettable, in which Augustine, shortly before returning to Africa, achieved a sense of transcending the created order and tasting the eternity of God. Most unusually for a mystical experience it was not a solitary one: he shared it with his mother, Monica. His belief in the possibility of overcoming the opaqueness of human minds to each other, and developing a mental world of shared experience, was not the romantic dream of a man unable to come to terms with the loneliness and isolation that separate human beings: it was born of an experience of warm human relations with his family and friends, and of a conviction that life in this world can receive a real if faint imprint of its goal – the communion of saints and union with God himself.

Imitating the Trinity

The Christian God is not some philosophical Absolute, so transcendent and pure in essence that he is unrelated to other beings: instead, he is intimately linked in love to the human beings he has created. Moreover, he is himself one God in three persons, Father, Son and Holy Spirit, united to each other in a bond of love. This enabled Augustine to relate his ideal of perfect human community to the Christian doctrine of God.

Augustine devoted to this doctrine one of his longest works – the fifteen books of *The Trinity*, which he worked at on and off for two decades (the 400s and 410s). In this work he insists that there are not three beings in God but a single reality or 'substance'. He had to accept the traditional formulation that Father, Son and Holy Spirit are three 'persons', but he insisted that the word 'person' in this context has no particular meaning: 'we say "three persons" not in order to say precisely that, but in order not to be reduced to silence' (T 5.9.10). Three 'persons' suggests, in ordinary language, three separate individuals with three different minds and three different wills: but in God there is only a single mind and a single will.

What, then, is the threefold element in the Trinity? For Augustine, the answer lies in the *relations* between Father, Son and Spirit. The relations in question are those of source and derivation: the Father is the source from whom the Son derives his being, while the Spirit derives his being from both the Father and the Son. Normally when we say a number of persons are related to each other, we mean that they exist as separate individuals who, as a distinct fact, are linked through being related to each other. But in the case of the Trinity, according to Augustine, relation has precisely the opposite function: it does not link what is otherwise distinct, but sets apart what in all other respects is indistinguishable. The persons are distinct *only* in being related to each other. The Son, in deriving his being from the Father, is necessarily distinct from the Father; but in every other respect, in mind and will, in qualities and activities, he is one and the same being. The same is true of the Holy Spirit, in deriving his being from the Father and the Son. In this way we distinguish the Father from the Son, and the Holy Spirit from both, while maintaining a strong doctrine of divine unity.

The fact that this account of the Trinity became standard in the west should not dull us to its extreme oddity. Augustine, in effect, invented a new and bizarre concept of relationship. The result was unfortunate: under his influence the doctrine of the Trinity became so artificial and so hard to grasp that it ceased to be part of the religion of the faithful, and retreated into the study of the professional theologian.

But in the context of Augustine's theme of Christian community his account of the Trinity takes on a new relevance. Most obviously, the oneness of will within the Trinity is a perfect model for the unity of wills in Christian community: as Father, Son and Holy Spirit possess in common a single will, so human beings are called to a perfect harmony of will, through sharing together the same desire to achieve union with God.

But Augustine's favourite argument relates not to the mere oneness of will in the Trinity but to the rooting of that oneness in a bond of love. The three persons of the Trinity form a single divine reality, or substance, with one mind and one will, but there remain distinctions between them: this means that the unity between them is to be defined not merely as identity of substance but as a bond of love, comparable to love between human persons. The Holy Spirit, in proceeding from both the Father and the Son, as the common source of the Spirit, can be called the bond of love that unites them. Augustine draws out the implications this has for human beings:

> *We are bidden to imitate this bond by grace, in our relationships both with God and with one another, in the two precepts [love of God and love of neighbour] on which the whole law and the prophets depend [MATTHEW 22:40]. In this way those three [Father, Son, and Holy Spirit] are one God, unique, great, wise, holy, and blessed. And we find our blessedness 'from him and through him and in him' [ROMANS 11:36], because it is by his gift that we are one with each other.* (T 6.5.7.)

In this passage Augustine begins with the theme of love within God – note that the phrase 'from him and through him and in him' is itself a Trinitarian formula. He then proceeds downwards, as it were, to the theme of love between human beings. But it is just as possible to reason in the opposite direction – to start with human love, and then move upwards to the love that unites the persons of the Trinity. This is really a better procedure, since it is precisely our human experience of love that enables us to gain some conception of divine love. It is the procedure adopted in the eighth book of *The Trinity*, where Augustine offers the following analysis of human love.

If I love my neighbour, I am conscious of the feeling of love and attach value to it. I can say that in loving my neighbour I love love itself. Three realities come together – the one who loves, the one who is loved, and the love that unites them. Moreover, since God is love, to love love is to love God. So my human experience of love of neighbour provides a mirror, or image, of God himself; and moreover this experience contains a threefold element, or trinity, that bears a resemblance to the divine Trinity itself. To use Augustine's own words:

> 'Yes, [someone will say,] I can see love and, as far as I can, conceive it in my mind; and I believe the scripture when it says that "God is love and whoever abides in love abides in God" [1 JOHN 4:16]. But when I see it, I don't see the Trinity in it.' Oh but you do see the Trinity if you see love ... For love stems from someone in love, and it is with love that someone or something is loved. Here we have three things – the lover, the object of his love, and love. (T 8.8.12–10.14)

Since the Holy Spirit is called in Scripture both the Spirit of the Father and the Spirit of the Son, and since he derives his being from both Father and Son, and is sent into the hearts of human beings by the Father and the Son acting together, it follows that he is the bond linking Father and Son. 'God is love' (1 JOHN 4:8), and within the Trinity it is supremely the Spirit who represents divine love: the Father and Son are lover and beloved, and the Spirit is the love that unites them. The Spirit is also the bond of love between God and his creatures: 'God's love has been poured into our hearts through the Holy Spirit that has been given to us' (ROMANS 5:5). It follows that Christian love is no less than a sharing in the Holy Spirit, in that bond of love that binds together the persons of the Trinity. In other words, Christian fellowship, as a union of love, is an image on earth of the Trinity; human community mirrors on earth the 'community' of the Trinity.

In the following part of the work (Book Nine) Augustine shifts the emphasis from this image of the Trinity in human community to a psychological one – the image of the Trinity within the human mind itself. Each human mind is a unity, since there is one 'self', and at the same time a plurality, since the mind performs all the time a variety of mental acts, especially the three acts of remembering, understanding and willing; this makes the mind like the Trinity itself, in which there is one substance and yet three persons. Augustine makes this shift from the community model of the Trinity to the psychological one for the following reason: the oneness in God is more fully echoed in the unity of a single human self than in the looser 'union' between a number of different human beings. Unfortunately, this has the effect of making the love that unites the Trinity look more like the self-love of a single individual than the Christian love of neighbour.

This does not mean, however, that Augustine went back on his teaching that love of neighbour echoes the love within God himself. Despite the unsatisfactory features in his doctrine of the Trinity, it remains the case that he saw a connection between the love that is the Spirit uniting Father and Son and the human love of neighbour perfected in Christian community. No reader of Augustine can fail to be struck by the real similarity between, on the one hand, his Trinitarian doctrine of three divine persons with one mind and will and, on the other, his ideal of community as described above – a union of friends who are one in heart and soul through sharing in fellowship the same thoughts, feelings and aspirations.

Conclusion

Augustine is not only the most prolific of the early Church Fathers but also the most wide-ranging. There are so many themes one could select as the heart of his message: I could have chosen, for example, his doctrine of the individual human being, made in the image of the Trinity, corrupted through the Fall, and refashioned through the grace of Christ; he does not preach community in a way that minimizes the value or responsibilities of the individual. Nevertheless, his stress on the community aspects of Christian life remains striking, and it has been the leading theme of this book. It arose partly from the influence of such African predecessors as Cyprian, with their emphasis on the doctrine of the Church, and partly as a response to the particular needs of his own time. But Augustine transcends his immediate context, and his treatment of Christian community remains a stimulus and a challenge even today. What, in sum, are its essential components?

We saw in chapter 1 how, according to Augustine, the basis of Christian teaching is the authority possessed by the Church as a community stretching back to the Apostles. Chapter 2 looked at Augustine's view of the Church as a community that binds together saints and sinners in a fellowship of sacrament and prayer. Chapter 3 treated his teaching on the relationship between the Church and the world, where, whatever the differences in motivation between sincere Christians and the rest of mankind, they are united by a common striving for peace. In chapter 4 we saw how, in the Augustinian doctrine of grace, human beings are united to each other through their equal dependence on the unmerited favour of God. Chapter 5 proceeded to Augustine's teaching on Christian marriage as the symbol, within a human relationship, of the love of Christ for his Church.

It is in his teaching on friendship and community that these themes find their richest development, in the notion of a shared spiritual life which heals and overcomes the isolation of the individual. Christian community on earth is a preparation for the communion of saints in heaven, where we shall be totally transparent one to another, and share the vision of God in union with each other. This, it transpires, is nothing less than a participation in the unity in plurality of the Holy Trinity itself. The deepest need of human beings is to be so transformed that we come to 'share in the very being of God' (2 PETER 1:5). To open ourselves to this transformation, we must grow in true fellowship, through developing bonds of mutual love and common hope. It is here, perhaps, that we today have most to learn from the message of Augustine.

Suggested Further Reading

Augustine's psychological perception and unusual self-knowledge make him one of the very few ancient writers whose works provide us with the material required for a modern biography. This has been provided by Peter Brown, *Augustine of Hippo*, Faber, 1967; though it is primarily an account of the life, quite exceptional for its insight and freshness, it includes discussion of most of the themes treated in this book. So does Gerald Bonner, *St Augustine of Hippo: Life and Controversies*, revised edition, The Canterbury Press, Norwich, 1986, which provides an admirably lucid, though uncritical, account of Augustine's case against Manichees, Donatists and Pelagians.

Meanwhile, Augustine the philosopher (and philosophical theologian) receives a sophisticated treatment from John M. Rist, *Augustine: Ancient Thought Baptized*, Cambridge University Press, 1994. Difficult but unusually stimulating is Christopher Kirwan, *Augustine*, Routledge, 1989, which does Augustine the welcome compliment of subjecting his ideas to sharp critical analysis.

There are excellent translations of the *Confessions* and the *City of God* in the Penguin Classics, by R. Pine-Coffin, 1961, and H. Bettenson, 1972, respectively; these two works are arguably the greatest of all Augustine's writings, but both are difficult reading for those unacquainted with ancient thought. The particular literary and historical problems of the *Confessions* receive a remarkably fresh and illuminating treatment in Gillian Clark, *Augustine: the Confessions*, Cambridge University Press, 1993. A reader who is impressed with my claim that it is immoral to condemn Pelagius without reading him should read *The Letters of Pelagius and his Followers*, translated and edited by B. R. Rees, Boydell Press, Woodbridge, Suffolk, 1991.

A new edition of the whole of Augustine – *The Works of St Augustine, A Translation for the 21st Century*, New City Press, New York – is in process of appearing, and already includes many volumes of sermons in a superbly racy translation. These sermons were largely preached extempore and taken down by shorthand writers at the time of delivery; this gives them a freshness and generally a simplicity that is likely to appeal to the modern reader more than the studied art of Augustine's more polished writings. Any volume of these sermons, plus the Brown biography as an overview, will provide the general reader with the wherewithal to enter more deeply into the mind of Augustine.

Two other books referred to in the main text of this volume and which may be of interest are: Aries, P. and Duby, G., eds, *A History of Private Life, Volume I: From Rome to Byzantium*, Harvard University Press, 1987; and Price, A.W., *Love and Friendship in Plato and Aristotle*, Oxford University Press, 1989.

FRANCIS &
BONAVENTURE

Paul Rout

Francis & Bonaventure

PAUL ROUT

Paul Rout is a member of the Franciscan Order of Friars Minor. He graduated from the University of Melbourne and continued postgraduate study at Heythrop College, University of London. His doctoral thesis, on Bonaventure and the religious experience of Francis of Assisi, was recently accepted by the University of London. Dr Rout presently lectures in Philosophy and Franciscan Studies at the Franciscan Study Centre, Canterbury, England.

To my family
Cecilia, Frank, Terry, Brian and Kevin
and to my Franciscan brothers and sisters.

Contents

Abbreviations

The following abbreviations are used in references to Bonaventure's works in the text:

B   *Breviloquium* (*The Breviloquium*)
H   *Collationes in Hexaemeron* (*Collations on the Six Days*)
I   *Itinerarium Mentis in Deum* (*The Soul's Journey into God*)
L   *The Life of St Francis* (*Legenanda Maior*)
SC   *Disputatae Quaestiones de Scientia Christi* (*Disputed Questions on the Knowledge of Christ*)
T   *De Triplica Via alias Incendium Amoris* (*The Triple Way or Love Enkindled*)

Details of editions cited are given in Suggested Further Reading

Date Chart

1253–4   Bonaventure's inception as Master at Paris. Writes *Disputed Questions on Mystery of the Trinity, Disputed Questions on the Knowledge of Christ*.

1257   Bonaventure elected Minister General of the Franciscans

1273   Bonaventure delivers the series of lectures *Collations on the Six Days* at the Unversity of Paris. Made Cardinal by the Pope. Travels to Lyon to prepare for the Council of Lyons.

1259   Retreat on La Verna. Writes *The Soul's Journey into God* and *The Triple Way*.

1259–73   As Minister General, journeys through most of Western Europe. Continues writing and preaching.

1274   Participates in Council of Lyons. Dies there on 15 July.

1482   Canonized by Pope Sixtus IV

1588   Declared a Doctor of the Church by Pope Sixtus V

Introduction

The medieval world of the thirteenth century was one of enormous social, cultural and religious change. Previous certainties were being questioned, controversies arose within political, academic and church circles. Within the hearts of many arose a new spiritual hunger which the traditional religious authorities seemed unable to assuage.

Into this world leapt one of God's special gifts to humanity, one who breathed with every fibre of his being a joy which could not be taken away, a peace which sank deep into the hearts of those whom he encountered. This man came from the Umbrian city of Assisi and his name was Francis. His life was living poetry. He was enthralled by God, the Divine Lover, and he lived out the reality of that relationship passionately, freely and joyfully.

Yes, Francis was captivated by God's love. This was the secret of his freedom, a freedom which put flight to fear and opened his heart to love in return. His was indeed a passionate love, one which reached out to embrace all his sisters and brothers, especially the lost ones, the outsiders, the poor and insignificant. It was a love, moreover, which extended to all of creation, which Francis saw as radiant with reflections of the divine glory.

The life and spirit of the little poor man of Assisi intensely affected the lives of so many of his contemporaries, people from all walks of life. One such person was Bonaventure. It might seem at first sight that Bonaventure would be far removed from the attractions of Assisi. He was the brilliant academic, the Master at the

University of Paris. The power and prestige of the academic world lay at his feet, and yet he chose to follow the way of Francis. His powerful intellect was energetically put to the task of relating the significance of the Francis-event to the concerns of the wider world. Bonaventure reflected on Francis' experience and, in a unique and powerful testimony to that experience, he produced works of theology which are permeated with the spirit of love, prayer and reverence which overflowed within the heart of Francis.

Francis stands as one who began with God and saw all else from there. Bonaventure's writings provide a Francis-inspired guide for the spiritual pilgrim, the one who is seeking God. It is a journey which is dynamic and relational. It is a journey which speaks so profoundly of the reality of God within our lives and of the meaning which God alone is able to provide for the concerns of human life. It is a journey which embraces this world and which emphasizes the dignity and sacredness of all creation. The spiritual journey of Francis and Bonaventure is not simply a record from the past. It is one which can continue to offer nourishment to spiritual pilgrims of our own day. It is hoped that this short book will open the door so that the reader may set out with confidence and with a joyful heart along the fascinating road of the journey into God.

Francis and Bonaventure in Context

Indeed, not so much of the water of philosophy should be mixed with the wine of Revelation that it should turn wine into water. This should be the worst of miracles. We read that Christ turned water into wine, not the reverse. (H 19.14)

The relationship between revelation and philosophy is no less an area of debate in our own time than in that of Bonaventure. Revelation involves God making known truths about himself and the universe to human beings. Philosophy, on the other hand, is a process whereby human beings use processes of logic to determine fundamental truths. In the thirteenth century medieval world of the University of Paris, controversy stirred in the academic faculties. The 'new learning' which had filtered into the universities carried with it a heavy influence from the recently discovered philosophical texts of Aristotle. Aristotle's philosophy was accepted as an essential element of University learning – the controversy surrounded the proper place of such philosophy within the academic process.

On the one side were those who saw in Aristotle a means whereby human reason would be 'set free' from the strictures of church tradition to think for itself. For example, Siger of Brabant (1240 –1284) separated revelation and philosophy, insisting on the right of the philosopher to follow human reason to its inevitable conclusions, even though it might sometimes contradict revelation. Religious faith was not to be dismissed, but its concepts were to be subject to the analysis of reason. Aristotelian philosophy, with its emphasis on the self-sufficiency of human reason, would bring about this liberation. Philosophy, not theology and religious tradition, would set the agenda for the new world.

Numbered among scholars who opposed such a stance was Bonaventure. In his mind, to separate philosophy from theology within university learning was to deprive human reason of that which made for its greatness, namely, the influence of divine revelation, the subject matter of theology. Bonaventure was convinced that reflection on the nature of human life could only take place within the context of reference to God as the origin and fulfilment of human destiny. To attempt to reason apart from this context, he claimed, was to deprive life of its essential vitality, a vitality which could be found only in God.

Bonaventure's stance was not due to mere academic preference. Just as the academic world of the thirteenth century had been heavily influenced by Aristotle, so the religious and social world had been unalterably shaken by the life of one man – not a philosopher but a poet, a mystic, a saint – Francis of Assisi. Bonaventure had been so affected by the story of this man that in Paris he entered the Order which Francis had founded. It was because of the experience of Francis that Bonaventure held to his academic conviction. He saw Francis as embodying truth and believed that this embodiment of truth was only possible because of Francis' experience of the transcendent God. To consider Francis outside of this experience, he affirmed, would be as life-giving as to change wine into water. Bonaventure understood Francis to have begun with God and to have reflected on all else in relation to that starting point. Similarly, he would insist, it was to be the truth of God breaking into human life which was to determine the truth of human thought; it was not human thought which was to determine the truth of God.

Bonaventure, the intellectual giant of Paris; Francis, the little poor man of Assisi. Miles apart, it would seem, yet their lives and destinies are inextricably linked in history. Indeed, it could be argued that it is because of the later events in Paris that the medieval spirit of Assisi survives and is of such relevance for today's religious and social world. This book will introduce the reader to the life and religious genius of St Francis and to the theological and philosophical reflection on that life which is to be found in the writings of Bonaventure. It will also suggest that from this medieval Franciscan experience, the contemporary world can draw much inspiration when seeking to address many of the pressing concerns of our own time.

Francis, the Poor Man of Assisi

Francis was born in the Umbrian town of Assisi in 1182. His father was a wealthy clothing merchant, and it seemed for some years that Francis was to play the role of the rich father's son. He is reported to have been the star of Assisi's young social set, and his natural exuberance found expression in pursuing a lifestyle which his wealth and social position enabled him to enjoy to the full. He dreamed of glory as a knight, and at twenty years of age set off to battle for Assisi in the war against the neighbouring city of Perugia. Francis' dream, however, took an unexpected turn. Taken captive in battle, Francis spent a year in prison in Perugia, a year which led him to reflect deeply on the direction of his life. His return from Perugia after his father had paid the ransom for his release was followed by a lengthy illness. His recovery took twelve long months, after which he sought to resume his earlier lifestyle. He set out once more for war in Apulia. But now the stirrings within him reached their crisis point. Francis realized he could no longer resist the changes in his way of life which were being called for from the depths of his heart. He could no longer continue to live a lie.

Despite the threat of social disgrace (for it was not proper for a knight to return from battle in this way), he returned to Assisi the very next day. This was to mark the final turning point. Francis was to leave behind family, wealth, social standing and material ambitions and to embark on a journey for which he willingly forsook all else, the journey into the heart of being captivated by God.

It was this experience of Francis, the experience of being overwhelmed and captivated by God's love, that was to transform so radically not only his own life but the religious and social world in which he lived. Francis was led into the most exciting of life's journeys. He became able to accept and even to love those dimensions of life which previously he had feared. In doing this, he gained true freedom. It was a freedom which marked out the path of his life. It enabled him to choose to live in radical poverty. Instead of seeking glory in war and conflict, he gloried in being the bearer of the good news of peace and goodwill, reaching out in compassion to touch the hearts of all. This freedom enabled Francis to embrace and reverence the whole created world. Someone who is in love sees everything which is associated with the loved one in a new light, in a spirit of devotion and appreciative joy. Francis, as the true lover, saw in a new light everything which God, the loved One, had made, and so grew to appreciate, to reverence and to rejoice in the realities of the world. Such was his sympathy for that world that, today, Francis is held up us as the patron saint of ecology. This freedom, which came from an unshakeable conviction that his being was held forever in the embrace of the God of Life, made it possible for Francis to say as he lay dying in 1226, 'Welcome, Sister Death.'

During his lifetime, Francis' irrepressible magnetism attracted followers who grew rapidly in number and were eventually to be recognized in the Church as a religious Order, the Franciscans. Francis was to later compose a Rule of Life for married people and others who were not members of the Order but who were inspired by his way of life. These were identified as the 'Third Order' and are now known as the Secular Franciscan Order. Today, tens of thousands of men and women throughout the world – within religious communities, as married couples or as unmarried – dedicate their lives to striving to capture and to express something of the joyful freedom which characterized the life of Francis, who, in giving away all for the One he loved, discovered that in giving, he was to receive immeasurably more than he could have ever conceived was possible.

Bonaventure, the Master of Paris

When Francis died, Bonaventure was still in his youth. Bonaventure was born John of Fidanza in Bagnoredgio, near Orvieto, in Tuscany around the year 1217. (His birth is dated by some as 1217 and by others as 1221.) There is relatively little historical detail concerning the circumstances of his life, particularly his earlier life. In around 1235, to prepare himself for a future career, he enrolled as a student for the Master's degree at the Faculty of Arts in the great medieval University in Paris. It was there that he would have come in contact with the early Franciscans. The Franciscans had moved into the university environment so as to have access to the academic facilities which, it was felt, would assist them to be more effective in their reforming mission within the Church. In 1236, a notable event took place within the University which would have deeply affected Bonaventure. The renowned Master within the Faculty of Theology, Alexander of Hales, joined the Franciscan brotherhood, and his Chair of Theology went with him. This event was to indicate to the young theology student that the Franciscan Order had indeed been especially inspired by God. As he wrote years later in a 'Letter to an Unknown Master':

I confess before God that the reason which made me love most of all the life of blessed Francis is the fact that it resembles the beginning and the growth of the Church. The Church, indeed, began with simple fishermen, and was enriched later with most illustrious and learned doctors. Thus you may understand the religion of blessed Francis was established, not by the prudence of men, but by Christ, as shown by

God himself. And because the works of Christ do not fail but cease-
lessly grow, it is God who has accomplished this work, since scholars
have not been reluctant to join the company of simple men, heeding
the word of the apostle [1 CORINTHIANS 3:18]: *'If any one of you*
thinks himself wise in this world, let him become a fool, so that he
may come to be wise.'

He was some short time afterwards to follow Alexander's lead,
joining the Order and taking the name Bonaventure. His own
academic abilities were recognized and he continued his study of
theology under Alexander of Hales and later under John of La
Rochelle, Odo Rigaldi and William of Meliton. The date of his
inception as Master of Theology is disputed, being given as early as
1248 and as late as 1254. Bonaventure continued teaching at the
University (Thomas Aquinas was a fellow academic) until 1257.
In that year he was called from his position as Master to serve as
the seventh Minister General of the Franciscan Order. In 1273,
Bonaventure was named Cardinal Bishop of Albano by Gregory X.
He died on 15 July 1274 while attending the Council of Lyons.

During his time in Paris, Bonaventure produced a number of
academic works on theology. Some of these works will be examined later in this book. After his election to the position of Minister General, his major writings were of a more deeply religious
nature. Nowhere is this exemplified more than in his work
Intinerarium Mentis in Deum (The Soul's Journey into God). When
Bonaventure became Minister General, the followers of Francis
were experiencing considerable difficulty in living out the spirit
of their founder. There was considerable tension between those
who sought an almost apocalyptic, spiritual interpretation of
Francis' message and those who wished to reduce the radical
nature of the Franciscan movement and make it more like the
already established Orders. Bonaventure's position as Minister
General drew him deep into the conflict, and for this reason
he withdrew in 1259 into the solitude of the Franciscan holy

mount, La Verna, in order to immerse himself more deeply in the spiritual world of the founder.

La Verna is situated some sixty miles to the north of Assisi. In 1213, Count Roland of Chiusi had given the mountain to Francis as a place where Francis could go for periods of solitude and prayer, just as, in the gospels, Jesus used to retire to the mountains to pray. It was during such a period of prayer in September 1224 that Francis, on the heights of La Verna, experienced the stigmata – in his own body were marked the wounds of the crucified Christ. It was here that Bonaventure composed the *Itinerarium* (*The Soul's Journey into God*), which was both the fruit of his earlier theological speculation and the paradigm for all of his later works. This contemplative and mystical work will provide the pattern for much of what is to be said about Bonaventure's unique contribution to Christian thought and practice.

Although history provides us with little detail concerning Bonaventure's personal life, it would appear that he was held in great respect and even affection by his contemporaries. Historical documents which appear to denigrate his role as Minister General of the Order are more the product of the bias of political infighting than of first-hand observation. Certainly the poetry, the artistry, the serenity, the beauty and piety which so often shine forth in the pages of his writings testify to a man who, like Francis, sought to live in peace and harmony with his God, his brothers and sisters and with the entire world of God's creation.

Francis and Bonaventure were both powerful witnesses in word and action to God's presence breaking into our world. It is time now to explore something of the experience which so enthralled Francis' heart and which so deeply affected the lives of Bonaventure and countless others.

The Inspiration: Saint Francis of Assisi

Most High, all-powerful, good Lord
Yours are the praises, the glory, the honour, and all blessing.
To You alone, Most High, do they belong,
and no man is worthy to mention Your name.

With these words Francis of Assisi begins his magnificent 'Canticle of Brother Sun', a song which burst forth from his heart and which reveals the unique nature of his inspiration. It is significant that the first verses of the 'Canticle' are caught up with praise of God, providing the focus of the central place of God in Francis' life. As in the 'Canticle', so in his whole life – Francis began with God and saw all else from there. The early medieval writings concerning Francis, both those which came from his own hand and those which were written by others, reveal him as one who was passionately in love with God and whose whole life was fired by this passion.

The Historical Sources

Much of our information concerning the life of Francis comes from a variety of early biographies termed *Legenda* – in medieval terms, a document to be read in public liturgical gatherings. Foremost among these were Thomas of Celano's *First Life* (1228); Celano's *Second Life* (1247); Bonaventure's *Major Life* and *Minor Life* (both completed before 1263); *Legend of the Three Companions* (first years of the fourteenth century); *Legend of Perugia* (1311); and the *Mirror of Perfection* (1318). Less in the style of history is the popular *Little Flowers of Francis* (composed between 1327 and 1342).

It is important to distinguish between the large collection of Franciscan writings which appeared within the century after the saint's death and those sources which we refer to as the writings of Francis. What we now recognize as the actual writings of Francis are to be found in the critical edition drawn up by Fr Kajetan Esser, OFM, and first published in 1976. Despite Francis' wish to have his letters and writings copied and preserved, many have been lost over the course of history. Nevertheless we have available to us today a collection of 36 separate writings, composed between 1205 and 1226. It would appear that most of the writings were dictated by Francis to a secretary who may have refined his imperfect Latin. Despite this, the writings serve better than do the biographical sources in providing us with a reasonably comprehensive view of Francis' life. They give us considerable insight into the nature of Francis' personal religious experience, into Francis' understanding of his relationship with God and the implications of this for his life in the world.

Francis was not a medieval philosopher who wrote according to abstract reasoning. His nature was more that of the Romantic, the poet, and, at his deepest level, the mystic. To appreciate the heart of Francis, more is required than a technical examination of his words. It is important to be caught up in the flow of the words, in the way that we might surrender ourselves and be caught up in the rhythm and movement of our favourite music. His religious experience is expressed not so much as theology as personal prayer. When Francis provides moral teaching, he does not leave us with a list of legal obligations, but challenges us to make a response which is motivated by love.

Awareness of the Divine

Max Scheler has written of Francis:

Never again in the history of the West does there emerge a figure marked with such a strength of sympathy and of universal emotion as that of St Francis.

Where lies the secret of such strength? It becomes clear in his writings that Francis had a direct awareness of the presence of God in his life. His religious conversion, he claims, was not simply a change in the way that he looked at life. Nor was it something which was brought about through the influence of others. Other people were very important to him and he was certainly one who knew his own mind. Yet, in these critical moments of his life, Francis was convinced that more was involved – he was convinced that his conversion experience was initiated through the action of God breaking into his life and shattering all his preconceptions.

In his 'Testament', dictated shortly before his death, he describes his conversion in terms of contact with a leper. The story is recounted as to how, while Francis was journeying on horseback, suddenly in his path there stood a leper. Francis had always had a revulsion for lepers and describes their presence as something ' ... bitter to me'. Certainly he had no inclination to go and work in caring for the lepers and would journey miles out of his way in order to avoid making any contact. He does not speak about his conversion experience as one of seeking out lepers but in terms of being '... led among them'. On being confronted by the leper, his natural instinct urged him to flee; instead he experienced a granting of strength and compassion which enabled him to reach out and physically embrace the leper, to embrace that which he had feared most.

> *The Lord granted me, Brother Francis, to begin to do penance in this*
> *way: while I was in sin, it seemed very bitter to me to see lepers. And*
> *the Lord Himself led me among them and I had mercy upon them.*

For Francis, the nature of the encounter lay beyond the power of
his own capacities; it was something 'granted' to him. He could
only explain this experience, an experience which changed his life,
through reference to the action of God erupting from beyond into
the context of his life. Later in the 'Testament', Francis writes:

> *And after the Lord gave me brothers, no one showed me what I should*
> *do, but the Most High Himself revealed to me that I should live*
> *according to the form of the Holy Gospel.*

At the time of his conversion Francis was a layman, not a cleric.
Within the context of medieval society, this would have created
two barriers between the Scriptures – 'the Holy Gospel' – and himself. In the first place, it is most likely that Francis did not have a
Bible at his disposal, both for reasons of cost and for reasons of
Church discipline. It was to the clergy only that the task of commenting upon the Scriptures was given. Secondly, the Scriptures
were available only in Latin. Although Francis had an excellent
command of his native Umbrian dialect, it is noted that his Latin
was poor. He would most likely have approached the Scriptures
through the mediation of a priest or one of the brothers well
versed in Latin.

It is tempting to try to explain Francis' conversion experience as
the result of the context in which he lived – to argue that the particular social and religious pressures which had been part of his
background created within his mind the feeling that God had
called him. This is not the way, however, that even at the end of his
life, Francis understood his call from God. As is evident from the
above passage from the 'Testament', he did not believe that his
particular calling by God had been created by somebody interpreting

Scripture for him. It was not as if he had been told by a priest that this was the meaning of the Scriptures and therefore that he should lead a certain way of life. On the contrary, Francis insists, 'No one told me what I should do'. Although he saw his conversion experience as unfolding within the church community and in the light of the Scriptures, the cause of the experience is not ascribed either to the community or to the Scriptures. Rather, his initial experience is referred to the action of God – 'the Most High Himself revealed to me'. This revelation was gradually clarified as he prayed, sought counsel from those he respected and as he heard the gospel read and explained within his church community. Francis believed in the reality of God's initial and personal call, and the meaning of this then unfolded for him within his social and religious environment.

It is important to remember that Francis never felt that his belief that God had called him directly justified him in 'doing his own thing'. He insisted that his conviction should be tested by the wider community of the Church and he sought confirmation of his calling from the Church's representatives – firstly, his local bishop, and later, the Pope in Rome. In 1209, Pope Innocent III approved Francis' Rule of Life. God may call individuals directly but it is very possible for people to be mistaken about the nature of such a call. In recent years we have seen tragic consequences following from the actions of self-labelled 'prophets' who were convinced that God had called them but who refused to submit their conviction for the approval of the wider religious or social community. Francis, however, realized that his calling was not meant to make him greater than God's people, but ever more a part of God's people. Just as yeast achieves its potential not by being separated from the dough but by being immersed within it, Francis immersed himself in the community of the Church and brought it new life.

Reversal of Values

It is this direct awareness of God's presence in his life which is the secret of Francis' strength. His strong sense of divine calling and of the working of God within his life led him to feel an intense yearning for God. He sought liberation from all that estranged him from God, and he found his model in Jesus Christ. Henceforth, his way of life was to be a literal following of Christ – a dying to self, a living for others, a willingness to give all for the sake of the One whose goodness and love were desirable about all else. There was now a reversal of values – what previously had taken prominent place in his affections left him dissatisfied, while a new system of priorities energized his entire being.

Such a reversal of values could only be achieved through radical dependency on the power of God's Spirit. Francis' use of the word 'Spirit' is akin to that of St Paul – a Hebraic sense of the spirit of the human person being seized by the Spirit of God. It was this power which Francis relied upon, not the power of his own efforts. He spoke of the need to live according to the 'Spirit', rather than according to the 'flesh'.

A servant of God may be recognized as possessing the Spirit of the Lord in this way: if the flesh does not pride itself when the Lord performs some good through him.

The 'flesh' is the egotistical self which sees its own end in itself and its own importance. It is the egotistical self which refuses to acknowledge dependency upon God. Francis identified such an attitude as sin, since it was essentially worship of self rather than worship of God. One who lives according to the 'flesh' is caught up in self-love, whereas one whose life is open to the Spirit dies to self and attributes all good to God.

Blessed is the servant who esteems himself no better when he is praised and exalted by people than when he is considered worthless, simple, and despicable; for what a man is before God, that he is and nothing more.

The living experience of the Spirit was crucial for the way of Francis and dictated his concern for God, his fellow human beings and all of God's creation. It is reported that on one occasion some of his brothers asked Francis whether or not they should feed hungry robbers who were coming to them out of the forests asking for bread. Francis urged his brothers to buy bread and wine, to lay out a supper for the robbers and to serve them with humility and good humour. While the robbers were nourishing themselves, the brothers were to gently speak God's word to them, requesting at first no more than that the robbers refrain from striking or harming anyone. This would bring the robbers, said Francis, to be won over by the charity which had been shown them and in this way they would be enabled to gradually change their style of life.

Whatever of the exact historical details of this story, it reflects an important aspect of Francis' character. He was very much aware of the 'robber' dimension within his own life – perhaps his earlier desires to be recognized before others, maybe to dominate others and to have power over them, or even the will to inflict hurt. He was well aware of the negative actualities and possibilities inherent in his own existence. When a brother asked him, 'Father, what do you think of yourself?', he answered,

I know that I am the worst sinner because, if God had shown some criminal all of the mercy he has shown to me, that man would be twice as spiritual as I am.

Francis' approach to the robbers reflected God's approach to him and the 'robbers' within his own life. His experience of God's Spirit had not been one of condemnation, but rather of welcoming patience and hospitality which gradually led him forward to a new way of life. He had been encouraged to accept his deeper self and to be at peace with that self. No longer did he need to prove himself before others, nor to be afraid when others might react to him in a hostile way. It was this experience which was to form the pattern of his teachings on how people ought to relate to one another, and which was to give Francis to the world as a model for peace, forgiveness and reconciliation.

There should not be anyone in the world who has sinned, however much he may possibly have sinned, who, after he has looked into your eyes, would go away without having received your mercy ... And if he should sin thereafter a thousand times before your very eyes, love him more than me so that you may draw him back to the Lord.

An Instrument of Peace

It was as peacemaker that Francis set out to meet Sultan Melek-el-Kamil. The setting was that of the Fifth Crusade and the fierce hostilities between the Christian world and the world of Islam. In 1218 the army of Crusaders landed on the coast of Egypt and laid siege to the city of Damietta. Their opponent was Melek-el-Kamil, Saladin's nephew, a man described as brilliant, highly cultured and religiously devout. In 1219, Francis came to Damietta in the Nile Delta determined to meet him.

A number of accounts exist of the meeting between Francis and the Sultan. What can be said with certainty is that Francis crossed the lines with the intention of seeking to convert the Sultan by preaching and returned unharmed to the Crusader camp. An Arab author of the fifteenth century also indirectly testifies to the encounter between the two men.

One such account is provided by Jacques de Vitry, who wrote while Francis was still alive and who actually met Francis in Damietta. De Vitry speaks of Francis continuing on from Damietta, unarmed, to the camp of the Sultan. On the way, Francis was taken prisoner, but with the proclamation, 'I am a Christian' and with a request to be led to the Sultan, he was taken to appear before Melek-el-Kamil. The Sultan appeared to be fascinated with Francis and listened to his preaching about Christ. Finally he guaranteed a safe passage for Francis back to the Crusader camp.

These records of the meeting would certainly not satisfy our present-day demands for first-hand, video-style news reports. The incident does, however, tell us much about the spirit which shone through Francis. He had come to the Sultan's camp unarmed, the man of peace. He had been able to cast aside the fears and prejudices which pitted armies against armies. In contrast to the crusader, Francis came to the Sultan's camp '... having no other protection than the buckler of faith'. He had left behind the Christian political structure which the Crusade symbolized, to preach the purity of his belief – faith in Christ and in the God revealed in Christ. He challenged the Sultan to do likewise, to go beyond the Muslim political structure in order to come to terms with his own purity of faith. The fact that the Sultan guaranteed Francis a safe return to the Christian camp indicated that Francis had obviously made a deep impression upon him. It was his deep trust in God which provided Francis with the strength to break down political and religious barriers and to become a model for religious dialogue. Such dialogue is a pressing concern of our own time and later in this book we shall return to examine the significance of this encounter more closely.

The Mystical Embrace – God and Creation

It is not possible to capture the spirit of Francis without understanding something of Francis the mystic. Central to this mysticism is a dying to the egotistical self in order to come to fullness of life in God. His mystical journey was indissolubly linked with his following of Christ, whom he believed in as the incarnational presence of God. Francis describes the mystical union in terms of being '...spouses, brothers, and mothers of our Lord Jesus Christ'. The closeness and tenderness of the mystical union is expressed not only in masculine images of fraternity, but also incorporates the images of married love and the intimate bonding between mother and child.

> *We are spouses when the faithful soul is joined to Jesus Christ by the Holy Spirit ... We are brothers when we do the will of His Father Who is in heaven ... [We are] mothers when we carry Him in our heart and body through love and a pure and sincere conscience; we give birth to Him through [His] holy manner of working, which should shine before others as an example.*

Note that Francis uses here the word 'joined' (*conjungitur*), a word often used in the Middle Ages to express the intimate nature of marital relationships. Francis is not writing abstract theology, he is recounting the overwhelming joy of a deeply personal experience. The intensity of his own experience of God bursts forth in the stream of adjectives of praise which follow.

> *Oh, how glorious it is, how holy and great, to have a Father in heaven! Oh, how holy consoling, beautiful, and wondrous it is to have a Spouse! Oh, how holy and how loving, pleasing, humble, peaceful, sweet, loveable, and desirable above all things to have such a Brother and Son.*

The mystical experience of Francis expressed itself in his relationship with all creation. We find this witnessed to in his 'Canticle of Brother Sun'. The 'Canticle', however, is no commitment to pantheism (the belief that there is nothing which is other than God, that the material universe cannot be separated from God). Nor is it mere aesthetic appreciation of the world of nature. What lies at the heart is Francis' claim that the God whom he has personally experienced is at the same time the Creator God whose goodness is reflected in all that has been created.

The major part of the 'Canticle' was composed by Francis towards the end of his life, at a time when he had been suffering from both physical illness and emotional anxiety about the future of his Order. Yet, as he reflected on his own relationship with God, he was overwhelmed by the persistency of God's goodness and this led him to see and experience the reflections of God's goodness in all created elements.

In the 'Canticle' he addresses the created world as 'Brother', 'Sister', 'Mother'. These attributes are not merely poetical personifications but expressions of spiritual relationship. He was able to enter into such a relationship since he respected all created things for the sacredness of the reflections they bore. His conviction that the Creator God is the highest good enabled him to perceive the world as a sacred reality, since it is a reflection of God's goodness. The praises of the 'Canticle' witness to one who was able, even as he lay ill in the Convent of San Damiano, to discern and feel the creative presence of divine love in all around him. Once again, fear was driven from his heart to be replaced with a deep-seated joy and confidence which none could take from him.

Most High, all-powerful, good Lord,
Yours are the praises, the glory, the honour, and all blessing.
To You alone, Most High, do they belong,
and no man is worthy to mention Your name.
Praise be You, my Lord, with all your creatures ...
Praised be You, my Lord, through our Sister Mother Earth, who
    sustains and governs us,
and who produces varied fruits with coloured flowers and herbs ...
Praise and bless my Lord and give him thanks
and serve Him with great humility.

St Francis is recognized today as the patron saint of ecology. In these final years of the twentieth century, the human race is realizing as never before the need to have respect and concern for the natural world in which we live. Without such respect, the ecological balance can be destroyed, resulting in tragic consequences for future generations. It is said that modern human beings often seem to live as strangers to the environment, unable to relate properly to the world in which they live. What Francis offers is the ability to recover the sense of our spiritual relationship with the created world through the conviction that all created entities contain within themselves reflections of God's creative goodness. As Francis' thirteenth-century biographer, Thomas of Celano, wrote in *The Second Life of St Francis*:

> *Francis sought occasion to love God in everything. He delighted in all the works of God's hands and from the vision of joy on earth his mind soared aloft to the life-giving source and cause of it all. In everything beautiful, he saw Him who is beauty itself; and he followed his Beloved everywhere by his likeness imprinted on creation; of all creation he made a ladder by which he might mount up and embrace Him who is all-desirable.*

Bonaventure, in his own major account of Francis' life, comments:

> *When he considered the primordial source of all things he was filled with even more abundant piety, calling creatures no matter how small, by the name of brother or sister, because he knew they had the same source as himself.* (L 8.6)

Francis' ultimate mystical experience occurred on the heights of the holy mountain, La Verna. As was noted in Chapter 1, Francis used to retire to La Verna for lengthy periods of solitude and prayer, and it was here that he experienced in his own body the wounds of the crucified Christ. His death to self in imitation of

Christ reached its fullest expression in this bodily identification with Christ's act of self-giving love in obedience to God. Brother Leo, Francis' close companion who had accompanied him on this occasion to La Verna, wrote:

After the vision and words of the Seraph and the impression of the stigmata of Christ in his body he composed these praises written on the other side of this sheet and wrote them in his own hand, giving thanks to God for the kindness bestowed on him.

You are holy, Lord, the only God, You do wonders.
You are strong, You are great, You are the most high,
You are the almighty King.
You, Holy Father, the king of heaven and earth.
You are Three and One, Lord God of gods;
You are good, all good, the highest good,
Lord, God, living and true.
You are love, charity,
You are wisdom; You are humility; You are patience;
You are beauty; You are meekness; You are security;
You are inner peace; You are joy; You are our hope and joy;
You are justice; You are moderation, You are all our riches
[You are enough for us]
You are Beauty, You are meekness;
You are the protector,
You are our guardian and defender;
You are strength; You are refreshment.
You are our hope, You are our faith, You are our charity,
You are all our sweetness,
You are our eternal life:
Great and wonderful Lord,
God almighty, Merciful Saviour.

Such was Francis' experience of God, an experience which transformed his life and was to set him aside as an inspiration and example for future travellers along the path of the journey to God. One such traveller was Bonaventure. He was to dedicate his God given gifts to expressing for the wider world what it might mean to allow oneself to be seized by the Spirit of God, as had the little poor man of Assisi.

Bonaventure's Intellectual Inheritance

*We should not believe that reading is sufficient without feeling, specu-
lation without devotion, investigation without wonder, observation
without joy, work without piety, knowledge without love, understanding without humility, endeavour without divine grace.* (I PROLOGUE 4)

Many stories and legends were created about Francis, although we
have relatively little remaining of his own writings. With Bonaventure, the reverse is the case. We have quite a large collection of his
own works, but very little written about Bonaventure by those
who knew him. His own writings are those of the scholar – at
times of a technical, philosophical nature, at other times, full of
the freshness and vitality of the poet and the literary genius. As
a scholar he was familiar with a wide range of earlier Christian
and non-Christian thinkers and drew on these to produce a
unique philosophical theology. None the less, the heart of his
inspiration, as we shall see, remained the life and experience of
Francis of Assisi.

Bonaventure's writings can be divided into two categories,
those of the time he spent at the University of Paris and those after
his election to the position of Minister General of the Franciscan
Order. Those which emerged from his period in Paris are in keeping with the accepted later medieval methods of argumentation.
The question under examination is firstly answered in the affirmative and supported with a presentation of arguments from accepted authorities, notably the Church Fathers and the writings of the

philosophers. Objections to this position are then considered, after which the Master puts forward his conclusion. Finally, he replies to the objections earlier raised. We see this structure in works such as *Disputed Questions on the Mystery of the Trinity* and *Disputed Questions on the Knowledge of Christ*. Following his election as Minister General, his writings tend to be of a more spiritual nature. We see notable differences in style and content in later works such as the *Itinerarium* or the *Collations on the Six Days*. He continues, however, to show familiarity with, and to draw upon, the academic authorities which were important in his earlier works.

Who were these academic authorities and in what ways did they influence the shape of Bonaventure's thought? Although Bonaventure drew on a wide range of such authorities, this book will concentrate on three key figures. From the early period of the Church, Bonaventure draws on traditions both from the West and from the East, notably, Augustine and Pseudo-Dionysius. From times closer to his own, he was particularly influenced by the thought of the School of St Victor.

Augustine

The writings of Augustine (AD 354–430) are voluminous and it is well beyond the scope of this book to attempt any critical analysis of them. What can be said, however, is that Bonaventure took from Augustine the fundamental starting point for his theological reflection. It was Augustine who wrote:

> *Believe in order to understand. Faith necessarily comes first and understanding later.*

This did not mean that people who profess to have faith do not need to reason about their faith. For Augustine, it was important to use the God-given gift of human intelligence in order to integrate the faith we profess with the concerns of our life in the world. There was to be no separation between the concerns of religious faith and the concerns of everyday life.

What Augustine wanted to stress, however, is that rational arguments will not produce faith. Faith is a fundamental conviction held by the human person, and no amount of reasoning can bring about such a conviction. Augustine urges that we begin with that conviction and then seek to understand it. This task of understanding will necessarily entail that we rationally reflect on our faith. Theology addresses this task as one of its major concerns. Consequently, Augustine affirms, the Church's theology must begin with the Scriptures, with revelation, the expression of faith convictions which have been handed down through the ages.

Like Augustine, Bonaventure believed that theological reflection must begin with faith. Not faith in the sense of belief in certain propositions, but faith meaning the individual's fundamental conviction that life finds its ultimate meaning and significance in the God who has created this world and who holds and sustains creation in being. The Scriptures or revelation, as the recorded experiences of faith recognized and officially accepted by the Church, were to be the springs from which theological thinking must first draw if it was to be fruitful. Having drawn from that wellspring, theology would then use reason to its fullest capacity. Bonaventure was convinced that when we use our reason with a spirit of humility before the greater knowledge which is the revelation of God, then it is possible to begin to formulate an understanding of faith which will answer the deepest aspirations of the human mind and heart.

Mind and heart – this was the secret of Bonaventure's theology. The terms he used were *intellectus* and *affectus* – intelligence and desire, especially the desire of love. When these combine what is produced is not just intellectual knowledge but wisdom – *sapientia*. Wisdom was, for Bonaventure, the aim of theology. One did not study theology in order to learn facts but in order to become wise. Theology must never be merely an intellectual exercise, it must become integrated into a way of life. This is an important lesson for today as well. Intellectual pursuits can all too easily become isolated from the rest of one's life. This is as true about theology as about any other discipline. What we learn from Bonaventure is that theology fails in its task if it remains a mere academic exercise. Its concerns must include the spiritual, moral and social needs of the human person.

One very important area of inquiry in today's world is the field of psychology, the study of the human person. Augustine was a very early Christian psychologist. It may seem to us, familiar as we are with the language of the Freudians and post-Freudians, that his analysis of the human person is rather primitive. Technically speaking, this is probably so, although this book is again inadequate to give a proper assessment of Augustinian psychology. What Augustine did grasp, however, was an extremely important religious insight – that when we delve into the mystery of the human person, we enter in some way into the mystery of God, since the human person is created in God's image. Indeed, much contemporary spiritual direction is based on this premiss. While Augustine's psychological analysis of the human person may appear a little simplistic, this does not negate the value of his fundamental insight.

In Augustine's writings, we are able to discover the outlines of the inward journey to discover God in the depths of the human psyche. Augustine's starting point is his conviction that the human person is essentially the 'image of God'. So when we look into the self, it is as if we are looking into a mirror in which the light of God shines. Imagine looking into a mirror. It is not the mirror itself that we are focusing upon. What draws our attention, rather, is the light that is reflected in the mirror. In the same way, claims Augustine, when we look into the self we are not focusing upon the self but upon the light of God which is reflected there.

Bonaventure takes up this theme in the *Itinerarium* (*The Soul's Journey into God*), particularly in the third chapter:

We enter into our very selves; and we should strive to see God through a mirror. Here the light of Truth glows upon the face of our mind. (I 3.1)

Chapter 3 of the *Itinerarium* concerns itself with a psychological analysis of the self. It is clear, however, that the journey into God is not to be equated simply with the attainment of self-knowledge. This would be to make a God out of psychoanalysis and to identify the religious quest with the psychological quest. Bonaventure does claim that his path will lead to a clearer understanding of the self – the self will only be fully understood in reference to God, who is its source and its final destiny.

Bonaventure's exhortation to journey into the self is an integral part of the journey into God. Those who wish to make the spiritual journey no doubt ask what it might mean to experience a God who cannot be seen. Bonaventure urges us to reflect on the psychological nature of the human self. Since the self is the image of God, it is possible to draw from those reflections analogies which help us to understand something about God. Reflection on the ability to inquire and to reason, for example, can create an awareness of the natural restlessness of the human heart. It is a part of human nature that we yearn to understand more about life and the world, that we have an unquenchable thirst to discover what is true. In using our ability to reason, we are demonstrating a desire to transcend the limitations of the present moment. We are naturally inclined towards the infinite – and therein the life of God is reflected.

Reflection upon the human ability to desire and to love reveals how, in loving, the individual is drawn beyond the self into the mystery of the other. In the wonder of that mystery, says Bonaventure, is reflected the wonder of the mystery of the Eternal Other. It is in this type of reflection on the nature of the self that we can begin to understand something of what it means to experience God.

Augustine's influence is evident in Bonaventure's writings. It is to Augustine that he looks to draw support for his conviction that human life cannot be understood without reference to God and that therefore there ought to be no separation between faith and reason, between theology and philosophy. It is also in Augustine that he finds the psychological model which enables him to expound his further conviction, that it is possible for the human person, made in the image of God, to discover and to experience God. Both of these convictions, however, have their foundational inspiration not in a study of theological volumes but in reflection upon the life experience of the little poor man of Assisi.

Pseudo-Dionysius

Bonaventure not only drew upon the Western tradition of Augustine but also appropriated the spirituality of the East, particularly that found in the collection of writings which has been entitled Pseudo-Dionysius. The true identity of the author is unknown. It would appear that at some stage an attempt had been made to give these writings substantive authority by claiming that they originated from a person who had been in contact with the Apostles, namely, Dionysius the Areopagite, who appears in Acts 17:34. Contemporary research seems to indicate that Pseudo-Dionysius was a Syrian who wrote during the first quarter of the sixth century.

The Pseudo-Dionysian texts draw extensively on imagery taken from Neo-Platonic thought. Neo-Platonism is the name given to a branch of thinking which is generally held to have begun with the thought of the third-century philosopher Plotinus. It is labelled Neo-Platonism because Plotinus, although heavily influenced by the work of the great Greek philosopher Plato, introduced a number of modifications into Plato's thought. This was particularly in order to make provision for some of the thoughts of Plato's student and (later) greatest critic, Aristotle.

Neo-Platonism described all reality as springing from an original source which was labelled 'the One'. All life flowed from the One. This flow of life from the One was called the process of 'emanation'. It accounted for the diversity which is found in life, the fact that things are separate and different. And yet, while we experience the world as diverse, we also have a yearning for unity. Such yearning lies, for example, behind the union of love found in marriage, where two different individuals, who are 'opposites' in so far as they are male and female, become one. For Plotinus, such yearning for unity in the midst of diversity will be fulfilled when everything returns to the One from which it has originated.

The writings of Pseudo-Dionysius reveal this fundamental Neo-Platonic structure, but within a Christian framework. The 'One' becomes the Creator God of the Book of Genesis. The work of creation is an 'emanation' or flowing forth from God. Creation is diverse and so displays various levels. For Pseudo-Dionysius, there are three levels:

- totally spiritual beings – the angels
- beings who are both spiritual and material – humans
- totally material realities – plants, rocks, etc.

Each of these levels are related to one another. The angels serve to communicate God's word to humans (for example, Gabriel communicating God's word to the Virgin Mary at the Annunciation). The material world of nature, since it comes from God, can also teach humans something about God. In this way the different levels of reality, through their inter-relatedness, serve to draw all closer to God. This is what Pseudo-Dionysius terms the operation of a 'hierarchy'.

The word 'hierarchy' comes from two Greek words: *hieros*, meaning sacred, and *arche* meaning source or principle. It basically describes the sacred principles which have been established by God in the work of creation in order to enable life to achieve its proper destiny, which is to return to God, the source of all life. Creation, then, is the emanation from God (and, for Pseudo-Dionysius, an overflow of God's essential goodness). God's creation manifests a hierarchical structure, or an essential inter-relatedness between all things. The purpose of this structure is to enable the proper completion of life's journey, which is the return to God. This return is spoken of in a technical sense as the process of 'divinization'.

Pseudo-Dionysius' vision of God and of creation is one where God is active, not a distant 'Unmoved Mover'. God is intimately involved with creation which is seen as God's free gift, an overflowing of the divine goodness itself. God desires that we should share to our utmost ability in this goodness, that we should become 'God-like'. God desires that we should be divinized through the process of the return to the divine source.

The Dionysian writings recognize that in speaking about returning to God, we are faced with two apparently contradictory notions. On the one hand, as St Paul writes, 'Ever since God created the world his everlasting power and deity have been there for the mind to see in the things he has made' (ROMANS 1:20). On the other hand, as found in the Gospel of John, 'No one has ever seen God' (JOHN 1:18). God can be discovered within creation and yet, at the same time, God is totally beyond all that has been created. Thus, while it seems true that we can say something about God which springs from our human experiences of life and the world, it also remains true that whatever we say can never capture the reality of the God who is essentially beyond all our experiences.

Pseudo-Dionysius addresses this problem by speaking of a 'twofold path' to God. It is possible for us to say something about God by giving God the names found in the Scriptures, names which have been revealed by God and are consequently part of the outpouring of God's goodness. The most prominent of these is that

God *is* goodness. To give God names is to affirm something about God. In saying 'God is good', for example, I affirm that God is not evil. In speaking of God as merciful, I affirm that God is not vindictive. Speaking about God in this way – making affirmative statements about God – is known as 'affirmative' or 'cataphatic' theology. The task of affirmative theology is to point the individual in the right way on the journey of returning to God.

However, since God is also the one who is essentially beyond description, it is not possible to identify God with our notions of goodness or mercy. If God were to be identified with these, then we would be able to understand God. God would cease to be mystery – God would cease to be God. If we wish to continue the journey, we must not stay in the one spot. Affirmative theology is like the setting up of a base camp on the ascent to Everest. It provides strength and sustenance. If we remain in the camp, however, we shall never complete the journey to the summit. We must leave behind the security of the camp and venture into the unknown.

This is the second of the paths which Pseudo-Dionysius speaks about. It is called the way of 'negation'. It means leaving behind the spiritual security which our affirmations about God provide and setting off into the unknown. It is possible to affirm that God is goodness, but God must not be identified with any experience of human goodness. In this sense, God is not goodness. This is not saying that God is therefore evil, the opposite of goodness, rather, it is an insistence that God is not to be equated with any *human* understanding of goodness. God is far greater than anything that we can conceive. The way of negation is a stepping into the darkness, and it calls forth an attitude of total trust. This is the way of negation, also known as the 'apophatic' way.

In chapter 5, we shall see in greater detail how Bonaventure integrated elements of Dionysian thought within the framework of his spiritual theology. Suffice it to say at this stage that in Pseudo-Dionysius, Bonaventure found a ready vehicle for his fundamental convictions. Through Dionysian concepts he was able to express his belief that God is not remote and abstract but a God of active goodness, intimately involved with the world, which is itself an overflow of that goodness. Moreover, the ultimate destiny of human life is to return to God. The return is to be completed through a journey which both affirms the goodness and the diversity of God's creation and yet at the same time moves beyond this to the origin and destiny of all created realities – the life of God.

The School of St Victor

Bonaventure's theological style was further influenced by writings which emerged from the School of St Victor. The Abbey of St Victor had its origins as a small hermitage community on the left bank of the Seine. During the twelfth century, the Abbey community came to be recognized not only as a leader in the efforts to renew monastic discipline but also as a centre of a vigorous, dynamic intellectual life. It was open to the theological developments emerging from the new schools at the University of Paris, and produced two of the leading intellectual figures of the latter part of the twelfth century, Hugh and Richard of St Victor. Bonaventure's Franciscan Master at the University, Alexander of Hales, highly respected the Victorine writings and his student came to share this intellectual devotion.

The Victorine tradition taught that theology must be concerned above all with symbolic representations of the sacred. In the work *In Hierarchiam*, Hugh of St Victor wrote:

> *It is impossible to represent invisible things except by means of those which are visible. Therefore all theology of necessity must have recourse to visible representations in order to make known the invisible.*

What we are caught up with here is the meaning of religious symbols. A symbol is more than a sign. A sign is able to give us certain direct information. The sign of an arrow pointing in a particular direction, for example, will inform people where to go. They do not think any further about the meaning of the arrow. A symbol, on the other hand, confronts those who encounter it and provides food for thought. Consider, for a moment, the ocean as a symbol of God. When the ocean is spoken about in this symbolic sense, we are not being provided with technical information about either God or the ocean. Rather, the reality of the ocean confronts us with its immensity, its seemingly eternal activity, its depth, its power, its serenity – the images appear endless. We are called to pause and to contemplate the ocean, to allow the ocean to engage our imagination and the depths of our own beings. As a religious symbol, the ocean confronts us and, through our engagement with it, can lead to a deeper appreciation of the unfolding mystery of God within the history and circumstances of human life.

Bonaventure very much appreciated the richness of the Victorine symbolic mode of thinking. He employed it to express Francis' vision that all created realities reflect God's goodness. Since creation itself is the outpouring of God's goodness, created entities contain reflections of that goodness and so are able to act as religious symbols. If we approach the created world in a spirit of prayer and contemplation, says Bonaventure, allowing that world to engage our imagination, we shall be able to discern the traces of God's footsteps which will lead us to the One whom our hearts desire. In chapter 2 of the *Itinerarium* he writes:

We can gather that the whole created world is able to lead the mind of the one who is contemplative and wise to the eternal God. (I 2.11)

We have been looking at a number of the significant influences which affected the nature and style of Bonaventure's theology. None the less, it is not possible to understand Bonaventure simply through an examination of these earlier authorities. Bonaventure not only drew on their thought, he moulded and reshaped it, producing a style of theology which was new and unique. In order to discover the secret which is at the heart of Bonaventurean thought, we need to understand how he fired all that he wrote with the inspiration of the poor man of Assisi, Francis. This will be the concern of the next chapter.

Bonaventure: Master of Paris, Disciple of Assisi

Bonaventure's religious world was deeply influenced by the founder of the Order which he entered. The great contemporary Swiss theologian von Balthasar describes the effect of the Francis-event upon Bonaventure in the following words,

> *When we speak of this event, we have at last mentioned the living, organizing centre of Bonaventure's intellectual world, the thing that lifts it above the level of a mere interweaving of the threads of tradition. Bonaventure does not only take Francis as his centre: he is his own sun and his mission.*

Bonaventure had been deeply impressed in his early years in Paris by the followers of Francis who were students and then Masters at the University. As mentioned in chapter 1, the entry of the great Master of Paris, Alexander of Hales, into the Order had been a catalyst for Bonaventure's own decision to join the Franciscans. No doubt he heard from the Franciscans with whom he associated many stories from the life of Francis. In Bonaventure's inquiring mind and poetic heart there must have developed a passion to understand what had seized and motivated the life of this remarkable man from Assisi.

Shortly after his election as Minister General of the Franciscan Order, Bonaventure went on retreat to the Franciscan holy mount, La Verna, where Francis had experienced the stigmata. It was here that he was to produce the *Itinerarium*, in which the basic pattern for all of his theology is found. The genius of Bonaventure lies in the way he grasps the experience of Francis and gives it philosophical and theological expression. This is what constitutes the uniqueness and value of the Bonaventurean theological method.

The *Itinerarium* is structured around the event of Francis' stigmata, when the wounds of the crucified Christ were imprinted upon Francis' body. As Bonaventure states in the Prologue:

> *While I was there reflecting on various ways by which the soul ascends into God, there came to mind, among other things, the miracle which had occurred to blessed Francis in this very place: the vision of a winged Seraph in the form of the Crucified. While reflecting on this, I saw at once that this vision represented our father's rapture in contemplation and the road by which this rapture is reached.* (I PROLOGUE 2)

The *Itinerarium* is basically a prayerful and reflective meditation which aims to lead the individual towards union with God. As Bonaventure emphasizes in its Prologue and again in the final section, the model for the successful completion of the journey is Francis. In this chapter we shall see the ways in which Francis acts as the inspirational model not only for the *Itinerarium* but for all of Bonaventure's theology.

The Way to God

The first six stages of the *Itinerarium* are spoken of as 'contemplations' or reflections. It could appear that Bonaventure is suggesting that it is possible for us to reason our way to God by, for example, elaborating arguments that will prove by the use of human reason alone that God exists. However, at the beginning of chapter 1, the author makes it clear that human effort by itself is not capable of leading to God. There must be assistance from God if the individual is to progress along the path of the journey:

No matter how much our interior progress is ordered, nothing will come of it unless accompanied by divine aid. Divine aid is available to those who seek it from their hearts. Prayer is the mother and source of the ascent. (I 1.1)

As with the life journey of Francis, Bonaventure's religious journey is not simply an ordered, textbook journey which we can undertake. It involves allowing God to break in from beyond into the reality of our lives, shattering even our most cherished conceptions so that we might be gifted with new vision and a new sense of purpose.

Like Francis, Bonaventure begins with God. In Bonaventure's writings, God is always the God of revelation, the Trinitarian God. But it is important to note the sources Bonaventure draws upon in developing his own understanding of the nature of the Trinity.

Firstly, Bonaventure uses the Trinitarian thinking of Pseudo-Dionysius with a particular purpose in mind. Dionysian thought speaks of an active Trinity. It begins with the conviction that God is the highest good. Goodness must, by definition, find expression – if it were never expressed, it could not be known as goodness. To say that God is the highest good is to say that God must express that goodness without limit. Where is there to be found such an unlimited expression? It cannot be found in the world of creation because, as we are well aware, those expressions of goodness, profound as they may be, are necessarily limited. Dionysian thought, however, speaks of God in terms of an active Trinity. It is within the life of God, within the relations between Father, Son and Spirit, that God's goodness is expressed without limit. God as Trinity did not need to create in order to express the divine goodness. The act of creation is an overflow of this expressive goodness, a free gift from a bountiful God.

But Francis experienced God not only as goodness but also, and perhaps more intensely, as love. It is for this reason that Bonaventure takes care to introduce the thought of Richard of St Victor into his theology of the Trinity. Along with Dionysius, Richard maintained that God is the highest good. But he went on to say that of all that is good, nothing can be said to be a higher good than love. Since it is the nature of God to be the highest good, God must be also the fullness of love. Consequently, argues Richard, there must be a number of persons within the Trinity, since love involves the relation of one to another. There must be more than one person within God, otherwise the communication of love would not be possible. Moreover, the fullness of love is to be found when the love which exists between two persons is shared with a third person. The life of God, then, as the fullness of love, is the life of the unending communication of that love between three persons, Father, Son and Spirit.

In integrating the thought of Richard into his theology of the Trinity, along with that of Pseudo-Dionysius, Bonaventure is able to speak of God not only in terms of expressive goodness but also in terms of a communication of love. In so doing he gives theological form to the experience of Francis. God is the good who is to be desired above all. God is the one who communicates, who reaches out and captivates the human soul in the embrace of love.

Francis was a mystic. When he spoke about his experience of God, he used the language of desire and of love. Bonaventure's theology is similarly mystical in nature. The final stage of the *Itinerarium* is entitled 'On spiritual and mystical ecstasy in which rest is given to our intellect when through ecstasy our affection passes over entirely into God'. Here we find the two prominent features of Bonaventurean mysticism, namely, that 'the intellect' is 'given rest', and that it is desire and love which finally lead the soul into God.

It is in keeping with the inspiration which Bonaventure received from Francis that he gives primacy to love. This is not to say that he downgrades the intellect, ignoring the place of rational reflection. The first six stages of the *Itinerarium* witness to the religious value of the exercise of human reason. But in so far as the final stage of the journey moves beyond rational reflection, the affective or emotional is ultimately pre-eminent:

> *In this passing over, if it is to be perfect, all intellectual activities must be left behind and the height of our affection must be totally transferred and transformed into God.* (I 7.4)

In this final stage, to experience God is not to think about our concepts of God, it is to directly encounter God in affective experience. As in the writings of Francis, the imagery Bonaventure uses for the movement towards the mystical state is that of marital love:

> *When it sees its Spouse and hears, smells, tastes and embraces him, the soul can sing like the bride. No one grasps this except him who receives, since it is more a matter of affective experience than rational consideration.* (I 4.3)

This conviction that love is to be the motivating power in the journey to God shines forth in Bonaventure's writings. In *The Triple Way* he writes,

> *Through love, whatever we lack is given to us; through love, an abundance of all good is given to the blessed; and through love, there is attained the supremely desirable presence of the Spouse.* (T 1.16)

It is this same love which is to be found at the heart of Francis' mystical experience of the stigmata. The stigmata are described in terms of the appearance of 'a winged Seraph in the form of the Crucified'. The Seraphs are to be found in the Dionysian writings on the angels. They exist at the highest level of the angelic hierarchy and their function is simply and totally to love God. Francis' stigmata, then, are fundamentally his experience of the overwhelming love of God and also the confirmation of his own love for God. It is in such an experience of divine love, Bonaventure asserts, that ultimate truth is to be found. As he writes in *The Triple Way*, 'Truth is to be embraced with caresses and love as pertains to the Seraphim' (T 3.14).

Even within the more technical of Bonaventure's writings, it is possible to discern a theological approach which is shaped and inspired by his reflections on Francis' experience of God. Towards the end of his tenure as Master at the University of Paris, Bonaventure produced the work *Disputed Questions on the Mystery of the Trinity*. Question 1 of the *Mystery of the Trinity* examines the issue 'Concerning the Certitude with which the Existence of God is Known'.

In his treatment of the topic, Bonaventure is concerned to demonstrate that it is possible for the human person to know God – his concern is experiential. His starting point is his conviction that God exists as the highest good and that the world is God's creation. Through his reflections upon Francis of Assisi's experience of God, he seeks to make this religious reality evident for us. That God *is*, Bonaventure surmises, is evident in the experience of Francis. If there were no God, the life of Francis would have no meaning. It would be irrational and without significance. But Francis, Bonaventure is convinced, does have meaning and significance for human life, and consequently so does the God who is at the centre of Francis' inspiration. Since God *is*, Bonaventure claims, and since the world and all it contains is God's creation, it is possible for us, as it was for Francis, to discover God's presence and so to desire, know and experience God.

Question I discusses ways in which we can come to know of God's existence. For example, in what he calls the 'second way', Bonaventure urges reflection upon the nature of the world as it is experienced. Such reflection will create an awareness of both the experience of limitation and the desire for perfectibility. This is the sort of awareness that we have in times of great happiness – 'I wish this could last for ever ...' And sadly, it does not last for ever. Bonaventure notes this limited nature of our experience. He then argues that we are only aware of limitation because it is possible for us to conceive of the state of perfection – 'This would be just perfect if ...' We have the capacity, if not for perfection itself, at least to know what would constitute perfection. Consequently, the argument moves on, we have the capacity to know God who is absolute perfection.

Bonaventure's 'ways' are not attempts at natural theology; that is, they do not aim to logically prove from verifiable premises that God exists in reality. Bonaventure is not claiming that his arguments would, for example, prove to someone who does not believe in God that God does really exist. He begins with the conviction of faith, the conviction that it is possible to experience the God who is spoken about in the Scriptures. This has been shown in the life and experience of Francis of Assisi. His life was such a powerful testimony and Bonaventure insists that it cannot make sense unless the God whom Francis claimed to have experienced actually exists.

In his theology, Bonaventure's intention is to lead us to say, 'Yes! Even though I cannot logically prove to a non-believer that God exists and that it is possible for us to experience God, I can see that God's existence does make sense for my life as a thinking human being, just as it made so much sense in the life of St Francis.' Bonaventure's theological approach to the question of God cannot be properly understood without the recognition that it is shaped and inspired by Francis' experience of God.

The Created World

The relationship which Francis experienced with God carried over into his relationship with all of creation. Captivated by God's goodness, he rejoiced in and reverenced the world around him since it constantly reminded him of the goodness of God from whom creation flowed. His 'Canticle of Brother Sun' provides ample testimony to this. Bonaventure's writings on the nature of the created world once again express in theological concepts what Francis experienced. Bonaventure presents a theology of creation which emphasizes the inherent goodness and sanctity of all created realities while at the same time directing us beyond those realities to the source of all creation, God.

In the first place, creation is both good and sacred since it flows or 'emanates' from God. Bonaventure employs the Dionysian concept of emanation which was discussed in the previous chapter. His vision of creation is expressed through the image of the life-giving flow of a river. In the thirteenth Collation of *Hexaemeron* he writes,

> It is written in Ecclesiastes: 'All rivers go to the sea, yet never does the sea become full. To the place where they go, the rivers keep on going. They derive from the sea, and they return to it.' (H 13.4)

The river is a powerful image of creation. It is the life-giving stream which comes forth from the limitless sea, the image for the bountiful and fertile life of God. Creation, then, has its origin in the action of God which constantly bestows life. The river flows through the earth, and, in the same way, the act of creation involves a journey through history. Just as the river finally returns to the sea, its source of life, so too is the journey of human history to find its completion in being reunited with its origin, the depths of the life-giving mystery of God.

Bonaventure sees the created world as having a sacred purpose. It is given to humanity as a 'home' and it is to serve humanity by awakening within the human spirit 'the fire of love' for God who is the Creator of all. Humanity, then, must respect and care for the created world, in the same way as we respect and care for the home in which we live.

> All material things exist to serve humanity by enkindling in human beings the fire of love and praise for the one who has made all things

and by whose providence all things are governed. They have been formed as a sort of home for humanity by the supreme architect until such time as humanity should arrive at that 'house not made by human hands'. (B 2.4)

The world is able to awaken within us the noblest qualities of love, peace, reverence, thanksgiving. As such, it is to be contemplated with reverence and not exploited for selfish purposes. Such was the attitude of Francis towards his world, a world with which he entered into a spiritual relationship, a world in the midst of which he rejoiced and walked in freedom because it spoke to him constantly the language of God's love and goodness. So it is with Bonaventure – it is the awareness of 'spiritual relationship' that must mark the interaction between humanity and the natural environment.

Francis' awareness of the sacred dignity of the created world finds further theological expression in Bonaventure's use of the term 'exemplarism'. An exemplar is an original model. Exemplarism is the process whereby likenesses are created of the original model. In artistic terminology, we could speak of the exemplar as, for example, the original painting of a Great Master. Exemplarism would be the process whereby prints of the original are produced. The prints are not the original but they are likenesses of the original. Bonaventure speaks metaphorically of God as the Divine Artist. The original 'model of God' (we are speaking here metaphorically) is the Trinity. The Trinity is the eternal exemplar. In the work of creation, the divine artist produces 'prints' of the original masterpiece. All created realities contain, in some way, likenesses of the Trinity. Moreover, to continue the artistic analogy, when we contemplate the work of an artist, we are able to learn something about the artist. The artist is expressed in some way in the work of art. For Bonaventure, the world is God's work of art. As such it expresses the life of its author and therefore contains within itself reflections of the life of God, the life of the Trinity. In contemplating

God's works of art, therefore, we are able to learn something about God. As Bonaventure writes in the *Breviloquium*, 'The created world is like a book in which its Maker, the Trinity, shines forth, is represented, and can be read' (B 2.12).

Human History – The Search for Harmony

Created reality is, for Bonaventure, essentially Trinitarian in structure. Like the Trinity, creation is diverse and we are well aware of its diversity. We are also aware that the experience of diversity can sometimes lead to conflict. When people are confronted by the 'other' who is different, the temptation can be either to destroy the other or to attempt to assimilate the other and to make the other the same. Bonaventure's Trinitarian vision of life, however, presents a compelling alternative. Within the Trinity, there is diversity, the opposites of Father and Son. Yet these opposites do not conflict, nor do they seek to make the other the same. They remain fully as opposites and yet exist in perfect harmony through the mediation of the Spirit, the breath of love and goodness which flows between Father and Son.

For Bonaventure, God contains at one and the same time both the harmony of Unity and the individuality of Trinity. Within the Trinity, the individual Persons are fully individual and different, yet are in harmony through the mediation of divine love. In the very depths of the life of God, unity exists in and through diversity. This is possible since the life of the Trinity is the life of active goodness in which are found relationships of love. These, then, are the qualities which should mark life in the world, life which is characterised by the experience of life's diversity, but which also yearns for unity and harmony. The human journey through history is to be a journey of reconciliation. It is to be a journey which recognizes the unique individuality of each and every human being while at the same time being actively involved in the task of peace-making. And again, the model for the journey is Francis, the Man of Peace.

I call upon the Eternal Father to guide our feet in the way of that peace which surpasses all understanding. This is the peace proclaimed and given to us by our Lord Jesus Christ and preached again and again by our father Francis. At the beginning and end of every sermon he announced peace; in every greeting he wished for peace; in every contemplation he sighed for ecstatic peace. (I PROLOGUE 1)

Bonaventure speaks of the journey of human history in terms of the image of the circle. In tracing a circle, the circle returns to its point of origin. The journey is complete when the circle is complete, when the return to the origin is accomplished. At the conclusion of his work on the Trinity, Bonaventure writes:

Eternal life consists in this alone, that the human person, who emanates from the most blessed Trinity and is a likeness of the Trinity, should return after the manner of a certain intelligible circle to the most blessed Trinity by God-conforming glory. (T 8 REPLY 7)

Yet we find from the experience of life that harmony and unity are not yet attained. The circle of harmony has not been completed. Bonaventure insists that it is impossible for humanity to complete the circle by itself. Humanity is lost, the circle of harmony has been broken and the centre of the circle cannot be found in order to complete the circle. It is here that God takes the initiative. God locates the centre for us. And how. asks Bonaventure, is the centre of the circle to be found?

How marvellous is divine wisdom, for it brought forth salvation through the cinders of humility. For the centre is lost in the circle, and it cannot be found except by two lines crossing each other at right angles. (H 1.24)

The two lines crossing each other at right angles stand for the crucified Christ. It is in Christ that we are put at rights once more.

When a life is centred around Christ, when it is Christ-like, the journey into God is renewed and the harmony for which the human spirit longs is restored.

The circle and the centre are no mere theological abstractions for Bonaventure. Once again, Francis is his inspiration. It is significant that Francis' religious journey began as he knelt alone in prayer before the Crucifix in the Church of San Damiano. It was here that Francis heard the words which were to motivate his life. Bonaventure writes in the second chapter of *The Life of St Francis*, the chapter which deals with Francis' conversion:

> *One day when Francis went out to meditate in the fields, he walked beside the church of San Damiano which was threatening to collapse because of extreme age. Inspired by the Spirit, he went inside to pray. Prostrate before an image of the Crucified, he heard a voice coming from the Cross, telling him three times: 'Francis, go and repair my house which, as you see, is falling completely into ruin.'* (L 2.1)

It is equally significant that the religious journey of Francis found its completion in his experience of the stigmata on the heights of La Verna – the experience in the very depths of his being of the overwhelming love of God poured out in the crucified Christ. Francis' journey began and ended in Christ, and in order to make that journey, Francis strove more and more to imitate Christ. It was an imitation not just in externals but one which flowed from a heart filled with love for the Crucified. This was why Francis placed so much emphasis on the humanity of Jesus, without ever forgetting that the Christ who is fully human is also the God-Man. The human life which Christ lived was, for Francis, the fullest expression possible of God's love. Francis sought to imitate that life as literally as possible, in the way that the lover seeks to take on a lifestyle in conformity with the desires of the beloved. Francis' lifestyle was never an external performance. Rather, it sprang so naturally from the heart of one who was challenged by the irresistible power of God's love.

This explains, then, the centrality of Christ within Bonaventure's fundamental vision of the fulfilment of our human destiny.

The Son of God, the very small and poor and humble One, assuming our earth, and made of earth, not only came upon the surface of the earth, but indeed to the depth of its centre, that is, He has wrought salvation in the midst of the earth. (H 1.22)

It is in the way of life which is revealed in the humanity of Jesus that we are able to find directions for the completion of the journey into God. The challenge is to become Christ-like, as Francis did, to be true imitators of Christ. This is not simply a matter of imitating the actions of Christ. It is a challenge which is addressed to the heart. The challenge is to become in our whole being 'other Christs'. The moral life is not a matter of following rules and regulations but to live as Christ lived, with all the radical implications that this entails for our attitudes and duties towards God and towards our fellow human beings. Bonaventure insists that such a radical style of life is possible. Moreover, it is not only possible, but it becomes a source of true and lasting joy, it becomes the way to a happiness which fulfils every yearning of the human spirit. And this is so because it has been lived and witnessed to in the life of the poor man from Assisi.

This was shown also to blessed Francis, when on the height of the mountain, there appeared to him a six-winged Seraph fastened to a cross. There he passed over into God in ecstatic contemplation. He became an example of perfect contemplation as he had previously been of action, so that through him, more by example than by word, God might invite all who are truly spiritual to this kind of passing over. (I 7.3)

The Journey into God

In some ways we might tend to feel that while it may well be true that Francis *did* experience God, and in a very powerful way, how could it ever be possible that *we* could experience God in even remotely the same way? The world we live in is very different from the world of thirteenth-century Assisi. Moreover, Francis was an exceptional person, one of the outstanding figures of history, and his experience must have been uniquely his own. We could certainly never have the audacity to lay claim to it.

Bonaventure recognized that Francis' experience was indeed special, even unique. Yet he believed that we could all learn from Francis in order to make our own way to God. Bonaventure had applied the great power of his mind and the resources of his heart to reflection on the life of the saint, and from his meditations arose writings in which he wished to teach that not only Francis, but all who believe, are able to make the same journey to God that Francis did – even if the conditions of our individual journeys might differ. If you like, Bonaventure maps out the road and the signposts mark the various stages through which Francis himself had passed. The person who embarks on the journey with an open heart and who takes care to be attentive to the directions will reach the same journey's end as Francis did. It is part of Bonaventure's enduring genius that the path he has mapped out can also enable people of our own time to make the journey into God.

Where can this map be found and what directions does it provide? This chapter will try to find the key which will unlock the spiritual treasure of Bonaventure's path for the journey into God. It will investigate a number of his writings and in particular will examine the insights which are to be found in *Disputed Questions on the Knowledge of Christ* (in the Latin, *De Scientia Christi*).

De Scientia Christi is one of Bonaventure's more technical works. It contains seven 'disputed questions' concerning Christ's knowledge. The teaching technique of 'disputed questions' was used extensively within the medieval universities. Basically, it was a form of co-operative teaching wherein the learning process took place by means of a debate between two opposing points of view. At the conclusion of the debate, the particular question under discussion would be resolved. The title of the work indicates that in this instance, the question under discussion is that of Christ's knowledge. Bonaventure takes as his starting point the Church's belief that Christ possessed both a fully divine and a fully human nature. One of the questions that subsequently arises is this: how was Christ, in his fully human nature, able to know God who is beyond all human understanding? Bonaventure supplies an answer to this question and his answer provides exciting insights into the question of how human beings in general can come to know God. It is important to note that from the outset, *De Scientia Christi* speaks of the journey to God in terms of coming to 'know' God and that, therefore, 'knowledge' is a key concept.

Created Knowledge

The first stage of the journey is arrived at when the individual acquires what is termed 'created knowledge'. Created knowledge is the knowledge which we gain when we rationally reflect on our experience of the world around us. Bonaventure is far from sceptical about the possibility of being able to know something about the fundamental nature of our world. He accepts that human knowledge can in some way give us access to the world as it really is.

What, then, is Bonaventure's picture of 'the world as it really is'? His vision stems from his religious convictions – that all created realities originate from God and are reflections of the essential goodness of God. Consequently, if we are to understand what something *really* is, we must come to understand it in terms of where it has come from, that is, in terms of its relationship to God. The principle Bonaventure applies is a familiar one – understanding a reality in terms of its origins. When someone tells a doctor, for example, that he has a pain in his side, the doctor tries to locate its source. When the origin is found, the doctor understands the real nature of the pain and is able to treat it. Similarly with the Bonaventurean method – when the origin of created realities is found, then we can start to properly understand the realities themselves.

In order to express these religious convictions, Bonaventure employs the theological concept of exemplarism, which we encountered in the previous chapter. In this particular instance, he speaks of the 'original model' in terms of the 'eternal reason' or the 'divine ideas'.

These concepts are no doubt very foreign to the contemporary mind and it is important to unpack them. To use once more the metaphor of God as Artist, it can be said that God has prior 'ideas' of everything that appears in the created world, in the way that the artist has a prior idea of that which he or she wishes to create. When the artist reveals the idea behind the work of art, it is possible for others to come to a fuller appreciation of the work. Bonaventure argues along the same lines. If we wish to fully appreciate created realities which are God's works of art, we must seek to understand them in the light of their origin as ideas in the mind of God. It is important to remember that we are involved here with metaphorical language which cannot be applied literally to God. What Bonaventure is seeking to emphasize, however, is that in order to *know* the reality of the world around us, it is necessary to recognize that it has a transcendent, sacred dimension, since everything has come from God.

When he talks of 'divine ideas', Bonaventure does not wish to imply that all knowledge is simply planted in the human mind by God. This would do away with human responsibility and indeed would drastically restrict any concept of human freedom. Bonaventure does not look to God as the one who *determines* what we must know, imposing dictates upon us. In the Conclusion to Question IV, he speaks of God as the one who 'regulates and motivates'. As Divine Artist, God is the one who firstly regulates or brings into a certain arrangement the patterns within creation. And just as the artist desires that others should appreciate the particular nature of his or her art, reaching out and motivating them to do so, so God is the one who reaches out and motivates us to appreciate and understand the world. Bonaventure teaches that the more one grows in awareness of the presence of God, the Divine Artist, the more one will be inspired in the quest to come to a fuller understanding of the meaning and purpose both of human life and of the world around us.

The image of God *regulating* and then *motivating* is one in which God co-operates with us in our search for knowledge. In his conclusion to Question IV, Bonaventure comments: 'The principle of knowledge is to be found in the eternal reason together with the proper created reason'. Again, these appear as abstract and difficult concepts. What is Bonaventure suggesting here?

The 'eternal reason', as already noted, refers to the knowledge which God has of the whole realm of creation. As Creator, as Divine Artist, God has the deepest possible knowledge and understanding of each created entity. Human beings also have knowledge of the surrounding world. When such knowledge is gained through our experience of things, both through our senses and through our power of reflection, Bonaventure calls it 'created knowledge'. In this latter respect, Bonaventure, as a philosopher, draws upon Aristotle's teaching that human knowledge is derived from sense experience when we reason about or reflect upon that experience.

Bonaventure insists, however, that there is much more to human knowledge than what we know through the experiences gained through our senses. What we do experience through the senses is of value. But its value is not to be found when it is taken as an end in itself. Its real value lies in the fact that it becomes the means to acquiring a knowledge, a vision of the world of our experience which is so much more inspiring and uplifting than the limited vision which our senses can provide. What is experienced through the senses is to be fully appreciated, but it is not an end in itself. It is experience which is designed to lead us forward to a vision of life which is greater than we could ever have imagined.

Consider, for a moment, the appreciation of wine. The person who has never tasted wine, but who desires to gain an appreciation of wine, may begin a course in wine tasting, sampling recent vintages. The experience of wine gained in this way is real and is to be appreciated. But it is not an end in itself. This initial experience will hopefully lead the would-be connoisseur onwards to an appreciation of the great and classic vintages. It is when this latter appreciation of wine is gained that joys which were unimaginable with that first taste of wine will be experienced. So it is with Bonaventure's vision of knowledge. When we appreciate that first taste of the world around us, he claims, we do not simply have to remain content with that. It is possible to gain an ever-growing appreciation of that which we savour, a vision of life which will be the source of a joy which cannot be taken away. It is this joy which filled the heart of Francis.

Learning to Read

How, then, are we to gain such an appreciation of the world of our experiences? Bonaventure argues that 'created knowledge'– the knowledge which is gained through the experience of the world – only finds its ultimate significance when it serves the purpose of leading us closer towards God. On Bonaventure's map, all created realities are signposts which show us the way. It becomes a matter of learning to read the signs correctly.

Bonaventure frequently uses this metaphor of 'learning to read'. In other places, he speaks of the world as a 'book'. When the book is able to be read, it will lead the reader to God. Unfortunately, Bonaventure comments, there are times when human pride and selfishness bring darkness upon the earth, so that the book is unable to be read. It is only when we allow ourselves to be enlightened by God, through listening attentively and reflectively to God's revelation, that the light is provided by which, once again, the book of creation can be read.

> *When Man had fallen, this book, the world, became as dead and deleted. It was necessary that there be another book through which this one would be lighted up. Such a book is Scripture which points out the symbolism of things written down in the book of the world.* (H 13.12–13)

Creation is an important part of God's revelation. It reveals something of the mystery of God and hence is a symbol of the divine. Bonaventure points out that an attentive reading of the Scriptures will give light to our experience of the world. It will reveal that what we experience through our senses also has a transcendent dimension and can speak to us of spiritual realities. This is so even when we might least expect it. Consider one example which Bonaventure uses, the phrase in the gospels, 'be as wise as serpents' (MATTHEW 10:16). Even the often dreaded serpent is able to act as a symbol of spiritual realities. Think about the willingness of the serpent to sacrifice other parts of its body in order to keep what is essential, namely, its head. In the same way we are called to be willing to give away the non-essentials in our lives in order to preserve what is essential, which for human life is the realm of the heart, the life of love.

Bonaventure is calling us to be aware of the importance of a symbolic way of thinking in order to help us to draw closer to God.

Our world is more than just the way it appears. When we contemplate that world and reflect deeply on its symbolic significance, we shall be taught lessons of the heart and realize that life does have more than a material dimension. Bonaventure's concept of 'created knowledge' is symbolic by nature. All created things have sprung from God and confront us as enduring symbols of the presence of divine love. This was what St Francis discovered. Drawing on his inspiration, Bonaventure calls on the believer to pause and to look beneath the surface of things, to recognize the world as a reflection of God's creative goodness. The world in which we live is for Bonaventure, as for Francis, a world which, when seen in reverence with the contemplative eyes of faith, can lead us along the way towards God.

Knowing God

Created knowledge can point people in the right direction on the journey to God. The journey, however, must proceed further, and it is necessary to move deeper and deeper into the heart of the mystery. In exploring further the thought of *De Scientia Christi*, it is possible to discover additional parts of the guiding map. It is in Questions V to VII that Bonaventure more specifically addresses the question: how can human beings who are finite come to know God who is infinite?

The first point to note may appear a little technical, but it is important. In the original Latin text, when Bonaventure speaks about knowledge in Questions I to IV, he uses the Latin word *scientia*. *Scientia* refers to intellectual knowledge such as that which is gained through the study of science. In Questions V to VII, however, when he speaks of knowledge, he uses the term *sapientia*. *Sapientia* was a word which he had earlier defined as the achievement of theology, since it is a knowledge which derives from both intelligence and love. It is important to recognize that love is integral to his understanding of how we come to know God. *Scientia* is the term employed in speaking about created knowledge. When the discussion moves on to specifically discuss the nature of our knowledge of God, Bonaventure employs the term *sapientia* – which we could translate as 'wisdom'. *Sapientia*, or wisdom, is a form of knowledge which is acquired, not simply through exercising the intellect, but through the involvement of human *desire*, especially the desire of love.

In Question V, we come across another of Bonaventure's seemingly complex distinctions, that between *created* wisdom and *uncreated* wisdom. It has already been noted that the realities of the created world are able to act as symbols which can lead those who search for God closer to their final destiny. This can only come about, Bonaventure advises, when the world is encountered in a spirit of prayerful contemplation. The contemplative heart grows in the ability to recognize this symbolic nature of the world, to see beneath the surface and to appreciate, deep within, the reflections of divine love. This, for Bonaventure, is the acquisition of created wisdom.

Once this state is achieved, the human person is shaped anew, just as the lover is shaped anew in grasping the deeper significance of the gift given by the beloved. It is time now to move beyond the appreciation of the gift to appreciate the very presence of the beloved. When the human soul acquires *created* wisdom, says Bonaventure, there now exists a capacity to receive the gift of the divine presence itself – and it is the divine presence which is *uncreated* wisdom. In coming to appreciate the realities of this world as symbols of the divine love, we are motivated and directed so that it is possible to be drawn ever more deeply into the life of God. The Franciscan way to God is not to flee from the world. It is, rather, to be immersed in reverent contemplation of the world, awake with patient desire, so as to be drawn to the Source who is God.

For Bonaventure, then, coming to know God means being *drawn* to God. The one who desires God will be captivated by God, as Francis was, and in this sense *knows* God. Bonaventure emphasizes that this is the nature of our knowledge of God. Indeed, it is the only way in which the finite human person can be said to know God who is infinite.

In Question VI of *De Scientia Christi*, Bonaventure observes that it is never possible for the finite human mind to 'comprehend' God, that is to fully and completely understand God. The human mind has its limits. God is infinite, without any limits, and the finite can never fully understand the infinite. Consequently, Bonaventure comments, our knowledge of God is not to be spoken of in terms of comprehending God. We are to come to know God, not by attempting to *understand* God, but by *desiring* God. We desire that which we see as good. And since God is the highest good, God is desirable above all else. In Question VI, Bonaventure argues,

> *The soul is not satisfied with any good which it grasps and comprehends, since no such good is the highest. It is satisfied only by a good of such a sort that the soul is taken captive by its greatness and superexcellence.*

Question VII of *De Scientia Christi* provides us with a new dimension of the nature of human knowledge. It is common to identify knowledge with 'comprehension'. The type of knowledge we have of God, however, is not comprehensive knowledge, says Bonaventure. It is *ecstatic knowledge*. In using this term, he draws upon the mystical theology of Pseudo-Dionysius, but gives the concept a flavour which is derived from the experience of St Francis.

What exactly, then, is ecstatic knowledge? It is only possible to acquire ecstatic knowledge when we put aside our customary way of looking at life and have an open mind, an open heart, so that we might be able to receive a new appreciation of the significance of our circumstances. This is not a new awareness which we create ourselves. It is a new way of understanding which is given to us from beyond, it is something which happens to us. In knowledge,

which comes through ecstasy, we *know* through being drawn totally out of ourselves by the object of our desire. Our heart longs for its
beauty and we yearn to experience it in the fullest way possible.

This is the type of knowledge which Bonaventure speaks of in
relation to our knowledge of God. We prepare to receive it by firstly being willing to put aside our usual understanding of ourselves
and of the world around us. Any renewed appreciation of life is
not possible for the person who is convinced that life *is* the way
that they think it is. But when the mind and heart are not closed
but open, Bonaventure claims that it is possible to be *enlightened*.
In such a spirit of openness, which is the attitude of contemplation, the world is able to disclose itself as what it essentially is – a
radiation of the beauty of its Creator. The contemplative soul
moves beyond the discernment of God's beauty reflected in creation to grasp the very presence of the divine beauty and wisdom
itself. At that stage, the lover surrenders in ecstasy to the presence of the Beloved, 'The soul is drawn to that Wisdom in Ecstasy'
(SC 6 RESPONSE).

In the Epilogue to *De Scientia Christi*, Bonaventure describes ecstatic knowledge as 'that ultimate and most exalted form of knowledge'. It is possible to know God, not through an intellectual
process, but through the experience of God. Remaining true to
Francis, Bonaventure stresses that what is experienced is the
boundless depth of God's love. To experience this is to have certain
knowledge, more certain than any knowledge which can be
arrived at through logic. The highest form of knowledge is to be
found in the personal certainty of the love relationship. Ecstatic
knowledge finds its consummation in the experience of God. It is
this experience which Bonaventure calls 'experiential wisdom'
and it is grounded in love. What is called for here are not words
but the expectant silence of the true lover, a silence which desires
not the understanding of the idea of love, but the ecstatic granting
of divine love itself. Bonaventure concludes the Epilogue:

This type of knowledge can be understood only with great difficulty, and it cannot be understood at all except by one who has experienced it. And no one will experience it except one who is 'rooted and grounded in love so as to comprehend with all the saints what is the length and the breadth, the height and the depth ... until you are filled with the utter fullness of God.' (EPHESIANS 3:17) *And if it is to be experienced interior silence is more helpful than external speech. Therefore, let us stop speaking, and let us pray to the Lord that we may be granted the experience of that about which we have spoken.*

In Questions V to VII of *De Scientia Christi*, Bonaventure describes how it is possible for the human person to know God. In the first place, our knowledge of God is not simply intellectual knowledge. It is *sapientia*, knowledge which involves both our intelligence and our desire to love. The first stage in coming to know God is the acquisition of *created* wisdom. Created wisdom is gained when we are able to approach our world in a spirit of contemplation. In seeking the deeper meaning inherent within those realities which confront us, we begin to discern the reflections of the Creative Goodness. This involves movement into the second stage, when God is firstly appreciated by the mind to be the Highest Good and then, as the Highest Good, is desired by the heart above all else. It is now possible to be drawn beyond ourselves through ecstatic knowledge towards the One whom we cannot fully understand but whom we desire from the depths of our being. In ecstatic knowledge, the ultimate and highest form of knowledge, we gain *experiential* wisdom. God gifts us with the overwhelming experience of the divine love, an experience which no words are adequate to express.

Desire and love are central to Bonaventure's approach to the question of our knowledge of God. We *can* know God, claims Bonaventure. This does not entail that we can understand God – for the finite human person, that is impossible. It is possible to know through love, however, without having to say we fully understand.

Through love, whatever we lack is given to us; through love, an abun-
dance of all good is given to the blessed; and through love, there is
attained the supremely desirable presence of the Divine Spouse. (T 1.16)

It is, indeed, the knowledge which is the fruit of love which is the
most certain of all knowledge.

The journey which Bonaventure maps out is the journey into
the heart of the mystery and the attraction of divine love. It was
the journey which Francis had travelled, in freedom from fear
and with deep-seated joy, drawn by overwhelming desire for the
beloved. It is a journey which still exerts its fascination for searching hearts within our own time. The following chapter will seek to
uncover the wealth of nourishment which Bonaventure's way to
God can offer to the spiritually hungry in these last years of the
twentieth century.

Bonaventure:
A Spiritual Guide for Today

As we approach the third millennium, there is no sign that interest in spiritual experience has faded. Our world abounds with individuals and groups who advocate various paths for spiritual enlightenment. Sometimes, unfortunately, the avenues which people are encouraged to follow lead to false idols. We only have to witness the tragedies of Jonestown or Waco to see the disastrous consequences which emerge when the spiritual impulse is misdirected.

Bonaventure offers directions to the spiritually lost, food to the spiritually hungry. It is food which is of substance, food which will sustain and nourish those who partake of it. His spirituality is grounded in the real world. It takes proper account of our ability to reason, to imagine, to love. The journey does not leave us stranded in isolation and aridity but brings us to the springs of living water which never fail to satisfy our thirst. This living water is the boundless beauty and goodness of the God who has created us and to whom we return. Bonaventure's way to God is designed for the person who is concerned for the well-being of the world in which we live. It accepts and indeed widens the human search for knowledge. Bonaventure emphasizes the value not only of intellectual knowledge, but also of that knowledge which springs from the attitude of love. His language, the language of the literary artist as well as of the scholar, challenges our imagination, awakening in us desires for beauty and harmony, longings which find their fulfilment in God. This chapter will explore the ways in which the philosopher-theologian of medieval Paris can continue to guide the footsteps of the spiritual pilgrim of our own time.

A Spirituality of Engagement

Many of the concepts which we examined in the previous chapter suggest that in our search for God, we are not to shun our experiences of involvement with the natural world and with other people. If anything, the desire for God should bring us to value ever more deeply all that God has created and should lead not to detachment from, but to engagement with, this world of which we are a part. For Bonaventure, religion ought never to be an isolated part of life. It is not a matter of going to church to find God and then, afterwards, forgetting all that and getting on with one's real life. No, for Francis and for Bonaventure, there ought to be no separation between faith and life. The experience of God is one which has meaning within the context of all our experiences, and indeed gives deeper meaning to them.

As was noted in the previous chapter, 'created knowledge', the knowledge which we acquire when we use our ability to reason, is an essential part of Bonaventure's theory of knowledge. As an integral stage on the journey into God, created knowledge enables us to begin to know God within the context of the other experiences of our lives. In the *Itinerarium*, the knowledge which we gain through reflecting upon our experience of the world is not a hindrance to knowing God. On the contrary, when seen with the eyes of contemplative faith, it is able to lead us to the depths of the encounter with God. When the person of faith contemplates the *significance* of what he or she knows, he or she is enabled to accept the realities encountered in his or her experience as symbols of God's presence.

Bonaventure's integration of created knowledge and created wisdom demonstrate how important it is that the human individual is not thought of as an 'isolated self'. Rather, the individual is necessarily engaged with the wider world of nature and of human society. Nature is not a mundane reality to be exploited by humanity but is itself a reflection of the sacred. We are challenged to positively engage with our environment so that we, and indeed all creation, might move towards final fulfilment in God. If we seek to experience God, claims Bonaventure, our engagement with the world of nature ought to be one whereby we 'present to ourselves the whole material world as a mirror through which we may pass over to God, the supreme Craftsman' (I 1.9).

Bonaventure's understanding of the natural world and our place within it is relational and dynamic. He puts to flight any understanding of life which portrays the human person as 'the isolated individual', set in the midst of a world of passive objects, completely detached from and a stranger to the surrounding environment. Rather we are presented with a powerful, challenging vision of mutual encounter between ourselves and our world. It is a vision in which we do not simply aim to manipulate that world, but are willing to humbly acknowledge that we have much to learn from our experience of the inherent sacredness of creation.

The Moral Life

Within the Bonaventurean vision, knowledge of God has an intrinsic social dimension. It is not simply a private affair between the individual and God but necessarily entails engaging with others. Travelling along the path of the journey into God entails living a moral life, a life which will be characterized by the practice of 'virtue'. This should not be understood in terms of following abstract or impersonal obligations. Virtue, rather, is a way of life. The virtuous life is one which enables both individual and social progress along the path of the journey to God. Just as the summit of the spiritual journey is to be found in the experience of God's love, so the summit of virtue is to be found in the practice of charity.

Justice alone, Bonaventure insists, is insufficient to ensure a virtuous society. The exercise of justice will bring about a certain unity, a certain sense of order. However, if that unity and order is to last, if it is not to deteriorate into disorder and fragmentation, love is required. Each member of society ought to desire the highest well-being of the other members of society.

This ideal is no doubt difficult to achieve. Yet such a way of life is possible, Bonaventure claims, since it has been expressed in the life of St Francis. It is Francis whose experience provides a model for moral and virtuous living (H 5.5). The exhortation to live morally is a challenge to respond to the demands of divine love. It calls for a willingness to embrace, as Francis did, a way of life which will have as its foundation the values expressed in the life of Christ. Above all, the moral life is one which is caught up in the mystery of God's love for humanity, the mystery which so captivated the heart of Francis. When one's whole being is seized by infinite Love itself, one cannot but love in return.

As soon as we acquire charity, all that pertains to perfection becomes easy: acting or suffering, living or dying. We must therefore endeavour to advance in love, for perfect love leads to perfection in all else.
(T 2:11)

Our own century has witnessed many calls for justice. Sadly, it has also sometimes seen such calls degenerate into hatred, violence, mass slaughter, the imposition of totalitarian governments. Unless the struggle for justice is imbued with the fire of love, the oppressed can so easily become the oppressor and the cycle of injustice is perpetuated. Bonaventure reminds us that at the heart of morality must be found genuine love, whose source and wellspring is a love which knows no bounds – the love which flows from the goodness of God.

Bonaventure does not establish a dichotomy between our experience of God and other dimensions of human experience. His works testify to the possibility of speaking about religious experience in a meaningful manner, in terms which address the issues which arise from our necessary engagement with our natural and social world.

The Quest for Knowledge

An essential part of human endeavour is the quest for knowledge. It seems to be a part of human nature that we are continually attempting to know more – about ourselves, other people, about the world in which we live. But how we attain knowledge is also influential in determining the attitude we end up having towards that which we know. If it is thought that the objects of knowledge are just there, to be used as people wish for their own benefit, then there will be little concern for the integrity of those objects themselves. They are simply there to be exploited. To separate human knowledge from the recognition that there exists a sacred relationship between the knower and that which is known cheapens the value of human life. It was such an attitude which, in the past, allowed the flourishing of the slave trade. Individuals were treated as objects and the fundamental relational values which ought to operate in any human society were ignored. Similar attitudes prevailed in the Nazi concentration camps of the Second World War. If knowledge means investigating, from a completely detached point of view, objects 'out there', then the world which will result will be a frightening, impersonal and valueless one.

Relationship is central to Bonaventure's theory of knowledge. To truly know, he insists, is to allow the use of our intellect to be guided by the spirit of love. The challenge is to acquire knowledge in its fullest sense of *sapientia*, wisdom. To have wisdom is to be able to recognize the deepest significance of that which is before us. This requires much more than the attitude of a detached observer and investigator of facts. In order to know, Bonaventure advises, it is necessary to become engaged with that which we wish to know, and to acquire knowledge through an attitude of contemplation and reverence.

This is illustrated in his use of the term 'ecstatic knowledge'. Ecstatic knowledge is not the end product of an abstract process of investigation. It demands firstly an attitude of standing back and contemplating. Through contemplation, the knower becomes engaged with the object, is fascinated by it and desires to know it more deeply. This desire to know draws the knower into engagement with the object of knowledge and leads to an increased awareness of its significance.

Education could become so much more fruitful if the essence of ecstatic knowledge could be captured and expressed within the educational process. Too often, education can become a matter of storing up information, storing up facts – perhaps even more so in this electronic age, when so much information is available at the click of a mouse. But what is required more than information is the ability to assess the value of that information for the life of the human family. This only comes through the acquisition of wisdom. Wisdom is not acquired through speed but through depth, and it is only in contemplation that one is drawn into such depth.

Bonaventure's understanding of the essential nature of knowledge can offer inspiration to the growing number of contemporary philosophers who cry out against the negative and devastating effects of the attitude of 'disengagement' or 'detachment'. Disengagement views the human person as the investigator observing the environment from a completely detached point of view. If disengagement becomes the norm for our theories of knowledge, ultimately, it becomes destructive. If we try to develop our theories about our environment in abstraction from the people who inhabit it, we will be left with a grey and barren world, devoid of personal meaning.

There is a call to dethrone the 'disengaged Man of Reason' who is caught up in the ultimately futile belief that knowledge is only possible through objective investigation. The Man of Reason, attempting to distance the self from the object of investigation, becomes alienated from the world of *human* activity, a world which necessarily must incorporate feelings and desires. Those who protest against the Man of Reason insist that if a theory of knowledge is to be faithful, it must incorporate an attitude of contemplation. We must question what it is that we care for, what it is that we love, if we are to discover who we are, if we are to give ourselves a sense of purpose for the future.

Bonaventure would join today's protesters against the Man of Reason. The attitude of contemplation is what he called for when he spoke of 'created wisdom'. He did not reject out of hand knowledge which is gained through rational investigation – knowledge which today is commonly called 'scientific knowledge'. Indeed, he recognizes the value of scientific knowledge, labelling it created knowledge, and allocating it a specific place in the journey into God. But scientific knowledge takes its proper place when it is supplemented by accounts of other ways in which we know – knowing through contemplating, through relating, through loving.

Within the Bonaventurean perspective, to acquire 'knowledge of God' is not in the first place to know a new proposition but to experience a relationship. This is true knowledge of God, Bonaventure claims, ecstatic knowledge, and it was witnessed to in the life of Francis. What follows from this is knowledge *about* God. This is knowledge gained by reflecting upon the meaning of the experience of ecstatic knowledge and it forms the subject matter of the first six chapters of the *Itinerarium*. Such knowledge, however, steps aside in the final instance in humble acknowledgement of that highest knowledge which is found in the mystical relationship of love between the soul and God:

> *In this passing over, if it is to be perfect, all intellectual activities must be left behind and the height of our affection must be totally transferred and transformed into God.* (I 7.4)

Bonaventure's theology offers insights for contemporary inquiry within the philosophy of religion. What type of philosophical inquiry is appropriate when approaching the question of knowing God? Perhaps the closest analogy is to be found in our understanding of how we know other people. Knowledge, however, has often been philosophically understood as that which is obtained through an attitude of critical detachment. Yet our understanding of other people naturally involves 'trust' and 'love'. If our knowledge of God is to be spoken of as in some way analogous to our knowledge of other people, then philosophers of religion are going to be forced to re-examine the philosophical understanding of knowledge and its relationship with love.

Philosophy needs to be freed from the restrictions which have been placed upon its understanding of knowledge. It needs to take into account the way people actually know. This includes, above all, that it considers the nature of the knowledge people have of each other. What then becomes clear is that there exists a reciprocal relationship between knowledge and love.

To say that we know through loving and trusting by no means entails that reason is excluded. When a person trusts someone or something, that person is said to believe in the other. Trust, however, can be misplaced. To state that I believe in some invisible person who will save my life if I step directly into the path of a speeding train can hardly be said to be a meaningful belief. It is, indeed, a dangerous belief. In order to decide whether a particular belief can be defended as meaningful for human existence, some form of rational assessment is called for. The issue of 'rationality' needs to be addressed. If a belief is assessed to be 'irrational', it could fairly be said that its value in providing meaning for human life would be discredited.

Discussion about the rationality of a belief has, however, often narrowed itself to an assessment of whether the belief accords to standards such as those formulated in the late nineteenth century by a certain W. K. Clifford: 'It is wrong, always, everywhere and for everyone to believe anything upon insufficient evidence.' According to Clifford, a proposition should be believed only when evidence can be produced which will immediately verify it.

This understanding of rational belief has been rightly questioned. Rationality pertains to *thinking persons* and Clifford's criterion is in fact quite remote from the way people actually think. Even when we are attempting to come to a conclusion on the basis of the evidence that is before us, our decision is influenced not only by the evidence but by many other prior assumptions and considerations that we bring to our assessment of the evidence.

Two historians, for example, may examine the same evidence but come to differing conclusions. We do not normally say that one of the historians is 'irrational'; on the contrary, we may hold that both positions are rational, and instead explain the varying conclusions in terms of the prior assumptions which the historians may have held and subsequently brought to their assessment of the evidence. We would only describe the conclusion as irrational if we were to make the judgement that the historians' assumptions or methods of argumentation were irrational. Such an assessment would entail a consideration of a very wide range of factors – an examination of the kind of evidence which the historian has admitted as evidence, the principles of historical interpretation followed within the tradition to which the historian belongs, and convictions about the purpose of human life which are accepted within that tradition. It will be in the light of the relationship to this wider framework that the rationality of the historian's belief that such and such was the case will be assessed.

The question of the rationality of beliefs is far wider than simply examining whether a particular proposition is justifiable according to detached and impersonal procedures of investigation. To illustrate this, the philosopher Basil Mitchell uses the example of the navigator and the lighthouse. The ship's watch believes he has sighted a lighthouse, despite the reckoning of the navigator that the ship is hundreds of miles away from land. The rationality of the watch's belief is not assessed, however, simply in isolation – his belief is wrong because the navigator's evidence contradicts it. When, a short time later, the lookout reports that he has sighted land, the watch's belief is seen to be more reasonable. We are not speaking about assessing whether an individual proposition meets the standards set by a specific investigative process – in this case, the process of navigational calculation. The rationality of a belief is to be assessed by means of an evaluation of an interacting network of factors which will defend or attack the truth of that belief.

Bonaventure's approach to the question of our knowledge of God is not structured around a process which aims to logically prove the proposition 'that God exists'. He claims, rather, that it is possible to experience God and that this experience has meaning within the context of other claims which arise from our engagement with the natural and social world. He shows that the experience of God does not cause irrational behaviour but rather has positive implications for our engagement with our environment and with our fellow human beings. Consequently his claim is acceptable in the light of other claims.

The quest for knowledge is a continuing quest. It is also one of the noblest quests undertaken by humanity. But if the quest is to be undertaken seriously, it is important to understand what we are searching for. We are not searching for mere facts – these can never satisfy the deepest longings of the human heart. We are searching for meaning, for relatedness, for that which will draw us beyond ourselves. In our search for knowledge of this kind, Bonaventure's insights can serve as a most helpful guide.

The Beauty of God

Bonaventure's writings, influenced as they are by Francis of Assisi, incorporate ways of thinking which are in keeping with the poetry and mysticism of Francis. It is not surprising, then, to find Bonaventure employing metaphorical, aesthetic language in order to

capture something of the reality of the God whom Francis so powerfully experienced. The Swiss theologian von Balthasar notes the
aesthetic character of Bonaventure's writings:

> *Of all the great scholastics, Bonaventure is the one who offers the
> widest scope to the beautiful in his theology: not merely because he
> speaks of it most frequently, but because he clearly thereby gives
> expression to his innermost experience and does this in new concepts
> that are his own.*

The Bonaventurean appreciation of the religious significance of
aesthetic experience is illustrated in the second chapter of the *Itinerarium*. The chapter is concerned with the contemplation of God
by means of what we perceive through our senses. Bonaventure
speaks of 'the senses taking delight' when we experience something's 'beauty', 'sweetness' or 'wholesomeness'. This experience
of delight can lead us to question what kinds of things cause us
delight, and what can cause us the greatest delight. We cannot be
satisfied, he claims, with finite objects as the highest cause of the
sense of delight, since the experience of delight draws us beyond
ourselves and our limitations. We are forever seeking deeper
sources of delight. For Bonaventure, this suggests (he does not
claim that it *proves*) that the ultimate source is to be found in the
infinite, which is the life of God.

> *In this way that which delights as beautiful suggests that there is pri-
> mordial beauty. It is obvious that in God alone there is primordial and
> true delight and that in all of our delights we are led to seek this
> delight.* (I 2.8)

Bonaventure speaks of 'the beauty of God'. It is important to note,
however, that he never *identifies* our experience of God with our
experience of beauty, as if religious experience can be explained
simply as a variety of aesthetic experience. No – our appreciation

of what is truly beautiful ought to be determined by our experience of God. Consequently, for Bonaventure, beauty can be found where many might see only its absence, for example, in Christ crucified. The crucified Christ is held up as the model of the truly beautiful because of the spiritual reality expressed there, the limitless outpouring of divine love. Beauty is not just what appears on the surface. True beauty is spiritual beauty. What makes a person beautiful is what comes from within.

> For many are those who love beauty. But beauty is not in externals; true beauty consists in the splendour of wisdom. (H 20.25)

When Bonaventure speaks of God as 'beautiful', he is not speaking of an abstract, conceptual beauty. God is beautiful because God is a dynamic, active God who captivates our desires, our affections, and so becomes our delight.

> God is powerful; and if powerful, beautiful also, for wisdom is the most beautiful form: therefore God is the Wise One. 'I was enamoured of her beauty'. (H 11.3)

Note the implications here: ultimate power is not the power of might and force but the power of attraction, the power of beauty. God does not force us into worshipping. Rather, God draws us beyond ourselves and is experienced as eminently desirable. In turn, this experience breaks in upon our normal understanding of what constitutes beauty and may radically alter this understanding. It becomes possible to discern beauty even in the darkness of the pit, even in the one who is broken and crucified.

Bonaventure's use of aesthetic language to refer to God can offer valuable insights in the quest to find meaningful ways to speak of God in today's world. Perhaps in this regard we could ponder on the distinction which Bonaventure makes in *De Scientia Christi* between *apprehension* and *comprehension*. We do not comprehend God, he says, but rather we apprehend or sense God's presence. Similarly, aesthetic experience is not a matter of comprehension but apprehension. It is impossible to analyse an experience of beauty and provide a list of logical reasons which completely explain why something is beautiful. The experience of beauty always remains more than the reasons which can be given for it. Nor does following set procedures automatically produce the experience of beauty. Rather, beauty is discovered; to use Bonaventure's terminology, it 'is sensed in some way'.

Sometimes, indeed, beauty overwhelms us, such as when we are struck by the beauty of the natural world in the overpowering majesty of a sunset, for example. In apprehending something as beautiful, we come to find it desirable. We are not involved in an intellectual exercise; it is more that we are drawn beyond ourselves and our rational concepts by that which is desirable. The language of such experience can help us to speak about God whose goodness and beauty overwhelms and captivates the one who seeks with an open and listening heart. It is language which can offer hope and meaning to those many who are growing disillusioned with the sterile world of clinical efficiency and are yearning for the eruption of the beautiful.

Bonaventure's language should not be read literally. Its aesthetic and metaphorical quality is there to lead us more deeply into the mystery of God, a God who has been experienced but who cannot be fully understood. After the stigmata, St Francis, overcome by the power of God's love, breathed this prayer to God, 'You are beautiful'. The God towards whom Bonaventure's language directs us is the God who is beautiful, the God who draws us beyond ourselves, captivates our desires and satisfies our spiritual thirst.

Authority within the Church

It is commonly held that authority is exercised within the Church because the Church is by nature hierarchical. When people think of a hierarchy within the Church, they generally tend to think of an identifiable group such as the Pope, bishops and priests who constitute *the* hierarchy. The term 'hierarchy', moreover, can often receive a bad press, since it is identified with the domination of one group over others.

This is a very static understanding of the notion of hierarchy and indeed is completely foreign to Bonaventure's use of the term. His understanding of hierarchy finds its inspiration in the writings of Pseudo-Dionysius. When Bonaventure speaks about hierarchical structures, his first concern is with the levels of spirituality *within the individual human person*. Each person is called to become 'hierarchized' in that each is challenged to grow to be 'like God' in attitudes and in actions. In the *Hexaemeron* Bonaventure comments:

> *The third part of contemplation consists in considering the hierarchized human mind. And this is understood through the stars, or through the light of the stars, which indeed has a radiation that is constant, beautiful, and joyful. The soul, when it enjoys these three is hierarchized.* (H 20.22)

Hierarchy has its origins not in the language of power structures, but in the language of spirituality or life with God. Hierarchy is concerned with the states of being of a person in terms of relationship with God. The individual is 'hierarchized' when that person shows certain spiritual qualities and the Church is hierarchized when it enables the flourishing and expression of such qualities.

What are these qualities? To be hierarchized, according to Bonaventure's understanding, is to live the relationship with God in a way that is constant, is beautiful and is joyful. Constant, in that the spirit of prayer, of contemplation, enables one to be focused on what is truly important in life; to be attentive, to be faithful, above all to be able to love with a love that is sincere. To be beautiful, not with the beauty of the external, but with a beauty which above all grows in prayer through the acquisition of wisdom. To be joyful, in the realization that one is called by God, inspired with the power of God, a joy which expresses itself in a life of enthusiasm in service of God's kingdom.

The Church is hierarchical in nature. This does not mean that the Church has an élite who are the hierarchy. On the contrary, *all* people within the Church are called to be hierarchized. Understood in this way, the Church's hierarchical structure is not a static reality, but rather a challenge. To be a hierarchical Church should have nothing at all to do with power and domination. Any group within the Church which claims hierarchical power can only substantiate that claim if the statements issued in the name of that authority are permeated with constancy, beauty and joy, and facilitate the growth of those same attitudes within the life of the community. To speak of the Church as hierarchical is a challenge to the Church as a community to live in such a way that God's world is able to be uplifted through the witness of lives which, like the life of Francis, are constant, beautiful and joyful.

Francis, the Sultan
and Interfaith Dialogue

In this final chapter we shall be concerned with one of the pressing issues facing modern society, that of dialogue between the religions of the world. The issue of interfaith dialogue is crucial for the future of humanity. It is only when there is peace among religions that there will cease to be war among nations. And if there is to be peace among religions, religions must engage in dialogue. As was noted in chapter 1, Francis and the Sultan engaged in interfaith dialogue in the early years of the thirteenth century. There is much we can learn from the nature of that dialogue, much which can help us to develop an educational model for the continuance and enhancement of dialogue between religions in the world of our own time.

Background to the Encounter

If there are seen to be obstacles in the path of interfaith dialogue today, there were certainly no fewer obstacles in Francis' time. The meeting between Francis and the Sultan took place within the context of the Fifth Crusade. The Crusades had been triggered by the Clermont Address of Pope Urban II in 1095, which called upon Christians to defend the Christian Holy Places against the Saracens. Successive Crusades were launched throughout the twelfth century, but despite the initial success of the First Crusade, politically they proved a failure. Islam, previously divided into warring factions, grew into a powerful, united force under the challenge of

European invasion. In 1187, Saladin recaptured Jerusalem, which was for Islam, too, a holy city.

The thought of a Crusade dominated the thinking of Pope Innocent III, who became Pope in 1198. In 1212, the victory of Las Navas over the Saracens in Spain confirmed Innocent in his plan of launching a new Crusade. The following year, he announced a Council and a Crusade, and in 1215, the Council fixed the Crusade for 1217. Innocent died in 1216 and was succeeded by Honorius III who possessed similar enthusiasm for the cause of the Crusade. In 1218 the army of Crusaders landed on the coast of Egypt and laid siege to the city of Damietta. Their opponent was Sultan Melek-el-Kamil and it was with El-Kamil that Francis entered into dialogue.

The nature of the meeting between Francis and the Sultan was briefly noted in chapter 1. Jacques de Vitry, who met Francis in Damietta, speaks of Francis continuing on from Damietta, unarmed, to the camp of the Sultan. On the way, Francis was captured and taken to appear before Melek-el-Kamil. The Sultan appeared to be fascinated with Francis and listened to Francis' preaching about Christ. Finally he guaranteed a safe passage for Francis back to the Crusader camp. De Vitry records that the Sultan asked Francis to pray that he might receive from God a revelation as to which faith is most pleasing in God's sight.

The Significance of the Encounter

Whatever the historical accuracy of De Vitry's account, it is significant that an encounter between a Christian and a Muslim be described in this way at this particular time. De Vitry shared in the mentality of his time and culture, which was a Crusade mentality. He rejoiced that the 'treacherous Muslim' had been chased from Damietta in 1220. Nor would De Vitry have presented the encounter in the way that he did on account of Francis being a holy man. Perhaps the most renowned of the twelfth-century saints, Bernard of Clairvaux (1090–1153), argued that it was better to kill Muslims rather than to risk the spread of their 'wickedness'. The killing of a Muslim was not seen as a crime; on the contrary, a knight who died in battle against the Muslims could be called a martyr.

Dr Vitry's account, written before the death of Francis in 1226, in a religious and cultural environment which viewed Muslims as evil, may be held as a significant witness to the true nature of the meeting between Francis and the Sultan. We can consequently draw from this some telling points concerning interfaith dialogue.

It should be noted that when Francis came to the Muslims, he did not try to contradict the teachings of Mohammed; rather, he preached Christ. His words as recorded by De Vitry – 'I am a Christian' – drew him apart from the political conflict of his time and placed him in the world of religious dialogue. It was not only the words of Francis that created such a setting but his whole bearing. In contrast to the Crusader, Francis came to the Sultan's camp unarmed. He had left behind the world of politics and diplomacy and came openly as a person of faith.

De Vitry reports that the Sultan 'was so overwhelmed by the countenance of this man of God that he was filled with tenderness. For many days he listened most attentively while he preached to him and to his own men the faith of Christ.' The Sultan's reaction implies that Francis did not insult his religion. Certainly, there is a contrast between this setting and the account De Vitry supplies of the treatment given to followers of Francis when they departed from his model of preaching:

As long as the Friars Minor preached the faith of Christ and the doctrine of the gospel, the Saracens willingly listened. But as soon as they openly contradicted Mohammed in their preaching, by treating him as perfidious and treacherous, the Saracens mercilessly beat them, expelled them from their city, almost massacred them.

The Sultan understood that Francis respected his religion, even if Francis told him that, from his point of view, the Christian way was more pleasing to God.

One further significant point emerges from De Vitry's narrative. Francis challenges the Sultan to go beyond the human structures and institutions which become entwined with religious belief and to seek the purity of religious faith. He challenges the Sultan to do likewise, to go beyond the Muslim political structure in order to come to terms with his own purity of faith. Although De Vitry presents the Sultan as being unable to do that, the story serves to highlight the essence of religious dialogue as being primarily concerned not with the human constructs which so often surround faith, but with the reality of what lies at the heart of religious belief.

The sources available do not allow us to gauge the extent of the impact of the meeting upon the Sultan. It is possible, however, to discern that the encounter had considerable impact upon the religious life and practice of St Francis. His writings after his visit to Egypt show that he went through an experience there which profoundly influenced his life. He is definitely struck by the religious attitudes of the Muslims, the call to prayer, the approach to a transcendent God, the deep respect for the sacred book of the Qur'ān.

The regular call to prayer proclaimed by the Muslim muezzin (crier or herald) deeply impressed Francis. In a letter to the Rulers of the People he writes:

See to it that God is held in great reverence among your subjects; every evening at a signal given by a herald or in some other way, praise and thanks should be given to the Lord God Almighty by all the people.

In an illusion to the Islamic 'salat', Francis wants the bells to be rung – the cry of the muezzin could be replaced by a bell or any other sign commonly used in the West to call people to prayer: 'At every hour and when the bells are rung, praise and honour may be offered to Almighty God by everyone all over the world'. In this way, Christians and Muslims all over the world, might be united in prayer – a powerful ecumenical sign in a society where so many were blinded by hatred for Islam.

Francis would have also observed the way Muslims prostrated themselves on the floor or with deep bows paid reverence to Allah. In a letter to the General Chapter he wrote, 'At the sound of His name, you should fall to the ground and adore Him, so that by word and deed you might convince everyone that there is no other Almighty God besides Him'. The latter expression is very similar to the Muslim 'halma': 'There is no other God but Allah'.

A deepening awareness on the part of Francis of the transcendence of God also became clear during this period. In his earlier writings, Francis had very much emphasized the humanity of Christ, as expressed in his creation of the Christmas crib at Greccio. Yet there is a clear shift towards the transcendent after his return from Damietta. In his Rule of 1221 he writes,

He alone is true God, without beginning and without end. He is unchangeable, invisible, indescribable and ineffable, incomprehensible, unfathomable, blessed and worthy of all praise.

Such language is indeed the language of transcendence. His encounter with Islam had caused Francis to ponder his understanding of his own faith – the result of this was not the abandonment of his earlier faith but the emergence of a deepened sense of awareness that God was not only immanent but also transcendent.

A further illustration of the way Francis' experience of Islam affected him is found in his exhortation to show reverence towards the pages and words of the Bible. He had observed the deep respect the Muslim had for the written word of the Qur'ān, and shortly before his death in 1226 he wrote in his 'Testament': 'Whenever I find writings containing His words in an improper place, I make a point of picking them up, and I ask that they be picked up and put aside in a suitable place'. Perhaps Francis' new attitude to the world of Islam is best expressed in his Rule of 1221 when he tells his brothers who wish to go as missionaries to the Muslims that they should testify to their Christian faith not by disputation but by a simple, peaceable presence and a disposition of service.

The Encounter as a Model for Interfaith Dialogue

The faith of St Francis was deeply influenced by his experience at Damietta. A new self-understanding arose as he grew to a new awareness of his religious relationship not only with his Christian brothers and sisters but with all people. While maintaining loyalty to his own religious tradition and openly proclaiming his faith in Christ, Francis opened himself to the goodness in the Muslim tradition and faith. Thus he sought to discover a deeper, transcendent meaning in his own faith through what he had encountered in the faith of Islam. Francis came to recognize the religious meaning and truth in Islam and so commissioned his brothers to go to the Muslims not as Crusaders but as Christians, obedient and submissive to all. In his own life, Francis entered into dialogue with Islam and through reflection on his experience, he urged his example of dialogue on those who followed after him.

What principles should guide the process of dialogue? In his Rule of 1221, Francis urges that those who go to the Muslims 'avoid quarrels or disputes'. Clearly what had occurred in his meeting with the Sultan was not argument concerning human constructs or propositions. Indeed, Francis placed himself outside this perimeter and urged the Sultan to do the same. Both men became concerned with what might be called a process of 'conversion to the transcendent', to borrow a phrase from the theologian Bernard Lonergan. It implies a turning away from faith in the human constructions which often surround religious commitment to a searching for the truth which lies in the heart of ultimate reality. Such a conversion involves a letting go and a radical openness to the future. It means 'allowing God to be God', seeing truth not as something we already fully possess but as a reality we are yet to grasp.

What we see emerging are the conditions for proper interfaith dialogue. In the process of conversion to the transcendent, there must be a readiness to avoid domineering behaviour and to give up false ideas – as Francis did in departing from the crusading norm of his time, and as the Sultan did in granting Francis hospitality and a safe return. There are no conquerors or conquered, but only an attempt to come to a mutual understanding of a higher Truth. Francis became convinced that Islam, too, has its place in God's plan. Each tradition realized that the other was in touch with the divine – the Sultan asks Francis to pray for him and Francis requests that Christians be united in prayer with people from all parts of the world. Dialogue has opened the way for continuing conversion to the transcendent.

The dialogue between Francis and the Sultan took place in an atmosphere of mutual respect. What may well have occurred in the first place was a respectful meeting of personalities. As individuals, both Francis and the Sultan were imbued with the spirit of *courtesia*, care and respect for the dignity of the other. Hence, the meeting between the two could well have been an initial meeting of spirits, a mutual respect for the identity of the other regardless of religious belief. Such respect meant that what occurred in the exchange was neither arrogant hostility nor overweening condescension. This basis of mutual respect allowed a wider selection of the religious world to affect one individual through the medium of another. In so doing, it allowed both to enter into the process of constructive interfaith dialogue.

What is essential in a particular religious faith can often be obscured during impasssioned theological disputes. Such confrontations are specifically forbidden by the Qur'ān and also found no place in the life of St Francis. As we have already seen, Francis exhorted his followers to make a point of avoiding all disputation. The essential task, he insisted, is to preach faith in God Almighty (the divine attribute given special prominence in Islam) and to witness to faith by a peaceful way of living.

By stressing what is essential in the faith of Christians, Francis proclaimed the universal Fatherhood of God as the source of a spirit of universal sisterhood and brotherhood, placing himself alongside the Muslim who sees the end of humanity's search for wholeness and integration in the fundamental Reality and the fundamental Unity which is God. Dialogue between the religious faiths as to how this universal reconciliation can be achieved enables a deeper and richer understanding of what it is to be human.

Within the Christian tradition, the latter part of this century has seen considerable development in ecumenism – increased conversation, understanding and co-operation between the different Christian churches. The twenty-first century will call for an ecumenism which extends its concerns to dialogue between *all* religious groups. Dialogue occurs in an exchange of views in which we do not set out to convert the other to our own beliefs, but rather strive for a deeper understanding and knowledge of the faith which the other professes. It entails a respect for the other's beliefs and world view. Dialogue is a process which calls for more than an objective study of the external facets of a religious tradition. To understand believers from another religious community, we must attempt to look at the world, so far as possible, through their eyes. What is required, consequently, is an opening of the frontiers which divide communities in order to allow for freedom of exchange. When Francis and the Sultan opened their respective frontiers, fruitful dialogue followed.

Interfaith dialogue should result in a process of 'conscientization', whereby each faith community is awakened to a greater awareness of its own participation in the life of God who transcends all human divisions. There needs to be a mutual recognition of the 'creative need for the other', a need which is not one-sided. Just as the Christian community, for example, should strive to share the insights of Christianity, so it should seek to learn from, as Francis did, what is distinctive in other traditions. Mutual enrichment occurs when, in faithfulness to our own tradition, we are able to accept what another tradition has to teach us. Francis never disowned his Christian faith. His dialogue with the Sultan, however, enriched him and led him to invest that faith with a new and deeper meaning.

In the world of today, which sees not only divisions between nations of different religious faiths, but also friction between people of varied religious traditions who live side by side, the need for greater understanding and co-operation is great. To immerse ourselves into the environment of Damietta and to be led through the stages of this ecumenical encounter will not simply teach us about religion. It is able to create within us a greater awareness of the opportunities for dialogue within our own immediate world. The meeting between Francis and the Sultan raises such questions as the development of understanding in the light of new experience; the willingness to share life stories and to do away with preconceived and sometimes false ideas; the necessity for mutual respect in order to avoid destructive conflict; the need to identify what one essentially believes in order to truly encounter another. Refusal to enter into dialogue is a form of totalitarian self-sufficiency. Such refusal, however, since it implicitly condemns others, condemns itself. Cut off from the wellsprings of growth, there stagnation and decay can only follow. Openness to dialogue, on the other hand, proclaims confidence in the truth already experienced and a willingness to continue the journey towards the fullness of truth.

Bonaventure's theological writings may appear far removed from the setting of the religious encounter between Francis and the Sultan. It is important to keep in mind, however, that the basic structure of Bonaventure's thought has been shaped by Francis' experience of God, an experience which, in Damietta, provided the grounds for dialogue. Like Francis, Bonaventure displays a keen awareness of the presence of God in all created reality – God is not restricted to the world of the Christians. The whole world, as an outpouring of God's creative goodness, reflects the divine presence, and can lead human beings towards God. Bonaventure's theology is essentially and unchangeably Christian, but never exclusivist. Ultimately, he claims, God is beyond all concepts, all imaginings, all the words of our theological systems. Bonaventure's fundamental metaphysical principle – emanation, exemplarity, consummation – is one which can, no doubt in varying ways, be grasped by all who search for God. This is so because the principle expresses the underlying conviction that this universe, in which all have their being, is not the result of random chance but rather the outpouring of divine goodness and love. The invitation is open to all people of faith to dispense with human pride and the desire for self-sufficiency, and to pray for enlightenment. And in this spirit of contemplation it will be revealed that our world indeed radiates with glimmers of transcendence, glimmers which guide the feet of those who journey along the path towards the fulfilment of every human longing in the discovery of the source of all truth, all goodness and all beauty, which is God.

Francis, the little poor man of Assisi; Bonaventure, the scholar of Paris. Francis' life experienced transformed the religious climate of his own time and continues to fascinate people today – people from all walks of life, people from a wide variety of religious faiths, and, indeed, people of no religious faith at all. Bonaventure breathed deeply the spirit of Francis and reflected intensely upon it. He has left us with a testimony as to the meaning of that experience for those who, like himself, are fascinated by Francis and who seek to discover the secret which will enable each of us, limited though we feel our personal spiritual resources may be, to follow the path which Francis has travelled.

Therefore, let us stop speaking, and let us pray to the Lord that we may be granted the experience of that about which we have spoken.
(SC EPILOGUE)

Notes on Sources

CHAPTER 2

The quotation from Max Scheler is from *Wesen und Formes der Sympathie*, quoted in Leonardo Boff, *Saint Francis: A Model for Human Liberation*, New York: Crossroad, 1982, 18.

Jacques De Vitry's account of the meeting between Francis and the Sultan (also cited in chapter 7) is to be found in F. De Beer, *We Saw Brother Francis*, Chicago: Franciscan Herald Press, 1983, 131–2.

Celano's *The Second Life of St Francis* (quoted on page 134) is to be found in *St Francis of Assisi, Writings and Early Biographies: English Omnibus of the Sources for the Life of St Francis*, edited by M. Habig, Second Edition, London: SPCK, 1979.

CHAPTER 4

The quotation from von Balthasar on page 149 is to be found in H.U. von Balthasar, *The Glory of the Lord: A Theological Aesthetics*, edited by J. Riches, translated by A. Louth, F. McDonagh and B. McNeil, 7 vols, Edinburgh: T. & T. Clark, 1982–91, vol. 2 (1984), 262.

CHAPTER 6

Basil Mitchell's example of the navigator and the lighthouse cited on pages 183–4 is taken from his book *The Justification of Religious Belief*, London: Macmillan, 1978, 112–3.

The quotation from von Balthasar on page 185 is to be found in *The Glory of the Lord*, vol. 2, 260–1.

CHAPTER 7

Lonergan's notion of 'conversion to the transcendent' (quoted on page 196) is treated in his work *Method in Theology*, New York: Herder and Herder, 1972.

Suggested Further Reading

The Writings of Francis

Francis and Clare: The Complete Works, translation and
introduction by R. Armstrong and I. Brady, The Classics of
Western Spirituality Series, New York: Paulist Press, 1982.

The Writings of Bonaventure

There are two series, each of five volumes, which provide English
translations of a large number of Bonaventure's works:

The Works of St Bonaventure, translated by Jose de Vinck,
Paterson, NJ: St Anthony Guild Press, 1960–70.
Works of Saint Bonaventure, edited by P. Boehner, M. F. Laughlin
and G. Marcil, 5 volumes, New York: The Franciscan Institute
Saint Bonaventure University, 1940–94.

The writings of Bonaventure which are relevant to this study are:

Breviloquium, translated by Jose de Vinck, *The Works of
St Bonaventure*, vol. 2 (1963).
Collations of the Six Days, *The Works of St Bonaventure*,
vol. 5 (1970).

De Reductione Artium Ad Theologiam, introduction and translation
by E. Healy, *Works of Saint Bonaventure*, vol. 1 (1955).
Disputed Questions on the Knowledge of Christ, introduction and
translation by Zachary Hayes, *Works of Saint Bonaventure*,
vol. 4 (1992).
Disputed Questions on the Mystery of the Trinity, introduction and
translation by Zachary Hayes, *Works of Saint Bonaventure*,
vol. 3 (1979)
The Soul's Journey Into God – The Tree of Life – The Life of St Francis,
translation and introduction by E. Cousins, The Classics of
Western Spirituality, New York: Paulist Press, 1978.
The Triple Way or Love Enkindled, *The Works of St Bonaventure*,
vol. 1 (1960).

Additional Reading

The widest selection of early writings on St Francis (including the
writings of Francis) is to be found in:

*St Francis of Assisi, Writings and Early Biographies: English
Omnibus of the Sources for the Life of St Francis*, edited by
M. Habig, Second Edition, London: SPCK, 1979.

The English language books that have been written on Francis
during this century are voluminous. It is unfortunate that the
same cannot be said concerning Bonaventure. It is to be hoped
that the rediscovery of Bonaventure's work within the English-
speaking world will lead to a plethora of volumes in the near
future.

A number of scholarly works are available to us, however, and
the following are recommended:

Balthasar, H. U. von, *The Glory of the Lord: A Theological Aesthetics*, edited by J. Riches, translated by A. Louth, F. McDonagh and B. McNeil, 7 vols, Edinburgh: T. & T. Clark, 1982–91, vol. 2 (1984), 260–362.

Bougerol, J., *Introduction to the Works of Bonaventure*, Paterson, NJ: St Anthony Guild Press, 1963.

Cousins, E., *Bonaventure and the Coincidence of Opposites*, Chicago: Franciscan Herald Press, 1978.

Gilson, E., *The Philosophy of Bonaventure*, translated by I. Trethowan and F. Sheed, Paterson, NJ: St Anthony Guild Press, 1965.

Hayes, Z., *The Hidden Centre: Spirituality and Speculative Christology in St Bonaventure*, New York: The Franciscan Institute St Bonaventure University, 1992.

JOHN OF THE CROSS

Wilfrid McGreal, O Carm

John of the Cross

WILFRID McGREAL

Fr Wilfrid McGreal, O Carm, studied Theology in Rome and English at University College Dublin. He joined the Order of Carmelites in 1957 and since 1990 has been Sub-Prior and Shrine Director at Aylesford Priory in Kent. The author of *Guilt and Healing* and of numerous articles for the *Universe* and *Priest and People*, he is also a frequent broadcaster on Radio 4 and Radio Kent.

Contents

Acknowledgement

I would like to offer my thanks to Ros Duddell, who did much to enable this book to reach its final form.

Date Chart

1562	St Teresa establishes the Reform at St Joseph's, Avila
1563	John enters the Carmelites at Medina
1567	John ordained at Salamanca
1568	John part of first community of Reformed friars at Duruelo

1571	Don Juan defeats Turks at Battle of Lepanto

1572–77	John confessor at the Monastery of the Incarnation at Avila
1577	Dec. – John imprisoned at the Priory at Toledo
1578	Aug. – Escapes from Toledo
1580	His mother Doña Catalina dies
1582–6	Prior at Granada where he writes most of his poems and commentaries
1588	Prior of Segovia and assistant to Nicolas Doria, the new head of the Reform

1588	Destruction of the Armada

1591	June – John destined to go to Mexico – loses all offices Sept. – Moves to Ubeda – already ill 14 Dec. – Dies at Ubeda

		1541–1613	El Greco
		1547–1616	Cervantes
		1564–1616	Shakespeare
1618	First edition of John's works		
1630	First complete edition of his writings		
1726	Benedict XIII canonizes him		
1952	Named patron of Spanish poets		

Introduction

This is a book about a man with a sublime imagination. He was the victim of misunderstanding by those who should have appreciated him. Faced with darkness and cruel treatment, he responded with great poetry that sings of the highest experience of love. The man is Juan de Yepes (1540–1591), known as John of the Cross. He came from Castile in the heart of Spain and lived most of his life as a member of a community of brothers or friars, the Carmelites.

John has a message and a vision of life that can have real meaning for people today. His poems, born in darkness and personal tragedy, even with a sense of the loss of God, find God in the midst of sorrows. For John, the healing presence of God could be found in dark, unlikely places. He also believed that our human longings, our deepest desires can only find fulfilment in God. John claimed to have found that closeness and fulfilment and wanted to share his experience and the possibility of that experience with others. The way to this intimacy with God is a way of letting go of what could seem dearest and most important in life. John's teaching is challenging but it is not abstract, it is not unreal. It comes from the heart and speaks the language of the imagination.

As John of the Cross, the man, is probably scarcely known in the English-speaking world, this introduction provides a biographical sketch. The section on John as a poet and mystic is meant to give a flavour of his poetic genius. John's poems spring directly from the moments in his life when he believed he was intimate with God. The rest of the book attempts to pick out the key themes and concerns which run through his other writings.

Can John say anything to people today? In his own day, John was concerned to be a genuine guide to people searching for personal growth and help in their quest for God. In an age when many guides and gurus prove to be bogus, does John offer a wisdom that transcends time? John was a passionate, caring person who wanted only the best for those he guided. This book will hopefully enable his voice to be heard by men and women at the end of the twentieth century.

John's Life and Background

The sixteenth century was an age of upheaval, discovery and change. It was the century of the Reformation and the time when Europeans ventured out to the Americas and the Indies. It was also the century of the Renaissance, an age of creativity in the arts and sciences. In England, figures such as Shakespeare, Drake and Elizabeth I stand out. In Spain, Philip II is a dominant political figure while John of the Cross is the great poet of the age and also an outstanding teacher for Christians searching for God.

John of the Cross deserves to be better known in the English-speaking world. He has a message for our age and he needs to be given a hearing. Up to now, John has not been well served by his biographers, most of whom have presented him as a remote, rather severe saint. John's humanity has been removed and religious clichés and miracles have obscured the real person.

To understand John's life and what he stands for means finding out something about sixteenth-century Spain. Spain was at the height of its power during John's lifetime. But it was also a new country, something like the United States is even today. Most of modern Spain was conquered by Islamic invaders from North Africa in the eighth century. It took six hundred years to drive the invaders out and it was only at the end of the fifteenth century that the south of Spain was reconquered.

The end of Moorish rule coincided with the discovery of the Americas and the establishment of an empire in Mexico and South America. Wealth flowed into Spain and the country flourished.

However, Spain was still a mixture of peoples. Germanic and Celtic people lived alongside Jews and folk with North African origins. There was also a religious mix – Christian, Jewish and Muslim. The official policy of the government was to expel Jews and Muslims or to force them to become Christians if they wanted to remain in Spain. There were, therefore, tensions among the different racial groups, and the Inquisition, which was very much an arm of the State, worked to achieve stability.

The Spanish Inquisition had originally been an organ of the Catholic Church, but from the sixteenth century onwards, orthodoxy, uniformity and national unity became part of an overall process. Philip II wanted to control the Church so that it served the interests of Spain first and foremost. This control and the fear aroused by the Inquisition was to cast a shadow over the life of John of the Cross.

Childhood

According to the latest research, John de Yepes, to give him his family name, was born in 1540 at Fontiveros in Castile, in the very heart of Spain. John did not have an easy childhood; he knew poverty and insecurity. His parents came from opposite sides of the social divide. His father, Gonzalo de Yepes, came from a prosperous business family who lived in Toledo. They were merchants dealing in textiles and enjoyed a comfortable life given the expanding economy. However, they had their insecurities as they were *Conversos*, Jewish converts to Christianity.

They had been Catholics for some generations, but there was always the fear that a business rival could rake up the information to do them down. The omnipresent Inquisition, which operated like a secret service, posed a threat. It was easy enough to be denounced by the Inquisition and end up penniless.

It was in the course of buying cloth that Gonzalo met his future wife, Catalina Alvarez. She was a weaver, living and working in

Fontiveros, near Madrid. Gonzalo's family were against the marriage, ostensibly because of the social gulf, but historians argue that there was another motive. It is claimed that Catalina lacked *limpieza de sangre* – purity of blood. She was, it is believed, of Moorish origin – a descendant of the Muslim invaders. Gonzalo's family were frightened and felt that such a marriage could put the spotlight on them and people would then discover their Jewish origins.

Gonzalo was unwilling to give up Catalina so they married, even though he was disowned by his family and the couple started out in life penniless. Gonzalo learned the skill of weaving from his wife and together they struggled to earn enough money to keep a roof over their heads.

John was the youngest of three boys born to this tenacious couple, but tragically, when John was five years old, his father died, a victim of the plague which was the scourge of the poor at that time. Gonzalo's family were unwilling to help Catalina and her three young sons, so she struggled as best she could to bring up the boys on her own. She moved north to Medina Del Campo, a busy market town, where she found a more secure outlet for her weaving. However, tragedy struck again when Luis, the middle son, died. John by now was eight years old.

Gifted and Caring

The plight of single parents then as now was hard. John was growing up on the wrong side of the tracks, and yet marvellous bonds of love and loyalty grew up between the boys and their mother. John was able to get some basic education at a school for the poor, the Colegio de la Doctrine. Medina was a vibrant, exciting place, and John loved to hear stories of the Americas and enjoyed the bustle of the market. He must have seemed a waif, he was so small – as an adult he was barely five feet tall. He was also dark-skinned, more African than European in looks.

When John was twelve, he was asked to work in a local hospital. The hospital administrator, Don Alonso, was to prove a generous friend. Las Bubas, as the hospital was called, housed patients with contagious diseases. John was asked to be a nursing assistant and so for the next six years or so he cared for the sick, feeding them, washing them and dressing their sores. This was a period when syphilis was rampant, so many of the patients were dying slow, painful deaths, shunned by family and locked often in deep anger and denial. The young John gave of his energy to care for those abandoned by society. He spent hours chatting, telling stories and singing the songs he had learned in the market-place. In addition to this caring, John helped raise funds and collected food for the hospital.

Don Alonso recognized that John was a gifted young man and paid for him to study at the newly established Jesuit College in Medina – perhaps John might become a priest and care for the sick. For the next three years, John studied literature, the classics and philosophy, enjoying the challenge of study and especially the chance to write. Here he had his literary formation, the future poet learning his craft.

The Carmelites

John still helped out at the hospital and it seemed natural that John should get ordained and become the hospital chaplain. John wanted to give his life to God but he felt that if he was going to be a priest he would like to belong to a community, a family. So, in 1563, he decided to join the community of Carmelite friars at the Priory of Santa Ana in Medina. Why did he join that community, and who were these Carmelite friars?

As to the why of his joining the Carmelite Community, the answer is probably quite simple. Pablo Garrido, who has specialized in the history of the period, believes that some of John's father's family had been members of the Carmelite Order at

Toledo. He cites Diego de Yepes and an Andres de Yepes, who were members of the Carmelite Community in Toledo in the early years of the sixteenth century. They could have been his forebears and perhaps were an unconscious influence.

The Carmelites were part of a movement in the development of Christianity which occurred in the early thirteenth century. The Church of the day seemed out of touch with the people, and the simplicity of the gospel seemed to have been lost. In this context, groups of Christians seeking to live a simple life based on the gospel emerged in Europe. One such group, centred on St Francis of Assisi, was the origin of the Franciscans, an order of brothers or friars who lived and preached the poverty of Christ. The Carmelites did not have a leader or founder, but the order grew out of a group of pilgrims who had settled on Mount Carmel. These pilgrims, who had journeyed to the Holy Land seeking a closer union with Christ, began to live as a community on Mount Carmel and were given a rule of life in 1208 by the Patriarch of Jerusalem. Like the Franciscans, the Carmelites lived as a group of brothers committed to prayer but also ready to go out and preach to the Christian groups in the Holy Land.

These men chose Mount Carmel as their home because it had links with the great prophet Elijah, and its beauty caused it to be seen as a symbol of God's grace. It was because the Order originated on Mount Carmel that its members became known as Carmelites.

The first Carmelites lived out their contemplative lifestyle in the Holy Land for some fifty years. They lived according to their rule, 'meditating day and night on the Word of the Lord'. The praying of the Scriptures and daily eucharist were at the heart of the life of these early Carmelites. They constructed little cells around the spring of Elijah and, because of their commitment, many pilgrims and Crusaders were drawn to what must have seemed an idyllic way of life.

However, the politics of the day broke in on this peaceful community. The Crusaders were forced out of the Holy Land and groups of Carmelites came to the West, refugees from violence. Once in Western Europe, the Order, which had received Papal approval in 1247, had to decide how they should live. At a meeting held at Aylesford in Kent in 1247, delegates representing the groups who had come from the Holy Land decided that their way of life should be one of serving the people by preaching the Gospel. The Carmelites decided, like the Franciscans, to go out among the people preaching in the market-places or opening churches in the new towns. They would depend for their livelihood on the people's generosity, they would be preaching brothers who begged for their living. The official Church was to call these groups – Carmelites, Franciscans and Dominicans – mendicant friars.

The Carmelites had their own distinctive vision which came from their origins in the Holy Land. When they came to Europe and became involved in active ministry in the growing urban centres, they brought with them memories and symbols. Mount Carmel, with its beauty and solitude, was a symbol of God's goodness but also a challenge. The challenge was to retain a sense of solitude and stillness so that even in the busiest of places there would be a space for God. Again, because Mount Carmel was associated with the great prophet Elijah, who was outspoken and yet close to God in prayer, the Carmelites have always tried to incorporate his spirit into their lifestyle. Finally, like all Christians in the Middle Ages, the Carmelites had great devotion to Mary the mother of Jesus. They admired her trust, her faith and they saw her as a model of discipleship.

The medieval Carmelites and their successors have tried to create a synthesis whereby they could be involved in the outreach of the Church but at the same time they have tried to keep alive a sense of reflective scriptural prayer and silence. The attempts to create a way of life which is rooted in silence and prayer and yet involves working in society as preachers, teachers and answering people's deepest needs have always created tensions.

It was this order of brothers, with its traditions rooted in the

Holy Land, that John joined in 1563 at Medina del Campo. The Carmelite friars in Castile were not numerous but were known for their faithfulness in keeping their rule. The Middle Ages had seen many communities of monks, nuns or friars become quite mediocre, but the Carmelites of Castile were a fervent group.

John was one of a group of young Carmelites studying and learning the traditions of the Order. Since the Carmelites, like other friars, were preachers, they needed a good formation. People looked to the friars to provide them with sound doctrine as so often in the Middle Ages the parish clergy were poorly educated. John and his contemporaries spent their year of initiation or noviciate learning about the Order's traditions and being helped to grow in their relationship with God. They would also have had classes in literature and philosophy, learning how to formulate and express ideas and also being given a sound cultural basis. From contemporary documentation it seems that John's fellow students were a lively and committed group. After a year of initiation, John and his companions moved to Salamanca to study theology. Salamanca was highly regarded as an academic centre on a par with Paris or Oxford. John's studies would have covered the Scriptures and he would have been introduced to great figures of Christian thought such as St Augustine and St Thomas Aquinas. His lectures would have been in Latin and the style of teaching, called scholasticism, was rooted in Greek philosophy. It might seem rather foreign to us, but it was intellectually challenging and gave John a means of expressing his ideas.

While John studied at Salamanca he also had a chance to read books written by Carmelites from the early years of the Order. These writers were to give John a thirst for journeying closer to God. *The Fiery Arrow*, written in 1270, not long after the Carmelites came to Europe, was the work of a French Carmelite who wanted his brothers to preserve the ideals of the Order's earliest days and not be swamped by over-activity. He also stressed the need for sound formation and intellectual vigour. Another book,

The Institutions of the First Monks, written by a Catalan Carmelite, Philip Ribot, stresses the role of reflective prayer and challenges his colleagues to aspire to close union with God – nothing less should be the goal.

The Influence of Teresa of Avila

In 1567, John was ordained as a priest in the Carmelite Order. It was at this stage that he met a remarkable woman who was to have as deep an influence on his life as his mother. The woman was Teresa de Alumada y Cepeda, better known as Teresa of Avila. Teresa was a Carmelite nun. The Carmelites, like most orders in the Church, had set up a way of life for women so they could live the spirit and inspiration of the Order. Teresa was a remarkable woman with a vision. She wanted to bring the Carmelite Order closer in spirit and practice to its earliest days in the Holy Land. She wanted communities where prayer and silence were high on the agenda. What she was calling for was a Reform or Renewal of life in the Order for both friars and nuns. The Prior General, the head of the Order, John Rossi, had given her permission to found convents where this more fervent living of the Carmelite ideal could be fostered. Teresa had won the heart of John Rossi, who commented that she was worth a hundred friars.

When John met Teresa she was already fifty, twice his age. She came from a well-to-do family, and as a girl had shown independence and a romantic nature. For many years she had lived an unremarkable life in her convent at Avila, but around the age of forty she had profound religious experiences which had a radical effect on her and gave her the energy to begin her work of renewal among the Carmelites. Teresa was also the author of books chronicling her experiences, her *Life* and *The Way of Perfection*. Teresa was impressed by John and saw that he would be a likely candidate to help her with her work. At this time, John was going through a spell of being shy and wanting to withdraw from the rush of life. Teresa persuaded him to go back to finish his studies at Salamanca but to keep an open mind about working for her project. Teresa's comment on John at this time makes play about his height: 'Though he is small in stature he is great in God's eyes'.

When John had finished his studies in 1568, Teresa approached the superior of the Carmelite friars in Castile, Alonzo Gonzalez, and asked him to allow some of his friars to live according to her renewed vision or Reform. In the first instance, she wanted friars who would help her nuns by hearing confessions and giving them guidance. John was willing to join in the project, as was Antonio de Heredia, who had been in charge of forming new members of the Order. However, Teresa wanted to make it clear that her Reform was not meant to be superficial – something measured by austerity and ascetic practices. She wanted a way of living with balance so that charity, detachment and humility mattered more than doing spectacular penances. Teresa was interested in creating environments where genuine humanity could flourish. She was to show John that what was vital was the development of the creative and the imaginative in the life of a Christian. She helped him see that academic life had overshadowed the playful, creative side of his nature. His love of music, of poetry, story-telling – these were rediscovered and became central in his development. As John was to grow as a great teacher, it was his creative gifts that enabled him to communicate his profound experiences.

The Reform

A new way of life began for John on 28 November 1568 at Duruelo, a small village between Avila and Salamanca. On that day, he, Antonio and Joseph celebrated mass, presided over by the head of the Carmelite Order in Castile, Alonzo Gonzalez. The three friars put on habits made of coarse cloth and promised to live by a vision of Carmelite life that would reflect its early years on Mount Carmel. They wanted to turn their backs on any mitigation of the original Rule of the Order. To mark this moment as decisive, John took a new name and was to be known as John of the Cross. This way of life eventually gained the title of Discalced Reform – the term Discalced means 'barefoot'. Being barefoot was a sign of reform in religious communities in the sixteenth century, although in the case of these Carmelites it meant wearing rough sandals.

The first priory of what was to be called the Reform was an old barn that the friars were to turn into a simple dwelling. John was delighted at the development. Living this simple prayerful life fulfilled his heart's desire. There was another reason for John to be happy as his mother volunteered to act as cook while his brother, Francisco, came over to help in the restoration of the building. John never lost close links with his family, loving to spend time with them.

The new way of life or Reform began to spread with new priories being founded. John was soon called to leave Duruelo to help care for the young friars who were studying for ordination at Alcalá, near Madrid. This was a role which John relished, as he had come to realize that the whole person had to be developed. Academic attainment was essential but these young men needed to value the traditions of the Order and be well-grounded in humanity if they were to help people.

Not everyone in this new movement among the Carmelites had the same balanced view of life. The new entrants or novices to the Order at nearby Pastrana found themselves under a novice master who had gone overboard with asceticism. In the name of the quest for holiness, the Novice Master had introduced bizarre and irrational practices. The spectacular had taken the place of the spiritual. John, mindful of Teresa's advice, was able to see the lack of balance. He realized the young men needed proper food and adequate sleep and reintroduced laughter into their lives. John knew that what really mattered was an inner conversion, and he believed God wanted a loving, generous person.

In 1572, John was given what proved to be a daunting task. He was asked to go to Avila to be confessor to the Convent of the Incarnation. This was the convent where Teresa of Avila began her life as a nun. It was a huge community of 130 nuns beset by poverty and full of factions. In 1571, despite the protests of the community, Teresa had been made Prioress, and Angel de Salazar, who was now in charge of the Order in Castile, gave her his full support. By January 1573, the convent was at peace and open to creative change. While much of the credit must go to Teresa, she could not have set so much change in motion without John's help. John lived in a small house near the convent and was to stay there until 1577. John gave of himself generously and won the confidence of the community. He was deeply sensitive in dealing with the nuns, recognizing each person's uniqueness. A typical piece of generosity was the famous drawing of the Crucified Christ which he made for one of the nuns, Ana Mary of Jesus. Centuries later, the drawing was to inspire Salvador Dali's masterpiece, *Saint John of the Cross*.

These five years at Avila were a time of mutual enrichment for John and Teresa. By this time, Teresa was deeply advanced in the mystical life – she lived sensing God's closeness to her. She shared many of her insights and experiences with John, helping him in turn make sense of the profound things happening in his life. Their friendship was a precious gift and perhaps can teach us today to value friendship and such creative intimacy. John and Teresa were obviously attracted to each other but in a way that respected the other's role and journey in life.

During this period in Avila, John continued to make time for the poor and disadvantaged. He was always ready to preach and spend time listening to people, especially the sick. He also remembered his own impoverished childhood and found time to teach poor children the basics of reading and writing. And, as ever, he found time for his mother and brother.

Punishment and Imprisonment

In 1577, John's life was turned upside down by events outside of his control. The Reform or Renewal of the Order which John had helped initiate was now the subject of controversy and suspicion. Originally, the leadership of the Order had supported the Reform, but they had imposed certain restrictions. One such restriction was to limit the number of priories committed to the new way, and also not to set up communities of the Reform in Andalusia. The reason behind these restrictions was the experience of similar reforms in Italy developing too quickly and being taken over by the immature and enthusiasts. These restrictions were now being ignored, chiefly because King Philip II began to interfere in the internal affairs of the Order. Philip had an obsession with Church affairs and wanted to exercise as much control over the Spanish Church as possible, resenting the influence of the Pope and any order coming from Rome. As a result of this interference, a whole tangle of misunderstanding developed among the Carmelites. Those friars who had not joined the Reform felt threatened by the growth of the new foundations, and the head of the Order in Rome, John Rossi, felt slighted. Communications between Spain and Rome were painfully slow, and letters which could have clarified matters arrived too late.

The perception grew both in Rome and among those in charge of the Order in Spain that the movement inspired originally to renew the Carmelite way of life was getting out of hand, and that certain personalities were becoming far too independent. It was in this context that John was seen as a leader of what was now viewed as a disobedient group. John became the focus of criticism because he had been among the first to commit himself to the movement which was now called the Reform.

In December 1577, John was forcibly taken by a group of friars from Avila to the Carmelite Priory at Toledo. Here, John was accused by the superiors of the Carmelite Order in Castile of being rebellious and disobedient. He was subjected to the punishments laid down in the Statutes of the Order of that time. These included solitary confinement and being flogged. Some biographers describe his imprisonment at Toledo in great detail, although such accounts are fiction, as we have few details about the eight months of John's imprisonment. However, the whole period must have been a time of terrible trauma. John must have wondered why he was the focus of such anger, why should people who were supposed to be idealistic act in such a harsh way? John's imprisonment and abduction seem very like the fate of modern-day hostages. What we do know is that during this tragic, cruel time John had profound religious experiences which he was able to express in sublime poetry. The long months of imprisonment brought him close to God and saw an awakening of a great artistic gift.

John managed to escape from his prison in the high summer of 1578. His captors grew careless, and in the middle of the night he managed to slip out of the priory. Nuns at a nearby convent gave him shelter, and with the help of friends, John found his way to a priory belonging to the Reform.

The tensions in the Carmelite Order diminished as misunderstandings were ironed out and the priories belonging to the Reform began to have their own organization and became more or less independent from those not wanting to embrace it. The Reform began to be called Discalced, or 'barefoot', while the rest were known as Observants.

Given this happier climate, John was able to get on with his life. He soon recovered from his imprisonment and was asked to help in a newly-founded Priory in Andalusia. John was to spend the next ten years of his life in the South of Spain. It was a totally different landscape to his native Castile, but John fell in love with the rugged countryside. Nature was to be an important part of his life from now on. He loved walking and would often walk up to fifty miles to see a friend. He liked nothing better than the feel of the wind and the sun, and his brother Francisco tells how the night sky fascinated him. He would often spend hours staring at the beauty of the stars.

During these ten years, John's life was rich and varied. He held many responsible posts in the administration of the Order. He taught many of the young friars and gave numerous lectures to the Carmelite nuns. This was the time when he wrote his poetry and composed his commentaries on the poems. From 1582 to 1588, John was Prior of the newly-founded Carmelite Priory in Granada. The Priory, called Los Martires, was built on the hill of the Alhambra. The Alhambra was a complex of Moorish palaces and fortifications, and even today it strikes visitors as one of the wonders of the world. John admired the delicate Moorish architecture and the beautiful flowers that covered the surrounding hills. Gardens, design and engineering were all important in John's life. He delighted in designing gardens for any newly founded priory or convent. When building was in progress, John loved to choose the stone and work along with the architect so that the building would be a home, not an institution. One of his great achievements was to design the aqueduct that brought water from the Alhambra to the Priory in Granada.

The only cloud in John's life during this time was his mother's death. He had loved her dearly and knew how she had struggled to give him and his brother the best possible home. John found time in these years to help many of the friars and nuns, guiding them in their search for God. He also proved a loving friend to a whole host of people. By the end of his years in Granada, John was at the height of his powers but also had flowered as a most loving and lovable man. Small, dark, intense, but also humorous, gifted and loyal.

Rebellious

The last years of John's life, between 1588 and 1591, saw the clouds returning again. The leadership of the Discalced Reform had passed to Nicholás Doria. Doria was a great administrator (he had been a banker before joining the Carmelites), but a man who loved discipline and abhorred laxity. Doria clashed with Jerome Gracián, a charismatic figure, a friend of Teresa of Avila and Doria's predecessor as head of the Reform. Gracián had been the dynamo at the heart of the Reform, responsible for its expansion. It had been Gracián's impetuosity in the 1570s which had created the situation that led to John's imprisonment.

Doria now wanted to contain Gracián, and the rift between the two came to a head when Doria expelled Gracián from the Discalced Reform. John, by this time, was back in the Castile Priory at Segovia and was Doria's deputy in the running of the Order. John saw the rift between Doria and Gracián as power politics and made it clear that this was no way to behave. Doria, a cold personality, saw John's attitude as rebellious and became very negative towards him.

A whispering campaign began against John, orchestrated by Diego Evangelista, one of Doria's lieutenants. Diego disliked John because in years gone by John had had to discipline him. The word went out that John's writings were heretical and that his behaviour was suspect. A posting to Mexico was mooted, but instead ill-health intervened. In 1591, John was sent to a remote priory in Andalusia where he settled down to live a simple life of prayer and to work on the farm attached to the Priory. Meanwhile, the whispering campaign continued, with hints that John's teaching on prayer was not in keeping with orthodox teaching.

Diego claimed that John was teaching people to be independent of the Church in their prayer lives. This was a period when any departure or seeming departure from orthodoxy was viewed with grave concern. The Reformation had fragmented Christianity so the need to preserve an embattled Church was paramount. Sadly, Doria did nothing to counter the rumours and this did little to help John's frail health. By the autumn of 1591, John was seriously ill. The indications are that John probably had some form of skin cancer which eventually became localized as a tumour on the spine.

John was transferred to the Priory at Ubeda where it was hoped he could receive some medical treatment. However, John's troubles were compounded as the Prior of the Community resented the presence of an invalid. He saw John merely as a financial burden. Eventually, John managed to penetrate the Prior's hostility and the resentment vanished. John died on 14 December 1591. On his deathbed, he asked the community to read from the Song of Songs, which was his favourite scriptural text. He found comfort in the words expressing sublime love, and his final words were ones of trust: 'Into your hands, Lord, I commend my spirit.' In his dying he found a peace that had often been elusive during his life.

John of the Cross emerges as a man who grew in humanity as he searched for holiness. His life as a Carmelite was not always easy but he came out of the trauma of his imprisonment without bitterness and turned the negative experience into a source of creativity. His last months were overshadowed by the whispering campaign and sheer insensitivity, but again he was able to rise above the pettiness. John had a strength and resilience that is really admirable. He was never one to show resentment but got on with the business of living. He did not allow other people to set the agenda for his life. His strength was his ability to rise above rivalries. What does emerge is a sense that he had a wonderfully warm personality and he really had a great love for people. He always valued his family, especially his mother, and after her death he found great comfort in his closeness to his brother Francisco and Francisco's wife. John, while he was a great poet and a wonderful teacher, always remained very domestic. He loved caring for people and when he had roles of responsibility, he used the position to make priories and convents happier places. He enjoyed organizing picnics on feast days, and, as has been noted, his practical talents included designing gardens and solving engineering problems. However, besides all this energy and giftedness, there was a basic grit and determination in the man. His early years, his awareness of poverty gave him a sense of realism and helped him survive persecution and hardship. John, though, was not remote or forbidding; he was gifted, lovable and single-minded in his love of God.

Doria died shortly after John and the whispering campaign petered out. Gradually, John's works were published and his teaching was recognized for its beauty and profundity. Official recognition came when the Church declared him a saint in 1726, while the literary world gave its accolade when he was named patron of Spanish poets in 1952.

Poet and Mystic

When John was imprisoned by his fellow Carmelites he under-
went profound religious experiences. In the middle of physical
suffering he had what he believed was an amazing experience of
closeness to God, so close as to be akin to a physical union. John
wanted to share this experience, and the result is his poetry which
is among the finest in the Spanish language. It reads as powerfully today as when it was first composed.

John's deep sense of union with the divine is often called 'mystical'. All the great religions of the world acknowledge the reality of
mystical experience. In fact, today many scholars find the mystical
an important bond between the great faiths. One such scholar is
William Johnston, a Catholic who lives and works in Japan and
has a special interest in Buddhism. He also sees John of the Cross
as a mystic who has an important message for people today.

In the modern world, while many people would have little to do
with organized religion, there is still a deep thirst for meaning in
life, for a relationship which could satisfy our deepest longings.
Can John of the Cross help such people, and can we find a language that will speak to people from different backgrounds as they
search for meaning?

If we go to John of the Cross we will find words like 'love',
'knowledge' and 'secret' having a great importance. John speaks
of a secret knowledge that comes through love: love is at the heart
of such knowledge and it is a gift. In the Christian tradition, the
relationship between the individual and God is always seen as

being initiated by God. It is God who loves us first and we gradually become aware of God wanting to be part of our lives. St Paul and St John the Evangelist both emphasize the primacy of God's love for us. St Paul writes to the first Christians at Ephesus: '... he chose us in Christ before the foundation of the world to be holy and blameless before him in love' (EPHESIANS 1:4). St John, in his First Letter, writes:

> *In this is love, not that we loved God but that he loved us and sent his Son to be the atoning sacrifice for our sins ...*
>
> *God is love, and those who abide in love abide in God, and God abides in them.* (1 JOHN 4:10,16)

At this stage, a reader could well ask what the link is between the idea of love used in connection with God and in peoples' everyday experience. Love between human beings can obviously have a wide range of expressions and meanings. The love a mother has for a child; love and care shown to the sick; love of friends, and sexual or erotic love. What is common to these different expressions of love is the way love brings us out of ourselves and establishes bonds, commitments and fulfilment. The love that we call erotic, flowing from our sexuality, is possibly the most powerful force in life and can either be creative and enhancing or a source of pain and confusion. In a relationship which develops and is personal, erotic love combines with friendship to enable a permanent commitment. What is important to our search to understand mysticism is that the capacity to love among human beings leads to happiness and fulfilment. It ends isolation and is a force towards building community.

The Language of Love

When we examine the writings of mystics, especially in the Christian tradition, it becomes clear that the language of erotic love is an important element in the expression of mystical experience. However, given the fact that Christianity has often seemed to be anti the body and against sexual pleasure this can lead to a sense of paradox.

A way in to resolving the paradox is to go to the Bible, in particular to the Old Testament book the Song of Songs. This book, which is a collection of poems, is in its literal sense a sheer celebration of the passionate love between men and women. The Song of Songs encourages the reader to appreciate the emotional experiences of love. The Song speaks of the joy of physical presence but also it reflects the pain of absence. Another theme is the mutuality of the feelings which draw women and men together. The admiration and yearning of the lovers in these poems is reciprocal and intense. The lovers praise each other's charms and issue passionate invitations to lovemaking. In these invitations, there is no sense of male domination – the woman's voice sounds loud and clear in the poem, ready to initiate as well as to respond to calls to love.

The Song is exuberant in its eroticism. The woman says in her desire for fulfilment in the arms of her lover: 'Let him kiss me with the kisses of his mouth ... We shall praise your love more than wine' (SONG OF SONGS 1:2,4), while the man is clear about his physical intentions, 'May your breasts be the clusters of grapes, your breath sweet scented as apples' (SONG OF SONGS 7:9). The poetry is erotic in its appreciation of sexual love, but there is never a hint of prurience. The poet conveys the feelings linked to love but does not depict clinical acts of lovemaking. The poet is interested in the whole person.

How did this collection of poems, which are sometimes attributed to King Solomon, come be included in the Bible? Well, the rapturous depiction of love between men and women shows that such activity is healthy, natural and good. If a theological warrant is needed to endorse the joy of the poem, then the first chapter of Genesis is the place to look. There in the story of creation we are told creation is 'good ... indeed ... very good'. That goodness includes our sexuality. Genesis also reminds us that the divine image is shown in the complementarity of the male and female. Sexuality is a good gift to be rejoiced in and part of God's design for human life.

God created humankind in his image,
in the image of God he created them;
male and female he created them. (GENESIS 1:27)

While the Song of Songs was intended to celebrate the gift and beauty of sexuality, other meanings were attached to the poem and they will be important in the understanding of mysticism. The Bible, both Old and New Testament, has often used the metaphor of marriage to express the relationship between God and people.

As the bridegroom rejoices over the bride,
so shall your God rejoice over you. (ISAIAH 62:5)

God initiates and maintains a loving relationship with those who accept his invitation. It is in the context of this key metaphor that first Jewish and then Christian teachers began to see the Song of Songs as being capable of expressing the love between God and humankind.

In the Christian tradition, Origen, writing in Alexandria in the second century, saw this love-song as expressing the union of the individual person with Jesus Christ. So the theologian took the poem that celebrates sexuality and gave it a meaning that places love on a different level. But the change of interpretation, or the allegorical meaning, to give it its technical name, leaves the notion of union and intimacy intact. Jesus is now the Lover and the individual Christian is called into an intimacy as intense as a sexual union, but at a level that goes beyond normal categories. But the crux is that such talk of union with the divine is only possible because we know of the reality of the intimacy that comes from our sexuality. If sexuality is perceived as a good gift from God, then it must be seen as crucial in any understanding of God loving us, and vice versa. To deny our sexuality or ignore it is no recipe for closeness to God, and yet much of what passes for Christian morality would take us down that road – that the way to God is to denigrate the body, our feelings and desires.

Origen's writings on the Song of Songs were to have a great influence down the centuries and affected such outstanding figures as Bernard of Clairvaux, Rysbroec (the great Flemish mystic), and Richard Rolle, the English author of *The Cloud of Unknowing*. We know that John of the Cross was drawn to the Song of Songs and it became his favourite Biblical text, so much so that he knew it by heart.

Another word that needs examining in relation to mysticism is 'secret'. In English, secret often means something special or esoteric. Perhaps the meaning that best relates to mysticism is 'a reality that has to be discovered'; it is beyond our normal grasp of things, and yet not irrational or magical. Dionysus, a Syrian theologian from the fifth century, was the first writer to develop this notion. He stressed the secretness or mystery of God. God is light beyond light and this light is usually perceived as darkness. He said this to emphasize his belief that the things of God are beyond the human eye and ear. This echoes the teachings of St Paul and is part of a tradition that asks us to avoid having a set image of God and to be open to the wonderful fullness of God. Rigid images of God can so often be barriers to the reality of God. Sometimes people say they can no longer believe, when in fact what they mean is they have gone beyond seeing God in a particular way.

The mystic is someone who has moved away from images of God to a point when they are open to a loving relation with a God whom they see as personal. The nature of that relationship is intense and beautiful, and often expressed in the language and images of sexual love. The high point of that experience is often described as ecstasy. Ecstasy is a state that occurs when, under the power of love, a person feels that he or she has been raised to a point of union with God. The mystic believes that this is made possible by the action of the divine. It is not a self-induced state, nor does the mystic use any form of drug. It is a state of standing outside oneself to be one with God. St Paul expresses this powerfully when he says, 'I live, now not I, but Christ lives in me' (GALATIANS 2:20).

Ecstasy is also linked to a deep sense of commitment and joy. Again the language of sexual love has to be brought to bear. Once the Beloved (God or Christ) is known then nothing else can satisfy the Lover (the mystic). Everything else in life pales into insignificance. In the gospels, the discovery of God as love is expressed in the parables about treasures and precious pearls. Once the treasure is discovered, nothing else matters, the only way forward is to sell everything and gain the treasure, the pearl beyond price. John of the Cross uses the words *nada* (nothing) and *toda* (all) in this context. For John even though his life was full of many and varied activities all of these were *nada* before the utter loveliness and wonder of the deep loving experiences of God that came into his life. God became all (*toda*) for John.

John believed, as all mystics do, that God gave him the gift of loving knowledge. He trusted, he believed that all this is possible. In the Christian tradition, this is what is called faith. It is, at heart, a sense of loving trust in God, in God's promise and what God can do in our humanity. However, while faith in God might not be easily acceptable today faith, trust among human beings is crucial to life. We trust people in so many ways, from our parents to our lovers, or to those who do practical things on our behalf. We have faith in the train driver, or the engineer who designed the bridge we are driving over.

It is commonplace to claim that we live in an era almost devoid of faith, but is that really the case? In the past, the social and cultural climate was favourable to belief in God. There was a community of values between art, science and religion. Dante, Shakespeare, Newton and Beethoven believed in values over and above their work. Today it would seem that nothing can be certain and that all values are relative. However, is that the full picture or is there a liberal establishment saying one thing while there are still many people who would be willing to risk believing? Perhaps it would be more realistic to say that right across society there are still many who believe in God and many more who would like to be helped to come to a sense of a personal God. Is the mystic someone who could speak lovingly to modern men and women, speaking of experiences that could resonate in their feelings, in their imaginations?

John the Poet

John of the Cross can certainly address our imagination because he expressed his deep religious experiences in poetry. He found a poetic voice which sang beautifully of his intimate experiences.

John had shown a great love for poems, songs and music when he worked in the hospital at Medina. He had a gift of easing the pain of patients by singing songs which he had composed. This gift seemed to go underground when he studied theology but was given a new lease of life by Teresa of Avila, who wanted him to break out of his seriousness. Teresa herself was no mean poet and she often challenged John to cap some poem she had written.

However, it was his experience of imprisonment at Toledo in 1577–8 that gave rise to his great poetic outpouring. The intensity of his suffering and his simultaneous awareness of God's love and goodness gave birth to an amazing lyric voice in John.

John's love of poetry had its roots in the popular songs he heard as a boy in Medina. Medina was famous for its market and the crowds were entertained by singers with their repertoire of love-songs. John also had a chance to study literature, first of all at the Jesuit College and then during the noviciate. He would have read the great Latin poets, such as Horace and Ovid, and also the poems of a contemporary Spanish poet, Garcilaso de la Vega. Garcilaso was a young man about the Spanish Court who cut rather an heroic figure. He died young, but his poems were full of invention and innovation. John was obviously impressed with his work, especially the sensitive way he wrote of nature. John loved nature and felt a kinship with Garcilaso's imaginative approach.

John's poetic output is not huge. In fact the totality of his works comes to about 40 pages in *The Collected Works*. His poetry dates from 1578, with 'The Spiritual Canticle' being among the earliest of his works, and with 'The Living Flame of Love', written in 1585, rounding off his poetic output.

Rather than talking about and around John's poetry it would be better to let John speak for himself. For this purpose, the poem 'The Dark Night' would be a good choice. The text and translation comes from *The Collected Works of St John of the Cross*, edited and translated by Kieran Kavanaugh and Otilio Rodriguez.

NOCHE OSCURA
Canciones de el alma que se goza de haber llegado al alto esta-do de la perfección, que es la unión con Dios, por el camino de la negación espiritual.

I
En una noche oscura,
con ansias, en amores inflamada,
¡oh dichosa ventura!
salí sin ser notada
estando ya mi casa sosegada.

II

A oscuras y segura,
por la secreta escala disfrazada,
¡oh dichosa ventura!
a oscuras y en celada,
estando ya mi casa sosegada.

III

En la noche dichosa,
en secreto, que nadie me veía,
ni yo miraba cosa,
sin otra luz y quía
sino la que en el corazón ardía.

IV

Aquésta me guiaba
más cierto que la luz del mediodía,
adónde me esperaba
quien yo bien me sabía,
en parte donde nadie parecía.

V

¡Oh noche que guiaste!
¡Oh noche amable más que el alborada!
¡Oh noche que juntaste
Amado con amada,
amada en el Amado transformada!

VI

En mi pecho florido,
que entero para él solo se quardaba,
allí quedó dormido,
y yo le regalaba,
y el ventalle de cedros aire daba.

VII

El aire de la almena,
cuando yo sus cabellos esparcía,
con su mano serena
en mi cuello hería
y todos mis sentidos suspendía.

VIII

Quedéme y olvidéme,
el rostro recliné sobre el Amado,
cesó todo y dejéme,
dejando me cuidado
entre las azucenas olvidado.

THE DARK NIGHT

Songs of the soul that rejoices in having reached the high
state of perfection, which is union with God, by the path of
spiritual negation.

I

One dark night,
fired with love's urgent longings
– ah, the sheer grace! –
I went out unseen,
my house being now all stilled.

II

In darkness, and secure,
by the secret ladder, disguised,
– ah, the sheer grace! –
in darkness and concealment,
my house being now all stilled.

III

On that glad night
in secret, for no one saw me,
nor did I look at anything
with no other light or guide
than the one that burned in my heart.

IV

This guided me
more surely than the light of noon
to where he was awaiting me
– him I knew so well –
there in a place where no one appeared.

V

O guiding night!
O night more lovely than the dawn!
O night that has united
the Lover with his beloved,
transforming the beloved in her Lover.

VI

Upon my flowering breast,
which I kept wholly for him alone,
there he lay sleeping,
and I caressing him
there in a breeze from the fanning cedars.

VII

When the breeze blew from the turret,
as I parted his hair,
it wounded my neck
with its gentle hand,
suspending all my senses.

VIII

I abandoned and forgot myself,
laying my face on my Beloved;
all things ceased; I went out from myself,
leaving my cares
forgotten among the lilies.

John wrote this poem in the months after his escape from Toledo. It is rich in symbolism and, while a translation can never capture the power of the original poem, there is more than enough to enjoy. The poem uses the symbol of night in a way that draws out a sense of mystery. The night recalls the darkness of John's prison cell and the times of darkness when he must have been torn by a range of conflicting emotions. Was he in prison because he was at fault? Why had his own turned against him? But night is also a time of mystery when deep feelings can well up, a time to begin a journey.

In fact, the opening stanza, which rejoices in the freedom of the Lover to leave the house, echoes the Song of Songs:

Upon my bed at night
I sought him whom my soul loves;
I sought him, but found him not ...
'I will rise now and go about the city ...
I will seek him whom my soul loves.' (SONG OF SONGS 3:1–2)

Because the Lover feels so passionately, the night is no longer a threat – the rapturous love inside her soul is like a light. The light in her heart is a better guide than a full moon. The burning love is not only a light but it seems like a guiding, homing beacon as she finds her Beloved. In stanza V, John introduces a new symbolic element as the poem sings of the night in language that echoes the great Easter hymn of light, the *Exsultet*. Stanza V begins:

O guiding night!
O night more lovely than the dawn!

while the *Exsultet* proclaims:

Of this night scripture says:
The night will be as clear as day:
it will become my light, my joy.

In stanza VI of 'The Dark Night', the Beloved rests and sleeps on the Lover's breast because the purification has been so complete that it has become the most fitting place for union and in that closeness the wound of union takes place. The union is beyond anything the senses can begin to describe or comprehend. The union is also expressed as a wound, as the immensity of love is painful to the human spirit as the finite is overwhelmed by the infinite. So it feels a pain at being unable to take in such love in its entirety. This is a state which Teresa of Avila also experiences and describes in her writings.

So the Lover, who stands for you and I as we journey to God, has found perfect union with God. The final stanza takes us to fulfilment and hints at the joy of heaven, the beatific vision. This state of union where only God matters is the mystic state, and John maintains that human beings can experience such closeness to God in this life. The poem, as it moves from the house to finding the Beloved, expresses a journey that is a wonderful risk. Perhaps John is trying to tell us that because we perceive the image of God in our humanity, then if we trust enough in who we are we can be passionately close to God. This sense of trust is implied in the closing lines:

I went out from myself,
leaving my cares
forgotten among the lilies.

These lines link the poem by allusion to the Sermon on the Mount, where Christ uses the beauty of the lilies of the field to emphasise God's care for us and our need to trust in that care:

> *'Consider the lilies of the field, how they grow; they neither toil nor spin, yet I tell you, even Solomon in all his glory was not clothed like one of these.'* (MATTHEW 6:28–29)

The technique behind 'The Dark Night' warrants examination and provides insights into the way John crafted his experiences. John once told a friend that when he tried to compose poetry, 'Sometimes God gave me words and sometimes I looked for them myself.' Obviously, a good working knowledge of Spanish is needed to appreciate the details of John's art, but with the help of translation the essence of the poems can still be touched.

What is obvious is the simplicity of the language. Adjectives are few, but the nouns and verbs carefully chosen – all have force. The word 'night' appears and reappears, growing richer and richer in meaning. It begins as the night that enables the Lover to start on the quest; gradually, by the third stanza, it is linked to joy, and by the fifth stanza it has become the means for the lovers' union. In the same stanza, there's the marvellous way the union is described – at once economical and also allowing the force of the words to underline the marvel.

> *Amado con amada,*　　　　　*The Lover with his beloved,*
> *amada en el Amado transformada!*　　*transforming the beloved in*
> 　　　　　　　　　　　　　　*her Lover.*

The reader just has to say the Spanish aloud to get the feeling of the union taking place, the very sound conveys a sense of amazing communion of ecstatic love.

Other Poems

One of the poems which John brought out of prison was a song of rejoicing in knowing God through faith. 'For I know well the spring that flows and runs, although it is night.' For John, this is an eternal spring with an unknown origin, full of beauty and abundance. On an obvious level, the fountain is the source of hope that kept John going while he was in prison. It could also be the river Tagus that ran close by, becoming a memory of freedom and life for someone cooped up in the savage Castilian climate. Fountains, of course, bring pastoral memories, places where lovers meet, and such images from romantic poetry would have echoed in John's mind. However, as a Carmelite, John would have remembered a classic text that was part of his formation, *The Institutions of the First Monks.* The author, the Catalan Philip Ribot, writes of Carmelite origins and envisages the life of the hermits on Carmel. The early Carmelites living on Mount Carmel lived by the fount of the prophet Elijah. Elijah was the one who drank from the abundance of the torrent Kerith in time of drought. Drinking from the torrent in this text is a metaphor for intimate union with God. It is a description of mystical experience, one which Carmelites down the ages were told could be part of their life, their prayer.

Besides all this – and part of the richness of John's work in allowing his memory to be quarried for his poems – are the allusions to the Scriptures. John evokes rather than quotes, and allows his various allusions to grow like a tapestry. Again, all of this was a creative process taking place in confinement, with memory as the sole source. The living and ever more powerful source of water echoes the visions of the prophet Ezekiel, but more than anything, the reader is aware of imagery inspired by the gospel according to John. The living waters and the living bread speak of baptism and eucharist, and the texture of the poem is at times dominated by Joannine themes. 'This eternal fountain is concealed from sight within this living bread to give us life' (CF. JOHN 4:7–15 AND 6:41–51).

Another prison poem is a ballad based on Psalm 137, 'By The Rivers of Babylon'. The prison in Toledo has become John's Babylon, his place of exile, and yet he lives in hope and trust. While he is in this harsh place he undergoes an amazing purification, as if by fire. Love strikes, and in the process of wounding him John finds that love is actually taking his heart over:

There love wounded me
and took away my heart.

This paradox is carried to a further stage:

I died within myself for you,
and for you I revived.

Here, John is echoing St Paul's teaching that those who come to know Christ want to die to anything that could separate them from God's love, and only want the new life that is Christ. John wants to risk everything to gain the great treasure – God. As he composes this poem in prison, John is realizing how radical the process of reaching real freedom is – the freedom to be really open to God.

'The Spiritual Canticle'

The great poem of his imprisonment in Toledo is 'The Spiritual Canticle'. The first 31 stanzas were written in prison and the last eight were added between 1579 and 1584. The 'Canticle' expresses the deep mystical experience that came out of John's time in prison. The expression of what, on one level, could be beyond words comes from John's memories, his subconscious and his deep knowledge of Scripture. An insight into the poem's composition from the twentieth century could help us understand the creative process behind this and other of John's prison poems. The various Beirut hostages, victims of the Lebanese conflict, kept themselves sane by reciting poems they remembered from child-hood or told themselves stories from whatever source their memories provided.

John gives this poem the subtitle: 'Songs between the soul and the Bridegroom'. The soul, the Bride, is called the Lover who searches for the Beloved who is Christ. The first two stanzas set the scene and also show the influences behind the poem.

I

BRIDE *Where have you hidden,*
Beloved, and left me moaning?
You fled like the stag
after wounding me;
I went out calling you, but you were gone.

II

Shepherds, you who go
up through the sheepfolds to the hill,
if by chance you see
him I love most,
tell him I am sick, I suffer, and I die.

The obvious influence is the Song of Songs, but what matters is the way John uses and transforms his material. The opening stanza reflects the conflict going on inside John in prison. He loves God and yet feels deserted. He has loved God as fiercely as any human lover and yet feels lost, alone. The wound is the wound of love and also a sense of loss. Who knows that during his imprisonment John did not go through a time of darkness and shock? Why was he misunderstood? At such times, fear, and perhaps even doubt about his relationship with God, pressed in on him. These two stanzas can operate on various levels of interpretation, but they are in one sense a great cry of pain from John, feeling abandoned and confused in his prison cell.

However, if the poem is John's reworking of the Song of Songs as an ecstatic poem, helping us to have images of the mystical, then the cry is the expression of the deepest desire for God. In this context, the wounding is not some pain inflicted by God but the sensation a human being has when exposed to fullness of God. Wounding is, for John, the sensation of ecstatic prayer, as it was for St Teresa. There is a famous statue by Bernini (1598–1680) that represents St Teresa of Avila in ecstasy, where Teresa is seen with arms outstretched while an angel pierces her heart with a spear.

The setting for the lovers' search is pastoral with shepherds and beautiful rolling countryside. The Lover is distraught and over-whelmed by the beauty and power of the Beloved, so much so that it seems that she can no longer survive. She cries:

Reveal your presence,
and may the vision of your beauty be my death

Then the beautiful stanza:

O spring like crystal!
If only, on your silvered-over faces,
you would suddenly form
the eyes I have desired,
that I bear sketched deep within my heart.

The Beloved appears, and the sense of union begins to emerge, with image after image impacting to create the joy of union with God. The Beloved is everything marvellous in nature and the Lover, having drunk of the wine, feels freedom. The Beloved giving his heart makes the Lover his bride and the soul is now totally given to the Beloved.

For now I practise love and love alone

The Lover knows that the Beloved is enthralled with her because even the hairs on the nape of her neck seem fascinating. This whimsical and yet deeply erotic image points up just how much God is involved with us. The next image shows how God's gazing on us changes us because we become imprinted with the grace and loveliness of the Divine. One of the most memorable images of the sheer delight and play that exist in a deep relationship between God and the one loved is in the following stanza.

Catch us the foxes,
for our vineyard is now in flower,
while we fashion a cone of roses
intricate as the pine's
and let no one appear on the hill.

Then the Bride enters into the long-desired and pleasant garden, lying at ease resting in the Beloved's gentle arms.

Fulfilment, rest, joy and peace. The apple tree is now a place of healing, in contrast to the tree in Eden. The garden image is both pastoral and biblical, but also a special one for John. Carmel means 'the Garden of the Lord', a space for God, and John's work in the Reform was to create true Carmels, true Gardens of the Lord. During his years of founding communities, one of his joys was to design and create gardens, places where friars and nuns could have space to enjoy the beauty of nature and find God. So it is no accident that the joy of union is found in the garden.

'The Living Flame of Love'

The last of the poems to be considered is 'The Living Flame of Love'. This was composed in Granada between 1582 and 1584. The poem and the subsequent commentary were written for Doña Ana y Peñalosa, a devout laywoman that John directed. The poem and the commentary speak of the summit of mystical experience.

The poem is in a different form, having six rather than five lines per stanza, and it has a sense of ascending movement, like a dance. It is full of cries:

Oh llama de amor viva ...	*O living flame of love ...*
Oh cauterio suave	*O Sweet cautery,*
Oh regalada llaga ...	*O delightful wound! ...*
Oh mano blanda	*O gentle hand!*
Oh toque delicado ...	*O delicate touch ...*
Oh lamparas de fuego ...	*O lamps of fire! ...*

The ecstasy is both painful and yet delightful. The wound, the burn hurts yet it is sweet and delicate, the hand is soft. The poem shows the paradox of comfort coming with pain and the sense of healing as the one searching for God goes beyond a certain stage.

The phrase 'lamps of fire' is also evocative of the Spirit coming down as tongues of fire (CF. ACTS 2:1–4). For John, in this poem, the one who is in union with the Beloved is also united with the Spirit, the bond of love between Christ and the Father. The Spirit is a living flame, but is also love and a comforter. It is because John, in expressing his sense of deepest union with God, takes us into the life of the Christian God who is one and yet three, that he begins to find communication difficult. He is looking into mystery which for him is reality and yet at the same time, beyond the grasp of reason and intelligence. Language reaches breaking point, and so the language of the poem, with its cries and a seeming absence of verbs, proclaims that a boundary has been reached. Perhaps this is why John changes from five to six lines per stanza, to hint at the abundance of the Spirit. John now realizes that his union with the Beloved, with Christ, is possible because the love of God is at work in him, effecting a painful and yet loving transformation.

Transformed, John is able to rest with the Beloved and experience what St Augustine hoped for in his famous saying, 'my heart shall be restless till it rests in thee'. In this poem, John shows us that under the influence of the Spirit, the event the great Augustine thought impossible can happen even in this life. Our humanity, because of its origins in God, is apt for union with God when we open ourselves in trust to our creator.

Reading John's poems, with their powerful descriptions of the mystic state, the union of a human being with God, the question that confronts us is: Where does all this fit in with contemporary experience? The twentieth century is a century that has witnessed sexual revolution, bringing with it a new freedom in talking about and expressing human sexuality. In that context, John's poems have something to say about the value and power of erotic interpersonal love. If the reality of erotic love gives the mystic images and a language to express the relation between the divine and human, then conversely the mystic wants to tell modern men and women to look again at their sexuality and their sexual relations. The mystic would want people today to place a high value on sexual intimacy and to value it as the highest possible form of communication, in which the whole person should be affirmed and enhanced. In the spirit of the Book of Genesis, John's poetry speaks to us today of the goodness of creation, the goodness of sexuality.

The Prose Works

John of the Cross wrote four great prose works which began as commentaries on his poems but in reality they provide his vision of how we achieve union with God. The four works are *The Ascent of Mount Carmel, The Dark Night, The Spiritual Canticle* and *The Living Flame of Love.* They were written between 1579 and 1586 and were meant to help friars and nuns of the Discalced Reform in their relationship to God. John, therefore, was writing for people who were committed to an ever closer union with God and were ready to be challenged by what he had to say. He usually knew the people he was writing for and felt free to be himself in what he said. Again, we must remember that the temperament of sixteenth-century Spaniards was vigorous – willing to be stretched and not satisfied with compromise. It is a whole mental universe away from the modern world, with its uncertainties and the need for most of life to be on the level of instant gratification. It was a world of faith, and for these nuns and friars, their Carmelite Rule presented the following of Christ as a core value.

John wrote in a plain, direct way. He did not indulge in flowery, rhetorical writing. There are frequent quotations from the Bible and, of course, there is the influence of scholastic theology and philosophy. Aquinas and Augustine are the theologians who formed his world view. However, what does make his prose works difficult are his long parentheses. He can be very wordy at times, wandering off his subject and leaving the reader quite bewildered. A sentence can end up being a paragraph long, and John was well aware of this tendency. Another problem was the fact that he often broke off from writing because of the various responsibilities he had in the Reform. When he came back to the text he would often retrace his steps, treating the same material twice over in slightly differing ways.

At this stage it would be helpful to have an overview of the prose works and then look at the key concepts in greater detail.

The Ascent of Mount Carmel is closely linked to *The Dark Night*. John wrote these treatises between 1579 and 1584 and their focus is his poem, 'The Dark Night'.

The text of *The Ascent of Mount Carmel* is prefaced by a sketch of Mount Carmel or the Mount of Perfection. It was originally drawn for the nuns at Beas, but copies were made for the friars in Baeza and Granada. It is meant to be a summary of the book and the verses that accompany it express the antithesis between *todo* (all) and *nada* (nothing) which is at the core of his thinking. This antithesis can seem off-putting, but in fact *nada*, or nothing, is part of a process that achieves deep personal freedom – the off-loading of baggage that prevents personal growth. The way of *nada* is part of the journey called the dark night.

Nada is not meant to imply anything life denying nor does it mean putting the created into second place. It is meant to be positive, it is about genuine growth. However, this journey is something John will explain in detail. At this stage, it is useful to compare the journey with gospel images. The way to God is by the narrow path or the narrow gateway, the broad highway is not the way to go (CF. MATTHEW 7:13–14).

John refers to four different 'nights', which are all phases of the dark night of faith by which the soul journeys to union with God. John's analysis is built on two pairs of terms: **sense** and **spirit**; **active** and **passive**.

The active night of the sense can be initiated by anyone who wants to be closer to God. This night consists essentially in correcting obviously sinful behaviour and self-centred gratification.

The movement from **the active night of the spirit** to **the passive night of the sense** is a movement from meditation to contemplative prayer. It is also a time when obvious consolations associated with prayer fade away and the individual is challenged to live by faith and to let God take control.

The passive night of the spirit is a final purification which leads to deep mystical experience. It demands patience and is a slow process. The individual can feel powerless, crushed; everything seems dark. It is as if God has abandoned the individual concerned. The other side of this night is mystical union.

John's ordered treatment of the 'nights' does not mean that everyone has to come to union with God in this precise way. It is important to remember that this scheme is not an absolute. It is something that takes place inside someone open to God. Therefore the teaching on the night only makes sense when we respect the uniqueness of the person and remember that God's action in our lives has a freedom and gratuitous quality that can never be analysed or predicted.

The Ascent was written after John had experienced such close union with God, first of all in prison, and then in the time that followed that harrowing period. He had journeyed and now, on the summit, he could see the best way to travel and wanted to share the joy he had found. He was also aware that there were many people who desired closeness with God but had no guides. He wanted, therefore, to give people solid, substantial doctrine to help them.

John introduces the concept of the dark night immediately as the way a person grows closer to God. He points out that what he has to say will not be easy and apologizes for his 'awkward style'. He stresses he is writing for people who are already taking all this very seriously – the friars and nuns of the Reform.

It needs to be made quite clear that John saw the dark night as being initiated by God, but that does not mean that the individual concerned is totally passive in the process. Another aspect of the dark night is the way a person so affected has the feeling that God seems to be absent, it is important to recognize that this is a seeming absence of God. It is not as if God has withdrawn from a person's life. Again it needs to be noted that not everyone in their journey to God passes through the 'dark night'. In an attempt to understand what John means by the 'dark night', the reader must always remember that the person who has entered this process has to play his or her part. John would not want to deny our basic freedom or our use of reason.

The 'dark night' is, then, a freeing of desires so that the individual is not caught up with lesser gods; this in a way is a joy and a gift from God. John is anxious that his reader's way of living is not habitually fixed on realities that would eclipse God. Creation is good, but it is the way we use it that matters and it is important to live under the rule of Christ's love to give life its proper focus. John then shows in Book I, Chapter XIII, that following Christ must be everything if the necessary purification is to be achieved. Echoing the Carmelite Rule, he stresses the need to reflect on Christ's life as found in the Scriptures. It is in that love for Christ, who is at the centre of our lives, that we gain the motivation to rid ourselves of desires and ways of living that are not open to God.

Books II and III are dominated by John's reflections on faith. For John, faith or the life of faith is a 'dark night'. Dark because it is beyond intelligence and the intellect is not equipped to cope with its light. It is like a night animal whose eyes are attuned to the dark but then cannot cope with the brightness of daylight. Faith is directed to Christ, who is light – this sense of Christ as light is a powerful image in the gospel of John. It is in this context then that union with God can happen, because a person becomes open to the possibility of loving knowledge – wisdom being communicated to the core of one's being.

John also makes the point that while union with Christ is the goal of this active purification, we all reach it in an individual manner, a way special to each one of us. An interesting aspect of

John's teaching is the way he wants to ground this faith journey in the life of the Church and how much he values the role of reason, not wanting people to go running off looking for apparitions and miraculous statues. He sees the restlessness implied in such activity as running counter to what matters, which is putting all one's energy into the union with Christ. John was conscious that in a society that was by and large illiterate, there was a danger that people could bestow magical properties on statues or paintings. For John, the Church in its teaching role had to call for objectivity in these matters. The phenomenon of weeping or miraculous statues is still common today, and bishops often become unpopular when they caution people against credulity.

The theological virtues – faith, hope and charity – are seen as crucial by John in the work of purification.

The intellect must be perfected in the darkness of faith, the memory in the emptiness of hope and the will in the nakedness and absence of every affection.

For John, these virtues empty the person of all that is not God and help prayer life to grow simple, moving from words and concepts to a sense of intimate friendship. *The Ascent* finishes abruptly since, for myriad reasons, John found he could not move onto the next area of teaching which concerned him – the passive purification. John saw the passive purification as the special way God acted on the human person so that radical growth could take place in the core of that person. In terms of commenting on the poem *The Ascent* only touches on two stanzas!

The Passive Night

The Dark Night covers material that John had wanted to deal with in *The Ascent* but never managed to achieve, namely the passive purification. It looks at God's action on the human person. John claims that in this commentary he will be more faithful to the poem itself. He is, to a great degree, but ends the work with a comment on the first line of only the third stanza. John is most interested in sharing the experience expressed in the first two stanzas of the poem. He wants to tell his readers of the joy of union with God and how he has escaped from all the negative aspects of his personality to reach that stage.

The commentary combines personal experience along with theological reflection. Book I looks at the passive night of the senses while Book II examines the passive night of the spirit. John makes it clear that while much of the journeying to full union with God is the result of divine action, this does not mean that the individual has nothing to contribute. It is a principle of Catholic theology that all the work of people being saved, achieving union with God involves human co-operation. While it is true that human nature is finite or limited, that does not mean it cannot be open to God, to the divine working on the human. What human beings have to do is to be willing to be open to God, and then God will achieve wonderful things in the individual. St Paul expresses the action of God on humanity in the letter to the Ephesians: 'Glory be to him whose power, working in us, can do infinitely more than we can ask or imagine' (EPHESIANS 3:20).

The signs of the passive night of the senses are:

1 There is no sense of consolation present in any aspect of life, definitely no consolation from prayer.
2 Trying to serve God but getting nowhere and feeling that they are far from God. The reason for this is that God is trying to move us from feeling good about God to a deeper awareness.

3 A movement from meditation to contemplative prayer. In other words the agenda for prayer comes from God, not methods and modes of our choosing.

The passive night of the spirit is described in Chapter IV of the Book II. Here, a new way of loving and understanding is achieved. The intellect, purified by God, no longer operates under its own vigour but by means of divine wisdom. The act of loving, which, for John, is rooted in the will, now comes from the action of the Holy Spirit. John sees this as the loving wisdom of God which purges and illumines a human being and prepares us for union with God. All of this is painful because it goes beyond our normal way of thinking and of being in control. The letting go, allowing God to have the initiative, brings a new freedom and a new sense of the presence of God through faith and love.

Again, John finished the commentary when he felt he had done all he could to help his readers. The rest is for us to apply to our personal situations. Let John speak as the commentary concludes:

> *Love alone, which at this period burns by soliciting the heart for the Beloved, is what guides and moves her, and makes her soar to God in an unknown way along the road of solitude.*

Mystical Understanding

The commentary on *The Spiritual Canticle* was written at the request of Mother Ana de Jesus, Prioress of the Discalced Carmelite nuns at St Joseph's in Granada, in 1584. Ana de Jesús was one of the great figures of the Carmelite Reform and a person of deep faith and commitment. She was a close friend of John of the Cross, having known him since 1575. In the latter part of her life she went on to France and Belgium where she founded a number of convents.

The fact that the commentary was written for the nuns at Granada indicates a high level of interest and understanding. The community under their idealistic superior would have been eager for help in their own lives. John often came to give talks to the community, finding them willing listeners, and it is out of this context that the commentary was born.

Contemporary sources show the nuns found the poem dazzling in its imagery and beauty. They would have recognized the links with the Song of Songs and known that the poem was an expression in lyric form of John's profound experience.

John states his intentions quite openly, almost naïvely, in writing in the prologue to the commentary.

> *These stanzas Reverend Mother were obviously composed with a certain burning love of God. The wisdom and charity of God is so vast, as the Book of Wisdom states, that it reaches from end to end [WISDOM 8:1] and the soul informed and moved by it bears in some way this very abundance and impulsiveness in her words ... It would be foolish to think that expressions of love arising from mystical understanding, like these stanzas, are fully explainable. The Spirit of the Lord, who abides in us and aids our weakness, as St Paul says [ROMANS 8:26] pleads for us with unspeakable groanings in order to manifest what we can neither fully understand nor comprehend.*

John goes on to say that detailed explanations are not possible as 'the abundant meanings of the Holy Spirit cannot be caught in words'. Again, John makes the point that the commentary aims to shed some light on the poem as he is conscious that the 'stanzas were composed in a love flowing from abundant mystical understanding'. Finally, John apologizes for using scholastic theology as a means of expression, even though he knows it could well be off-putting. John would have been aware that by using too much technical language he would have lost half of his readers. The Carmelite Friars who studied academic theology would have been conversant with such language, but the nuns would not have had access to university faculties. John would be delighted to see in the twentieth century that men and women had equal opportunities in these areas.

There is one problematic factor with John's commentary. Two editions of the commentary are extant. The first or A text is favoured by Fr Lucien, a French Carmelite who writes on John in *La Dictionnaire de Spiritualité,* and by many other experts, including Gerald Brenan in his perceptive work, *St John of the Cross: his life and poetry.* However, Kieran Kavanaugh of the American Carmelite school favours the B text, in the edition of John of the Cross's works published in 1991 by the Institute of Carmelite Studies, Washington. There is an important difference between the two editions. The A text follows the original shape of the poem, where the intimate union with the Lover and the Beloved takes place in this life. The B text alters the order of the stanzas, suggesting the fullness of union between the Lover and Beloved as being a reality that occurs in the Beatific Vision, in other words in the next life.

Why did the changes take place and what importance can be read into the new edition? Perhaps John made the changes as a result of conversations with the nuns, or perhaps he was anxious that his ideas, once they were in the public forum, could be criticized by the Inquisition. Whatever the reason, many experts would favour the A text because it allows for a greater optimism about the possibility of an intimacy with God in this life. It would indicate a sense that our human nature working with God can achieve the sublime here and now.

In some ways, the commentary on the 'Canticle' is disappointing. John admits in the prologue that his poem comes from love and mystical experience. Once he starts to explain this and that aspect of the work, there is a feeling that the poem is being dragged down. There is a whole world of difference between inspiration and interpretation. Another problem arises out of John's need to see or explain everything as allegorical so that mountains for instance stand for virtues. The poem is beyond allegory, it is stating a deeply personal experience. It is about love at its most sublime.

The 'Canticle', if it can be explained, must be seen in the light of its relationship to the Song of Songs, but even then there are complexities. John had so made the biblical text part of his life that the Song of Songs was part of his mind's eye and would have influenced his poetry and been quarried at a subliminal level. It was like the air he breathed.

The commentary, then, needs to be seen in its context – a guidebook to help the nuns he loved so much both achieve the joy of union with God and avoid pitfalls along the way. His friend St Teresa would in these circumstances have written a treatise. John prefers a commentary on his poem, but in the end the poem rather than the commentary is the best guide.

Spiritual Marriage

Both the poem 'The Living Flame of Love' and the prose commentary were written for Doña Ana y Peñalosa. Doña Ana, a widow, lived in Granada, and when the first Carmelite nuns came to Granada, Doña Ana allowed them to use her house until their convent was ready. Doña Ana became a close friend of Ana de Jesús, the Prioress, and subsequently got to know John of the Cross. John of the Cross was to become the guide of this generous woman who wanted help in her prayer life. It was quite unusual for a laywoman to be helped in this way, but it was a case of two generous people meeting. At the time, the whole question of meditation and contemplative prayer was under scrutiny by the Spanish Inquisition. This body, anxious to preserve both Church and national unity, was always suspicious of anything that was not initiated by the institutional Church. Gifted people like John could and did come under investigation as there were always people who could be jealous. It is interesting to note that when John does go public in his commentaries he is very careful to show modesty and deference to the Church's authority:

> *Only the faults and mistakes of this commentary will be mine. Submitting it to the judgement and better opinion of our Holy Mother the Roman Catholic Church, by whose rule no one errs, finding my support in Sacred Scripture.*

John was not a person who sought any conflict with the Church authorities. However, misunderstanding often arises when people bent on bureaucratic action examine the work of someone gifted. The functionary can be well-versed in law but perhaps fails to recognize the depth and beauty of the visionary. In our present era, great Christian thinkers like Yves Conger and Teilhard de Chardin have been misunderstood. John had to cope with people who were on the defensive, suspicious of anything that was out of the ordinary.

In the commentary on 'The Living Flame of Love', John treats each stanza of the poem in detail. In many ways what he writes is a continuation of his teaching about the possibility of perfect union with God, or Spiritual Marriage. In *The Spiritual Canticle*, John describes Spiritual Marriage as:

> *a total transformation in the Beloved in which each surrenders the entire possession of self to the other ... The soul becomes divine, becomes God through participation in so far as it is possible in this life.*

St Paul expressed the intimacy of this union when he says: 'I live, now not I, but Christ lives in me' (GALATIANS 2:20). At the core of *The Living Flame* is the activity of the Holy Spirit, the flame. For John, people purified by the flame live even now on the threshold of eternal life. The action of the Spirit seems to be ready to take us out of this life.

> *With ardent desire the soul tells the flame the Holy Spirit to tear the*
> *veil of mortal life now by that sweet encounter in which he truly com-*
> *municates entirely what he is ... That is complete and perfect glory.*

John stresses in this work the glory that the human person can encounter, and the beauty of the relationship that is possible with the triune God, Father, Son and Spirit. Faith is no longer dark, the veil is almost transparent and light floods in. In short, a state of perfect love has been achieved.

John wrote this commentary over quite a short period, in between carrying out his varied tasks as a superior in the Reform. In the last months of his life he revised the texts influenced by his prayer life, eager to tell people that God has amazing gifts for those who turn to him with all their being.

Letters

No account of John's prose works would be complete without reference to his letters. We have only 33 of his letters. The reason there are so few is that a campaign of vilification was mounted against John in the last years of his life. The climate of fear that was generated and the ever present reality of the Inquisition caused friends and disciples to destroy his letters. We know that, but for a change of climate in the Reform following John's death, it was possible that all of his works could have been lost. As it was, his works were viewed with suspicion until Clement X declared him blessed in 1675 and Benedict XIII canonized him in 1726.

The letters that remain, and sadly there is no correspondence with his mother and brother, show John as a loving, tender person. Some commentators have seen John as austere and negative, yet nothing could be further from the truth. Many of his letters are meant to help nuns and friars as they journeyed to God, but the tone is warm, immediate – as if he were there in the room talking. At times he shows how much he misses people when he has to move to different tasks in different parts of Spain. He also gives advice on business, especially when he sees the nuns being treated unfairly. He is not beyond telling them to give businessmen a dose of their own medicine! He also warns the Prioress of Cordoba against having strict observance for its own sake.

Two letters survive written to Doña Ana y Peñalosa in August and September 1591, shortly before his death. John is living in the remote Priory of Peñuela and describes something of his life and feelings.

> This morning we have already returned from gathering our chickpeas and so the mornings go by. On another day we shall thresh them. It is nice to handle these mute creatures, better than being badly handled by living ones. God grant that I may stay here. Pray for this, my daughter. But even though I am so happy here, I would not fail to come should you desire.

These comments are an amazing insight into the feelings of a loving man, free to express his emotions and obviously valuing his friendship with Doña Ana. John particularly valued friendship more and more as he grew older. Why? Because as he experienced closeness to God he became more fully aware of his own worth and the worth of others. He was, in the language of his poetry, free to leave the house and to go out finding love from God and his contemporaries.

In September he received a packet of letters from Doña Ana. Already his last illness is overtaking him. He has a slight bout of fever that means he has to visit Ubeda for medicine. He ends the letter: 'I am closing on account of the fever, for I would like to write at greater length'.

The last letter we have of John's is a fragment from a letter written to a nun in Segovia whose identity is unknown. John was writing only days before his death and these words say so much about the man and his message.

Have a great love for those who contradict and fail to love you, for in this way love is begotten in a heart that has no love. God so acts with us, for he loves us that we might love by means of the very love he bears towards us.

Nada, the Night and the Twentieth Century

John of the Cross was shaped by his experience of being a Spaniard living at a time of change. Spain in the sixteenth century was a great power, but it was also a country of extremes and a definite fierceness. However, John was moulded by elements that transcend time and place: his Christian faith and the Carmelite tradition. What then does John have to say today to twentieth-century people, be they friars, nuns, or anyone seeking meaning in life?

To understand John of the Cross, we have to see him to some degree in the context of his time and we also have to acknowledge the influence of his scholastic formation. However, while John's intellectual framework may have been superseded, his writings do relate to the perennial in human nature. What is basic in John is basic to Christianity. John wants each person to allow God to be God for them, a God of love, of freedom, one who is turned towards the human race and asks that people relate to him and each other. It is in the context of this love of God that all of John's teaching about *nada*, the night and purification has its foundation. John proclaims the personal God of the Bible, the God of Abraham, Isaac and Joseph, the God revealed in Jesus Christ.

John of the Cross is like the prophets of the Old Testament in so far as he was impelled to proclaim the living God, and to show that there is no other God and the only way is God's way. Anything else or any other way for John is idolatry. In this he is like Elijah of old, who destroyed Jezebel's idols and journeyed to Mount Horeb where he encountered the living God (CF. 1 KINGS 18,19).

However, in the twentieth century, the denial of God is more common than his proclamation. Alongside this we find men and women filled or rather overwhelmed by uncertainty. The problem of the modern world is that nothing seems certain and, as a result, the transcendent is unthinkable. The rejection of God seems to go hand in hand with the rejection of our fellow human beings. The only relationship that seems consistent is my fascination with my computer and the hope that the next package will give me a window on reality I have never known before. But the computer is only an extension of myself and if anything it absorbs me to such a degree that all other possible relationships can be excluded.

The rejection of God and the breakdown of relationships mean that community suffers – our leaders even question if such a thing as society exists. The result can be a blind egotism that becomes impervious to injustice. The absence of God, the rejection of values, can mean a world of self-absorbed individuals driven by technology, achieving commercial success but with no feeling for the planet and no sense of a social audit.

It is in this context that people today need to hear John of the Cross's uncompromising message and to ensure that the essence of its content is made accessible to all. It is a teaching with substance. Even if at times John can sound fierce, pessimistic or demanding, what he has to say has a value that gives him every right to challenge his reader. He is a teacher whose message brings freedom, the freedom that allows each human being to realize their self, their person, in its fullness. John of the Cross would echo the gospel saying, 'The truth will set you free' (JOHN 8:32).

The Reality of God

What John wrote had its roots first and foremost in the Scriptures. The Carmelite tradition has always been one of immersing oneself in the Scriptures. Present-day Carmelites have been helped to continue this tradition by members of the Order who are biblical scholars. Their insights help their fellow Carmelites in their praying the Scriptures. John's theological formation and his studies at Salamanca offered a solid basis in theology. It is true that he did not go on to extra years of academic study but his overall formation was sound. Finally, John drew on his own experience of prayer and the traditions of the Carmelite order. Mention has been made of works like *The Institutions of the First Monks*, a fourteenth-century treatise which challenged Carmelites to see union with God as their *raison d'être*.

The Order's tradition holds that we can all experience the reality of God in this life. A modern Carmelite who expounded that reality was the Dutchman, Titus Brandsma. Titus, an academic and a journalist, proclaimed his beliefs in the face of Nazi domination of his homeland, Holland. On his way to the death camp after his arrest by the Gestapo, his meditations on the cross led to his own experience of mystical union that enabled him to face physical death in Dachau.

Titus was strongly influenced by John of the Cross and he gave many courses of lectures on the Saint at Nijmegean University. Christ's cross – indeed the whole Paschal Mystery – is at the heart of John's teaching. The Paschal Mystery, for Christians, concerns the life of Jesus, his suffering, death on the cross and resurrection, through which God has established a new intimate relationship with the human race. The first great relationship was established as the Israelites passed over from slavery to freedom under Moses. Jesus suffered, died and rose at the time the Passover was being celebrated, hence he is the new Passover and the event is known as The Paschal Mystery.

What is at the core of Jesus' saving work is the reality which reaches its triumphant outcome in the resurrection. The new fullness of life is only achieved by embracing the cross, offering oneself in loving obedience to the Father, even in death. For John of the Cross, the Paschal Mystery and its central role in Christian life was vital. Not for nothing when he entered the Reform did he add 'of the Cross' to his name. The cross stands for loving trust of the Father. It states that we will allow God freedom in our lives, and that suffering and love lead to the moment when, as in *The Living Flame*, we encounter God's Holy Spirit, the personification of divine love. It will lead to the possibility of union with God in this life and resurrection after physical death.

The diagram of the Mount of Perfection which John made for the nuns at Beas showed that following the narrow path of the gospel we can journey to the place where God's glory dwells. However, if we want to attain union with the One who is everything we have to travel by the way of *nada*, that way of detachment which brings true freedom. God is the one who lovingly invites us into this union and our response given in unquestioning generosity is the way of *nada*, allowing God freedom.

It is at this point that many commentators have found John austere, even objectionable. He has been called a fakir, and Abbot Chapman, an English Benedictine, thought of him as a Buddhist. It is easy to see his use of *nada* (nothing) as a way of escaping from the material world into a world of the mind, a world of rigorous self-discipline. Here we have a paradox, because John loved nature and obviously loved a whole variety of people – his relatives, his brother friars, the nuns and people who were special to him like Doña Ana and Teresa of Avila. He loved walking, feeling the sun and the wind on his face, and his poems show how the Spanish countryside with its wild beauty touched his heart. He loved gardening, he appreciated the very texture of stone used in building new priories, and to put a stop to outbreaks of seriousness and false austerities among the friars he would organize impromptu picnics and shake the over-zealous out of their self-importance. John could be strict on himself because he knew himself and knew his own limits. However, when it came to his confrères, he would advise them to live the rule of the Order and if they decided to live a more austere way, to remember the call to moderation which is at the heart of the Rule. Austerity, asceticism for its own sake, could end up as an ego trip.

John did not ask that those he was guiding should turn their back on life. What he was saying was that God is everything; nature and people in themselves, are as nothing. The way to come to love people and value our planet is to see them as God sees them in a loving, sustaining gaze. John does not want people to lose their identity, because after all it is the unique person that God loves and is calling into the relationship. What John is against is putting anything before God. He wants everyone to be free so that they can soar on eagles' wings, as even a silken thread can hold an eagle down. *Nada* is the true freedom that is meant to take us away from all that is negative in our lives and, above all, free us from alienation.

Denial

For us in the twentieth century, it is not just our own personal wrongdoings which prevent us putting God at the centre of our lives. It is the way society is structured. The way it operates with its presuppositions and at times its blindness. The market economy and the freedom that is supposed to follow in its train is great for some but brings suffering to many others. Certain things become essential and dominate lives. The motor car is a symbol of independence and freedom, yet it can be at the cost of ruining the atmosphere and at the expense of public transport.

Besides such obvious idols there are also the shadows and burdens of human inheritance. Over fifty years on, the world has yet fully to come to terms with the events of the Second World War. Few have been willing to acknowledge the crimes that both sides committed. We remember Nazi or Japanese atrocities, but talk of Dresden or Hiroshima is still regarded as unpatriotic. The shadow of the past still encourages violence in Northern Ireland and elsewhere, with people's fears fuelled by leaders who glory in violence. The West, through NATO and the UN, cannot always be honest. Nowadays, when we kill civilians in military operations we hide behind phrases such as 'collateral damage' – we cannot face facts and say a hospital was bombed by mistake.

John in his age knew of comparable denials. The cruelty of the Conquistadors in the Americas, the social inequality of which he had been a victim, and the imposition of orthodoxy by the Inquisition. John would want all of us, whether sixteenth-century nuns or twentieth-century folk, to be free from idols and totally open to God.

For John, *nada* was a God-given value, enabling us to see how everything speaks of the glory of God. Time and again in his poetry, Gerald Manley Hopkins (1844–1889) speaks of the glory of God in creation. 'The world is charged with the grandeur of God,' he proclaims in 'God's Grandeur'. This is no romantic cry but rather the prayer of a poet who could see the vision of creation. James Joyce (1882–1941), who felt that there was an essential conflict between poet and priest, often spoke of 'Epiphanies'. These were moments of sudden beauty, like the sheen of the sun on a wet slate roof, a sudden unexpected beauty which surely John of the Cross would have loved.

Ross Collings, an Australian Carmelite, in a recent study on John of the Cross reminds his readers that if they have a good theology of creation they can better understand how, for John, *nada*, the way of renunciation, does not clash with his joy in created beauty. Creation is not something in the past, nor is redemption, the process of God's saving work. They are both a process going on all the time with the love of God wanting to touch our world.

John reminds us of something basic to human experience, that two contraries cannot coexist. We have to give ourselves to God's sovereignty because if we give our hearts to the limited we will be limited. The heart has to be free to grow in God's love. As Jack Welch, an American Carmelite, says: 'We were made for great loves, little loves diminish us.' John is asking that in faith we surrender ourselves to the mystery that is God. God wants right relationships with us and we need to have a singleness of purpose and a clear vision so that we can attain the summit of the Mount of Perfection. John prefers, in his way of *nada*, the difficult to the easy, and he sees life that costs as the way to bring out our true humanity. In all of this we do not lose our identity but gain freedom from slavery. Also, if we discover our true identity through closeness to God then we can begin to value people more profoundly and our relationships will be based on an awareness of human dignity that flows from our being like to God. We are, as St Paul says, 'God's work of art' (EPHESIANS 2:10).

The Way of the Night

The way of *nada* is the way of the night, the way of faith. The word 'night' is perhaps one of the most powerful in John's teaching and yet it can be off-putting. The night is not a denial of life, but rather through the night we seek a way that will lead to union with God, the Beloved. This is a union that can best be described as a Mystical Marriage. Night stands as a symbol for purification, for escape from all that is negative, and it is also a place where true light is encountered. Again, to understand what is really meant by night in John's writing then the reader must see what is implied by faith.

Faith, for John, was part of our deepest self that is willing to accept truths revealed by God, truths that transcend natural light and exceed human understanding. In a multi-faith society, the question can be asked, Whose revelation do we accept? This book is based in the Judaeo-Christian tradition, the tradition that also formed John. However, that in no way means that other traditions are to be dismissed. John believed that faith was a gift by which God allows us to go beyond reason into the reality of the divine, and that gift is received through praying the Scriptures and living in the community of the Church. Faith is a personal, loving relationship with God, and becomes the bond that links us to other believers. While it is beyond reason, faith, through theology, can be articulated in a coherent manner. But because it does go beyond reason, faith is like a light that is brighter than anything we know.

The way into the experience of the night is the way of *nada*. While John talks about the night under a fourfold division, everyone experiences the night in their own personal, special way. The night can be seen as a path we join as we journey to God, a path which could take us all our middle life. As Dante wrote in *The Divine Comedy*, 'In the middle of life I found myself in a Dark Wood'. For Dante, the end of his journey was at the core of Paradise.

The night can also be likened to *kenosis* – the self-emptying of God in Jesus. When God sent his Son into the world he was willing to empty himself of all that was special and lived as we do, entering into the world of faith, travelling through the night of misunderstanding. Eventually he came to the ultimate night, the darkness of the cross, where his obedience brought him to the deepest sense of desolation, when he felt abandoned and cried out: 'My God, my God, why have you forsaken me?'

John's teaching on the dark night is found in *The Ascent of Mount Carmel* and *The Dark Night*. His inspiration for writing these commentaries had been the way he saw so many people who were supposed to be wise guides being far from helpful, not recognizing where people were at nor giving them the necessary challenges.

The most straightforward part of the journey is the active night of the sense. This involves facing up to ourselves and, because we want God to be the focus of our lives, becoming open to change. This is not a question of personal will-power, rather it is a willingness to recognize what has to change so we can grow as a person. We need, as *The Book of Common Prayer* expresses it, to be willing to acknowledge 'the devices and desires' of our heart. These 'devices and desires' can include all the games people play, ranging from power games to procrastination, or the way we misuse sexuality. Another aspect of facing up to ourselves is acknowledging our feelings, seeing what they are telling us and using them positively. It is well-nigh impossible to grow as a person if we allow our feelings of anger, jealousy or whatever to tick away inside us like a time bomb. Facing up to our feelings and taking appropriate action is a positive way to change and to grow as a person.

The active night of the sense also involves being honest about relationships. Positive relationships are good, but so often we can be possessive or destructive in our treatment of people. A true respect for human dignity will ensure that people are not used and abused. Even more negative is the way people can be idolized so that they feel trapped. The person who has put them on a pedestal is really signifying their own immaturity, as that sort of relationship diminishes both parties.

If a person is willing to be realistic and to allow growth, it is also necessary to face up to one's shadow side. John of the Cross would not have known of this technical term (one which features prominently in the psychology of Carl Jung), but he would recognize the concept easily. All during our life we have pushed underground aspects of reality either because we were told to keep quiet or our super ego was conditioned to behave in certain ways. Often this was to please people, to be correct, to be seen in a good light. We perform, live the roles but can never feel comfortable or really at ease. Anger, frustration and longings simmer away and we can pass a lifetime like this. Brave faces and bleeding hearts! Part of the resolve of the passive night of the senses would be, with the help of wise guidance, a willingness to face up to this baggage, this shadow side. It often means letting go of conventions, it can lead to confrontations but it does mean a healthier and more honest approach to life.

The active night of the spirit is again an area where the individual is involved in making choices that open us up to a more authentic union with God. John is conscious that people can relate more to a concept or an image of God than the very person. He is asking those who have experienced conversion, who have been drawn to God, to take steps to deepen and mature their faith. I believe in our own day John has an important message to those who have experienced a conversion and perhaps are living on a spiritual high. This can be seen in many groups but especially those of a Pentecostal or Charismatic nature. Such groups are found in all the mainstream churches and often in independent churches. At the point of conversion and for an indefinite period afterwards it is possible to feel great satisfaction in the new relationship with God. The fellowship of the group is vital and certain ways of praying and worshipping take on great importance. It then becomes possible to go to services, to engage in devotions because they are satisfying and become an end in themselves. For Catholics, there is also the bias towards visions – apparitions and certain places can be invested with immense importance. Also, ways of prayer become 'canonized', and the day is incomplete without having said this or that prayer.

John does not see this type of prayer life as deepening faith or bringing a person out of themselves so that they can be touched by the flame of the Spirit's love. What he proposes at this stage is a willingness to give up reliance on what the individual does and begin to practise contemplative prayer, which consists of a trusting waiting on God. John would also want us to move towards a reflective reading of Scripture. And in all this there should be a willingness to be still before the mystery of God. John, in stressing the Scriptures and inner peace, was going back to his Carmelite roots and to the traditions of prayer that had come down through the Middle Ages, such as *Lectio Divina*, the practice of quiet, reflective reading of the Scriptures. It is likely that he would have known of the exercises of St Ignatius as he had attended a college directed by the Jesuits, and by 1580 Ignatius' methods would have been widely diffused. John, however, would have seen the exercises as a step towards contemplative prayer, vital for beginners, but too systematic for the vision he had of a deeper immersion into the mystery of God.

John's attitude to a great deal of piety was firm. While he would have understood the value of popular religion, he was against the one-upmanship that went with running after the latest vision, miracle or whatever. He had nothing against people having a favourite image or finding a certain place helpful for prayer but all these things were in the end relative.

The passive night of the spirit and sense can seem daunting, and I believe it is important to see the end they are meant to achieve. This purification is a gift from God and enables us to reach a close-ness to God that is beautiful and beyond our human conception. This stage in a person's growth is therefore, like anything to do with faith, a gift. It is a time of longing for God, filled with a sense of absence. It calls to mind the words of the Psalm:

As a deer longs for flowing streams,
so my soul longs for you, O God. (PSALM 42:1)

John's experience of the night occurred during his imprisonment and when he came close to God in an amazing union. So John is not retailing some system but making sense of his own life and hoping that what he has to say will benefit others. Also, it must be noted that each of us will make our own journey according to our unique being.

The passive night affects the whole of the person, and John asks that we trust in what is happening so that God can be God for us. The way into this period is a time when prayer becomes almost impossible. It can feel that God is abandoning us and the pain of feeling you have lost the Beloved becomes almost unbearable. Peace and joy depart and are replaced by depression and loss of self-esteem. As in any state of loss, we can feel bewildered and wonder just what has gone wrong. This is the time when we are being asked to share with Christ in a death by which we say yes to God in an unconditional way. In the dark there is a light, but as yet we are unable to grasp what is beyond our comprehension. John is, as it were, displacing death and its fear from its usual biological moment to a place in the life of faith. He is reminding us of the theme of John's gospel, that to believe in Christ is to have eternal life. The act of belief for John is radical, the consequence is to taste now the beauty of the fullness of life.

What is interesting about John's experience of night is that it occurred when he was being persecuted, misunderstood. He became powerless on every level. John was imprisoned because in the midst of an all too human tangle, his goodness became threatening. John was in fact trying in all simplicity to live an ideal, he was wanting to be prophetic and faithful to the gospel. His predicament reminds us of so many great figures in Christianity who have suffered for their love of God either through persecution or being misunderstood. Titus Brandsma and Edith Stein, both Carmelites, were people of faith who were overwhelmed by the darkness of the Nazi ideology and yet through the cross they achieved a marvellous union with God. But what about the many others who have suffered at the hands of the Church because their message was not understood, because they were pioneers. In our own century, figures like Yves Congar and Bernard Häring spring to mind. Again, the diaries of Anne Frank and many of the Beirut hostages show journeys akin to the dark night. In particular, Brian Keenan's book *An Evil Cradling* tells a story that John would have understood.

The night, then, is a time of powerlessness and with a sense of the gulf between oneself and God's holiness. The feeling of isolation and of seeming failure makes the figure of Job seem an apt comparison. How could anyone love this wretchedness and failure?

John, however, would not want us to see this process as some terrible ascetic ordeal. One thing must be clear – the passive night is God's action and the key is to trust and wait and believe in the dawn. We live in the hope that God will possess us.

The way of *nada* has then been well-trodden through the experience of the night. The journey has been freely entered upon and the motive for the journey has been love. We know that nothing can take the place of God in satisfying our needs and the night has shown the deep caverns of our being that only love can fill. And the experience of the night has been the end of false gods. We recognize the aching and longing which only God can satisfy.

Close to God

The purpose of the journey has been love, and the Lover in 'The Dark Night' and the 'Canticle' can go out in full freedom to find the Beloved. The search is possible, union can take place. Love is the God-given energy and that love is the Spirit's gift. But it is also a purifying flame which takes away any obstacle to union with the Beloved – we can now be close to God. Love makes us like God as sin is destroyed, and that same love has given us the trust to journey open to God's ways, even when the whole affair has felt like utter risk.

Obviously, the joy of coming into a close relationship with God is something that few people can articulate. John's poems have done that through powerful symbols and because he was able to find words that even surprised him by their power. However, what stands out in John's writings is the language he uses about our union with God. It is the language and images of the most tender and fulfilled human loving. This is powerful news for our own times because it tells us that human love at its most sublime is the best image we can find for how God and ourselves can relate. It also raises the question of whether we need some experience of human tenderness to begin us on the journey to God. I believe that how we love each other and how we love God is reciprocal, the one affecting and enhancing the other. The journey into God which John shows us is a journey where possessiveness goes and faith, trust and love find freedom to flourish. It is because true human growth and freedom is realized that we can come close to God. If growth and maturity has occurred in our innermost being, then we are able to take up our human relationships in a mode that is gentler, deeper and more understanding of the other.

John's life was one that gave space and time to love and friendship. He felt a freedom in intimacy, he neither wanted to possess nor be possessed. He could celebrate friendship and was honest in the joy such relations brought him. The mystics, because they are open to the loving wisdom of God and allow the love of the Spirit freedom, achieve a humanity that is creative, sensitive and spontaneous. Perhaps one of the great contributions of teachers such as John of the Cross for today could be that in enabling people to grow in loving trust of God and experience unconditional love, men and women would gain confidence in the possibility of achieving a fully loving relationship. Mysticism could well be a school for marriage!

There has never been more talk about relationships and yet there has never been greater difficulty it would seem in living them out. It appears we do not know what we want from each other and the hurt and the anger all this causes is terrible. Can John's *nada* lead to a *todo* for people wanting to find love and deep relationships? I believe it can, because John will help us discover the other in all their beauty and he has so much to say to the devices and desires of our hearts.

John and Spiritual Direction

John of the Cross was concerned that people seeking union with God had good guides or spiritual directors on their journey. He was aware of the harm that unwise, bad advice could have on a person. People seeking God, trusting another in the most intimate longings of their beings, need genuine guides. John's concern is perhaps even more valid today when we see the damage that can be done by enthusiasts, charlatans and so-called guides who in the end can abuse the power and trust afforded to them.

In writing about John as a spiritual director I must acknowledge a debt to the work of two North American Carmelites, Kevin Culligan and Denis Graviss. Denis Graviss analyses the hallmarks of John's work as a spiritual director, while Kevin Culligan explores the interface between John and modern client-based therapy.

Spiritual direction is perhaps as old as Christianity. People have always sought help in their journey to God from contemporaries that they perceived as having deeper experience. It is a ministry of one Christian to another so that they can journey well. Over the years, Carmelites have been sought out as guides in matters of the spirit. English medieval Carmelites were directors to people such as Margery Kempe.

John was concerned that those who helped people towards union with God should be qualified and sensitive. John saw a good director as an exceptional person because, as he observed in *The Living Flame of Love*, 'They must be more than wise and discreet, they have to be experienced'.

John, however, believed that the first and best guide was always God. He often talks of God's guidance using or naming the ways the various persons of the Trinity act in us. Jesus teaches us by example, the Holy Spirit brings wisdom into our lives, while God the Father draws us to a substantial union. The key way in which God helps us is by allowing his wisdom and love to take over in our lives and liberate us from negative feelings and desires. However, John understands that we often need help from another human being to make sense of what is going on in our lives. It is all too easy for us to misinterpret the reality of what God is doing in the core of our being.

The spiritual director has a crucial role which requires immense sensitivity, since he or she is concerned with the complete experience of the person they guide. The director has to be sensitive to the person and able to discern the meaning of God's action in the person's life. John realizes that the director's work has many facets – teaching, parenting, guiding. A guide who supports is perhaps the best shorthand for what is entailed in this work. This means the director has to have an excellent interpersonal relationship with the client, one of respect and awareness of the uniqueness of that person. John sees Jesus as the role model – our brother, our companion on the way. Jesus always listened and would ensure that in every sense he was alongside the person with whom he was involved. A director is a brother or sister, a soul friend. For John, ordination was not a prerequisite for this work; any man or woman with the right qualities could be a spiritual director. The qualities are experience, wisdom and discretion.

Experience means that a person has lived life in a full sense. Nobody can communicate what they have never experienced. The director should be someone who has come close to God in love and also has deep love for people. Experience breeds sensitivity and a way of understanding that can best be described as intuition. Sensitivity means drawing out the other person's gifts and not imposing one's own opinions. A good director leaves room for the Holy

Spirit and is not possessive. When a client may need help from someone other than the director, they should be free to do so.

Wisdom, for John, was a gift of the Holy Spirit. Wisdom came not from some intellectual process but it was special knowledge of God, a way of loving. It also involves having that sort of imagination which prevents us missing what is really going on in a person's life. Wise directors are always reflecting back to their own relationship with God so that they can act as creative channels for God's love to be transmitted into another person's life.

The third quality John looked for was discretion. Discretion was linked to prudence. It meant that the individual and the individual situation were given their proper value. Clear thinking is required when assessing a person's motivation. If necessary, it could mean that mistaken motivation had to be highlighted and corrected.

The wise, prudent, experienced director makes sure that boundaries are set and respected in the relationship. These boundaries are important as they prevent misunderstanding and any hint of the relationship being abusive. What matters is that room is left for Christ and Christ always remains the goal and the model.

Contemporary Psychology

John, writing in the sixteenth century, worked out of a psychology linked to medieval theology. John refers to our faculties the will, the intellect, the memory, whereas modern psychology is based on perception. Is John's approach foreign to how we deal with people today, or can bridges be built? Kevin Culligan sees the possibility of modern therapeutic psychology casting new light on John's work of spiritual direction. He sees behavioural science adding insights to established practice in spiritual direction.

The question is, How can a synthesis be made between John's teaching and the work of contemporary psychology? In his writings, Culligan cites the work of Carl Rogers, which is client-centred, as a possible point of contact. Rogers, like John of the

Cross, proposes definite criteria which should underpin the work of a therapist. The therapist should be genuine, caring and understanding towards the client. For Rogers, the aim of his work was to enable whoever he worked with become a fully functioning person. Along the way to that goal, he saw the need to help his client find a unity between experience of life and their concept of self – the need to bridge the gap between reality and how I perceive reality. He also explores how the potential within us for realizing our self can be tapped and developed. The therapist helps create conditions for growth through care and understanding and by the commitment to being genuine.

If we look at John's teaching, he would stress that God working in us through the ordinary processes of our humanity helps us towards union with God and the attainment of peace. John, like Rogers, has a goal, and his insistence on criteria such as discretion are not unlike Rogers' criteria. A director should care and should, by their understanding, enable the client to realize their potential.

Rogers, when insisting on congruence between the self and experience, is asking for realism. John states that our well-being flows from the quality of our conscious relationship with God. Our being can flourish if it is grounded in the reality of God and not some image we have created. Again, often a spiritual director has to point out to a person that they are not quite so advanced in their journey, that there is a lack of congruence between where they are and their perception of themselves. It is easy to be deluded about holiness.

The caring and understanding of the director then enables the real work of change which will help towards genuine closeness to God and appropriate behaviour to begin. The quality of the relationship between director and client is crucial. The director does not impose anything but creates a climate where the client begins to recognize the shortcomings in their life.

The notion of 'congruence' found in modern therapy corresponds to a sense of realism in our relationship with God. Our models of holiness have to bear some relationship to our experience, otherwise we can be into dysfunction, displacement activity and denial. A married person cannot act like a monk, nor do external practices guarantee inner growth. In this context, being counselled towards self-denial is not something exotic but rather a call to greater realism. This is also being genuine – to face up to truth about ourselves.

Caring, by which a client is accepted as a unique person and valued for what they are, ensures that the person is respected. This respect is not unlike the New Testament *agape*, a non-possessive yet deep love for the person as they are. Understanding – in the sense of experiencing the other person's inner world 'as if' it were our own – is yet another aspect of non-possessive love. The result of such an attitude is the growth of a trusting relationship which can become a model for other relationships. In spiritual direction, the sense of love and trust generated in this process helps people believe they can be loved by God. The more a person feels helped the more they can believe they can relate to God. Feelings of unworthiness and inadequacy can be left behind.

Experience

Both John and modern therapy value experience. For John, everything has a validity in helping us journey towards God, while Carl Rogers would see the here and now as the seed-ground of values – the building blocks for personal fulfilment. For Rogers, as we develop we should become more open to experience and, as a result, more trusting and creative.

John would see us moving away from negative desires and letting go so that the full reality of God can break out in our lives. Rogers values the energies that let us move from rigidity into a deeper sense of freedom. For John, the journey to God in love helps us become a real person, as we let go of religious conventions. John saw rigidity and misplaced piety as obstacles to union with God.

He would agree with modern therapy that rigidity is a barrier on the way to being the person God wants us to be. Spiritual direction leads us to a genuine relationship with God, and this must include a greater knowledge of ourselves. Prayer and therapy can both claim to bring us to greater self-knowledge. We see ourselves as we are. Prayer helps us see ourselves gaining our worth from our relationship with God and knowing we have deep worth helps us respect and value others as that is how they are in their turn before God. Self-awareness and a coherent sense of our own worth are crucial, and both come from having a goal realized objectively, and this can happen both in therapy and in the way of the mystic. The two are not in opposition, nor are they liable to contradiction.

Over the years, John developed a great capacity for observing where people were at in their search for God and in trying to find overall meaning in life. His deep, genuine love for the people he was guiding meant that he grew more and more sensitive in understanding the process by which they tried to grow. His ability to be so empathetic – so willing to be caring and understanding – created a wonderful climate of trust. It was through that warmth of approach that those helped by John felt able to explore their inner selves and so grow and develop. People are often very shy, diffident and uncertain in talking about what is going on in their inner lives. John because he cared, allowed people to express their feelings and he was then from his own experience able to guide such people with genuine understanding and respect. Also, John would be enriched as he was allowed to observe God's working in that person's life. Being a companion to a person on their inner journey is a privilege, allowing others to see the variety and beauty of people's experience of God. Often the sharing between a spiritual director and their client can produce insights that have a validity for the world at large. The understanding of the reality of God can be enriched by these encounters and have greater mean-ing than abstract theological studies. The translation of such ex-periences needs the language of imagination.

If the director works creatively with the person being directed, there is deep respect and the danger of misuse of power in the relationship is never in question. Genuine caring and discreet work will never descend into manipulation or the imposition of the views or opinions of the one who could claim to be more experienced. This point needs to be emphasized, because all too often we read of religious leaders or teachers who use power over people and direct their inner lives in ways that are destructive and can even end in death. John of the Cross offers a way of guidance which has a perennial wisdom, based on a deep respect for the person being guided. For John, the spiritual director and client are companions on the journey, and the treasure, the relationship with God, cannot be compromised by anything that comes in the way of God's work.

Modern therapy emphasizes the need for quality in our interpersonal relationship at whatever level of life. Where good relations exist, whether at work, in the home, in education or in the Church, then growth and positive change take place. We can let go and move if we feel trust in the environment in which we operate. Where relationships are lacking in quality and depth, then we have problems – life goes askew and, so often, inappropriate or dysfunctional behaviour flourishes. Spiritual direction is an interpersonal relationship, and, if we focus on John of the Cross, we see he is a reliable guide because he is so concerned to be caring and understanding with the people he helps.

John, through his wisdom and experience, worked to respect the individual and create the atmosphere where the person is at ease. This is a far cry from any system being imposed or the individual being used or abused by some guru. No, once a person feels recognized for who they are, they feel at ease and the world of their spirit can be explored. Spiritual direction in this sense, as it discovers the world of the human spirit, takes us beyond the senses, showing us that there are realities in the human person that go beyond our normal perceptions of time and space. They are not quantifiable in scientific terms, but they are real because they represent what goes on in the core of our being. Behavioural experts like Rogers admit this possibility, and the work of spiritual directors inspired by John of the Cross give us insights into the mind, body and soul relationship which are crucial.

John and those who continue his work in spiritual direction take us into the mystery of God. Whenever there is talk about attempting to understand God we are always brought back to our attempts at understanding the human person and how that person can relate to God. It is this specialized work of exploration that is the particular remit of spiritual direction. Such work takes us towards the transcendent, what John might call the 'secret'. The spiritual director in the twentieth century who is in dialogue with those who work with client-based therapy will want to talk to the world of behavioural science and ask that world to take note of his findings. Because the spiritual director is moving into areas of experience which do not fit easily within received categories, is this research to be dismissed, or is it to be seen as a new field for the behavioural scientist to examine? It has always been held by Christian thinkers that there is only one truth. Spiritual direction, client-based therapy and other disciplines can help in developing our understanding of what it is to be human, and also the possibility of being open to the transcendent.

Suggested Further Reading

John's Own Works

The Collected Works of St John of the Cross, translated by Kieran Kavanaugh, OCD, and Otilio Rodriguez, OCD, ICS Publications, 1991.

The Dark Night of the Soul and *The Living Flame of Love*, Fount Paperbacks, 1995.

St John of the Cross Poems, with a translation by Roy Campbell, Penguin, 1960.

Other Works

Brenan, Gerald, *St John of the Cross his life and poetry*, Cambridge University Press, 1973.

Collings, Ross, OCD, *John of the Cross*, Michael Glazier, 1990.

Culligan, Kevin, OCD, *A Comparative Study of John of the Cross & Carl Rogers*, Carmelite Studies 2, ICS Publications, 1982.

Graviss, Denis, O Carm, *Portrait of the Spiritual Director in St John of the Cross*, Institutum Carmelitanum, 1983.

Johnston, William, *Mystical Theology*, HarperCollins, 1995.

Matthews, Iain, OCD, *The Impact of God*, Hodder and Stoughton, London, 1995.

Murphy, Roland E., O Carm, *The Song of Songs*, Fortress Press, 1990.

Welch, John, O Carm, *When Gods Die*, Paulist Press, 1990.

THOMAS MORE

Anne Murphy

Thomas More

Anne Murphy is a member of the Society of the Holy Child. She studied History and Theology at the University of London, and obtained her doctorate from the Gregorian University, Rome. She currently lectures in Reformation Studies and Systematic Theology at Heythrop College, University of London. Her previous work includes *The Theology of the Cross in the Prison Writings of Saint Thomas More*.

For
Elisabeth Jupp and Jared Wicks

Contents

Abbreviations

The following abbreviations are used in references given in the text:

CW	The Yale Edition of the *Complete Works of St Thomas More*
CW5	*Responsio ad Lutherum*, ed. J. M. Headley
CW6	*A Dialogue Concerning Heresies*, eds. T. Lawler, G. Marc'hadour, R. Marius
CW8	*The Confutation of Tyndale's Answer*, eds. L. A. Schuster, R. Marius, J. P. Luscardi, R. J. Schoeck
CW12	*A Dialogue of Comfort against Tribulation*, eds. L. L. Martz and F. Manley
CW13	*Treatise on the Passion*, ed. G. E. Haupt
CW15	*In Defence of Humanism*, ed. D. Kinney
DC	*A Dialogue of Comfort against Tribulation*, ed. F. Manley
EA	*Essential Articles for the Study of Thomas More*, ed. R. S. Sylvester and G. Marc'hadour
Gogan	B. Gogan, *The Common Corps of Christendom*
Harpsfield	Nicholas Harpsfield, *Life of More*
HR3	*The History of King Richard III & Selections from Poems*, ed. R. S. Sylvester
Kenny	A. Kenny, *Thomas More*
LW	*Luther's Works*, eds. J. Pelikan, H. T. Lehmann
Martz	L. Martz, *Thomas More: The Search for the Inner Man*
Moreana	*Moreana, Bulletin of Amici Thomae Mori*, Angers 1963–
Roper	W. Roper, *The Life of Sir Thomas More*
Rogers	*The Correspondence of Sir Thomas More*, ed. E. F. Rogers
SL	*St Thomas More: Selected Letters*, ed. E. F. Rogers
TW	*Thomas More: The Tower Works*, ed. G. E. Haupt
U	*Utopia*, ed. G. M. Logan & R. M. Adams

Full bibliographical details of these and other works are given in Suggested Further Reading.

Date Chart

Early Life

1477/8	Born in parish of St Lawrence Jewry, city of London
c.1492	Oxford University
1496	Admitted to Lincoln's Inn, London
1499	First meeting with Erasmus on his visit to England
1505	Married Jane Colt; four children: Margaret, Elizabeth, Cecily, John
1509	Accession of Henry VIII
	Erasmus writes *In Praise of Folly* in More's house
1510	Under-Sheriff of London. Elected to Parliament
1511	Wife died; remarried to Alice Middleton
1513–18	*History of King Richard III* (English and Latin versions)

Public Life

1515	Flanders mission. Book 2 of *Utopia* written in Antwerp
1516	*Utopia* completed and published
1517	Became a member of the King's Council
1523	Elected Speaker of the House of Commons
1525	Appointed Chancellor to the Duchy of Lancaster
1527	Proceedings to annul Henry VIII's marriage to Catherine of Aragon
1528	Licensed to read, retain and confute Protestant writings
1529	Succeeded Wolsey as Lord Chancellor of England
1532	Resigned as Chancellor

1533   Henry married Anne Boleyn

1534   Imprisoned for refusing oath to Act of Succession

Polemical Writings

1521   Luther condemned at the Diet of Worms

1523   More's *Responsio ad Lutherum*

1526   *Letter to Bugenhagen*
       Tyndale's translation of New Testament reaches
       England

1529   *A Dialogue Concerning Heresies* (revised 1531)
       Supplication of Souls

1532/3   *Confutation of Tyndale's Answer* (about 500,000 words)
       Letter to John Frith

1533   *Apology*
       Debellation of Salem & Bizance
       An Answer to a Poisoned Book

Prison Writings

1534   *A Treatise on the Passion.* Begun, possibly finished before
       prison
       A Dialogue of Comfort Against Tribulation

1535   *De Tristitia Christi* (original manuscript found in 1963,
       Valentia)
       Letters from prison, prayers, annotations in Psalter
       Trial proceedings and execution July 1535

Posthumous Reputation

1935   Canonization of John Fisher and Thomas More

1963–1996   Yale edition of *Complete Works of St Thomas More*

Introduction
The Controversial Thomas More

*I cannot tell whether I would call him a foolish wise man or a
wise foolish man.*   (EDWARD HALL, CHRONICLER)

Thomas More is remembered most often as the author of *Utopia*, a
classic of political thought, and as a former Lord Chancellor of
England, executed for treason against Henry VIII because he
refused to take an oath against his conscience. In time the manner of his dying, with courage and understated humour, won him
the admiration of those who did not share his religious convictions. Jonathan Swift regarded him as 'a person of greatest virtue
this kingdom has ever produced'; Macaulay, who could not
understand the beliefs for which More died, regarded him as 'one
of the choice specimens of human wisdom and virtue'. Most
would agree that More is someone whose life and thought will
always reward greater study, because of their continued relevance to our own human choices and situations.

Contemporary scholarship, however, has revealed that Thomas
More was a far more controversial figure in his life, death and
posthumous reputation than we might have been led to believe.
When he was beheaded in the Tower of London on 6 July 1535,
few, if any, of his family and friends understood why his 'scruple of
conscience' should have brought about his death. His friend, the
Dutch scholar Desiderius Erasmus, commented: 'Would that he
had never become involved in such a dangerous matter, and had
left theological business to theologians.' His daughter, Margaret,

herself took the oath he had refused. His wife, Alice, put the family point of view most vigorously: 'Master More, I would marvel that you, that have been always ... taken for so wise a man, will now so play the fool.' Most of More's contemporaries agreed with Alice's common-sense view.

It was only slowly and with hindsight that More's family and close friends came to understand the religious and political consequences of Henry VIII's quarrel with the Pope, his claim to Royal Supremacy over the Church in England, and so the reasons for More's resistance. As they lovingly preserved his relics and collated his writings, they began to interpret More as a Catholic martyr who died for the orthodoxy of his faith. To make this saintly More better known and loved, they published More's English works (1557) and his Latin works (1565). The saintly image of More influenced William Roper's first family 'memoir' of his father-in-law, and the four subsequent 'biographies' written between 1557 and 1631. As English Catholics were reduced to a persecuted minority at home, or were forced into exile, they came to see More through the lens of their own suffering, and kept alive the memory of More as martyr and saint. However they neglected or played down his reputation as humanist writer and friend of Erasmus.

In the earlier part of their lives (c.1500–20), More, Erasmus and their circle of friends had aimed at the reform of the Church in 'head and members'. This involved quite strong criticism of many aspects of Christian life and practice. But from 1517 onwards, the coming of Martin Luther and the Protestant Reformations meant that the language of reform became suspect in Catholic circles. More's orthodox reputation would not be helped by mentioning his closeness to Erasmus, whose writings were put on the Roman list of books forbidden to be read by Catholics (1558). Some of More's own earlier views on the papacy and the reform of Christendom were either toned down or edited out of his writings. It was the Basle edition of More's works

(1563) that presented him again as humanist writer and reformer. Contemporary scholarship has paid most attention to this tradition of More.

In his highly successful play *A Man for All Seasons* (1960), Robert Bolt presents More as a man with 'an adamantine sense of his own self'. What fascinated him was the drama of an individual conscience holding out against the power of a tyrant. In the present century we are interested in human rights and the freedom of the individual conscience, in ways that would have been very unfamiliar to More. Bolt admired More as a 'hero of selfhood'. But More saw the human self as 'in the hands of God', not as independent or free-standing. This raises the problem of how far we are justified in interpreting More in the light of our own interests and concerns. His context may be like, but does not replicate, our own.

With the exception of *Utopia*, which has received much attention, More's contribution as a Christian thinker and writer has been neglected until relatively recently. In 1963 Yale University initiated a project to provide a critical, scholarly edition of the *Complete Works of St Thomas More*. This is just nearing completion (1996) and has enabled a much fuller appreciation of all More's writings – humanist, polemical and devotional. We can evaluate him as a humanist who argued for moral, social and religious reform, and as a lay theologian whose views on the nature of the Church were rich and creative. But we may be less appreciative of the combative and adversarial style he used when he wrote in defence of his faith. The devotional and religious intensity of his prison writings belong to the finest of that genre within the whole Christian tradition.

In the light of this 'new' material, a revisionist school of historians has set out to uncover the 'real Thomas More', sanctified and exalted by a series of admiring and uncritical biographers, from Roper (1557) to Chambers (1935). They challenged the traditional view of More as a humane, wise, heroic 'man for all seasons'. In his biography (1985) Richard Marius wanted to discover the 'man of flesh and blood able to take his place in his real world, and ours.' An extreme revisionist thesis affirms that the 'real Thomas More' was a singularly unattractive character, ambitious, intolerant, reactionary and guilt-ridden, a 'man who tried to salvage his failing reputation by a final act of stage-managed heroism'.

While this exercise was long overdue, it is itself deserving of criticism. 'The all too human More of the revisionists constitutes as great a travesty as the all too saintly More of the hagiographers' (B. Bradshaw, 'The Controversial Sir Thomas More', *Journal of Ecclesiastical History*, 1985, 536). Recent studies have moved beyond the somewhat sterile arguments surrounding the 'real Thomas More', and recognize that thirty years of research have cleaned away the overlay on his traditionally gilded portrait. The process has revealed details obscured or unknown to previous generations. The restored portrait is the same portrait, 'warts and all', not an entirely new painting. The revisionist challenge has, if anything, enhanced our appreciation of the creativity and humanity of an outstanding Christian thinker, whose fate it was to have to test his ideals and thought in the public arena of practical politics and religion.

Early Life and Marriage
1478–1515

More is a man of an angel's wit and singular learning; I know not
his fellow. For where is the man of that gentleness, lowliness and
affability? As time requireth a man of marvellous mirth and pas-
times; and sometimes of as sad gravity; a man for all seasons.
(RICHARD WHITTINTON, 1520)

Thomas More was born in London in 1477 or 1478, in the last
years of the reign of Edward IV (1461–1483), and he lived there
for most of his life. Its sights and sounds and common talk were
to shape the direction of his thought, which was urban and
community-centred, and salted with earthy common sense. Both
his parents came from the upwardly mobile London merchant
class, which was ambitious to acquire land and status from its
newly acquired wealth. His father, John, became a judge, and chose
the legal profession for his son, living until 1530, proud to see
Thomas as Lord Chancellor of England. He appears in family portraits and was given marked respect and honour by More. We hear
very little about More's mother, Agnes, who died sometime before
1507.

More's education began in St Antony's, Threadneedle Street, a
leading London school. Then he was sent to serve as a page at
Lambeth Palace, the household of John Morton, Archbishop of
Canterbury. This was a training in court life – waiting at table, listening to the conversations of the great and powerful, taking part
in amateur dramatics and court entertainment. It gave More a

lifelong sense of familiarity and ease in such circles. Morton's patronage enabled him to spend about two years at Oxford University, until his father recalled him to legal studies in London, first at New Inn and then at Lincoln's Inn. He became familiar not only with the principles of English common law but with the 'putting of cases', and the weighing of both sides of an argument. He qualified for the bar in about 1501, and was soon appointed as reader in Furnival's Inn, instructing young students.

Between 1501 and 1505 More 'lived without vow' at the London Charterhouse, home of the Carthusian monks. It was not unusual for young graduates to be associated with this monastery while continuing with their professional lives. Charterhouse was known for its strict observance, religious orthodoxy, and practical piety, and it had a lasting effect on More's spirituality. A time of withdrawal for prayer and reflection was built into his daily and weekly schedule. It is probable that for a time he was attracted to the monastic way of life, but finally opted for marriage and a life of public service.

More, therefore, had four distinct strands to his formal education: court life at Lambeth, Oxford University, legal studies, and a period sharing monastic life and prayer. To this he now added a fifth area of interest, which came to inform and colour his whole outlook. From 1499 onwards he joined a number of friends who were critical of the somewhat sterile and unimaginative educational methods current in schools and universities. Under the influence of John Colet, Dean of St Paul's Cathedral, and a generation of scholars who had been educated in Italy, More and his circle began to share the views of a wider, more diffuse, European movement which later generations labelled **Christian Humanism**. (This is explained more fully in Chapter 2.) They became convinced that any serious renewal of religion and society must begin with a renewal in education, and a retrieval of classical and Christian sources. When the Dutch humanist scholar Desiderius Erasmus visited England in 1499, he forged a lasting friendship with More, and provided a strong link with continental humanism.

More and his friends set about perfecting their Latin and learning Greek. They read the pagan and Christian classics not only for content, but also for form and style. They wanted to be 'men of letters', able to communicate through a well-turned phrase, a good public speech, or a well-constructed letter. Humanists aimed to influence the language or discourse of school, university, pulpit and court – the communications media of the day. They admired the old classical writing styles, especially that of Cicero. So since style was 'the dress of thoughts', More began his humanist career by practising the art of writing and speaking well, in English, Latin and Greek. He translated poems and epigrams, wrote his own poetry, translated the life of Pico della Mirandola (a leading figure of the Italian Renaissance), and wrote the *History of King Richard III*. He also began to read the classics of early Christian theology, especially Jerome, Ambrose and Augustine. This explains why More, a layman, gave a series of lectures on Augustine's *City of God* in a London church *c*.1501.

But More's humanistic studies and writings were only one part of an increasingly busy professional life. He was elected to Parliament, and became Under-Sheriff in the City of London in 1510. As such he was a permanent adviser to the Sheriffs, and sat as judge in the Sheriffs' court at the Guildhall.

In 1505 More married Jane (or Joan) Colt and had four children by her: Margaret, Elizabeth, Cecily and John. They made their home in the Old Barge, Bucklersbury, and it was here that Erasmus wrote *In Praise of Folly* (1509) while More's guest, and where More's *Utopia* was completed (1516). Within a month of Jane's death in 1511, More married Lady Alice Middleton, a widow with one daughter, and known to Jane's family circle. Henry VIII's secretary, Andrea Ammonio, called Alice a 'beak-nosed harpy' and she has had a bad press ever since. The standard view has been that More chose a mere step-mother/housekeeper for his children, and an additional hairshirt for himself. But Lady Alice turns out to have been considerably younger than was thought, wealthy, attractive and fashion-conscious. She was a kinswoman of Henry VIII through the marriage of her cousin, Mary Bohun, into the Tudor family. It would seem that More made an exceptionally advantageous second marriage, which undoubtedly furthered his career, and may have been a spur to his political ambitions.

Whereas Jane had been somewhat in awe of her clever husband, Alice was made of sterner stuff and gave him as good as she got. More certainly enjoyed her company and her repartee, and she often made him laugh – even when he was in prison. She tried to smarten up his appearance and to humanize the rigorous order of the household. But she was also very ambitious for her husband and may have put pressure on him to enter public life. More's epitaph, written (c.1532) for his tomb in Chelsea, makes a succinct statement: 'The one so lived with me, and the other so liveth, that it is doubtful whether this or the other were dearer unto me... O how well could we three have lived joined together in matrimony, if fortune and religion would have suffered it. So death shall give us that thing which life could not.'

Together More and Alice supervised the studies of the children, at least until 1516, when outside tutors were hired. More loved his garden, his aviary and his small menagerie, and he encouraged his children to take an interest in plants and animals. When they were older he also encouraged them to undertake some form of work for the less fortunate. For example, Margaret Giggs, his adopted daughter, visited prisoners in Newgate prison. More himself had a special understanding of, and sympathy for, the mentally handicapped and those with suicidal tendencies.

A Family Portrait

In about 1525 the family moved from their city home to a larger house in Chelsea. Hans Holbein the Younger was welcomed into the house for a time between 1526 and 1528, and painted the famous group portrait of Thomas More at the centre of his family. (Sadly, the original is lost, though the preliminary sketch survives in Basle.) Renaissance portraits are not as innocent as we might once have thought. Such paintings were commissioned and bought to be displayed as indicators of family wealth, position and importance. The Holbein family painting shows how More wished to be remembered by posterity. Every detail included has its special significance.

Erasmus was to describe the household in Chelsea as Plato's Academy in Christian form. The group portrait projects a united and exceptionally gifted family. Old Judge John More holds an honoured position at his son's right hand. More's wife, Alice, and his daughters, hold books, indicating their learning. Musical, mathematical, and astronomical instruments are present in the room, indicating a breadth of interests. Later versions of the portrait include a dog and a pet monkey. The group is arranged in a semi-circle as if gathered for morning prayer. But most members are busily occupied – no room for idleness or boredom here. This is a devout but learned Christian household, well ordered, living in harmony and peace, the perfect retreat for a busy statesman. Most significantly, the family represents the young and the old, the wise man and the fool, the richness and variety of human life, centred on commitment to God, source of all life.

The integration, rather than the separation, of human and religious activity, pleasure and morality, devotion and learning, was characteristic of humanism. Since this is how More wished to portray what he held to be most precious in his life, it would be helpful to examine More's Christian humanist thought and ideals, especially in relation to marriage, family, education and friendship.

In Defence of Humanism
Early Writings 1500–1519

Nothing is more humane – and humanity is the virtue most proper to human beings – than to relieve the misery of others, assuage their griefs, and by removing all sadness from their lives, to restore them to enjoyment, that is, pleasure. (THOMAS MORE: *UTOPIA* BOOK 2)

The modern word *humanism*, first coined in 1808 by a German scholar, was derived from a similar word *humanista* (Italian: *umanista*), used in the fifteenth and sixteenth centuries for professional university teachers of the five humanities (or liberal arts): grammar, rhetoric, poetry, history, ethics. Humanists, sometimes dubbed 'mere grammarians', were prepared to go back to the basics of the Greek and Latin languages so as really to understand, and enter the thought world of, the great classical writers of the past. By being in touch again with the best that human thought and action had achieved, they felt they could come to know what it was to be truly human, and put it into practice in their own lives. Humanists despised scholars who lived only on quotation or translation, because they were not equipped to read the complete text in the original language. Humanists wanted to read the whole text in its living context, not in isolation from it. For them, language was an expression of living experience.

The term 'humanist', initially restricted to the professional academic, came to be applied to many of their students who chose careers outside the university setting. These could be churchmen, royal councillors, secretaries to kings or city councils, schoolmasters, or interested lay men (rarely women) with time and leisure to study. More belonged to this network of lay humanists, who often had a distinctive contribution to make to civic and public life. These men had an interest in political thought and practical ethics as a guide to civic humanism. Their ideal of a 'sound classical education' as a preparation for public life, passed into the (English) public and grammar school systems, and dominated educational practice until our own century.

At its core humanism was neither religious nor irreligious, but most humanists were believing Christians and many were committed to the reform of Christendom. The rebirth (*renaissance*) of interest in classical sources came to include a rebirth of interest in biblical and early Christian sources, and a conviction that Christianity could be renewed only by returning to its roots. If the pagan classics put a person in touch with the best expression of what it was to be 'truly human', the Christian classics put one in touch with what it was to be 'truly Christian', rooted in the actual life of Jesus Christ himself. Humanists were concerned with integrating, not separating, the human and the Christian. They sought to deepen their understanding of both in a secular, not a cloistered, setting.

The teachers of the humanities and the new biblical theology increasingly challenged the teachers of theology, who used the older methods of the medieval academics (or scholastics). Their rival arguments about method and content in education became increasingly bitter and acrid. Humanists regarded speech as *the* most characteristic human gift. Knowledge remained private and sterile unless shared with another. To be able to communicate well was essential for the preacher or teacher, councillor or politician. It was not without significance that Christ, the supreme teacher, had been the *word* (or speech) *of God made human*. And his word moved human hearts. What was at stake for Christian humanists was the pastoral strategy needed to revitalize Christian thought and practice.

Humanism in its English context began earlier and continued later than has been supposed. The historian Denis Hay has drawn attention to the 'density of humanist activity in England'. There were many more humanists than one influential group operating in London. But it seems that while they were influential educators and editors of texts, they published no outstanding humanistic writings. Their hopes and promises were fulfilled in the lay amateur, Thomas More. Arguably the first two masterpieces of English renaissance humanism were his *History of King Richard III* (*c*.1513–1518), and *Utopia* (1516).

To understand More as a humanist expert in the art of speaking and writing well, with a preference for dialogue over systematic thought, provides the best interpretative framework for all his subsequent writings. More is urbane and witty in *Utopia*, vitriolic in his polemical writings, and devotional in his prison writings. Some scholars regard these differences as evidence for a deeply divided and ambiguous personality, bordering on imbalance. But a humanist was one trained in the art of using language and speech appropriate to the occasion. More could turn as easily to polemic as to eulogy, to satire and ridicule as to compassion, to earthy, bawdy Chaucerian farce as much as to other-worldly spirituality. This means that More's thought can never be separated from the context in which it was conceived. His thinking was at its best when interacting with people and concrete situations. His writings can only be understood in the light of his life and experience, and his life in relation to his writings.

'Learning Joined With Virtue': More's Household

More's vocation as a Christian humanist began in his home, and it was here that he first put his educational ideals into practice. A household in his time consisted not just of wife and children, but also of many attendants and servants. If we agree with the judgement that 'domestic hierarchy in late medieval England both reflected and reinforced political values' (LAWRENCE STONE), then More's home was also the foundation of his political and civic values. Youth was 'the seed-time on which the state depends for its future growth' (ERASMUS).

In many ways More's was a conventional Tudor patriarchal household, where a husband and father had almost unconditional rights over property, and had a duty to 'control' an unruly wife, children or servants. Stone points out that a father ruled his household much as a king ruled his court, and that both institutions were 'mutually supportive' in stressing the importance of docility, obedience, and respect for authority. More's may have been a fairly benign rule, and his preference for 'citizen' rather than 'subject' in the political order, is reflected in the love, equality and companionship he showed to members of his family. But rule it was; he was the undisputed head of the household.

More differed from his contemporaries in the importance he attached to the formal education of his children. Erasmus, as an observant visitor, saw More's household as a place of education:

> *You would say that in that place was Plato's Academy. But I do the house an injury in likening it to Plato's Academy. I should rather call it a school or university of Christian religion. For there is none therein who does not study the branches of a liberal education. Their special care is piety and virtue'.* (ERASMUS TO JOHN FISHER)

Piety and *virtue* are words which do not commend themselves to us today. For Erasmus, *piety* meant a loving, practical religion, and *virtue* meant the moral strength of an informed conscience, which could make good choices in the business of every-day life. But *virtue* also carried within it the old Roman, classical sense of 'virile energy', strength to stand up and shape destiny, rather than remain helpless or passive in the face of the inevitable. Again and again More's moralism included praise of *industry* and hatred of *idleness*. He declared he would give up public life rather than 'allow his children to be idle and lazy'. Idleness or inactivity was the bain of domestic, spiritual, intellectual or political life. Life at all these levels was something human beings could energetically create, in collaboration with the grace of God. 'We may not expect ... to get to heaven in feather beds', he declared when the going was tough; and a little later: 'God sent people here to wake and work' (CW 13). But the activity of play or pleasure was also a 'work'.

Erasmus and More shared an almost unlimited optimism about the power of education to shape mature, moral, industrious, religious persons, and to provide an antidote to the damaging effects of the 'original sin' of our first parents. A good education gave the best possible start 'for the whole scope of human life – which is to have a sound mind in a sound body' (SL 31). They also shared a perception of life lived in an upside-down world of human folly. Human beings were not so much sinful as foolish or stupid. Life was a comedy of errors, because so often people were taken in by appearances, empty promises, or flattery. Education was the chief means of acquiring true wisdom and avoiding folly. It was the 'natural' foundation upon which the grace of God could build.

More hired distinguished tutors for his 'school', which included others besides his own four children. His justly acclaimed interest in the education of woman was at least partly due to the accident that there were more girls than boys in his household and among family connections. He supervised every detail of their education, wrote to them during his absence from home, and expected them to write to him daily, as a kind of formal exercise. More's letters to one tutor, William Gonell (*c*.1518), express most clearly his hopes and fears for his children. He wants them to be able to

> *put virtue in the first place, learning in the second, and in their studies to esteem most whatever may teach them piety towards God, charity to all and Christian humility in themselves.* (SL 20)

He is pleased, he told Gonell, that Elizabeth has made so much progress, and that she has not allowed it to go to her head.

> *Let her understand that such conduct delights me more than all the learning in the world. Though I prefer learning joined with virtue to all the treasures of kings, yet renown for learning, if you take away moral probity, brings nothing else but notorious and noteworthy infamy, especially in a woman. Since erudition in a woman is a new thing and a reproach to the sloth of men, many will gladly assail it, and impute to learning what is really a fault of nature ... On the other hand ... if a woman, to eminent virtue of mind should add even a moderate skill in learning, I think she will gain more real good than if she obtain the riches of Croesus and the beauty of Helen ...* (SL 20).

The reward of wisdom depends on 'inner knowledge of what is right, not on the talk of men'. More is concerned with the formation of conscience, and with good judgement in ordinary life. 'Warn my children not to lament that they do not possess what they mistakenly desire in others; not to think more of themselves for gaudy trappings, nor less for the lack of them' (Rogers 129). He is afraid that if the children are praised too much for their efforts, they will become dependent on the good opinion of others and be easily deceived by flattery. So Gonell must be sparing with praise, and direct them to understand that 'the whole fruit of their endeavours should consist in the testimony of God and a good conscience'. Poor children, we might say, if we did not know that More also made learning fun for them: he taught them to read by shooting arrows at letters, and sought useful aids to memory, and methods to make study easier. And he found it hard to punish them except with the lightest tip of a peacock's tail.

Margaret grew up to become one of the most learned women of her day, informally accepted as a member of Erasmus' circle. Elizabeth, Cecily and John were also educated in Latin, Greek and science. Family prayer and religious education – a heavy diet of reading from the early Christian writers – were also part of the structured day. More's ideas on the education of women directly influenced the first important treatises on the subject: Juan Luis Vives' *On the Instruction of A Christian Woman* (1523) and Sir Thomas Elyot's *Defence of a Good Woman* (1540). (Elyot's wife had been one of the children at More's school.) More's experiment proved to his friends that women were as capable as men of benefiting from higher education. And though an educated wife was a good investment for a man, it was also important for the woman herself. More encouraged Margaret to continue her studies even after her marriage and the birth of her first child. Her role was not to be purely domestic. So in many ways More's views were innovative, creative and well ahead of his time.

More's early poetry contains some elegant tributes to women he admired: for example, 'An Apology to a certain noble lady', or 'He expresses his joy at finding her ... whom he had loved as a young boy'. The latter was a tender, almost romantic, poem, expressing regret at the passing of time and young love, but also its enduring power in the human memory. A 'Rueful Lamentation' (1503) was an elegy written on the occasion of the death of Queen Elizabeth of York, wife of Henry VII. More imagines Elizabeth regretting her untimely death and reluctant to leave her family. He allows a woman's voice to express the sadness of human mortality, and the inevitable separation from those we love.

More's views on women are ambivalent and contradictory. In the letter to Gonell cited above, he also suggests that though women are as capable as men of being educated, they actually need it more: 'A woman's wit is the more diligently to be cultivated, so that nature's defect may be redressed by industry'. Here More shares a common view within the Christian tradition, about the 'special' nature of women, who seem to be especially prone to foolishness or folly, because less amenable to reason. Education will help them not to follow their emotions, or indulge in trivial gossip or idleness. In an epigram, 'To Candidus: how to choose a wife', More advises him to be guided in his choice by reason, not considerations of beauty or money: 'Let her be either educated or capable of being educated', for learning can foster a sound judgement and self-knowledge. A good wife can become a source of goodness for others:

> *Armed with this learning, she would not yield to pride in prosperity, nor grief in distress – even though misfortune strike her down ... If she is well instructed herself, then some day she will teach your little grandsons at an early age to read ... When she speaks, it will be difficult to judge between her extraordinary ability to say what she thinks and her thoughtful understanding of all kinds of affairs.*

Those who have researched the images of women, real or fictional, in More's writings, have noted that while his early humanistic poems and letters present a positive attitude, the traditionally negative one lies very near the surface. More's 'modernity' frequently slips back into traditionalism. The anti-feminine discourse of the medieval sermon, or 'merry tale', is part of his inherited outlook. More loved to mock and ridicule, and women were often the special targets of his wit.

In his later polemical works, the vitriolic language meted out to his religious opponents is matched by his abusive language about women. In these writings women are likely to be seductive, idle, garrulous or foolish, and are generally inferior to men. As More saw it, 'unruly' or disordered women seem to reflect the disorder in the Church, or to embody danger in a very specific way. The exceptions are the good, no nonsense, articulate women, who hit the nail on the head by sheer common sense, and are a match for their men. These would seem to mirror Alice, his wife. His later Tower writings mark a return to civility and normality. When he was in prison, and with his life in danger, his beloved daughter

Margaret begged him to conform and save himself by taking the required oath. He compared her to the 'temptress Eve'. She was not the usual, dutiful daughter; she argued with him and presented her case very ably. Despite the poignancy of their situation, he could be proud of her independence of mind.

It would seem that in all More's writings he spoke little about the institution of marriage, but much about the family as the foundation for a good society. It was assumed that husband and wife entered a life-long relationship for the sake of the family they were founding. Their joint responsibilities extended to all

that are belonging to our charge, by nature as our children, by law as our servants in our household. If servants fall sick in our service, so that they cannot do the service that we employ them for, we may still not in any way turn them out of doors and throw them aside comfortless, while they are unable to work and help themselves. For this would be a thing against all humanity.

(DC 2 17)

In another letter he wrote: 'Even if I do not leave myself a spoon, no poor neighbour of mine shall suffer any loss through any misfortune which happened in my house.' A well-ordered household reflected the principles of justice and equity, which should also be found in a well governed state.

More was to speak in wonder of the natural miracle of human coupling which resulted in gestation and birth. He remembered two young people in his own parish:

It happened, as it does among young people, that they fell in love and were married at St Stephen's. And within a year she gave birth to a fine boy ... I cannot understand why we should consider it more wonderful to revive a dead man than to witness the conception, birth and growth of a child into a man. (CW6 1 79)

He also had a robust and earthy attitude to human sexuality, which may offend the pious or puritanical, but which most know to be fairly typical of his time and social class. More knew himself to be blessed in his family relationships, and he influenced a movement for the education of women. His humanistic ideals were sometimes overshadowed by his inherited attitudes about the nature of women and the role of the father in a Tudor household. But his ideals for the education of his children, his conviction that family life was the foundation of civic and political life, and that it embraced friends, neighbours and the less fortunate, have few recorded parallels within the long history of the Christian tradition.

In Defence of Humanism

More's interest in education extended beyond the family to higher and university education. He shared in the humanist struggle to reform educational practice, in which certain power groups had a vested interest. His ideas are most clearly expressed in four long letter-essays: to a theologian, Martin Dorp (1515), to Oxford University (1518), to a monk (1519), and to Edward Lee, future Archbishop of York (1519). Certain themes are common to all four letters, but in the first two More was directly intervening in the inter-faculty feuding at two universities; Louvain and Oxford. The feud was between the humanists (teachers of the liberal arts) and the scholastics (teachers of theology). The humanist-scholastic debates were a replay of the old classic Platonic debates about the respective merits of rhetoric and philosophy.

Martin Dorp, a member of the theological faculty at Louvain, was a 'lapsed' humanist, and so his criticism of Erasmus was all the more hurtful. In an exchange of letters, Dorp took Erasmus to task for undermining the authority of the Church in two ways: firstly, by undertaking his own translation of the New Testament, Erasmus would downgrade the old, authoritative text of Jerome's

Latin translation, known as the Vulgate. Secondly, in his *Praise of Folly*, Erasmus had ridiculed and made fun of people who held authority in the Church (monks, bishops, popes, rulers) whom, he said, acted from self-love, not charity. Criticism of either authoritative text or persons was dangerous and damaging. But Dorp had further reservations: pagan or secular studies were a threat to true piety, and rhetoric was too sophisticated for the simple message of the gospel. Humanists should stick to their linguistic skills and not presume to move into the area of the professional theologian. What was at stake was the nature of 'true theology' and who was qualified to practise the discipline.

More, a layman outside the academic forum, wrote to Dorp in defence of Erasmus, and of the whole humanistic enterprise. He tried to do so more in sorrow than anger, and in a way which would persuade, rather than alienate, those for whom Dorp was a spokesman. His long letter (forty-seven pages) seems to have brought Dorp back into line. More argued very forcibly that those who went back to the original Greek text could improve on the accuracy of Jerome's Latin Vulgate. A knowledge of Greek (and if possible Hebrew) was an indispensable tool for biblical studies. Indeed, he wrote, linguistic skills were a better preparation for penetrating the meaning of revelation contained in the biblical text than the debating skills of the scholastic theologian.

More argued for a return to 'positive theology', by which he meant a simpler, more reflective, pastoral theology which had been used by the early Fathers of the Church. A true theologian was one who could comment and preach on the biblical texts, so that hearts could be moved and lives transformed. True theology was based on a loving appropriation of the texts which, by constant familiarity, came to colour one's whole life. This was quite a different approach to that of an academic, who used texts as a source for the defence of a doctrinal position. Dialectical skill had its place in argument and debate. In fact 'dialectic and rhetoric [are] as closely akin as fist and palm, since dialectic infers more concisely what rhetoric sets out more elaborately' (CW 15 17). But in the matter of moving and persuading Christians to deeper faith and practice, the extended palm of friendship was to be preferred to the clenched fist of disputation and argument. Hence the new humanist method in theology was to be preferred to the medieval approach, and the persuasive power of ordinary language was preferable to the academic jargon of the scholastic theologian.

In 1518 More wrote to the Senate of the University of Oxford, intervening to solve similar tensions and difficulties. A group of Oxford theologians had begun to call themselves 'Trojans', indicating their opposition to Greek, and to the liberal arts. More had heard that the leader of these Trojans had chosen, during a lenten sermon, 'to blather all too liberally not only against Greek learning and stylistic refinement in Latin, but against all the liberal arts' (CW15 135). More appealed to the university authorities to end such factions and encourage all learning, including Greek. He reminded them of the progress being made at Cambridge, 'which you have always outshone', and asked them to restore peace. A university racked by contention will not prosper.

In these letters (1515–1519) More made a vigorous defence of pagan or secular learning. Christian humanists tried to give their answer to the age-old question of Tertullian (c.200): 'What has Athens to do with Jerusalem?' For them human nature and divine grace were in harmony, in that the human search for excellence was an integral part of the Christian search for holiness. Humanists opposed two powerful 'anti-intellectual' trends in sixteenth-century Christianity. Firstly, there was a *spiritual* tradition of 'holy ignorance' which believed that a simple, faithful soul was taught by the Holy Spirit and had need of no other teacher. Secondly there was a *theological* tradition which separated the 'supernatural' activities of faith from the 'natural' activities of reason. In fairness to More's scholastic opponents, they were not against human reason (anti-intellectual) since they valued classical philosophy very highly; but they disliked pagan poetry, literature and history.

Philosophy was useful for Christian theology; the rest was not. So More was defending human culture as expressed in the liberal arts against the 'barbarian' theologians, who thought such learning was at best an irrelevance, and at worst actually harmful.

But for More a major task of a Christian was 'the business of learning the best way to live in the world'. Christian belief had to be translated into every-day practice. 'It is a thing of less labour to know what they should believe, and to believe it when they know it, than it is to work well,' More argued against Tyndale. To know something about human life in all its complexities was important for every Christian and every theologian. This was the context in which faith was operative. The common experience of human beings was most poignantly and eloquently expressed in literature, poetry and history. The study of such writings was not a pretentious distraction, but rather allowed human wisdom to become a sure foundation for Christian wisdom and insight.

The History of Richard III: A Study in Tyranny

In his letter to Dorp, More had asserted that the foundation of theology is a knowledge of human nature and the human situation 'which apart from poets and orators can be best learned from historians'. More was interested in the springs of human motivation and behaviour. One subject was beginning to take hold of his political imagination: tyranny as the corruption of good government. It had already been addressed in several of his Latin poems, and was to recur again in his future thought, and in the dramatic events of his own life. Erasmus wrote that More 'always had a special loathing for tyranny and a great fancy for equality'. In about 1513 More began to work on *The History of King Richard III*, a version of events which had taken place in London in 1483 when he was a boy, and which were still fresh in the memory of Londoners. We now recognize that *Richard III* was in the process of being written, but lay unfinished, as More turned to write his classic work on

The Best State of a Commonwealth and The New Island of Utopia
(1515). *Richard III*, a study in tyranny or the corruption of good
government, is the dark underside of the ideal of good government
proposed in *Utopia*. How human beings acquire the one, and avoid
the other, was the core of his political thought and action.

Once again More was interested less in the abstract principles of
good and bad government than in concrete examples of both. He
had them ready to hand. Richard was an example of a king who
was knowingly and deliberately unjust. He was a tyrant because
he usurped power, and because he subsequently acted unjustly.
More's version of the events of 1483 has been criticized for its historical inaccuracies; but he reconstructed the popular London
account, and knew personally some of the participants in the
drama, such as Archbishop Morton. *Richard III* is a study of how a
country, blessed with good government under Edward IV, slipped
quickly into bad government because of the ambitions of one
man. Richard's predecessor, Edward, had not been innocent; he
had also usurped the throne and had blood on his hands (the murder of Henry VI). But experience had taught him to bring wise
government out of its dubious origins. Edward died leaving his
country in peace, but warning all parties that this could be lost.

Richard set out to seize the throne from his nephews, the legitimate heirs. In a series of calculated steps he dismantled the legitimacy of their claims (by declaring them bastards), denied their
right to the protection of sanctuary, or to their mother's household,
and their right to the loyalty of their subjects. Richard sought and
eventually secured the compliance of the nobles, clergy and judges
– those whose job it was to uphold civic liberties. Initially tyranny
had to try to assume the trappings of legitimacy, while those who
suspected what was happening had to be quietly eliminated.

The key question raised within the dramatic dialogue of *Richard
III* is: what does an individual do when he or she witnesses the ero-
sion of civil and ecclesiastical liberties? More suggested that most
remain passive and do nothing:

And so they said that these matters be but kings' games, as it were stage plays, and for the most part played upon scaffolds, in which poor men be but onlookers. And they that be wise will meddle no farther. For they that sometimes step up and play with them, when they cannot play their parts, they disorder the play and do themself no good. (HR3 83)

The poor have no power to influence events, and the wise think it best to keep a low profile. More's metaphor of the stage/scaffold brilliantly illustrates how the stage of public life can so often turn into a scaffold for a political victim. He exposed the double standards of political life: Edward's mistress, Jane Shore, had to do public penance for having lived openly with the king, while Richard's dark deeds of murder were committed in private and went unpunished. She was disgraced, he was honoured.

Why did More select this subject in 1513? He shared with other humanists a keen perception of the driving ambitions of renaissance princes, who spent much money on flamboyant lifestyles, and ambitious wars of self-glory, while neglecting their real responsibilities. When Henry VIII succeeded his father in 1509, the new reign raised many hopes. Four years later these hopes were proving illusory. So More began his reflections on the nature of good and bad government, and the misuse of power. He drew on his knowledge of the great classics of political thought: Plato's *Republic*, Cicero's *De Officiis* and Augustine's *City of God*.

Good government must include respect for the life and liberty of the subject and for the legal, civic and ecclesiastical liberties of the realm. What happens when good government is threatened or breaks down? We would love to know More's answer, but he never finished his manuscript, which ends as Archbishop Morton moves to take action against Richard. (The traditional view is that church or state authorities have the right and duty to remove a tyrant by force.) But by 1515/16, More was considering entering the king's service; so a treatise on how to rid the nation of a prince who had overstepped his rights was hardly politic. By that time he was working out another answer in *Utopia*. The philosopher or wise man must neither remain a passive spectator of events, nor use force to change them:

> *But there is another philosophy, more practical for statesmen, which knows its stage, adapts itself to the plot, and performs its role neatly and appropriately.* (U BOOK 1)

If you cannot change events, then at least work to make them less harmful than they might have been.

In a very real sense *Utopia* provides the answer to the unfinished dilemma posed at the end of *Richard III*. More could not continue to air his misgivings in a historical narrative, which looked like repeating itself in contemporary events. He had to find another mode of discourse and a less provocative way to continue his reflections on the nature of good and bad government. And so *Utopia* was conceived: an imaginary island, perhaps somewhere in the New World, where citizens had arrived at a form of government which put Christian Europe to shame.

Utopian Vision
1515–1516

Our own age and ages to come will discover in his [More's] narra-
tive, a seedbed, so to speak, of elegant and useful concepts from
which men will be able to borrow.   (WILLIAM BUDE, 1517)

In May 1515 More was sent to Flanders as part of a diplomatic
delegation, probably in connection with the English-Flemish wool
trade. The delegates met in Bruges, but negotiations were
adjourned in late July. As More did not return to London until 25
October, he had three months of unexpected leisure at his disposal, so he began to set down his thoughts on the nature of good government, and the role of a good councillor. Having some business
in Antwerp, he took the opportunity to meet Peter Giles, city clerk
to the town council, and humanist friend of Erasmus. More and
Giles clearly enjoyed each other's company, and their conversations formed the factual background to the fictional setting of
More's embryonic book. With the help of his friends, More soon
found a novel and creative way of entering into contemporary
humanist debates on what constituted good government, and
what was the price to be paid for entering public service.

Introducing *Utopia*

Antwerp was a major European port, crowded with ships and
travellers from the New World, which had been discovered by
Columbus less than twenty-five years earlier (1492). One day

Peter Giles supposedly introduced More to a Portuguese traveller, Raphael Hythloday, recently returned from the Americas. They were invited back to More's house. 'There in the garden we sat down on a bench covered with grassy turf, to talk together.' Their day-long conversations formed the setting and subject matter of *Utopia*, with an interlude for dinner between Book One and Book Two.

The longer name for More's new book was *The Best State of a Commonwealth and the New Island of Utopia*. Because the title has been shortened to *Utopia*, many readers have focused on the fictitious island of Book Two, and paid less attention to the real island – sixteenth-century England – described in Book One. But both books are equally important; to focus on the second is to miss the point. *Utopia* (meaning Nowhere) was in many ways a mirror image of a very real place: Tudor England. By creating a hypothetical world which could be set against the actual world, More hoped to stimulate thought and provoke debate and discussion. *Utopia*, thus conceived, was a realistic tool for political change and reform, and not idealistic (or Utopian) at all.

We now know that Book Two was probably composed first, and while More was in Flanders; Book One was completed on his return to England. More sent a copy of the completed work to Peter Giles, with an explanatory letter, which is probably the best guide to the author's enigmatic intentions. *Utopia*, written in Latin for a European readership, was first published in Louvain in December 1516, and was so well received that it was reprinted in Paris (1517) and in Basle (1518, two impressions). After the 1518 edition, there was to be a curious gap of over thirty years, before it was translated into English (1551). This undoubtedly reflected the difficult period of the early Reformation, when such a work, inviting critical reform, could be misunderstood in Catholic circles.

Though there is no substitute for reading the text of *Utopia* itself, opinion is so divided about its meaning and purpose, that a brief guide to conflicting interpretations may be helpful. One view is that *Utopia* should be read at its face value, and expresses More's blueprint for an ideal state. An alternative view is that *Utopia* is a highly enigmatic, ironic discourse, which partly expresses More's ideal and partly does not. This view is supported by those who would locate More's thought within broader humanistic concerns. *Utopia*, they would argue, is a trip to 'nowhere' (the Greek *ou* + *topos*), narrated by Hythloday, whose name means 'expert in nonsense'. So *Utopia* is partly More's ideal, and partly a model which he recognizes has severe limitations. A further view is that *Utopia* was a *jeu d'esprit*, something tossed off by More, and never intended to be taken seriously. This is the least convincing of the three approaches.

Book One: The Dialogue of Counsel

The fictitious setting for *Utopia* is a garden in Antwerp, where two friends, Morus and Peter Giles, come together to hear about Raphael Hythloday's travels. (More, the author, must be distinguished from his semi-fictional persona, Morus.) Hythloday is no ordinary traveller, but a man in search of the truth about political life, comparing the customs of one country with another. The friends are so impressed with the knowledge he has acquired as a 'political' tourist, that they press him to consider entering the service of a prince, and using his gifts as a good councillor. So almost immediately the friends are diverted from their main purpose – hearing an account of Hythloday's travels – into how he can best use his expertise back in Europe. Hythloday presents a strong case for not entering public life, since its business affairs disturb the tranquillity and leisure of mind necessary for thought – the highest form of activity open to human beings. Morus presents the case for such an engagement, since he considers the highest human activity is to be able to put one's gifts at the service of others for the common good.

Humanists were frequently called upon to give political advice to rulers. So they often discussed the topic of good counsel under two aspects. Firstly, how can a ruler secure good advice and distinguish true from false friends? Secondly, how can a philosopher engage in politics without loss of integrity and loss of that 'leisure' time necessary for thought? There were further pragmatic considerations: does good advice actually affect any policy directly? Do rulers ever take advice which goes against their self-interest? Is it better to concentrate power in the hands of a single ruler, or to share power among an elected group of magistrates? Does the common good ultimately depend on the kind of government which is in place? In discussion on *The Best State of a Commonwealth*, humanists drew heavily on classical political philosophy, especially the thought of Plato, Aristotle and Cicero. They were in agreement about what constituted the best state: one which had just laws, promoted the common good, and enabled its citizens to live well, happily and with human dignity. They differed about the means best suited to achieve this end. *Utopia* is concerned with all these questions.

In Book One of *Utopia*, Peter Giles speaks rarely. In its uneven dialogue Hythloday (the idealist) argues for non-involvement in public life, Morus (the realist) for involvement. Hythloday describes a supposed visit he made to England and a meal in the household of Archbishop Morton of Canterbury. Morton's 'table talk' turned to urgent issues in contemporary England: the widespread use of hanging for minor theft, which was both unjust and ineffectual; the number of crippled war veterans who swelled the ranks of beggars; the parasitic lifestyles of nobles living off the labour of others; the menace of nobles and retainers trained for war; the cruelty of enclosures forced by those who saw sheep as more profitable than smallholders or villagers; the disparity between the extravagantly rich and the destitute poor. In contemporary England individuals were motivated by self-interest, not by justice or equity. It was an example not of the best, but of the worst state of a commonwealth. When Hythloday tried to offer good advice, it fell on deaf ears. He was not attracted to the role of being a permanent councillor.

Following this trenchant social analysis of the state of contemporary England, Morus reminds Hythloday that Plato taught that commonwealths would be happy only when philosophers became kings or kings became philosophers. 'No wonder we are so far from happiness when philosophers do not condescend even to assist kings with their counsels' (U 28). Hythloday replies by imagining himself to be present at two kinds of royal councils. For example, were he to be present at the council of the king of France, could he dissuade him from pressing his claims to Milan, or Naples, or Flanders or Burgundy? Could he prevent the sham diplomacy and offers of peace which really served royal war aims? If he were to join another royal council (England thinly disguised), could wise counsel prevent unjust and manipulative ways of raising taxes, or stop judges from declaring in the interest of the king? Such councils are dishonourable and immoral. There is no place for the philosopher at the council of kings. A true philosopher must remain aloof from the corrupt world of politics.

Morus disagrees: there may not be a place for the academic philosophy of the schools in public life, but there is a place for a more practical, applied philosophy, which accommodates itself to the task at hand. Any society, including contemporary England, has less than desirable features. But you have to work with what you have, since politics is the art of the possible.

That's how things go in the commonwealth and in councils of princes. If you cannot pluck up bad ideas by the root, or cure longstanding evils to your heart's content, you must not therefore abandon the commonwealth. Don't give up the ship in a storm because you cannot direct the winds. And don't force strange and untested ideas on people who you know are firmly persuaded the other way. You must strive to influence policy indirectly, urge your case vigorously but tactfully, and thus what you cannot turn to good you may at least make as little bad as possible. For it is impossible to make everything good unless all men are good, and that I don't expect to see for quite a few years yet. (U 36)

Hythloday again argues the opposite case; accommodation to existing reality will not work. The moral (*honestas*) is not compatible with the expedient (*utilitas*):

When you say I should 'influence policy indirectly' I simply do not know what you mean ... In a council there is no way to dissemble or play the innocent. You must openly approve the worst proposals and warmly urge the most vicious policies. A man who went along only half-heartedly would immediately be suspected as a spy, perhaps a traitor. (U 37)

Hythloday continues: good government is impossible unless the evils of money and private property are rooted out, and people hold all things in common. Drastic remedies are required if things are really to change. A good state can be judged by what its citizens admire, or what conduct they think most deserving of praise and honour. Contemporary England operates on a false scale of social values. People attach enormous prestige to noble birth, wealth and its trappings, living in magnificent and showy splendour. A nobility trained for chivalry, thinks it honourable to go to war, or to pursue martial arts, or to hunt down animals for a pastime. The root of all these evils is private property and self-interest. And the riches of the few condemn the vast majority to a life of unrelieved poverty and unhappiness.

But things can be done differently. Hythloday has seen a society where there is no private property, where wealth is distributed evenly and citizens live in peace and happiness. He has seen this at work in the island of *Utopia*. His disbelieving friends suggest they adjourn for lunch before hearing any more.

It has been well argued that one of the multi-layered meanings of *Utopia* is pride as the source of social evil. Pride 'is not just feeling good about yourself. It is feeling good because you feel *superior* to someone else' (OLIN, *INTERPRETING THOMAS MORE'S* UTOPIA 41). Pride feeds on the envy or adulation of others. It needs the trappings of wealth, power, and position. It spawns the time-server and the flatterer. Pride is the special temptation of the ruler, who is not satisfied with the land he possesses, but undertakes wars of self-aggrandizement for dynastic reasons, bringing untold misery to others. Pride is the source of social sin, the political aspect of humanity's fall from grace. White argues that the central theme of Book One is this connection between pride and social evil (the problem), and that Book Two suggests how this evil might be eliminated (the solution). This is the essential connection between both books and the reason for the long digression of Book One.

Book Two: The New Island of Utopia

Hythloday's travel tale makes use of the intense contemporary excitement and public interest in the 'discovery' of the New World (1492). He supposedly made the outward journey with Amerigo Vespucci (1504), but stayed behind for some years of further travels. He arrived at *Utopia*, and was an open-minded observer of another culture. Hythloday describes a community of human beings untouched by either pagan classical civilization or Christian religion. Yet through their use of human intelligence and ingenuity, they had not only arrived at an advanced state of civilization, but held highly developed beliefs in God, providence, morality, and the immortality of the soul. Rational religion and philosophy were able to shape a just and equitable society, in many ways more advanced and admirable than contemporary Christian Europe. Utopian fiction was another way of expressing humanist belief that human beings had the power to shape their destiny, and had options open to them. Life was not a fate to be endured, but a future to be created, and in this, most of all, human beings resembled their creator, God.

GEOGRAPHY OF *UTOPIA*

Utopia is imagined as an island which, geographically and socially, is a mirror image of England. Its founder, Utopus, ordered a channel fifteen miles wide to be cut to separate the island from the mainland – and from contamination from the outside world. Utopia has fifty-four city states, and a capital, Amaurot, where three representative citizens from each city meet once a year. Every town is situated within at least a twelve-mile radius of farm land. Citizens have to work at least two years in a farming household on a rotating basis. (This is in direct contrast to Europe, where manual labour was held in contempt.) Rural households number forty or more adults, and are organized into groups of thirty, under a leader. The groups are self-sufficient, and either barter or share their surplus goods with their neighbours.

Amaurot, the capital, is a walled city on a tidal river, with an arched stone bridge (like London). Amaurot and all cities are carefully planned. The citizens enjoy piped water, good defences, wide streets, open doors and large gardens. 'In a sense gardens are symbolic of *Utopia* itself, a means of modifying the harm done in an earlier lost garden, and the delight taken in them is an anticipation of paradise regained', (*MORE'S* UTOPIA, 1991, D. BAKER-SMITH 160). Every ten years citizens exchange houses and gardens, as there is no privately owned property. Citizens are good tenants rather than property owners. Houses are comfortable, three-storeyed, faced with brick or stone, well decorated, and with glass or oiled linen in the windows.

GOVERNMENT

The Utopian form of government is a federation of cities which manage their own internal affairs. The basic group is the household. Once a year each group of thirty households elects a leader, and each group of ten such leaders elects its own representative (a tranibor). Only the tranibors may be re-elected. When needed, all elected officials come together, to choose a magistrate or governor from four men nominated by each area of the city. The governor holds office for life, unless 'suspected of aiming at tyranny', when he can be removed. The tranibors consult daily with the governor, and each time bring two different leaders with them to the senate. All matters of importance are discussed with a general assembly of elected officials, who also consult their households. Utopian city government tries to avoid an aristocracy, and to involve citizens in decision-making on democratic lines. But it is decidedly 'paternal', which reflects More's own family values. Governor, senate, and representative assembly relate in ways designed to block both tyranny and plotting factions. Strangely, in *Utopia* there is no positive enjoyment of politics; political structures exist to facilitate the 'good life', but are not really part of it.

OCCUPATIONS

Each citizen has two occupations: farming, which all must share in turn, and a choice of crafts or trades. Women work at lighter crafts, and sons usually follow their father's trade. Each citizen works for six hours a day, three before noon, and three after a siesta. Spare time is given over to intellectual pursuits. They have a period of recreation after supper for music or conversation, but they never gamble. They go to bed early, sleep eight hours, and rise early for public lectures before daybreak. (Commentators have noted the quasi-monastic structure of the Utopian day, and its resemblance to More's own household regime.)

Short working hours provide amply for their needs, as they do not have to provide luxury goods or inessentials. Some leaders may be exempt from work but often choose not to be. Scholars are exempted, and from this intellectual class are chosen the ambassadors, priests, tranibors and the governor himself. Only the learned may hold high public office, but in case they become a privileged group, their number is limited to about five hundred. Buildings last a long time and are kept in good repair. Back in Europe clothes locate a person socially, and are an indicator of rank and wealth. But the Utopians opt for the equality of uniform clothing, and use simple undyed fabrics (wool and linen), avoiding extravagance and waste.

SOCIAL AND BUSINESS RELATIONS, TRAVEL

Households are patriarchal, under the rule of the oldest male, and are limited to between ten and sixteen adults. On marrying, a woman joins the household of her husband. If a city exceeds six thousand households, it plants a new colony, preferably in uncultivated and unoccupied land. If the population shrinks, citizens are brought back from the colonies. *Utopia* is not a money economy. Heads of households collect what they need from area markets. Families dine in common dining halls assigned to each ward of the city, thirty families to each hall. Their women take it in turns to prepare meals, and nurses and infants are assigned a separate area. Stewards collect the food for halls and local hospitals. Citizens serving penal time as slaves do the chores and heavy work. The leader and his wife sit at a high table, with two elders or the priest. Seating is arranged in fours, with young and old interspersed. Children and unmarried young people either wait at table, or wait for food to be given them by adults. In remote rural households, meals are taken at home.

Citizens may only travel to other districts with permission, and must earn their own keep. There are no wine-bars, ale-houses, brothels or spots for secret meetings: they live in full view of all. If they make a trade surplus abroad, it is kept against a contingency such as war. They do not prize gold or silver but use them to make chamber pots, humbler vessels, and even the chains and fetters of slaves. Gems are used as playthings for children until they know better. Visiting ambassadors, who wear ostentatious dress and jewels, evoke surprise and ridicule, rather than honour and respect. In general, Utopians are amazed to meet people who value others for their wealth or dress, rather than their virtue. Both their way of life and their study confirm these views.

PHILOSOPHY: IN PRAISE OF PLEASURE

In the descriptive opening narrative of Book Two, Hythloday is not trying to describe the maximum desirable features of this state, but rather the minimum *necessary* for the happiness of its citizens. Even so, certain physical, constitutional or economic choices must be made to attain even minimum goals, and there is the recognition that even in the best state there may be conflict between valid goals. This may explain, or make sense of, some puzzling aspects of the work: the fact that More's commonwealth is a flawed one, and in places at variance with his own ideals.

Utopia is imagined as an inclusive society based on collective security, rather than on inequality of fortune founded on individual endeavour. However, it becomes clear that the equality, which guarantees satisfaction of basic needs and time for leisure, is very restrictive of personal liberty and choice. *Utopia* may be highly moral, but it is also exceedingly dull and uniform. And yet these people who live 'according to nature' are in essentials Epicureans (lovers of pleasure) rather than Stoics (those who make virtue the highest good). They discuss the nature of both virtue and pleasure, but their chief concern is *human happiness, and whether it consists of one thing or many. They seem rather too much inclined to the view that all or the most important part of human happiness consists of pleasure. And what is more surprising, they seek support for this comfortable opinion from their religion ... for they never discuss happiness without joining to their philosophic rationalism certain principles of religion. Without these religious principles they think that reason is bound to prove weak and defective in its efforts to investigate true happiness.* (U 67–8)

There is an opposed school in *Utopia* which argues that virtue itself is happiness, whether it leads to pleasure or not. They say virtue means living according to nature.

Nothing is more humane (and humanity is the virtue most proper to human beings) than to relieve the misery of others, assuage their griefs, and by removing all sadness from their lives, to restore them to enjoyment, that is pleasure. Well, if this is the case, why doesn't nature equally invite us to do the same thing for ourselves? ... Thus, they say, nature herself prescribes for us a joyous life, in other words pleasure, as the goal of our actions; and living according to her rules is to be defined as virtue. And as nature bids men to make one another's life cheerful ... so she repeatedly warns you not to seek your own advantage in ways that cause misfortune to others ... she cherishes alike all those living beings to whom she has granted the same form. (U 70)

Utopia is an attempt to create a society and culture where the pursuit of pleasure (self-interest) and virtue (consideration for others) are not mutually exclusive. Utopians believe that the goal of life, or happiness, consists mainly in the cultivation of the mind, and depends on domestic order and freedom from conflict. The enjoyment of pleasurable activities (in moderation) is compatible with virtue. But in *Utopia* the rational devices used to curb and control human ambition and greed screen out much of the variety, richness and unpredictability of human living. The state knows best how to provide for education, training, communal goods, family and civic life. It is a uniform, grey civilization, and perhaps reflects More's pessimism, that it is not really possible to create a 'good' society on earth.

Paradoxically, however, Utopian communism is close to the spirit of the early Church, where Christians held all things in common, 'and had but one mind and one heart' (ACTS 4:32). 'If the entire second book has a symbol, it is that of the common dining hall which abounds in good things and pleasures. Each meal taken together stands for the triumph of justice and equity, and represents the equality and communion of all the citizens' (E. SURTZ, CW, *UTOPIA*, XXV). To us the lack of privacy and freedom of choice seems contrary to our notions of human dignity. But the sixteenth-century household knew little privacy, and even less about individual (as opposed to communal) entitlement and rights.

Utopian practices are to be preferred to many features of contemporary Europe. Utopians dislike ostentatious dress, and cannot understand those who are taken in by flattery, empty ceremony or honours. They count these, as well as gambling, dicing and hunting, as false pleasures.

> *If what you want is slaughter, if you want to see a living creature torn apart before your eyes, then the whole thing is wrong. You ought to feel nothing but pity when you see the hare fleeing from the hound, the weak creature tormented by the stronger, the fearful and timid beast brutalized by the savage one, the harmless hare killed by the cruel hound.* (U 73)

There is pity for animals here, but also a hatred for pastimes which are considered honourable by the European nobility, but which brutalize, and are a form of training for the martial arts.

CONTROVERSIAL FEATURES OF UTOPIAN SOCIETY

Utopian society has slaves, either taken as prisoners of war, or citizens deprived of freedom for their crimes. Utopians are not born into slavery, and so there is no 'slave class' by birth or nature (an improvement on classical times). Sometimes foreign criminals condemned to death in another country, or foreign vagrants, are imported as slaves. Slaves are not essential but rather convenient to the economy, as they perform the lowliest tasks such as butchery. Slavery is a punishment for a severe and public crime. 'Slaves are permanent and visible reminders that crime does not pay ... But if they are patient they are not left without hope' (U 82). Their sentences can be commuted, although rebellion means instant death.

Though the sick are well cared for, the priests and public officials encourage the terminally ill to consider ending their own lives.

> *They never force this step on a man against his will; nor if he decides against it, do they lessen their care of him. The man who yields to their arguments, they think, dies an honourable death; but the suicide, who takes his own life without the approval of priests and senate, they consider him unworthy of either earth or fire, and throw his body, unburied and disgraced, into the nearest bog.* (U 81)

Though marriage is normally for life, and adultery severely punished, the Utopians allow divorce in rare cases, where it can be proved the marriage has broken down completely. Before marriage 'the bride-to-be is shown naked to the groom by a responsible and respectable matron; and similarly, some respectable man presents the groom naked to his prospective bride' (U 83). Though the custom seems absurd to the visitors, the Utopians regard it as essential to be legally protected from deception or physical deformity before the marriage takes place.

Utopians despise war 'and think nothing so inglorious as the glory won in battle'. They only go to war for good reasons: self-defence, to repel invasion, or to liberate an oppressed people. They dislike a victory won at too high a price. There is no standing army, but a civilian militia (including women) called up when needed. But some of their practices are highly dubious: to save their own citizens, they prefer to hire mercenaries; they use their surplus money, acquired by trading but not usable at home, to destabilize the enemy and reward hit killers; they enslave prisoners of war, take money and estates as war indemnities; they turn the inhabitants off land they conquer or need for colonies. Utopians do not regard foreigners as equals with civic rights, and their foreign policy is expedient rather than moral. So, although *Utopia* works well insulated from the outer world, contact through war or colonization brings a host of unsolved problems. (Does More intend his readers to pick this up and to realize that his ideal state had less than ideal features? He seems to leave these matters enigmatically open.)

RELIGION AND RELIGIOUS TOLERANCE

Utopians have moved from more primitive mythic religions to a form of rational deism. Different forms of religion are tolerated throughout the island but the vast majority of Utopians

> *believe in a single power, unknown, eternal, infinite, inexplicable, far beyond the grasp of the human mind, and diffused throughout the universe, not physically but in influence. They call him father, and to him alone they attribute the origin, increase, progress, change and end of all visible things; they do not offer divine honours to any other.* (U 96)

All citizens share in a similar form of public temple worship, and hold simple basic beliefs in common: a belief in the divine government of the world and in the immortality of the soul. Some religious diversity is allowed within the household rites. Utopians inherited a tradition of religious tolerance from their founder, who thought that:

> even if one religion is really true and the rest false, the true one will sooner or later prevail by its own natural strength, if men will only consider the matter reasonably and modestly ... so he left the whole matter open allowing each person to choose what he would believe. (U 98)

In such matters Utopus 'was not quick to dogmatize,

> because he suspected that God perhaps likes various forms of worship, and has deliberately inspired different men with different views. On the other hand he was quite sure that it was arrogant folly for anyone to enforce conformity with his own beliefs by threats or violence.'

Utopus even allowed a man to try to make converts, provided he did so 'quietly, modestly, rationally and without bitterness towards others. If persuasion failed, no man might resort to abuse or violence, under penalty of exile or slavery.' But it is a toleration within strict limits: anyone who denied the minimal basic beliefs in divine providence, or the immortality of the soul, was denied public office and held in disgrace. 'Yet they do not punish him, because they are persuaded that no man can choose to believe by a mere act of will ... and they are confident that in the end his madness will yield to reason' (U 99).

When Utopians heard about Christianity they were well disposed towards it, and many were baptized. But 'those who have not accepted Christianity make no effort to restrain others from it, nor do they criticize new converts to it' (U 97). An unruly, over-enthusiastic convert who 'created a public disorder', was exiled, not punished: 'it is one of their oldest rules that no one should suffer for his religion' (U 97).

In view of More's later controversial writings and intolerant attitude towards those who did not share his beliefs during the Reformation, it is important to grasp the social and civic limits to a Utopian form of religious toleration. A citizen who did not believe in God or an after-life was a civic threat, and had to be exiled from the community – but not physically punished. It is also of interest to see the Utopian priesthood as limited in number, inclusive of women, and characterized by great personal holiness. Priests exercise no power 'beyond that which derives from their good repute' (U 102). By implication, this is a criticism of worldly, powerful and corrupt clerics in Christian Europe, and expresses a desire for clerical reform.

Back to Reality: The Uses of *Utopia*

Hythloday (the idealist) finishes his praise of *Utopia* by comparing 'this justice of the Utopians with that which prevails among other nations', especially in Christian Europe. He ends where he began, listing the deeds of social injustice prevalent in contemporary society. 'When I run over in my mind the various commonwealths flourishing today ... I can see in them nothing but a conspiracy of the rich, who are fattening up their own interests under the name and title of the commonwealth' (U 108). The root cause is human pride. Morus (the realist) is very suspicious of the cure: Utopian communism. But Hythloday is tired – and inclined to be touchy. Morus tactfully guides him in to supper, and leaves his criticisms for another day.

How does More intend his readers to react to his Utopian fiction? Are we expected to share Hythloday's enthusiasm for a society based on common ownership? Or do we come away like Morus, impressed but convinced it is an impracticable dream?

Meanwhile, while I can hardly agree with everything he said ... yet I freely confess that in the Utopian commonwealth there are many

*features that in our own societies I would like, rather than expect,
to see.*   (U 111)

Is More happy to have sown the seeds of possible ways of acting,
and to leave it to his readers to decide whether some (or any) of
them can be transplanted into the politics of the real world? If, in
this real world, private property is retained (the indications are
that More thought this to be inevitable), did he intend us to see
that the price to be paid is very high? More intended Utopian society to be a reminder of the limitations we may have to place on
unrestricted human freedoms, in the interests of the good of others, and of living in harmony in a community.

At almost exactly the same time, and unknown to More, his
contemporary Niccolo Machiavelli was writing his famous political work, *The Prince* (1513). He wrote:

*Many have imagined republics and principalities which have never
been seen or known to exist in reality; for how we live is so far
removed from how we ought to live, that he who abandons what is
done for what ought to be done, will rather learn to bring about his
own ruin than his preservation.*   (THE PRINCE)

More and Machiavelli would have agreed that 'how we live is ... far
removed from how we ought to live' because human beings are
essentially self-interested and self-regarding. But Machiavelli went
on to state that the art and logic of acquiring and maintaining
political power meant manipulating and using human self-
interest. 'A man who wishes to make a profession of goodness in
everything must necessarily come to grief among so many who
are not good.'

This is precisely Hythloday's reason for not engaging in the corrupt world of politics. The moral (*honestas*) is incompatible with
the expedient (*utilitas*). Hythloday wanted to retire from a life of
public service to one of tranquil thought – unless self-interest can

be neutralized, as in Utopian society. He opted for the moral. Machiavelli wanted to withdraw from 'making a profession of goodness in politics'. He opted for the expedient. More remained committed to a strategy which struggled to combine the moral and the expedient: for virtue and honesty in public life are their own reward. Politics is the art of the possible. A good man cannot abandon the public sphere, and those who need protection from injustice. By being there he can at least temper its severity: 'what you cannot turn to good, at least make as little bad as possible' (U 36).

The struggle to relate the moral and the expedient was to be severely tested at least twice in More's public life. What does a Lord Chancellor do when citizens refuse to obey willingly the laws against heresy? Is he morally justified in using force, even violence, to get compliance? And what happens to a loyal servant of the crown when he has to choose between the moral and the expedient – either refusing an immoral oath or conforming to the wishes of his prince? The issues raised theoretically in *Utopia* were to become real in More's own public and personal life.

The King's Servant
Public Life 1517–1532

*In your counsel-giving unto his grace, ever tell him what he ought
to do, but never what he is able to do … For if a lion knew his own
strength, hard were it for any man to rule him.* (THOMAS MORE
TO THOMAS CROMWELL)

Thomas More was appointed to the King's Council sometime in
1517. He joined his father John, and his humanist friends, John
Colet and Cuthbert Tunstall, who were already members of the
council. He did not tell Erasmus for some time, and then gave him
to believe that he had accepted the office with some reluctance.
'No one has ever been so eager to get into court as More was
to stay out of it,' wrote Erasmus to a friend. But More's supposed
reluctance to assume office has been reassessed; we now believe
that though he did not accept office lightly, he chose it and
wanted it.

There was a high price to be paid. When More sent his finished
Utopia to his friend Peter Giles (1516), he complained in an
accompanying letter how difficult it was to find time to write :

*Most of my day is given to the law, pleading some cases, hearing
others … I have to visit this man because of his official position and
that man because of his lawsuit; and so almost the whole day is
devoted to other people's business; and what's left over to my own;
and then for myself – that is my studies – there is nothing left.
For when I come home I must talk with my wife, chat with my*

children, and converse with my servants ... and this has to be done
unless one wants to be a stranger in one's own home. (U 4)

More concludes that he can only snatch time to write from ' the
time stolen from sleep and food'. This situation could only get
worse as he entered public life and assumed public responsibilities. Apart from a brief period in 1528–1529, More rarely had
leisure for writing, reading or research. He did not merely observe,
but was deeply involved in, the political issues of the day. Before
assessing his polemical and devotional writings, this chapter will
briefly consider the public context of his life which shaped, but
also put quite exceptional constraints on, his literary output.

Councillor, Diplomat, Secretary (1517–1529)

Henry VIII disliked the routine of government, which he left to his
councillors and to his chancellor, Wolsey. This meant that there
were two centres of politics: this King's court in royal progress
from one residence to another, and Wolsey's household operating
from York House or Hampton Court. Wolsey effectively governed
England, though he had to keep the King informed of state business, secure his signature for documents, and appear to defer to
his will. Wolsey was rarely in attendance on the King, and lived in
constant fear that resident courtiers would work to erode his
influence and power. In such a situation it was essential to have
councillors trusted by both King and Chancellor. More fulfilled
this role with integrity and skill for twelve years, before his own
appointment to the chancellorship.

In 1523 Wolsey pressed Henry VIII to give More a generous fee
for services rendered, because 'he is not the most ready to speak
and solicit his own cause'. In this More lived out his Utopian
ideals. The real interest, however, lies in the question put in
Utopia: can a wise councillor actually influence political events, or
make any substantive contribution to public life, if he is unwilling

to fight political battles and get his hands dirty? In practice, how did More balance the claims of the moral and the expedient?

At first Henry used More mainly for his humanist skills as a secretary, orator and diplomat. As an orator he welcomed foreign visitors to court, and as a diplomat he accompanied the King or the Chancellor on foreign missions, and took part in negotiations. But it would seem that he was an adviser rather than an influential shaper of foreign policy. Wolsey frequently used him as his direct intermediary with the King. When at court Henry often sent for More to discuss astronomy, geometry or theology, and More probably had a hand in preparing Henry's *Defence of the Seven Sacraments* against Luther (1521). More's contribution to court entertainment was so valued that he found it difficult to escape to spend time with his wife and family. But he had no illusions about the permanence of royal favour. When his son-in-law Roper was unduly impressed after the King's visit to their home in Chelsea, More remarked 'Son Roper, I may tell thee I have no cause to be proud thereof, for if my head could win him a castle in France ... it should not fail to go' (ROPER 208).

More was elected Speaker of the House of Commons in 1523, a task to tax his principles and political skill. The Speaker spoke for the Commons: its members expected him to be their spokesman and to defend their liberties. But the Speaker was also the king's servant, expected to manage the Commons and get his business through. In 1523 More had to commend heavy war taxation to the House, while defending its right to speak its mind freely. Through the voice of its Speaker, the House did not capitulate to royal bullying. More's legal duties continued. With the court in progress, he dealt with the bills of complaint brought to the king. At Westminster he sat as judge in the Court of the Star Chamber, and was active on various reform committees.

In July 1525 More was appointed Chancellor of the Duchy of Lancaster, which involved residence at Court, with intervals away on Duchy business. He emerges as a 'hardworking administrator, a peacemaker more concerned to get at the causes of violence in the countryside, that to inflict harsh punishments, a protector of the weak against the strong, and an astute lawyer who could cut through the mass of detail to the heart of the matter in hand' (EA 118, M. HASTINGS). The Chancellorship of the Duchy was to be an invaluable preparation for the Chancellorship of England. However, More had no expectation of this in 1525; on the contrary, he was aware that Wolsey had promoted him 'sideways', to an office with more status but less influence and less remuneration.

From 1527 onwards, the question of the King's divorce from Catherine of Aragon was to prove the single most intractable political problem of the coming years. But though the King's 'great matter' was worrying, in More's view the growing influence of imported Protestant writings was even more serious. His friends convinced him that his gifts and reputation as a writer could be of incalculable use in combating heresy. So in March 1528 More accepted a licence from Tunstall, now Bishop of London, to acquire and read Protestant writings in order to refute their contents. He partly withdrew from public life to devote himself to this task. These writings will be considered in the next chapter.

Chancellor of England (1529–1532)

In June 1529 More was asked by Wolsey to help to negotiate the Peace of Cambrai. Within a few months Wolsey himself fell from power (October 1529), and after an interval of several days More emerged as a compromise candidate for the office of Lord Chancellor. His relative lack of power, aversion to faction and intrigue, and proven suitability for the judicial work of the office, made him a more acceptable choice than other rival candidates. More hesitated to accept, but was ordered by Henry to do so, the King promising 'never to molest his conscience' in the matter of the royal divorce. Shortly after receiving the seal of office on 25/26 October 1529, More launched a bitter attack on all that Wolsey had stood for. Perhaps this was a public exercise in damage limitation, since Henry (through More) had to explain Wolsey's sudden departure. Yet this unexpected attack on his disgraced former master does More little credit.

More's term of office as Chancellor was short, difficult and enmeshed with events which were part of the emerging Protestant Reformation in England. According to his biographer Roper, More desired three goals for Christian Europe, or as he thought of it, Christendom: perpetual peace between kings, extermination of heresy, and a 'good conclusion' to the King's divorce case (ROPER 210). The fragile Peace of Cambrai lasted until 1538; extermination of heresy was to be pursued by More as writer and as enforcer of the law; the 'conclusion to the King's divorce' was to be politically and personally disastrous for More. Inevitably More's views on universal Christendom clashed with the evolving ideas on the nature of a nation state, sovereign in all matters, spiritual and temporal. And More's (private) views on the royal divorce cast him as the political opponent of the king he tried to serve. 'The wonder is surely not that More ultimately failed but that he ever believed he might succeed' (GUY, *THE PUBLIC CAREER OF SIR THOMAS MORE*, 112).

More and the Law: Equity and Justice

More spent a great part of his life practising as a common lawyer and judge. 'It was as a judge, not as a politician, that his reputation stands highest' (GUY 93). When he became Lord Chancellor, More held the highest law office in the land, and in thirty-one months made a distinguished contribution to the development of impartial justice in the English legal system. Unfortunately he did not write a treatise either on English common law or on church canon law. Many of his own personal papers were either lost or confiscated. However, what he thought about either system of law, and its application to particular circumstances, including his own, is crucial for any appreciation of More as a Christian thinker. It has to be gleaned from his other writings, from court records, and from what we know of his life.

Roper gives us some insight into More's thought and practice. When More was Chancellor, some common law judges came to him, complaining that he was too free in issuing injunctions from the Chancery, which overruled their court judgements. More invited them to dinner, listened to their complaints, and offered a compromise: if, after thought, and acting on their own discretion, they could 'mitigate and reform the rigour of the law themselves', he would issue no more injunctions. When they refused his offer he declared he had no alternative but to continue to issue injunctions 'to relieve the people's injury' (ROPER 221).

As is evident from *Utopia* Book One, where Hythloday is critical of the entire English system of justice, More thought that the strict application of the common law to particular cases was often unjust and unfair. 'Extreme justice should properly be called extreme injury' (U 22, CITING CICERO). For example, using the death penalty for theft was unjust because disproportionate to the nature of the crime. It was also ineffectual, since it failed to deter. Those who enforced the law rarely considered the root causes of crime. Yet many people were driven to steal in order to survive, since society provided them with no alternative. If in turn their children grew up to be thieves, society (not malice) was to blame for making them criminals. The strict application of the law, irrespective of the social causes of crime, 'may look superficially like justice, but is in reality neither just nor practical' (U 21). Hythloday (More) challenged the 'law and order' school of thought, which regarded punishment as a debt the criminal owned to society, but never looked at what society owed to the criminal: moral and social rehabilitation (U 24).

More was convinced that the administration of English justice was often slow, cumbersome, and biased in favour of the rich, who could afford lengthy litigation. The criminal laws were like 'cobwebs, in which the little nits and flies stick still and hang fast, but the great bumblebees break them and fly quite through' (D 230). Much of English law was case law, not framed in universal terms, but relying on the precedents of previous judgements. It often involved very rigid procedures, which needed to be simplified and processed more quickly. Judges also needed to be guided by the spirit of equity (the desire to be fair) and to balance the spirit against the letter of the law.

The tendency for common lawyers to stick to the strict application of the rigid procedures of the common law, was checked by the growth of new equity courts (the Star Chamber and Chancery), especially under the Tudors. More's predecessors as chancellor, Archbishops Morton, Wareham and Wolsey, all felt that the common law was too inflexible and failed to respond to changing circumstances. They used the Chancellor's Court, which had no jury, to cut through the technicalities of the common law and give justice more swiftly. More did not so much innovate as extend their practice, by making still greater use of these courts of equity. The prospect of making justice more available to the poor probably attracted him to working with Wolsey in the first place.

In 1528 a distinguished common lawyer, Christopher Saint German, began to develop his arguments for greater use of the principle of equity, in a treatise later expanded and published under the title *Doctor and Student*. What we know of More's thought and practice indicates his broad agreement with Saint German on the equity principle. (They were to agree on little else, as we shall see.) Saint German argued that too much attention to the procedures of the law tends to legalism, and can obscure common sense and ordinary fair-mindedness. He wanted to reorder and reform the rather messy and diverse traditions of the common law, and to re-examine them in the light of conscience. As he inherited and understood the concept, conscience was the practical faculty which mediated between universal law and particular act. It involved assent to the universal rule (an act of the reason) and application to a particular case (an act of the will or judgement). 'And this is the nature of the equitable; correction of law where it is defective owing to its universality' (ARISTOTLE). Equity could be described as conscience in action in the field of practical or applied justice (M. FLEISHER, *RADICAL REFORM AND POLITICAL PERSUASION IN THE LIFE AND WRITINGS OF THOMAS MORE* 24).

Where Saint German tended to set out in detail the ways in which law could be evaluated in the light of conscience, More moved directly to equity – the will to act justly. True justice does not exist in the abstract, though a good lawyer must have thorough grasp of its principles. True justice lies in the application of just principles. This is practical justice, comparable to More's practical theology (which must be pastoral), or practical philosophy (which must be ethical or political). The common lawyer, like the canon lawyer, the theologian, or the philosopher 'must abandon the formal letter in order to uphold the human being' (FLEISHER 29). Even more importantly, equity reflects the way in which a just and merciful God deals with sinners. It embodies the 'new law of mercy', where God rules us 'as a father rules his children', not by the strict enforcement of law (U 22).

In *Utopia*, there were few laws, no lawyers, and no private property. In England, much of More's time was taken up settling disputes over property, and he tried to prevent the kind of continuous litigation which refused to take a court settlement as final. More's integrity and reputation as an 'incorruptible judge' were widely respected. William Daunce, his son-in-law, remarked that he did not gain financially from being related to More, as others related to those in high office seemed able to do. More congratulated him for his honesty, but ironically indicated there were more subtle ways open to the unscrupulous than accepting bribes: dropping a word or writing a letter in a friend's favour, hearing his case earlier, appointing a biased commission to hear his suit, returning a favour with another favour. More ended :

I assure you on my faith, that if the parties will at my hand call for justice, then ... were it my father stood on the one side and the devil on the other, his cause being good, the devil should have right.
(ROPER 220)

More and the Extermination of Heresy

In view of More's constant concern that the strict application of the law must be mitigated by mercy and equity, his vigorous campaign against the Protestant Reformers, whom he regarded as heretics, is difficult to understand. During Wolsey's time as chancellor, not a single person was put to death for his or her religious beliefs. During More's time of office (October 1529–May 1532), six men were burned at the stake as heretics, and More was personally involved in the detection of three of them. The accusations that More flogged heretics against a tree in his Chelsea garden, or stole property from them, must be discounted. More denied them and defended his integrity with great dignity in his *Apology* of 1533; there is no good reason to doubt his word. Yet the burning of heretics, the banning of heretical books, and the humiliating public penances for those found with them, were repressive measures which seem strangely at odds with More's earlier belief in religious toleration. The Utopians, we were told, held that 'no one should suffer on account of his religious beliefs' (U 97). Did More abandon his humanistic ideals because dangerous times required difficult decisions? Did he lay aside the radical vision of his younger days, to meet the demands of real politics? The answer is both difficult and complex.

More was proud of his campaign against heretics, and he mentions it in the epitaph he wrote to sum up his life, where he describes himself as 'grievous to thieves, murderers and heretics'. He wrote to Erasmus:

As to that statement in my epitaph that I was a source of trouble for heretics – I wrote that with deep feeling. I find that breed of men absolutely loathsome, so much so that, unless they regain their senses, I want to be as hateful to them as anyone can possibly be; for my increasing experience with those men frightens me with the thought of what the world will suffer at their hands. (SL 46)

One of the most damaging allegations made against More by revisionist biographers, such as Richard Marius, is that More 'cried out' for heretics to be burned. 'This fury was not a bizarre lapse in an otherwise noble character; it is almost the essence of the man' (R. MARIUS, *THOMAS MORE* XXIV). Though Marius exonerates More from personally torturing heretics in his house, such exaggerated rhetoric is not supported by the evidence. More viewed heresy much as a modern magistrate might view racism: as a repulsive and divisive civil and ecclesiastical danger (KENNY). He wanted a 'clean cutting out' of the infected part of the civic body, to ensure the survival of the rest. The evidence seems to point to More's having shouldered a grim responsibility, in the firm conviction that he was doing right, but not to any rejoicing or fanatical pleasure.

More's deepest reasons for prosecuting heretics were theological and religious: heresy was a kind of treason of the soul, and endangered the eternal salvation of other Christians. As More saw it, to put the soul of another person in jeopardy risked cutting that person off from God for all eternity. Such an action, he thought, deserved the death penalty, and with it the forlorn hope that it might produce a last-minute recantation.

By our standards the processes of the age were cruel and repellent. Nevertheless, More's fierce intolerance towards heretics, and the part he played in persecution, cannot be defended, and are at odds with his Utopian ideals. They are the negative side of his vision of a Christian society – a society united in religious allegiance and sharing a common life. The notion that a unified society depends on common values remains valid even today. In More's time this seemed to most people to exclude religious dissent. While we may understand his reasons, it remains deeply distressing that in this matter More was a man of his time, not a 'man for all seasons'.

Common Law, Canon Law and the King's Divorce

More and his legal contemporaries operated within two distinct systems of law, the common law of England and the canon law of the universal Church. More's immediate predecessors as chancellor had been canon lawyers. More was a common lawyer with a working knowledge of canon law. To More the common law represented the accumulated wisdom, grounded in human reason, of a temporal kingdom. Canon law represented the accumulated wisdom of spiritual authority, grounded in divine law or revelation. Kings as heads of their kingdoms, and the Pope as the visible head of the universal Church of Christ, held their power from God, and represented God to those they ruled. More believed he owed allegiance to each as part of the divine ordering of temporal and spiritual society.

Canon law, like common law, needed to be simplified and reformed. More naturally believed that the proper authority to do that was the Church, not the state. The failure of the Fifth Lateran Council of 1512–1517, a general council of the whole Church, to undertake the reform of canon law was a source of scandal which contributed to the Protestant Reformation. Many lawyers of the time thought that King and Parliament should intervene, especially if there was a conflict of jurisdiction. But More upheld the liberty and privileges of the Church, which must administer its own legal system. To do otherwise would subordinate the law of the universal Church to the law of one kingdom. So More, the modernizing reformer of the common law, was seen as the conservative defender of canon law.

Tension between the two systems of justice was very evident with regard to heresy trials. Two notorious cases occurred in the early years of Henry VIII's reign: those of Richard Hunne (1514) and Henry Standish (1517). Hunne was found hanged in his cell two days after his canon law trial for heresy. Then, as now, death while in custody aroused popular indignation; arguments for and against his possible suicide or judicial murder rumbled on for years. Standish was cited before a church court for arguing that a papal decree had no validity in England unless 'received' by Parliament. The King's discreet silence at the trial implied his agreement with Standish. The case was dropped.

Anti-clerical, or anti-papal, feeling was spasmodic rather than endemic in England, but could easily be aroused. There was a strong perception that English men and women should not be subject to 'foreign' laws, that many clerics were motivated by self-interest, not justice, and that canon law gave clerics an unfair privileged status. There were battles within the legal profession about the procedures adopted in the church courts. The Hunne case haunted popular imagination. More returned to it in five of his polemical works, each time defending the action of church authorities. His harsh policy against heretics was unpopular and fanned criticism of the Church.

An alleged heretic was brought to trial in a church court, and if found guilty and sentenced to death, was handed over to the secular authority for execution. This meant that someone accused of heresy was tried by one system and punished by another. Church courts used an *inquisitorial* system, where the judges sought to elicit the truth, sometimes requiring a suspect to take an oath of innocence or be tried as a heretic. Common law courts used an *adversarial* system, where the case for and against the accused was argued, and then judged by a jury. Both systems had advantages, and both were open to abuse. To most ordinary people the English jury system seemed preferable. From 1529 to 1532 More, as enforcer of the laws of heresy, had to defend them and canon law practice, and so was perceived as pro-clerical and traditionalist.

The issues of common law and canon law were to be focused most sharply in the matter of the King's request for an annulment of his marriage to Catherine of Aragon. Marriage questions were clearly within church jurisdiction. Not normally a patient man, Henry had suffered delays of three years (1526–1529), going through the usual ecclesiastical channels. He had no male heir, he had fallen in love with Anne Boleyn, and he thought he had grounds in canon law for declaring his first marriage illegal. When in June 1529 the ecclesiastical tribunal at Blackfriars declined to find in his favour, and referred the case to Rome, his anger knew no bounds. He was a sovereign king, used to getting his own way. Was he to appear as an ordinary plaintiff in a foreign court likely to find in his wife's favour?

Henry played the anti-clerical card to put pressure on the Pope. Wolsey had failed to get the King's divorce, so Wolsey had to be replaced. More, a layman, was appointed in his stead. Henry canvassed the opinions of European universities on the divorce question, and anxiously awaited the outcome. However, from late 1530 onwards new and more radical ideas began to spread. Could a king of England be lawfully summoned to a court outside his realm? Was not the King both Emperor (temporal leader) and Pope (spiritual leader) within that realm? Could he not empower Parliament to grant the divorce, irrespective of papal permission? These ideas were as yet tentative but were to gain ground steadily, especially among the supporters of Anne Boleyn, who brought them to Henry's attention. Above all they were very ably presented by an anonymous writer, who we now know to have been the brilliant lawyer, Christopher Saint German. Impeccably orthodox in his doctrinal beliefs, he was to become More's polemical and political opponent, because he denied the long-standing tradition of the legal and juridical independence of the Church.

The slow and tentative emergence of the concept of the royal (rather then papal) supremacy of the Church in England was clearly bound up with Henry's need for a divorce. It coincided with the ideals of emerging Protestant thinkers who had religious grounds for breaking with Rome, and of common lawyers who disliked the dual systems of justice. This More saw very clearly, but there was very little he could do. Once again he found himself defending the religious and constitutional *status quo.*

Henry had to find a way to put pressure on the English clergy to support his case. By February 1531 the clergy had been charged under an old statute for having exercised their spiritual jurisdiction directly from the Pope, bypassing the King. They begged pardon, paid a fine and acknowledged Henry as Supreme Head of the Church in England, 'as far as the law of Christ allows'. A year later, on 15 May 1532, the Convocation of the Clergy (except for John Fisher, Bishop of Rochester) submitted to Henry's authority as Supreme Head, without a proviso. The following day More handed his seal of office back to Henry on grounds of 'not being equal to the work'. More agreed with Fisher that 'the fort had been betrayed even by them that should have defended it'. He later declared that the King had been allowed to get his own way because of a 'flexible Council ... and a weak clergy', who had failed in their duty to give him the advice he had not wanted to hear. Since More could not prevent the divorce, nor the religious and constitutional changes needed to provide it, he had no alternative but to resign.

More's resignation from public office and public life was not only an admission of political defeat; it marked the end of his trial of 'practical philosophy', and his desire not to abandon the ship of state when it ran into a storm. The moral and the expedient were clearly incompatible. He could not be part of a government which declared that a lay ruler had spiritual jurisdiction over the Church of Christ – even that part which was his realm. As More saw it, what Henry proposed to do was to cut a living branch off the tree that was a united Christendom. At his trial More expressed his position clearly:

This realm, being but one member and small part of the church, might not make a particular law disagreeable with the general law

*of the Christ's universal church catholic, no more than the city of
London, being but one poor member in respect of the whole realm,
might make a law against an act of Parliament to bind the whole
realm.* (ROPER 248)

Henry and Anne Boleyn were secretly married in January 1533.
Henry was granted an annulment in an English church court by
Cranmer, now Archbishop of Canterbury, and on Whit Sunday
1533 Anne was crowned Queen of England. More, living in
impoverished retirement at Chelsea, refused to attend her coronation, even though Tunstall and others had begged him to do so. In
his reply to them, he cited an old story about an emperor bound by
a law which prevented him from carrying out a death sentence on
a virgin. It did not take long to find a way around the law 'by first
deflowering her and then devouring her'. More pointed out that by
attending Anne Boleyn's coronation, the bishops were compro-
mising their integrity. 'Now my Lords it lieth not in my power but
that they may devour me. But God, being my good Lord, I will
provide that they shall never deflower me' (ROPER 230). More's
imprisonment was only a matter of time.

In retirement, More had only one weapon left: to continue to
write in defence of the faith of Christendom. The next chapter will
consider More as a polemical writer, a role he assumed from 1523
onwards when he first wrote against Luther.

In Defence of Christendom
Polemical Writings 1523–1533

To insult anyone does not demand any skill; it is neither a gentle-manly thing to do, nor the mark of a good man.   (MORE TO DORP 1515)

The writer of polemic is of necessity ungenerous and unfair. (LOUIS MARTZ)

In the same year in which Thomas More entered the King's service (1517), Martin Luther published his famous theses against indulgences at the University of Wittenberg. By 1521 he had been summoned before the Emperor Charles V at the German Assembly, or Diet of Worms. He refused to recant, declaring 'Here I stand and can do none other'. But for the protection of his prince, Luther would almost certainly have been handed over to the secular arm and burned as a heretic. Martin Luther and Thomas More were each to make a famous stand on conscience, in the consciousness that before God they could not act otherwise. This they were to do from different sides of the religious divide.

Luther's excommunication from the universal Church took effect from 1521; his most famous Reformation writings date from the previous year, and their contents had spread rapidly. His treatise *To The Christian Nobility of the German Nation* called on the German Princes to remember their priestly vocation, given at baptism, and to act decisively to reform the Church. *The Babylonian Captivity of the Church* was an attack on the authority of the papacy and on Catholic teaching concerning the seven sacraments. On 21 May 1521 Luther's books were publicly burned at St Paul's Cross in London – a symbolic act affirming England's loyalty to the papacy and to orthodoxy. Henry VIII wanted to make his contribution to the rebuttal of heresy; he wrote (with help) his *Assertion of the Seven Sacraments* against Luther's rejection of five of the seven. Henry took such a high view of papal authority that More cautioned him, suggesting he amended the text and 'more slenderly touched' papal power (ROPER 235).

Luther replied to Henry in an unpleasant and vituperative pamphlet to which a king could not respond without loss of dignity. A substantive theological answer to Luther had already been written by Bishop John Fisher. More was allocated the task of demolishing the enemy in a more popular and accessible way. He did so (using a pseudonym) in his *Responsio ad Lutherum* (1523) and in language hardly less restrained than Luther's. Though at first reluctant, he was soon drawn so passionately into the controversy that he produced a second and expanded edition. Luther's attack on the institutional church had touched a topic central to More's beliefs and religious commitment: the nature and identity of the Christian Church. It was More's first major work of popular religious polemic, written in Latin for a continental audience, and part of a sustained official programme to discredit Lutheranism.

Theological Method: The Nature of Polemic

As a young humanist More had been intensely critical of the older, scholastic theology of the late Middle Ages, because it was combative, proffering the 'clenched fist' rather than the 'outstretched palm' of friendship. His preferred mode of theology was the dialogue, or conversation among friends at table or in a garden, where shared insight stimulated discussion. But what happens when there is no dialogue and no sharing of minds? The tolerance of the 'good pagans' in *Utopia* was based on the presumption that when Christianity was preached to them they would come to accept it. By 1523 More was aware that what he and Erasmus had written as reforming humanists before 1517 could be taken out of context in later, more difficult times. He would rather burn his books, or those of his friend, than cause scandal or misunderstanding.

Humanist theology broke down when friendly discussion failed to convince or persuade. Ironically it then had to revert to the adversarial style, and the polemical method of rebutting arguments, used by medieval theologians. It was generally accepted, by all sides, that error had no rights, and that to persist in error indicated either wilful blindness or great stupidity. The appropriate response to heresy was to root it out, since dissent from truth was potentially subversive. Polemical theologians tried to discredit not just the beliefs but the motivation and integrity of the enemy; almost any verbal tactic was admissible. As has already been said, a humanist was well equipped to make this shift from the dialogical to the polemical method, for he was not simply a man of peace but one trained in the art of using language appropriate to the occasion (MARTZ 21).

Many humanists found it hard to adapt their rhetoric of persuasion to the demands of controversy. The need to defeat became more urgent than the desire to persuade; the defence of doctrine more urgent than the pastoral needs of the individual. More, far more than Erasmus, found himself abandoning his humanistic programme for the duration of the Reformation emergency. In his polemical writings, More's attitude 'is not that of a judge standing above the contest and weighing carefully both pleadings. It is rather that of a barrister or advocate who has taken the position that the defendant is guilty' (HEADLY, INTRODUCTION TO CW5 813). In 1523, when More took on Luther, he had not had an opportunity to read very much of his opponent's writings. He relied on hearsay and rumour, and was probably influenced by contact with Thomas Murner, a German Franciscan, then in England and at court.

More Versus Luther (1523)

In the more open and tolerant climate of today we find the violence and intolerance of Reformation polemic very hard to understand. More's language is often immoderate, unfair and even scurrilous. In the *Responsio* More portrayed Luther as 'Luder', the buffoon (Latin, *ludere*, to play), or as Lewder, the shameful.

> *Men will recall and say that once long ago there was in a former age a certain rascal by the name of Luther who ... in order to adorn his sect with fitting emblems, surpassed magpies in chatter, pimps in wickedness, prostitutes in obscenity, all buffoons in buffoonery.*
> (CW5 684)

But beneath the unpleasant polemic, More began to shape his own contribution to ecclesiology (discussion on the nature of the Church) in answer to Luther's attack on the visible, institutional Church. More believed in a Church which he identified with the common, known, visible multitude of believers, spread throughout the world and down the ages. This visible community was the bearer and interpreter of revelation, of what God had revealed to us in Jesus Christ:

> *The common, known, Catholic people, clergy, lay folk and all, which whatever their language be ... do stand together and agree in confession of the one true Catholic faith.* (CW5 1 139)

More saw this living tradition as enduring in the Church. The Church is a living community, embodied in time and space. His preferred description of this was the *common corps of Christendom*. In the Middle Ages the concept of Christendom had developed as the Christian equivalent of Islam, and was primarily a religious concept; but for all practical purposes it was geographically located in Europe, and transcended national boundaries and interests.

Under the spiritual leadership of the Pope, it became a visible expression of the unity of Christian faith and practice, in a culture which equated baptism with full citizenship. The enemies of Christendom were the *infidel* (outside the corporate body) and the *heretic* (within the corporate body). The infidel was most usually seen as the Ottoman Turk.

More saw the Church as a common (or ordinary) Church of saints and sinners. More's belief in the *consensus* (or *common* sense) of faith and practice, was somewhat similar to his belief, as a lawyer, in the *consensus* of the people of England embodied in the common law of the land. More remained in touch with the ordinary folk who thronged into his courts seeking justice. These people made up the *City of God* on earth. Jesus Christ had given this living community of faith the gift of the presence of the Holy Spirit. The Spirit was the guarantor of its fidelity to its origins, despite the clear evidence of the sinfulness of many of its members, including some of its leaders.

This Spirit of God was present not only in the *collective* consciousness of the community, but in the *individual* consciousness of each baptized Christian. More, like Luther, believed in the gospel written by God in the hearts of all Christians. But he stressed the reciprocity between the community of faith guided by the Spirit, and the individual inner response to that same Spirit. 'The inner gospel [of the heart] was for More, at least at this time, the primary means by which divine revelation was transmitted from generation to generation within the believing community' (GOGAN 92–3).

On the heart, therefore, in the Church of Christ, there remains the true gospel of Christ which was written there before the books of all the evangelists. (CW5 1 100)   *The gospel is written with the greatest certainty in the hearts of men.* (MARGINAL GLOSS TO RESPONSIO)

More could not accept Luther's rejection of the living tradition of the Church, in order to return to the 'pure word' of Scripture. He constantly paraphrased Augustine's dictum that 'he would not have believed the gospel were it not for the authority of the Church'. The gospel has come down to us in and through tradition. It was written in the hearts of those who received the good news, before it was written down in a book. For More, Luther's stress on the written, necessarily external word, was a return to the old law, and a movement away from the gospel of the new covenant:

> *Is not Luther moved at all by the words of God, mentioned also by the Apostles: 'I will put my laws upon their hearts and upon their minds I will write them'? He wrote the old law first on stone, later on wood, yet always externally. He will write the new law inwardly by the finger of God on the book of the heart ... what he has written on the heart will last indelibly.* (CW5 1 100)

In the warmer ecumenical climate of today, we can see more clearly what divided More and Luther, two great Christians. More never had any insight into, or understanding of, what made Luther reject the institutional Church. Luther's experience of the human face of the Church had led him to doubt whether it could be a vehicle for divine revelation. He came to see the papacy and the papal administration as something which had developed during the history of Christianity, with no sure foundation in Scripture. The papacy, its legalistic canon law, and the burdens it had laid on the Christian conscience, had obscured rather than mediated the Christian gospel. Luther considered that if he could 'get behind' the barnacles of accumulated tradition, and reclaim the simple message of the gospel, he could hear the true word of God. This word would touch the heart and change the direction of Christian life. It followed that the 'true Church' consisted of those who heard the word of God here and now, and kept it by God's gift of faith.

Luther's Church was an invisible Church of the 'elect', known only to God.

More attacked Luther's 'Church of the Elect', which was utterly different from his 'Church of all common folk'. More could be *sure* that the Church was the bearer of Christ's teaching because of its organic continuity from apostolic times to the present. Luther could only be *sure*, if the word was preached and heard here and now, in a community ready to accept it. An unreformed, 'ungodly', community was unable to 'hear' the Word of God. Both men sought *certitude*. There was little room for compromise since these were truths necessary for salvation. More strongly opposed Luther's attempt to define the true Church according to its invisible, interior and purely spiritual nature.

More's attitude to the papacy needs special attention. He never held a high authoritarian view of the pope, though his later stand against Henry VIII invited this interpretation. He naturally inclined towards papal primacy, rather than the papal sovereignty. Only Christ the Lord held 'sovereignty' over human persons. The pope was Christ's visible representative on earth. More insisted that he would ever have brought up the question of papal authority if Luther had not entangled it with the nature of the Church, and so forced him to do so (CW5 1 139). After the Council of Trent (1545), post-reformation Catholicism naturally turned to popes and General Councils for guidance in matters of faith. The touchstone for More was not so much teaching authority 'from above' as the universal faith of the Christian community, spread through space and time. More was the heir of the theology of the early Church Fathers, who appealed to 'what has been believed everywhere, always, and by all' (RULE OF VINCENT OF LERINS). This was the criterion of orthodoxy which it was the duty of leadership to preserve and uphold. This was the essence of what it meant to be *Catholic* or *universal*. It was for this *Catholicism*, (under papal primacy) that More was eventually to die.

Luther's distinction between law and gospel, and his exaltation

of gospel and condemnation of law, presented particular difficulties for More. As a lawyer, More valued the function of common
law as a guarantor of liberty, and the exercise of equity where it
might fail to do so. Luther claimed that the justified man needed
neither the guidance nor the restriction of the law 'but accompa-
nies the law through a love which is rooted in faith'. Luther tended to agree with Plato (*Politics*) that the rule of a gifted magistrate
might be preferable to a body of laws. To More, the common
lawyer, this was sheer madness. He regarded Luther's treatise on
The Freedom of the Christian as a recipe for anarchy, and feared its
socio-political consequences. His worst fears seemed to have been
realized when the so-called Peasants' Revolt broke out in Germany (1524–1525). Later More was to blame the horrendous
sack of Rome (1527) on Luther's rabble-rousing language. (In fact
Rome was sacked by the mercenaries of the Catholic Emperor
Charles V.) Luther feared social anarchy as much as More did. But
Luther's rhetoric of Christian freedom forced More into giving a
greater emphasis to the role of all authority, including papal
authority.

More had a special dislike of those who 'broke their word'; in a
civilized society a man's word was his bond. He constantly
returned to the theme of perjury as a breach of faith, a misuse of
the common language of trust, or the breaking of a solemn undertaking. He wrote a memorandum on the topic while in the Tower.
One form of perjury he particularly disliked: the breaking of religious vows (CW5 11 763–9). His most strongly worded invective
against Luther concerned his marriage, for Luther had been a
friar who abandoned his vows. One of the reasons More
denounced heretics was that they had deliberately 'broken faith'
with their baptismal promises.

More was intent on demolishing Luther's arguments: he gave
less attention to the systematic exposition of his own. However,
these were the early years of formulating a Catholic response to
the Reformers. More developed his ideas further is his *Letter to*

Bugenhagen (1526), friend of Luther and pastor in Wittenberg. In these Lutheran controversies he first forged his great themes on the nature of the Church: the common corps of Christendom, the common sense of the faith held by all Christians, the guidance of the Spirit, the gospel written in the hearts of the faithful, the law which is not opposed to the freedom of the gospel, the papacy as embodying Christian unity. However, from 1526 onwards More's most urgent task was to confront English rather than continental reformers.

More Versus William Tyndale (1526–1533)

By 1526 the work of English evangelical Reformers was taking firmer shape and influencing a wider circle of English men and women. The bitter exchanges between Thomas More and William Tyndale, two gifted Englishmen, were a tragedy. Tyndale, a brilliant linguist and translator of the Bible, was exiled from England, settled in Germany and became deeply influenced by Luther. In 1526 his pocket-sized translations of the New Testament in English were smuggled into the country, and ruthlessly hunted down by church and state authorities. But in spite of this, many of Tyndale's apt and memorable phrases passed into the English of the Authorized Version (1611) and so into our common Christian understanding: 'Let there be light', 'we live and move and have our being', 'fight the good fight', 'the salt of the earth', and many more. The words of the familiar English biblical stories of creation or the teaching of Jesus are usually Tyndale's. This was the best possible vindication of the humanist desire to make the Bible available to the 'ploughman at his plough', and in his own language. More did not object to the Latin translation of the New Testament which Erasmus published in 1516. So why did he so bitterly attack Tyndale's English translation some ten years later?

Tyndale's translation was part of the Reformer's rejection of tradition in favour of a return to 'pure' Scriptures. Tyndale's key words and annotations were theological choices, favouring a Reforming, evangelical interpretation of Christian life and practice. More took issue with Tyndale over his substitution of new, for well known, translations of six key ecclesiastical terms: 'love' for 'charity', 'congregation' for 'church', 'senior or elder' for 'priest', 'favour' for 'grace', 'repentance' for 'do penance'. More was less interested in the exact origin of a biblical word than in its common usage and understanding. As More saw it, Tyndale was not a humanist making the Scriptures available in the vernacular, but a Reformer tilting his translations in support of his new beliefs.

Tyndale followed the success of his translation of the New Testament with *The Parable of the Wicked Mammon*, on justification by faith alone, and *The Obedience of a Christian Man*, on princely sovereignty. These were worrying developments. So in 1528 Tunstall, Bishop of London, officially commissioned More to read prohibited books and to defend the Catholic position. More's *A Dialogue Concerning Heresies* was first published in 1529 and revised in 1531, when he was Chancellor. It is written in English and is usually considered the best of his polemical works.

Like Utopia, *A Dialogue Concerning Heresies* was cast in the form of a fictitious conversation. A friend of More's supposedly sends his children's tutor as a 'Messenger' or go-between, to discuss with More disturbing aspects of popular religious opinion. The Messenger is himself attracted to some of these new reforming ideas and is 'confused'. He senses (possibly shares) the strong public distaste for the hunting down of heretics, and the mood of anti-clericalism. In this book More intends to address the 'common citizen' of London, capital of the book trade and a main source for obtaining heretical books from abroad. The *Dialogue* is filled with references to events known to Londoners, such as the case of Richard Hunne, and to places like St Paul's Cross, where heretical books were burned. There, in 1526, Thomas Bilney and the fire steelyard merchants had been forced to abjure and to carry faggots to the great bonfire. The opinion of Londoners was a crucial factor in the war of religious and political propaganda. The Messenger, a 'representative Londoner', is drawn into the domestic space of More's home and subjected to his 'gentle' art of advocacy (CW6 INTRODUCTION).

The *Dialogue* has many of More's best merry tales, proverbs and witticisms, and is clearly a work for popular consumption. More and his questioner would have had *The Canterbury Tales* in mind as they discussed the merits of going on pilgrimage. The *Dialogue* deals with the criticisms directed by the Reformers at popular piety: the cult of saints, belief in miracles, use of relics, images, pilgrimages. It tackled criticism of a supposedly corrupt and ill-educated clergy. Central to all these arguments was the question of the nature of the Church.

More expounded his conviction of the abiding presence of Christ and his Spirit in the living community of the Church from generation to generation. This living tradition includes beliefs and also customs, and every aspect of the corporate life of the Church (GOGAN 143). It included

all the devout rites and ceremonies of the church, both in the divine service as incensing, hallowing of the fire, of the font, of the paschal lamb, and over all that the exorcisms, benedictions and holy strange gestures used in consecration or ministration of the blessed sacrament, all which holy things great part whereof was from hand to mouth left in the church, from the time of Christ's apostles and by them left to us. (CW6 55–6)

More was well aware that not all custom dated from the early Church, and that change was part of natural growth. But he had an instinctive respect for the social and religious power of customs and rites, both to bond a community and to transmit the faith. His was a strongly sacramental view of the world: human beings needed the tangible and the material through which the spiritual could be disclosed. He was aware of the shift from the medieval visual culture to the new 'book culture' of the printed word. But what are words but verbal images, and what are names but images of personal identity? (CW6 46) Traditionally, visual images were the layman's book for those who could not read. Elsewhere More argued that *all* Christians, whether literate or not, needed visual images. He would have agreed with a modern definition of human beings as image, or symbol, makers.

> *For as I somewhat said unto you before, all the words that be either written or spoken, be but images representing the things that the writer or speaker conceiveth in the mind; likewise as the figure of the thing framed with imagination and so conceived in the mind,*
> *is but an image representing the very thing itself that a man thinketh on.* (CW6 46)

Recent research has revealed once more the desolation experienced in many English parishes when uncomprehending parishioners were stripped of their religious customs and popular forms of piety during the English Reformations (CF. EAMON DUFFY, *THE STRIPPING OF THE ALTARS: TRADITIONAL RELIGION IN ENGLAND 1400–1500,* 1992). This is not to underestimate the criticisms of those who saw the lush abundance and uncritical piety of some late medieval devotion as quasi-magical, and superstitious. But the reform of custom and rite is not the same as its abolition, and contemporary social anthropologists are much more wary of dismissing popular piety as 'mere superstition'. More's defence of many aspects of popular practice should not be seen as just traditionalist, hard-line and predictably anti-Reformer. He regarded all customs as part of the warp and woof of society. If here and there threads were pulled out, the whole was unravelled and spoiled.

Another of More's concerns in these controversies was Tyndale's conviction that the souls of the dead remained asleep in the 'bosom of Abraham' until the day of resurrection. Luther had proposed this far more cautiously. Such a belief did away with the Catholic doctrine of purgatory, or belief in a place of purification for souls after death and before admission to heaven. If the souls of the dead were not conscious they could not be helped. Equally the saints could not help the Church on earth because they too were in 'soul-sleep'.

The point here is not to rehearse arguments which divided Catholic and Protestant thought, or which may not interest a modern reader. But for late-medieval people the concept of 'kith and kin' extended beyond the grave. Saints were friends who could intercede in heaven for family and friends on earth. Religious confraternities, and chantries or chapels where mass was said for the dead, expressed a continued bondedness with an extended family, which had passed from this life to the next. The belief in the Church as a Communion of Saints, on earth, in heaven, and in purgatory, was part of common ecclesial understanding. To deny the existence of purgatory, or the cult of the saints, demolished what Berger has called the 'sacred canopy', which gave people their bearings and their world-view. More was convinced that this was destructive and dangerous to both religion and society, and had no warrant in tradition. The Reformers felt such practices had no warrant in Scripture.

More took issue with Tyndale over his belief in justification by faith alone, which seemed to More to deny a role to 'good works'. Luther and Tyndale were reacting against what they saw as self-reliance rather than God-reliance in Christian faith and practice. Their Reformation insight was the joy of discovering that faith and justification were God's pure gift, not something merited by human effort. In doing so they denied a role to the human will and to co-operation with God's grace in the process of human redemption. This ran counter to humanist belief in the power of human beings to shape their own destiny, and to be co-workers with God in creating a civilized world and society. To live life was a 'work' given us by a creator God, who would always give the grace to cope with any circumstance. More dismissed Tyndale's 'feeling faith' as subjective and morally dangerous: how could human beings *not* work out their salvation with the help of God's grace? In life, and in his crisis in the Tower, he had a strong sense of God 'ever at his elbow', enabling and strengthening his purpose. There were to be misunderstandings on both sides in discussion on this burning issue.

Tyndale replied to More's *Dialogue Concerning Heresies* in a treatise of about ninety thousand words, published in Antwerp in 1530. More replied in a massive work of controversy: *The Confutation of Tyndale's Answer*, in nine books and half a million words. To the modern reader such length is tedious beyond belief. Yet these books, and especially the *Dialogue*, contain important ideas. There is no doubt but that the pressure of political events and his resignation affected the quality and sharpness of More's writing. But he still managed to produce passages of brilliant wit and persuasive power, and to use digression as a strategy to bring the wandering mind back to the heart of the argument. More's mind had not disintegrated (as some critics have suggested), but his world was in the process of so doing, and the strain showed.

In Defence of The Doctrine of The Eucharist (1533–1534)

During the last months before his imprisonment (autumn 1533 to April 1534), More wrote four books in defence of the doctrine of the eucharist. It is possible that the last two were completed in prison; they were unpublished in his lifetime. Why was the doctrine of the eucharist so central to More during these last months of freedom? More, like Fisher, did not regard the eucharist primarily in devotional or individualistic terms but as *constitutive* of the unity of the Church. The primary sense of the 'real presence' of Christ was his whole body, the Church. The 'real presence' of Jesus in the eucharist allowed Christians to enter into this truth more fully. It was the sacramental celebration of what God had done for us in

Jesus Christ. Political opposition to royal supremacy, and theological opposition to the English Reformers who denied the doctrine of a *real* presence, were two distinct but related ways of confronting those who sought to break up the unity of Christendom.

In October 1532, John Frith, an associate of Tyndale, was imprisoned in the Tower, and wrote there a short treatise on the eucharist. A copy came into More's hands and he prepared a reply. In April 1533 an anonymous tract, *The Souper of the Lord*, appeared, defending Frith's approach to the eucharist, that is as a meal of remembrance. (Either Tyndale or George Joye was the anonymous author.) After Frith was burned at Smithfield on 4 July 1533, the debate became a major political issue. During the autumn of 1533 More prepared part one of his *Answer to a Poisoned Book* which he published in December, together with his *Letter to John Frith*.

Dubbed 'Master Mock' by his unknown opponent, More in his *Answer* named him 'Master Masker', ridiculing one who hid behind the mask of anonymity, although More had done this himself against Luther. The theme of 'masks and realities' was brilliantly exploited by More, both linguistically and theologically. A mask *hides* the reality of the human person; the eucharistic sign *discloses* the mysterious reality of the Christian's incorporation into Christ, and the 'loving connectedness of all things' in God's providential plan for humankind. Belief in a *real* and not merely *signified* presence was crucial for More's understanding of the gathering together of the many into the one body of Christ, both on earth and in heaven. More did not rely on scholastic arguments: the medieval word 'transubstantiation', meaning the change of the substances of bread and wine into the body and blood of Christ, was never mentioned. More used scriptural and early church sources to support his thesis. When he returned to these sources he used the latest translations and critical editions of the texts. Here was More, the humanist, retrieving the ancient tradition by the most modern scholarship.

More's last eucharistic writings have come to us under the titles *A Treatise on the Passion* and *A Treatise to Receive the Blessed Body of Our Lord*. Together they may have been intended to be the second part of his *Answer to a Poisoned Book*. Whether or not they were partly composed in the Tower, they belong to the devotional and (almost) non-controversial discourse that characterized More's Tower writings. Between December 1533 and his imprisonment on 17 April 1534, More had personal reasons for linking his own situation with the eucharist, Christ's gift to his disciples on the night before he suffered. More wrote that henceforth all his energies would be focused on the passion and death of Jesus Christ, and on his own passage from this world. In the end More, like Tyndale, turned to the comfort and consolation of the scriptural word of God, as he prepared the defence of his conscience.

Facing Defeat

By early 1534 More was exhausted. As a statesman and writer he had failed to stem the tide of change. Once Roper had congratulated him on his success against heretics. More had replied enigmatically:

> And yet, son Roper, I pray God that some of us, as high as we seem to sit upon the mountains treading heretics under our feet like ants, live not in the day that we would gladly wish to be at league and composition with them to let them have their churches quietly to themselves, so that they would be content to let us have ours quietly to ourselves. (ROPER 216)

More did not want mutual tolerance, a day when Christians of differing persuasions would agree to live and let live, because it would mean acknowledging the breakup of Christendom, which he held to be most precious. But the breakup of Christendom into the new nation states, each with their own state church, was at hand. And, unbelievably, there would come a day when a future pope, John Paul II, would declare Luther to be 'a man of faith' for all Christians (1983). A new kind of Christian unity would be painfully forged from the collapse of the old.

Both More and Tyndale were to die for their religious beliefs. Tyndale's imprisonment in Vilvoorde, outside Brussels, was to overlap with that of More, and he was to be strangled, then burned as a heretic, just one year after More's execution as a traitor.

In Defence of Conscience
Tower Writings 1534–1535

I die the King's good servant, but God's first.   (MORE BEFORE HIS
EXECUTION)

In May 1533, when Archbishop Cranmer pronounced the marriage of Henry VIII and Catherine of Aragon null and void, More
remarked to Roper: 'God give me grace, good son, that these matters within a while, be not confirmed with oath.' On 12 April
1534, More was summoned to Lambeth Palace to swear an oath
of allegiance to the new Act of Succession, which proclaimed
Anne as rightful Queen, and the issue of the second marriage as
rightful heirs. On Monday, 13 April 1534, More attended mass at
his parish church in Chelsea, said goodbye to his family at the gate
to his garden, and took his barge downstream to Lambeth. After
some time in silence, More turned to Roper and whispered: 'Son
Roper, I thank God the field is won.' Roper only understood later
that More did not expect to come home again, and that parting
from his family was the hardest part of his long battle.

At Lambeth, More was the first, and the only layman to have
the oath tendered to him by Archbishop Cranmer, and Cromwell,
the King's secretary. More read the documents carefully and
found himself able to swear to the Act of Succession itself, since
the King in Parliament had the absolute right to determine who
should succeed to the throne. But in conscience he could not subscribe to the preamble to the Act, which implied royal headship of
the Church in England. He also refused to give his reasons for

refusal. He was sent away to think things over, and from an upper room saw many of his clerical friends come and go, having no qualms about taking the oath. The only other person to refuse was John Fisher, Bishop of Rochester. More wrote a full account of his interrogation to his daughter, Margaret, a few days later:

> But as for myself in good faith my conscience so moved me in the matter that though I would not deny to swear to the succession, yet unto the oath that there was offered me I could not swear without the jeoparding of my soul to perpetual damnation. (SL 54 219)

More was called back for further questioning. The commissioners argued that this was a matter where More was bound to obey his sovereign Lord and King. More replied that

> this was one of the cases in which I was bounden that I should not obey my prince, sith that whatsoever other folk thought in the matter (whose conscience and learning I would not condemn nor take upon me to judge) yet in my conscience the truth seemed on the other side. Wherein I had not informed my conscience neither suddenly nor slightly but by long leisure and diligent search for the matter (SL 54 221)

It was pointed out to More that he had cause to fear setting his own opinion against the Parliament of the whole realm. More appealed to a wider General Council of the whole Church: 'I am not bounden to change my conscience and confirm it to the council of one realm, against the council of Christendom.' As for the oath:

> I never withdrew any man from it, nor never advised any to refuse it, nor never put, nor will, any scruple in any man's head, but leave every man to his own conscience. And methinketh in good faith, that so were it good reason that every man should leave me to mine. (SL 54 222)

More was given four days to reconsider his position. Refusing the oath yet again, he was sent to the Tower of London on 17 April 1534. For the next fifteen months More continued to refuse the oath, and to maintain official public silence about his reasons for refusal. Yet all his prison writings and recorded conversations were related indirectly to the defence of his conscience, as he tried to explain to family and friends why he had to make this stand. He had to do so in a way which was discreet, so that nothing he said or wrote could be construed against him in court. In the privacy of his prayer and personal meditation, he had to continue to discern whether he was taking the right action or not. This *outer* dialogue, with friends, and *inner* dialogue, with God and his conscience, pursued within a strategy of legal prudence and hardheadedness, constituted the core of his prison experience. His prison writings in defence of conscience, and in preparation for death, are among the finest in the whole Christian tradition.

Conscience and Consciousness

The role of conscience in the imprisonment and trial of Thomas More assumed an importance in sixteenth-century religious history only comparable to that of Martin Luther (1521). On that occasion Luther had said:

> *Unless I am convinced by the testimony of the scriptures or by clear reason, I am bound by the Scriptures I have quoted and my conscience is captive to the Word of God. I cannot and I will not retract anything, since it is neither safe nor right to go against conscience.* (LW 40 201)

For Luther and for More, conscience was not formed from a sense of the human rights of an individual person, but from a sense of the inner being of each human person as open to the scrutiny of God. For Luther, the freedom of the Christian conscience lay in being 'captive to the Word of God' addressed to the human heart. For More, the ultimate dignity of all human persons lay in the capacity of the 'eye of the heart' to see and act upon God's will. For both, God's ultimate and final judgement was all that mattered. Conscience was not self-determined, as in our contemporary understanding, but determined between the self and God. Peace, assurance and certainty of conscience lay in the grace of God towards human beings, for God alone is true and reliable, especially when all else fails.

In the sixteenth century the word *conscience* (derived from the Latin *scientia*, knowledge) stood not only for *inner*, moral self-awareness, but also for *outer* consciousness of the self in relation to the world and reality. There was no separate word for this outer consciousness; conscience stood for both inner and outer awareness; integrity was precisely the integration of both. If a person spoke, acted or wrote something which was not consistent with inner conviction, he or she lacked integrity and acted in bad conscience. In their different situations both More and Luther were asked to subscribe to something at variance with inner conviction. On trial and under oath, they were being asked to call upon God to attest to the truth of what they were saying, that is to perjure themselves. In More's case, a former judge was being asked both to perjure himself and to betray his profession.

More's prison writings constitute one of the most moving accounts of a Christian conscience striving to act morally and truthfully in a difficult situation. For More, conscience was firstly an activity of the intellect: the power to judge the past (what has been done), the future (what should be done), and the present (the reliability of one's convictions). But it was also an activity of the will: the power not only to judge but to act. As such the will was subject to many searing emotions: fear, anger, resentment, tedium, love of family, suicidal despair. More understood that these emotions had to be recognized and dealt with. But worst of all there was the experience of one's whole familiar world falling apart, and life itself threatened. How does conscience operate then? What are its compass bearings? How can one be sure of anything, or what comfort can be offered then?

The 'Little' Dialogue of Comfort: More and Margaret

The most poignant defence of More's conscience appears in the thirteen prison letters which survive – eight written to his daughter, Margaret, and five to friends. The longest and most significant was a further one supposedly written by Margaret to her stepsister Alice Alington, but in all probability composed by Margaret and More together. Alice had accidentally met the new chancellor, Lord Audley, and tried to plead More's cause. By means of a friendly warning, conveyed in two fables of Aesop about foolishness, Audley told More, via Alice, that by differing from the commonly held opinion of his peers, he appeared to most to be an obstinate fool. The Council considered More's refusal of the oath to be a foolish scruple over a mere trifle. Put succinctly, Audley's coded message to More was: try to find a way to trim your conscience to political reality, and save us all embarrassment.

Alice wrote to Margaret, who brought her letter to More in prison. Together they argued the case and composed an answer in which the word conscience appeared more than forty times. More and Erasmus had often enjoyed the use of a pun on More's name, which in Greek was close to *Moria* or folly. Erasmus' *In Praise of Folly* (1509) was written in praise of that Christian foolishness which turned out to be wisdom, but also in praise of his wise friend Thomas More, who so enjoyed playing the fool. More remembered this as he read the letter and weighed his arguments carefully, and it provided him with a line of defence.

If Audley conveyed his message by way of two parables about fools, More replied in kind. His was a story about an honest but slow-witted juryman who refused to perjure himself with the majority. In a court of law, even a fool was entitled to his conscience; and in a court of law, as the Council well knew, More was no fool. More tried to put Margaret at ease by laughing off foolish public opinion, before getting down to the serious part of his argument. A matter of conscience is no trifle, no mere scruple, no wisp of straw, but the very heart of what it is to be human.

More and Margaret discussed how he had arrived at his decision, of how dissent from a majority opinion might be, but also need not be, the mark of a misguided, foolish or obstinate mind. But for all More's awareness of the communal and communitarian aspects of human and Christian living, he believed that in the matter of conscience each human person was answerable to God alone. At the final judgement no one can take another's place or accept responsibility for another's conscience. 'And since I look in this matter only to God, it matters little to me that men ... say it is no conscience but only a foolish scruple.' In coming to his decision he had not even been influenced by his distinguished fellow prisoner John Fisher, one of the most learned in the land.

> Verily, daughter, I never intend (God being my good lord) to pin my soul on another man's back, not even the best man I know this day living; for I know not whither he may happen to carry it. There is no man living, of whom while he liveth, I may make myself sure ... If mine own conscience allowed me [to take the oath] I would not fail to do it though other men refuse, so though others refuse not, I dare not do it, mine own conscience standing against it. (ROGERS 206)

As for the law of the land, though each citizen is required to obey it, 'yet there is no man bound to swear that every law is well made'. Laws can be changed, improved, reformed, or revised. New laws can be brought in which some may think good, and others bad. But those who disapprove cannot be made to act against conscience. More would only allow one case where the individual should strive to conform conscience to a broader majority decision: that of a decision passed by a lawfully assembled General Council of the whole of Christendom. To dissent from such a law should be an occasion to 'move him, yet not compel him to conform his mind and conscience unto theirs'. More concluded:

> *This is like a riddle, a case in which a man may lose his head and have no harm ... And therefore, mine own good daughter, never trouble your mind for anything that shall ever happen to me in this world. Nothing can come but that which God wills. And I am very sure that whatsoever that may be, however bad it may appear, it shall indeed be the best.* (ROGERS 206)

A Dialogue of Comfort Against Tribulation

In the following months of enforced solitude, More wrote a longer defence of his conscience in *A Dialogue of Comfort Against Tribulation*. He gave great care to both the form and content of this work, now regarded as a classic of Christian prison and consolation literature. We know that More owned a copy of Boethius' famous prison work, *Of the Consolation of Philosophy*, written before his execution in about AD 524. For More *comfort* was a derivative of the Latin word *fortis* meaning strong. He understood it to be that which can give strength or courage to endure in a time of acute human suffering. Comfort or consolation literature was the medieval equivalent of modern counselling techniques used to deal with trauma and stress. In Christian spirituality and theology the Holy Spirit was understood as the true Comforter, the one who gave courage, strength and hope to the human heart.

More needed to comfort (strengthen) his family, and yet he had no easy solution nor the hope of quick release to offer them. He owed them an explanation for an apparent act of folly, which would profoundly affect their lives, and leave them financially destitute. He had to convince them that his death would not be a tragedy – as he was a public figure, his fall from power and probable execution had all the elements of a classic tragedy. He returned to the theme he had explored with Erasmus twenty-five years earlier: Christian wisdom which appears folly to the worldly-wise. *A Dialogue of Comfort* (1534) was More's version of his friend's *In Praise of Folly* (1511), but written in circumstances they could never have envisaged.

Because his writings could be confiscated at any time, and used against him, More had to conceal his real purpose under a semi-fictitious setting. He devised a story set in Hungary, then under siege by the Turks. The date he chose was 1527, just after the first invasion of Hungary by Suleiman the Magnificent, and just before the second devastating battle. These recent, terrifying events under a Turkish tyrant, and their indirect application to More's situation under Henry VIII, would be evident to his family. In the story an elderly uncle, Antony, and a young nephew, Vincent, try to face up to their situation. The old man is sick in bed, in a city (Buda) ringed by enemy troops. What comfort can one take facing a hopeless situation of prolonged siege, defeat, captivity, and almost certain death? What can one rely on when one's world is falling apart? *A Dialogue of Comfort* is a parable or story about how one terrified Christian (Vincent) is enabled to make a transition from paralysing fear, to one of total trust in God, whatever the future may hold.

As More saw it, his beloved 'common corps of Christendom' was threatened from the outside by the Turk, and from the inside by the heretic and the unjust tyrant. More wanted his personal battle for integrity to be seen as part of a wider battle between good and evil being fought in other parts of Christendom and the wider world. Tribulation or suffering is part of the human condition, whether it is experienced as international disaster, as family loss, or as inner anguish. So at the literal level (for the casual reader) More's story was about the recent, calamitous, Turkish invasion; at a deeper level he was writing to help his family and friends make sense of his choice and their fate; at the deepest level his own stronger self (Antony) dialogued with his weaker self (Vincent), or his Christian soul dialogued with God, by means of the comfort of Scripture, God's true word. More was also writing to comfort and strengthen himself against his coming ordeal.

Because of its multi-layered meanings *A Dialogue of Comfort* is not an easy book to read. The reader needs considerable help to understand its literary form: suffering or 'tribulation' considered from the perspectives of **Faith** (Book One), **Hope** (Book Two) and **Charity** (Book Three). More intended to show how it was possible for a Christian to move from a mood in which the mind is gripped by fear and despair, to one in which the *mind is* redeemed by faith, the *memory and imagination* by hope, and the *heart* by charity. At its core is a central fear or conflict: fear of persecution, physical torture and 'a cruel and shameful death'. The actual discussion of this central fear is suspended until book three, but it is before the 'eye of the imagination' throughout. The conflict is resolved only when the fearful human emotions are exorcized by love and the promise of eternal life, the only true comfort in adversity.

In **Book One** (On Faith), Antony and Vincent discuss the comfort which the collective wisdom of the human intellect can offer in time of suffering. The classical Stoic philosophers gave sound advice: on how to accept adversity with dignity, on being indifferent to the swings of fortune, or to wealth, reputation, even good health. But natural wisdom can only offer partial comfort; belief in God, and in God's word revealed in Scripture, is a further necessary step towards possessing sure comfort. However tiny the seed of faith is in our hearts, it can grow into a force that can move a mountain of tribulation. But it has to be an active, lively faith that *wants* God's comfort, a faith that does not get swallowed up by listless sorrow or raging anger.

So Antony outlines that kind of faith which builds upon, but goes beyond, rational human efforts to meet adversity. He gives some of the traditional theological arguments for accepting suffering as part of God's providence: suffering can be medicinal, or educative, or corrective. God can use suffering to chasten sinners, to purify the good, to deepen the superficial. The problem of undeserved suffering is faced. If we suffer this patiently, our reward will be great. Vincent is impressed, but not entirely convinced. Is it possible to pray for suffering to be removed or avoided? Yes, replies Antony, provided we leave the outcome to God, because from the perspective of faith, some suffering may be a gift.

The great contribution of **Book Two** (On Hope), is More's recognition that the human mind, especially in time of anguish, will not be satisfied by purely intellectual arguments. So in Book Two, Antony tries a different strategy with his nephew, moving from what may be *read in books*, to what may be *seen and heard* in the rich complexity of human living. True comfort is related to hope, that gift of the human imagination which can help to redeem the mind from fear. Book Two stresses the importance of relaxation and 'proper pleasant talking', and is full of merry tales and jokes. But it also explores black humour and the darker side of life without hope. It is deliberately long and rambling, full of digressions which may irk the contemporary reader. But it must have delighted More's family, who knew well his method of rambling off at a tangent, only eventually to target what he really wanted to say.

For More, Christian hope ultimately meant hope that there would be life after death. And more immediately, it was grounded in the conviction that God's enabling grace would support the Christian in all circumstances of this present life, without exception. Evil, understood as the activity of a personalized devil or demons, was part of More's mental world; the subversive activity of the 'princes and potentates of these dark regions' put the human soul in grave moral danger. The devil, rather than the Grand Turk, the English king, or the heretic, was the real enemy. The Christian life is a wrestling match or struggle between the forces of good and evil: God alone is the ground of our hope that good will prevail.

The ability to hope and to endure was also related to sound common sense and healthy human psychology. The mirth and the many tales about human folly and absurdity were intended to relax both Vincent and the reader. Laughter is itself transformative and has its role to play in adjusting perspective, especially a tragic perspective. Antony admits that he is of 'nature even half a giglet [jokester] or more'. Merriment is good sauce for the meat, or a sweetener for the medicine, of theological discussion. So the very structure of their conversation sets out to be an act of hope in the middle of tribulation.

Antony and Vincent now concentrate on 'the anxiety which assaults the mind when a man is brought to trial', or to a time of acute testing. He addresses four kinds of temptation, suggested by Psalm 90:5–6: 'You will not fear the terror of the night, nor the arrow that flies by day, nor the pestilence that stalks in darkness, nor the destruction that wastes at noonday.' The element common to all four temptations is fear. The first temptation, the night fear, suggests the inner reality of a soul trapped in an anxiety state, with the possibility that it may ultimately be driven to self-destruction. Next comes the 'arrow by day' or pride in all its forms. Then the 'pestilence that stalks by darkness': the covetousness, lust and entanglement of worldly business. Finally the noonday devil, or open persecution and the threat of a violent and painful death. Armed with the shield of God's truth, the Christian can fight these four temptations.

Under the image of the 'terror of the night', Antony and Vincent explore the psychology of fear and anxiety in its many forms: presumption, scrupulousness, cowardice, despair and suicide. Reason is brought to bear on each problem by directly confronting it. The author gives more attention to suicide than to any other form of temptation in the entire work. Arguably it is the first significant treatment of the topic in the English language. Antony (More) has had considerable experience of would-be suicides: 'Many have I heard of and with some have I talked myself that have been sore encumbered with that temptation, and marked I not a little the manner of them'. Like most of his contemporaries, the author attributed the temptation to suicide to the suggestions of the devil. Yet his experience and intuitive insight were far greater than either the psychological and theological tools at his disposal for correct diagnosis.

To what extent was suicide More's own personal temptation, especially considering his fear of torture? He clearly tried to exorcize the fear by considering what drove people to it. He noted that war and invasion can pose exceptionally difficult moral choices, and that in extreme circumstances some felt justified in taking their own lives. Others chose suicide because they were subject to forms of religious self-deception or derangement: the widow who 'arranged' her martyrdom so that she might be canonized; the deluded monk who 'aspired' to martyrdom; the grisly example of a carver who asked his wife to crucify him so that he could literally follow Christ.

Evidence from the prison letters suggests that More was worried most by the possibility of self-delusion. The problem of the self-deluded person was indirectly related to the problem of martyrdom. Martyrdom, if self-chosen, or hastily entered into, or in any way directly sought, could be regarded as a form of self-destruction. Right discernment in the events which finally bring a person to a choice between life or death, has to be very careful. The act of human self-destruction is the triumph of death in every sense, and the antithesis of Christ's salvific act, which is a triumph of life. A Christian martyr has to make a very finely balanced choice. Was More's personal choice *really* necessary, or was he deluding himself that he had no other choice?

The arrow that flies by day, pride, and the pestilence in the darkness, acquisitiveness, are temptations of prosperity, so they provide a short dramatic interlude before the final terrible onslaught of the noonday devil: when the worst befalls.

Book Three (On Charity) moves beyond faith and hope, to the only sure comfort in extreme adversity: the love of God anchored in the human heart and made visible in the passion and death of

Jesus Christ. It begins as a calm and rational meditation on how to preserve moral courage in the face of death. Poverty, disgrace and death are not to be compared to a virtuous life; the short act of execution can be quicker and less painful than a long and lingering disease; physical imprisonment is only an intensified instance of life in a world which is quite like a prison anyway, and full of suffering. Such rational arguments were intended to prevent the tendency to over-dramatize the situation, or to fall into self-pity.

Gradually Antony and Vincent, who is by now much stronger, draw less comfort from rational arguments, and more from the biblical examples of those who kept faith in God, especially those unjustly imprisoned: Job, Joseph, Daniel, John the Baptist, Stephen, Peter, Paul. But above all there is the example of Jesus the prisoner:

> *Our saviour was himself taken prisoner for our sake, and prisoner was he carried, and prisoner was he kept ... unto the end of his passion. The time of his imprisonment, I grant well was not long, but as for hard handling which our hearts most abhor, he had as much in that short while as many men ... in much longer time.*
> (DC 286)

Book Three gradually becomes *an experience* of receiving strength and comfort through an extended meditation on the passion and death of Jesus the prisoner. He also felt fear and anguish, but overcame both. He is our pattern of moral integrity and of trust in God. His victory can strengthen and empower those facing acute suffering and a shameful death. The conversion of Vincent's mind by faith, his will and imagination by hope, and his heart by charity or the redeeming love of Christ, turns him into a conqueror (Latin *vincens*). When the discerning heart, conscience, is in the hands of God, love can conquer all, even sickening fear, and lack of courage.

> *Let us be of good comfort, for since we be by our faith very sure*
> *that holy Scripture is the word of God, and the word of God cannot*
> *be but true and we see that ... if God makes us and keep us good*
> *men, as he hath promised to do ... then saith holy Scripture: Unto*
> *good folk all things turn to good (Romans 8:28). God is faithful,*
> *which suffereth you not to be tempted above that you may bear but*
> *giveth also with the temptation a way out (1 Corinthians 10:13).*
> (DC 254–5)

Gethsemane: More and the Sadness of Christ

The real ending of *A Dialogue of Comfort Against Tribulation* lies
beyond his writing, in More's trial and execution. Until the very
point of martyrdom, he could not be certain that he would not
betray himself in some way. The fear of what was to come constituted his Gethsemane: his own agony in the garden. Not surpris-
ingly, More turned again to meditate on the passion of Christ. His
last work was *On the Sadness, Weariness, Fear and Prayer of Christ*
before his Passion, usually referred to as *The Sadness of Christ*. This
is really a commentary on the texts of the four gospel accounts of
Christ's agony in the garden, interspersed with personal prayer
and reflection. Either by design or accident, it stops at the point of
Jesus' arrest.

More wrote it very quickly, probably in about twenty-five sit-
tings, in May/June 1535. He wrote in Latin, and so for an educated audience, probably the same as that for which *Utopia* had been
intended. More focused not on the physical but on the mental
anguish and human feelings of Jesus during the time in the Garden of Gethsemane. More had always held that human beings
have the power to shape their own destiny, with the help of God's
grace. The freedom of following conscience was to him their
ultimate dignity. For a Christian giving witness by his own death,
this involved being refashioned in the likeness of the suffering
humanity of Jesus Christ.

Humanist theology more usually affirmed the dignity and greatness of human beings made in the image and likeness of God. In the agony in the garden it was the vulnerability and weakness of the humanity of Jesus Christ that were revealed. God can, and does, raise up 'brave champions' who publicly confess their faith and expose themselves to a martyr's death with great heroism. But God, in his mercy, has given Christians the example of Christ, who in his weakness and reluctance to face his death, sought his strength from God alone. More need not be ashamed to follow such a master.

More meditated on Jesus in the garden, praying in the darkness in agony; the apostles were sleeping, like many church leaders since; Judas was awake, doing the evil that would lead to his final despair. During those hours Jesus fought and won his battle. More focused his meditation on the moment when Jesus freely decided and knowingly accepted his destiny: passion and death. He imagined Jesus about to be taken captive, foreseeing the sufferings of future Christians, his comrades-in-arms, who will fight against the prince of darkness and all his human agents.The whole of history, not merely the hour of Christ's passion, is an 'hour of darkness'. This imagined speech of Christ is a triumphant, classical oration, covering eleven pages of the original manuscript. The moment of betrayal and arrest seems to be defeat, but in reality the time of the power of darkness is very short. Jesus confronts his enemies:

> *But this hour and this power of darkness are not only given to you now against me, but such an hour and such a brief power of darkness will also be given to other governors and other Caesars against other disciples of mine. And this too will truly be the power of darkness. For whatever my disciples endure and whatever they say, they will not endure by their own strength or say of themselves, but conquering through my strength they will win their souls by patience ...* (TW 284)

Judas betrayed his master by an acted lie, which was the opposite of what it was meant to signify: an act of friendship. Jesus dealt with what he knew to be treachery, with patience and gentleness. After Jesus' arrest 'all his disciples abandoned him and fled'.

On 12 June 1535, the Lieutenant of the Tower and others came into More's cell and ordered the confiscation of his writing materials and books. Judas also entered his cell in the person of Sir Richard Rich; it was his version of the subsequent conversation between himself and More that was the cause of More's final conviction. Between 12 June and his trial on 1 July, More closed the shutters of his window and announced that his shop was closed.

The Morean Synthesis

No part of his life is more frequently or more gladly spoken of than his cheerful death. (MORE IN *UTOPIA*, ON THE DEATH OF A GOOD MAN)

Trial and Execution

On 28 June 1535 Thomas More was formally indicted for treason, and on 1 July appeared on trial in Westminster Hall, the place where he had sat so often in judgement as Lord Chancellor. Treason trials were unfair and their conclusions predictable. More was not given a copy of the grounds for indictment before his trial, and only had it read out to him in court. He had to conduct his own defence, could call on no witnesses, and could expect the jury to comply with the wishes of the bench. More did not complain of his unjust hearing; this was usual practice in treason trials. His intention was to defend himself as well as he possibly could, with all his skill and ability as a lawyer. Because of his ill health and infirmity More was allowed to remain seated while conducting his defence.

That defence was that he had never disclosed to anyone the reason for his refusal of the oath attached to the Act of Succession. In common law and in natural justice a man could not be tried for his thoughts. Silence was normally interpreted as consent rather than disapproval. Nevertheless, by his silence More was accused of 'falsely, traitorously and maliciously' depriving the King of his title of Supreme Head of the Church, 'to the contempt of the King and against his peace'. More replied:

> *Ye must understand that in things touching conscience, every true and good subject is more bound to have respect to his said conscience and to his soul than to any other thing in all the world ... when his conscience is in such sort as mine is, that is to say when the person giveth no occasion of slander, of tumult and sedition against his prince, as it is with me; for I assure you that I have not hitherto to this hour disclosed and opened my conscience and mind to any living person in all the world.* (N. HARPSFIELD, *THE LIFE AND DEATH OF SIR THOMAS MORE* 186)

It has been rightly said that 'More is that rare figure ... an establishment martyr' (Kenny). He feared sedition, or any act that would destabilize lawful government. Throughout his trial he always spoke of the King with love, respect and loyalty. He did not seek to influence others, so what he *thought* in his innermost mind was known only to God. As he had previously said to Cromwell:

> *I am the King's true and faithful subject ... and pray for his highness and all the realm. I do nobody no harm, I say none harm, I think none harm ... but wish everybody good. And if this be not enough to keep a man alive, in good faith I long not to live.* (SL 63)

More was condemned because of the evidence of Richard Rich, who swore that in a conversation with More in prison, the latter had broken his silence and declared that Parliament could not make Henry VIII Supreme Head of the Church in England. More insisted that they had spoken of hypothetical cases, not of the matter before the judges. Rich's word was believed, without a corroborating witness. Only after More had been condemned did he finally break his silence and reveal the reasons for his stand in conscience. He had been charged on an indictment insufficient to condemn any man, under the terms of an Act of Parliament which was itself unlawful, since it failed to uphold the liberties of the Church as stated in Magna Carta (1215). Finally, he argued that the universal law of Christendom had a prior claim on his obedience above that of the law of a single realm. According to one biographer, More gave one hint as to the real reasons for his trial: 'I call and appeal to God whose only sight pierceth onto the depths of man's heart to be my witness ... it is not for the supremacy that you seek my blood, as for that I would not condescend to the marriage' (HARPSFIELD 186).

More was condemned to death, and his sentence was 'mercifully' commuted to beheading. It was carried out on 6 July 1535, on Tower Green. His final prison letters to his family and friends were free of rancour, bitterness or self-regard, and were full of concern for those who had suffered so much because of his decision. He had recovered his peace of mind and sense of humour, so often absent in his controversial writings. His last prison prayers and the annotations on the side of his well-used psalter, testify to the depths of his faith and to his trust in God's grace that he would be faithful to the end. He died, as he had lived, 'the King's loyal servant, but God's first'.

More's Life and Thought: An Assessment

More's trial proceedings, and his subsequent execution, are so well known and recorded that they must constitute a final statement about what he thought, in relation to conscience and the human person. More's famous refusal to allow the state to dictate what he thought or believed in his innermost mind, because a *cause célèbre* in Europe within weeks of his execution. A Paris newsletter was in circulation by mid-July 1535, and his biographers, Roper and Harpsfield, had access to eye-witness accounts and to family memories. The political and constitutional implications of More's final act have passed into the English parliamentary heritage.

More's discreet and political silence has made the precise cause of his death a little difficult to pinpoint. Henry VIII and his secretary Cromwell regarded the sovereign action of the king in Parliament, embodied in statute, as the highest expression of binding law. They were, in modern parlance, 'little Englanders'. More took the older view that English law should be tested against the law of nature, and against the consensus of Christendom embodied in the decrees of General Councils. England was not just an island 'sovereign unto itself'; it had its rightful independence but had also to consider its relationship and responsibilities to the wider community of which it was a part. More believed in the unity of Christendom, symbolized by the leadership of the pope. He died because he refused to play his part in any process which might dismantle or harm that unity. This seemed to many of his political colleagues to be traditionalist, bigoted and against the nation's best interests.

It does not detract from the integrity of More's stand to say that it is now generally recognized – with hindsight – that the breakup of European Christendom, and the emergence of the nation state, was part of an inevitable shift from late-medieval to modern European society. Christendom broke up for political, economic and social reasons as much as for religious ones. In each country, and in many cities throughout Europe, the self-interest of prince or city council played its part in the reception or non-reception of religious reformation. England was no exception. Ironically More had most in common with those whom he implacably opposed: religious leaders like Luther and Tyndale, who were motivated by a genuine desire to preach the gospel.

More's religious vision of a united Christendom was inseparable from his political vision of a Europe united by a shared heritage and a common culture. He constantly expressed his hatred for war, which disrupted the internal and external peace of European nations. While Christendom in its late-medieval shape can never be revived, the idea that the nation state belongs to a greater whole – either the European or the world community – is a vision many can share today. Thomas More was not only a great Englishman but also a great European; he perceived that England's national interests were served by belonging to, rather than being in isolation from, the rest of the continent. His Utopian vision embraced the whole world.

More made no claims to be a professional theologian or philosopher, and positively disliked abstract thought. He claimed to be a Christian humanist interested in every aspect of human life as it related to the Christian vocation. More's thought was always directed to practical action; for him a Christian was called to serve God 'especially in the mind' as directed outwards towards the complexities of life. In the journey through life there are no blueprints, no exact precedents telling men and women how to act in any situation; there are only general principles which have to be applied to particular situations. A good Christian had to work out, with the aid of reason, the help of God's grace, and the collective wisdom of the Christian community, how to discern right action. Conscience as right discernment applied to all More's life, not only to his decisions as a judge, or to his final choice.

As this study has shown, More's thought and action fall into three distinct phases: early humanist, public life, and the prison experience. As a young humanist More relished belonging to a circle of friends with whom he shaped his political, educational and literary ideals. His early writings include pithy epigrams, English poetry, four long letter-essays in defence of humanism, and a *History of Richard III*. *Utopia* was to be the greatest and most enduring expression of his political ideals, and is a work which continues to challenge and to invite criticism of social injustice, which is the consequence of human greed and self-interest.

In More's second period, that of his public life, he provided an enduring example of honesty and integrity in the exercise of his duties. More's time as Chancellor was marked by concern for the poor and for the reform of common law; but it was also marked by harshness and intolerance towards heretics, to whom he denied the freedom of conscience he was soon to claim for himself. The limitations of a good man under pressure, as his world falls apart, are evident in More's controversial writings, of which the best must be his *Dialogue Concerning Heresies*. These polemical writings are difficult for a modern reader, and are the least relevant for contemporary life.

More's Tower experience yielded the devotional writings and letters of a great Christian who was prepared to suffer the loss of everything – position, wealth but most of all his beloved family – rather than compromise his conscience. He defended his choice with dignity, courage and lack of bitterness. Failed politicians usually are not noted for 'letting go' of public life and the part they may have played in it. More had played his part and now wanted to 'set the world at nought' and prepare himself to face God, his final judge. The depths of More's faith and spirituality were the fruit of a lifetime habit of prayer and of referring all things to God. He was discreet and humble about his spiritual life, though there are hints in his prison writings of the times he experienced joy and consolation during his lonely vigils. He had asked, 'The things good Lord that I pray for, give me thy grace to labour for'. The good works of human living had to be laboured for, but God was always at hand.

More's final gift to his family and friends was his conviction that this was not the end. 'Fare well, my dear child, and pray for me, and I shall for you and all your friends that we may meet merrily in heaven.' (SL 66) The best things in life: love, friendship, homely conversation, shared insight, festive meals, would be part of life with God in heaven, where we 'shall need no letters, where no wall shall separate us, and where no porter shall keep us from talking together' (SL 65).

Suggested Further Reading

More's Writings

The Yale Edition of *The Complete Works of St Thomas More*, 1963–1996, 15 volumes.

The Yale Edition of *Selected Works of St Thomas More* (with modernized spelling). Where possible these have been used in the present study.

St Thomas More: Selected Letters ed. E. F. Rogers 1961.

Utopia ed. E. Surtz (see below for alternative text), 1964.

The History of King Richard III, and

Selections from the English and Latin Poems ed. R. S. Sylvester, 1976.

A Dialogue of Comfort Against Tribulation ed. F. Manley, 1977.

The Tower Works: Devotional Writings ed. G. E. Haupt, 1980.

Thomas More's Prayer Book, 1969.

The Correspondence of Sir Thomas More ed. E. F. Rogers, Princeton, 1947.

Alternative edition of *Utopia* ed. G. M. Logan & R. M. Adams, Cambridge Texts in the History of Political Thought, 1989. Cited in text.

Biographies

Roper, William, *Life of Sir Thomas More* in the Everyman Edition, ed. E. E. Reynolds, or in *Two Early Tudor Lives* ed. R. S. Sylvester & D. P. Harding, Yale University Press, 1962. Cited in text.

Harpsfield, Nicholas, *The Life and Death of Sir Thomas More* (1557), Everyman edition with Roper's life, as above.

Stapleton, Thomas, *Life of Sir Thomas More* (1588), Burns & Oates, 1928.

Chambers, R. S., *Thomas More*, Jonathan Cape, 1935, Penguin, 1963.

Reynolds, E. E., *The Life and Death of St Thomas More: The Field is Won*, Burns & Oates, 1963.

Kenny, A., *Thomas More*, Oxford University Press, 1983.

Marius, R., *Thomas More*, J. M. Dent, 1985. Fullest revisionist study.

Martz, L. L., *Thomas More: The Search for the Inner Man*, Yale University Press, 1990. Four reprinted articles.

Humanism/Utopia

Bradshaw, B., and Duffy, E., eds. *Humanism, Reform and Reformation: The Career of Bishop John Fisher*, Cambridge University Press, 1989.

Fleisher, M., *Radical Reform and Political Persuasion in the Life and Writings of Thomas More*, Geneva, Libraire Droz, 1973.

Hexter, J. H., *The Biography of an Idea*, Princeton, 1952.

McConica, J., *Erasmus*, Oxford University Press, 1991.

McCutcheon, E. and Miller, C. H., *Utopia Revisited*, Moreana 118–19, Angers, 1994.

Olin, J. C., ed. *Interpreting Thomas More's Utopia*, Fordham, 1989.

Skinner, Q., 'Sir Thomas More's *Utopia* and the Language of Renaissance Humanism' in *Languages of Political Theory in Early Modern Europe*, Cambridge, 1987.

Baker-Smith, D., *More's Utopia*, HarperCollins Academic, 1991.

Public Life/Reign of Henry VIII

Duffy, E., *The Stripping of the Altars: Traditional Religion in England 1400–1580*, Yale University Press, 1992.

Guy, J. M., *The Public Career of Sir Thomas More*, Harvester Press 1980.

Gwyn, P., *The King's Cardinal: The Rise and Fall of Cardinal Wolsey*, 1990.

Rex, R., *Henry VIII and the English Reformation*, Macmillan, 1993.

Later Writings

Fox, A., *Thomas More: History and Providence*, Oxford, 1982. Particular attention to More as writer.

Gogan, B., *The Common Corps of Christendom: Ecclesiological Themes in the Writings of Sir Thomas More*, Brill, Leiden, 1982.

Luther, M., *Luther's Works*, eds. J. Pelican et al., St Louis & Philadelphia, 1955–.

Reynolds, E. E., *The Trial of St Thomas More*, London, Burns & Oates, 1964.

Articles and Collections

Introduction to each volume of the Yale Editions of the *Complete Works*. This study is especially indebted to

Martz, L. L. and Manley, F., introduction to CW12, *A Dialogue of Comfort Against Tribulation*, xix-clxvii.

Sylvester, R. S. & Marc'hadour, G., eds. *Essential Articles for the Study of Thomas More*, Connecticut, 1977.

Bradshaw, B., 'The Controversial Sir Thomas More', *Journal of Ecclesiastical History 36:4*, 535–569, 1985.

LUTHER

Hans-Peter Grosshans

Luther

HANS-PETER GROSSHANS

Hans-Peter Grosshans teaches systematic theology and philosophy of religion at the faculty of Evangelical Theology at the University of Tuebingen (Germany), where he is also deputy director of the Institute for Hermeneutics. He studied theology at the universities of Tuebingen and Oxford, and served in the ministry of one of the member churches of the Evangelical Church of Germany for several years. His most recent book is *Theologischer Realismus: Ein sprachphilosophischer Beitrag zu einer theologischen Sprachlehre* (Mohr Verlag, Tuebingen, 1996).

For Barbara

Contents

Abbreviations

The following abbreviations are used in references given in the text:

LW   *Luther's Works*. American Edition, ed. by J. Pelikan and
H. T. Lehmann, published by Concordia Publishing
House (St Louis) and Muhlenberg Press (Philadelphia)
in 55 volumes.

WA   *Martin Luthers Werke. Kritische Gesamtausgabe*
(*Weimarer Ausgabe* = WA), Hermann Böhlaus
Nachfolger (Weimar). Not all texts of Luther have been
translated into English. Quotations of the WA, which is
the main critical edition of Luther's works, are
translated by me. In the references to WA, the first
number refers to the volume, the second to the page,
and the third to the line.

Full bibliographical details of other works cited are given in
Suggested Further Reading.

Date Chart

1521	April, Diet of Worms
	4 May, Luther arrives at the Wartburg, where he stays until March 1522
	26 May, edict of Worms: Luther regarded as a convicted heretic and outlawed
	Autumn, evangelical mass with wine to laity; tumult in Wittenberg
1522	Justus Jonas, minister of the Castle Church at Wittenberg, marries
	March, Luther returns to Wittenberg
	September, Luther's German New Testament published
1524	Erasmus, *The Freedom of the Will*
1525	Conflicts with anabaptists and peasants; peasant war
	13 June, Luther and Katherine von Bora marry
	December, *The Bondage of the Will* (against Erasmus)
1526	20 May, birth of first child, John (died 1575)
1527	10 December, birth of daughter Elisabeth (died 3 August 1528)
1528	Publication of the *Confession of the Lord's Supper*
1529	4 May, birth of daughter Magdalena (died 20 September 1542)
	Protest of the princes following the Reformation at the Diet of Speyer
	The Small Catechism; The Large (German) Catechism published
	1–4 October, Marburg colloquy with Zwingli
1530	Diet at Augsburg; presentation of the Augsburg Confession by Philip Melanchthon
1531	9 November, birth of son Martin (died 1565)
1533	28 January, birth of son Paul (died 1593)
1534	Publication of the translation of the complete Bible into German
	17 December, birth of daughter Margarethe (died 1570)
1537	First volume of Luther's German works published
1545	First volume of Luther's Latin works published
1546	23 January, journey to Eisleben
	14 February, Luther's last sermon
	18 February, death in Eisleben

Introduction

Martin Luther was a preacher and teacher who based his theology and his understanding of Christianity on what he considered to be the truth of the Bible. For centuries, he has been highly influential on culture, politics and the Church. He changed the world not by political means but through his words and ideas. Martin Luther had a message which hit a nerve in his time as well as in the hearts and the minds of many of his fellow people. It was this message, in combination with the ideas of fellow reformers like Jean Calvin in Geneva and Huldrych Zwingli in Zürich, which produced those changes in the history of our world we now know as 'the Reformation'.

Luther was a pious man and he had a spiritual message. It was his piety and his spirituality which led him into the monastic life, but it was this same piety and spirituality that led him to criticize the Church and which, later, led him to strip off his monk's habit and to live a civil Christian life.

Luther was a fascinating character and an extremely vital and passionate person. In this book there is only space for a short glance at Luther's biography and some of the main events of his life, before we concentrate on the most important of his ideas and doctrines. Luther's spiritual ideas have had a great and far-reaching influence. The Christian faith was given a new definition by him, and by this faith people were enabled to gain a new understanding of themselves – this new understanding shook the world of his time.

The main critical edition of Luther's works contains more than a hundred volumes, and therefore a short presentation of Luther's theology such as this one will inevitably be fragmentary. However, there is no substitute for reading Luther's main writings or selected works for oneself, and hopefully this volume will encourage such wider reading.

I would like to start by thanking three people without whom this book would not and could not have been written. My thanks are offered to Peter Vardy who has edited it. I am sure he did not realize the extent of the work he would have to do when he asked me, a German, to write a book in his series. His encouragement throughout has been essential, and his criticisms forced me to concentrate on the main ideas of Martin Luther and to present them as clearly as possible. That the whole book may not hurt the eyes of the English-speaking reader is the result of an enormous effort by Anne Vardy, who improved my English in style and grammar. I owe a great debt of gratitude to her. My thanks also to the Revd John Handford, whose excellent knowledge of Luther's theology was of great help and whose comments on the manuscript were pertinent and sharp, but always kindly given.

Luther's Life

Martin Luther was born on 10 November 1483 in the small Saxon town of Eisleben, the son of a miner, Hans Luder, and his wife, Margarethe. He died in the same town on 18 February 1546. Throughout his life, he stayed in his native country: he grew up in Mansfeld, another small town in the kingdom of Saxony; he studied in Erfurt; and he held a chair in theology at the new University of Wittenberg.

Martin Luther was a typical child of his time. It was a time of great change, in which the Middle Ages had reached their end, with major new developments and discoveries in economics, culture, politics and science. Politics was dominated by the Austrian house of Habsburg, in which Charles V (1500–1558) ruled a huge empire that covered central Europe, Spain and the new Spanish colonies in America. It was said that 'the sun did not go down' on his empire. There was a tremendous economic boom and a more pervasive capitalism appeared. Many citizens developed successful smaller companies of their own, and Hans Luder, father of Martin Luther, was an example of this, starting as a miner, but becoming a successful and independent self-employed entrepreneur. Through hard work he became wealthy, and financed the education of his son through both school and university. In the cultural arena, the Renaissance had reached its height, with artists like Michelangelo being sponsored, for example by the popes. With increased wealth and an emerging middle class, education generally became significantly more important, and many new schools and universities were founded, among them the University of Wittenberg (1502).

In these times of tremendous change and such a variety of new activities and innovations, Martin Luther acquired a sound education at school followed by philosophical studies at university. He then – as was his father's wish – began law studies, with the aim of taking up a professional career, and it was as a student of law that he experienced a profound change of heart. One day in July 1505 he was unexpectedly caught in a violent thunderstorm during which he experienced extreme fear and in his anguish made a request and a promise to St Anne, the mother of the Virgin Mary, who was at that time a fairly new and popular saint of the miners: 'St Anne, help me! I will become a monk.' Against strong opposition from his father, Martin, seeing himself bound by his vow, broke off his law studies and, after a farewell party with some friends, entered the Augustinian monastery at Erfurt, which was well known for its ascetic life. Luther chose a life which the Church regarded as the surest way to salvation. The search for a gracious and merciful God was part of the Augustinian understanding of being a monk. When a novice presented himself to an Augustinian congregation the first question the prior asked him was: 'What seekest thou?' And the candidate had to answer: 'God's grace and thy mercy'. Martin Luther entered the monastery in order to make his peace with God and to gain knowledge about God's gracious and merciful will. He spent his days in prayer, in song, in meditation and in quiet companionship. But this peace was shattered by a spiritual experience. His superior selected Luther for the priesthood, and on 2 May 1507 he had to say his first mass. In that mass he experienced the majesty and holiness of God, and this he found terrifying. In the midst of the mass he experienced the terror of the Holy and the horror of the Infinite. The Prior had to persuade him to continue with the mass. What had happened? In the introductory part of the mass Luther had to say: 'We offer unto thee, the living, the true, the eternal God'. Later Luther reported:

At these words I was utterly stupefied and terror-stricken. I thought to myself, 'With what tongue shall I address such Majesty, seeing that all men ought to tremble in the presence of even an earthly prince? Who am I, that I should lift up mine eyes or raise my hands to the divine Majesty? ... At his nod the earth trembles. And shall I, a miserable little pygmy, say "I want this, I ask for that"? For I am dust and ashes and full of sin and I am speaking to the living, eternal and the true God'. (QUOTED IN R. H. BAINTON, *HERE I STAND* 30)

With that experience the possibility of a peaceful and quiet life as a monk faded away. Luther now agonized over the question how he, who was unworthy, could stand before the divine majesty. And how could he, who again always transgressed the divine law in thought, word and deed, confront the divine Holiness? These questions now dominated his spiritual life. Terrified by God's holiness and majesty, his search for God's grace and mercy became more desperate. He experienced trial and desperation. And seldom was he at peace with God. Some years later, however, he had another strong spiritual experience: the experience of the true meaning of the righteousness of God, which opened to him the gates of heaven again (see chapter 2).

Shortly after his first mass, Martin Luther was selected by his superior for the study of theology. In 1510–11, whilst still in the Augustinian monastery in Erfurt, he was sent to Rome where he was for the first time confronted with the very worldly side of the Church. As a pilgrim he walked over the Alps to Italy, but the months in Rome were a shock for Luther. None of his high spiritual expectations were fulfilled. On the contrary he got the impression that in Rome, in the very centre of the Church, there was almost no Christian spirituality. Luther's later attacks against Rome and the Pope were partly the result of this journey.

On his return from Rome in 1511 Luther moved to the Augustinian monastery in Wittenberg, where he became vice-prior in 1512 and later an overseer of other monasteries in the region. After completing his theological studies by gaining his doctorate, he became Professor of Biblical Studies at the University of Wittenberg in 1512, a position he held until his death.

In those years Martin Luther came to know a man who was to be a strong influence on his development, the Vicar General of the Augustinian Order, Johann von Staupitz (1468–1524). In him Luther found his ideal spiritual guide and a strong support for his academic interests as well. Johann von Staupitz, who was fifteen years older than Luther, became almost a second father. Luther could complain to him about all the trials of his faith and his difficulties with Christianity as it was taught by the Church at that time. With this understanding of God and human faith he found that he could gain no certainty about his salvation. He always saw the need to confess his sins and to do penance. Luther agonized with doubt as to whether he was one of the elect destined for life in heaven. Staupitz counselled him, advising him to cling to Jesus Christ and to understand God only through Jesus Christ as recorded in the Bible. It was significant for the development of Luther's theology that Staupitz tried to answer all spiritual and theological questions in this way. Indeed, Luther was to set the Bible and Jesus Christ at the centre of his theology. In later years Luther praised Staupitz as the father of the Reformation, although Staupitz did not follow Luther away from the Catholic Church:

> My good Staupitz said, 'One must keep one's eyes fixed on that man who is called Christ'. Staupitz is the one who started the teaching [of the gospel in our time]. (LW 54, 97)

Luther reported that for the daily readings in the cloister during meals Staupitz wanted only the Bible to be read, and not other spiritual or theological writings and, again, this influenced the young Luther.

When he was appointed to the professorship in biblical studies, Luther had to concentrate on the biblical texts themselves and to develop his theological ideas by interpretation of the Bible. Early signs of Luther's new thinking were already evident in his first lectures. In 1513 he started to lecture on the book of Psalms, in 1515 he lectured on St Paul's Epistle to the Romans, in 1516–1517 he treated the Epistle to the Galatians. In intensive discussion with the theological and philosophical traditions; Luther highlighted the problems there and tried hard to find a new understanding of the Gospel which would meet the needs of his time as well as the turmoil in himself. In those biblical texts he found a new view of God: the holy God, who terrified him, is the All Merciful too. The cross of Jesus Christ shows that there is a reconciliation of God with the world. The God whose holiness and majesty had made Luther feel totally unworthy, had been revealed as a God who deeply loved the world as well.

Beside his duties as professor, Martin Luther was also director of studies, he preached at the castle church of Wittenberg, was an overseer of eleven monasteries, and a parish priest in a village church. It was there that he got to know the disastrous effects on ordinary Christians of the practice of indulgences. People could buy letters of indulgence which were supposed to grant them remission not only from punishment for their sins, but also freedom from their guilt as well.

In 1516 Luther began to criticize this practice in sermons and in academic discussions. In October 1517 he stepped into the limelight with his publication of ninety-five theses which vehemently attacked the ecclesiastical practice of indulgences (see p. 23). The well-known story is that Luther nailed his theses on to the church door at Wittenberg in order to create public interest and discussion. However it is not certain that this did happen. Irrespective of the actual events, however, knowledge and interest in the ninety-five theses spread rapidly across Germany, causing sharp counter-attacks from clerics and lay people. These counter-attacks did not defend the practice of indulgences nor attempt to answer the theses, but tried to accuse Luther of lacking belief. The theses were forwarded by Archbishop Albert of Mainz to Pope Leo X, who first tried to have the problem clarified within the Augustinian Order. This might have been the reason why in 1518 Luther was invited to defend his theology in a disputation before the chapter of the German Augustinians, meeting that year in Heidelberg. But the Augustinians did not want to suppress their brother Martin, who was a true follower of the theology of Augustine (354–430). So it was left to their rivals, the Dominicans, who followed the theology of Thomas Aquinas (1225–1274) which was strongly influenced by the philosophy of Aristotle, to present the case against Luther. In the summer of 1518 the Dominicans succeeded in convincing the Pope to cite Luther to appear in Rome within sixty days to answer charges of heresy. It is important to remember that in those days heretics were normally burnt, and so Luther was in a highly vulnerable position. However, Luther received the assurance of Elector Frederick the Wise, the prince of Saxony, that he would not have to go to Rome, and because of this protection the case against Luther had to be transferred to Germany.

In October 1518 the Pope sent Cardinal Cajetan to interview Luther about his theology and to prove the charges of heresy. The meeting in Augsburg was a disappointment, because Cajetan did not allow Luther to debate the issues, but only gave him an opportunity to recant. When the interview was finished rumour reached Luther that the Cardinal was empowered to arrest him, so by night Luther escaped from Augsburg. His prince, Frederick the Wise, rejected the appeal of Cardinal Cajetan either to banish Luther from his territories or to send him bound to Rome. In the only document he ever sent to Rome on Luther's behalf, Frederick wrote:

As for sending him to Rome or banishing him, that we will do only after he had been convicted of heresy. His offer to debate and submit to the judgement of the universities ought to be considered. He should be shown in what respect he is a heretic and not condemned in advance.
(QUOTED IN R. H. BAINTON, *HERE I STAND* 78)

After this letter, in which Frederick effectively declared Martin Luther his personal protégé, the attacks on Luther moderated. The Roman curia now tried diplomatic means to settle the affair. A series of negotiations and debates followed, culminating in Luther's hearing before the German Diet (or Parliament) in the town of Worms in 1521. However, Rome had already pre-judged the issue without waiting for the hearing, and in the second half of 1520 a papal bull was sent to Luther, declaring that he was a heretic and was excommunicated by the church. The bull also said that all his books should be burnt. Just before he received the papal bull in October 1520 Martin Luther had made a last attempt to come to peace with Pope Leo X. He addressed a diplomatic letter to the Pope expressing great sympathy with him, and with it sent a short treatise on *The Freedom of a Christian*, which he regarded as a summary of his theology. Leo did not react to this letter.

Luther's books were burnt in some cities of Germany in accordance with the papal edict. Fortunately, however, only his books could be burnt. Luther himself remained safe as long as he remained in Saxony, where Frederick could protect him. Luther's excommunication was the beginning of the division in the Church which was to lead to the formation of the new Protestant Churches, and was to influence dramatically the political history of Europe and beyond. As a result of the Reformation the Christian Church was divided into Protestant and Catholic, as well as the Orthodox Church which resulted from the earlier division in 1054.

The new emphasis on German as the national language, the realization that every citizen was a free individual, the importance of individual education and the value of freedom of conscience are ideas that are fundamental to Luther. He has influenced the history of the Western world, because of his unwavering insistence and fight for truth in the cultural, political and religious areas. One of the best-known examples of his determination to hold to his beliefs occurred in 1521, when he appeared before the

German Diet and Emperor Charles V in Worms to defend his position. Luther's refusal to recant in spite of his examination by the German authorities made a marked impression on believers well beyond the boundaries of Germany. In his defence Luther said:

> *Unless I am not convinced by the testimony of the Scriptures or by clear reason (for I do not trust either in the pope or in councils alone, since it is well known that they have often erred and contradicted themselves), I am bound by the Scriptures I have quoted and my conscience is captive to the Word of God.* (LW 32, 112)

He completed his speech in front of the most powerful men of the nation and the emperor Charles V:

> *I cannot and I will not retract anything, since it is neither safe nor right to go against conscience. I cannot do otherwise, here I stand, may God help me. Amen.* (LW 32, 112–13)

In the final edict the majority of the Diet of Worms decided to follow the ecclesiastical lead and to regard Luther as a convicted heretic. He was declared an outlaw. Nobody was allowed to give him further protection. Frederick the Wise, however, decided not to remain loyal to his emperor Charles V and to the German Diet, and he secretly broke the edict of Worms in order to protect and hide Luther. Frederick arranged for him to be kidnapped on the way back from Worms, and secretly Luther was brought to the Wartburg, a castle in Eisenach, where he stayed unrecognized for ten months. Almost nobody knew where he was or even whether he was dead or not. During those months Luther translated the New Testament from its original Greek into German – this was the first time this had been done and was significant as, with the invention of the printing press, the Bible now became available to ordinary people. At the same time many changes were taking place in the

Church all over the country. Luther's friends and followers tried to reform the Church according to his ideas. In Wittenberg the Lord's Supper was now celebrated in a new form by giving wine to the laity. Church liturgy was changed; paintings in churches were destroyed and church music was abolished; monks left their cloisters and the first priests got married. Although still outlawed as a declared heretic, Luther returned to Wittenberg in March 1522, under the protection of Prince Frederick, in order to oversee the reforming process. The Reformers had become more and more radical and had thus begun to threaten the whole process of reformation. Luther's return to Wittenberg was a political signal as well, because it now became obvious that Frederick and other German princes were not obeying the edict of Worms or the Emperor Charles V. Luther had divided the German princes and cities into two: some were loyal to Charles and the Roman Church whilst others protected Luther and began to reform the Church.

There followed very hectic years in which Luther wrote much. He was asked for advice on many and varied matters, and also continued his normal university teaching. He became involved in many conflicts – and the position he took was not always consistent with the teaching of Jesus. For example, when the peasants rebelled in 1525 Luther strongly supported the princes and he justified the butchering of the peasants.

From 1517, academic theological debate began to be increasingly important to him. One example of such disputes occurred in 1524–1525 regarding freedom of will. The debate was between Luther and the most famous scholar at that time, Erasmus of Rotterdam (1467–1536), who was a humanist as well as a moderate Catholic with reforming ideas. Another example was the dispute with his fellow reformer Huldrych Zwingli (1484–1531), which culminated in the Marburg colloquy in 1529 regarding the understanding of the eucharist.

In 1524 Luther left the Augustinian Order and gave up his monastic vows. A year later in 1525, at the age of forty-two, he married the former nun Katherine von Bora (1499–1552), who had asked him to marry her. As a result of Luther's criticism of monastic life, many young monks and nuns had left their monasteries. Katherine was one of these and she had come to Wittenberg, but two years later she was still in domestic service. There were unsuccessful attempts to find her a husband, and in the end she asked Luther if he would not marry her. At first he did not respond seriously to the suggestion but shortly afterwards he agreed. 'I am not infatuated' he was later to say, 'though I cherish my wife.' However he did care for her:

> *I would not exchange Katie [as Luther called her] for France or for Venice, because God has given her to me.*

With Katherine he experienced the joys and trials of family life alongside his work and writing in church, university and political matters. The family was continually short of money, partly because Luther always had guests at their home but also because Katherine, as a former nun, was without property and Luther's only possessions were his books and clothes. Until his marriage Luther had no personal salary because, according to the statutes of the University of Wittenberg, his monastery had to supply his needs. Once he abandoned the cowl, he was no longer entitled to the revenues of the cloister. After his marriage he was given a regular, though small, salary for his professorship by the new Prince, John. He had no other income, because he refused to take royalties from his books or other writings. In later years the couple acquired a small farm which Katharine managed. Her home-brewed beer was highly praised by her husband. Katherine bore six children, two of whom died young – Elisabeth, aged six months, and Magdalena, aged thirteen, whom Luther loved very deeply. As a family man Luther was more involved in the midst of everyday life than most priests and monks.

The years were filled with theological disputes about doctrinal questions, with the ordering of the new Protestant churches, and with the first moves in the Counter-Reformation – which was the Roman Catholic counter-attack to the Reformation. When Luther died on 18 February 1546, he was by accident in the same town where he had been born, Eisleben. He was there to give advice in some conflicts, when he had a heart attack. He died a few hours later, aged sixty-two.

Luther was not a quiet and diplomatic man. In arguments he liked to use the robust and powerful language of his native countryside. However, despite his abrasive attitude, he was not arrogant and did not claim to be the only person to know the truth. Luther was, rather, a fierce fighter for the truth of the Bible, and it is here that his most important contribution to the Reformation lies. He placed Holy Scripture and its truth at the centre of the life of the Church and of theology. Indeed it is fair to say that Luther did not see himself as a reformer, rather he wanted Scripture to be the reformer of the Church. One of the great disappointments of the Reformation is that the opponents of Luther did not take up his challenge to fight for the truth of the positions they held, but instead resorted to condemnation and the exercise of authority, rather than addressing the issues and the need for reform. This was a missed opportunity as well as a failure to stand up for Luther's vision of a search for truth.

We can now turn to address some of Luther's ideas.

The Evangelical Experience:
The Righteousness of God

Martin Luther developed his ideas and religious convictions during and through his interpretation of the Scriptures. He was concerned with the relation of God to human beings and, from this relationship, with human self-understanding. At the heart of Luther's faith and theology is a discussion about the righteousness of God. For Luther it was essential to know how he was to be judged by God after death. In the violent thunderstorm in 1505, he experienced the God who had created him but who also threatened his life as well, and it was this thunderstorm that made him vow to become a monk. When he first said mass in 1507 he experienced the terrifying majesty and holiness of God. In the following years, this sense of the holiness and majesty of God increased. By living a very ascetic monastic life and trying to follow strictly all the monastic rules, Luther tried to become more virtuous. However, he never was satisfied with his spiritual efforts and never had the feeling that he lived up to God's holiness. It was during his study of the Bible that he realized he had misunderstood what God's justice and righteousness meant, and this brought him to a new and deeper understanding.

Luther's realization of the true meaning of God's relationship with human beings has been described as his 'Tower Experience', since it came to him in his study in the tower of the Augustinian monastery in Wittenberg. It was Luther's third major experience of God, and can be called his evangelical experience of the righteousness of God. According to some scholars, Luther had this experience during the first years of his biblical lecturing in 1513–1515, but Luther himself said that this happened in 1519, when he began to interpret the Psalter anew after having lectured on St Paul's epistles to the Romans, Galatians and Hebrews. Luther explained how he had been captivated by an extraordinary desire to understand Paul's Epistle to the Romans. His stumbling block to an understanding of this epistle was the phrase in chapter 1:17, 'In it the righteousness of God is revealed through faith for faith.' In a kind of autobiography written near the end of his life, in 1545, Luther wrote about his 'Tower Experience':

I hated the words 'righteousness of God' which according to the use and custom of all the teachers I had been taught to understand ... as the ... active righteousness ... with which God is righteous and punishes the unrighteous sinner.

Luther wrestled with this phrase to understand what Paul's true meaning and message was.

At last, by the mercy of God and meditating day and night, I gave heed to the context of the words, namely 'In it the righteousness of God is revealed, as it is written, "He who through faith is righteous shall live".' There I began to understand that the righteousness of God is that by which the righteous lives by a gift of God, namely by faith and this is the meaning: the righteousness of God is revealed by the Gospel, namely, the passive righteousness with which merciful God justifies us by faith, as it is written, 'He who through faith is righteous shall live.' Here I felt that I was altogether born again and had entered paradise itself through open gates.

The word 'righteousness of God' over which Luther had so agonized and which he had come to dread and hate, became for him the 'sweetest word with a love as great as the hatred with which I had before hated the word' (LW 34, 336–37).

If the righteousness of God was to be understood in the sense of a law, then the just God would be a God who accuses, judges and punishes the human person, and by so doing would be true to the law which demands justice and goodness. Considering the fact that all human beings are sinners and therefore do not live up to the requirements of God, then if God acted justly, this would mean condemnation of all human beings. God would be acting justly in condemning the unjust. This was Luther's understanding prior to the 'tower experience', and it was this that led him to make every possible effort to become a just and holy person. His new theological 'discovery' was that the biblical concept of the righteousness of God was not to be understood by seeing God as a judge, but instead as a truth revealed in the promises of the Gospel. The Gospel promises God's everlasting love and faithfulness to all human beings who have faith. In such a vision of the Gospel the same God who stands against a person as judge and measures the individual according to the commandments of God's law also stands close to the person and supports him or her.

By realizing that God comes close to human beings and accepts them unconditionally, it becomes clear who God is and what his righteousness involves. The righteousness of God does not condemn the unjust, but makes an unjust person righteous. The justification of the nonbeliever and sinner is evident in the words of promise and hope – words like 'Come to me, all who labour and are heavy laden, and I will give you rest' (Matthew 11:28) or 'God so loved the world that he gave his only Son, that whoever believes in him should not perish but have eternal life' (John 3:16). This is not a human but a divine idea of righteousness, which becomes a reality and is valid for all human beings through faith. A person cannot become righteous by his or her own efforts and activities, but is made righteous only by trusting in God's unconditional acceptance and love.

Sin

For Luther Scripture describes:

> ... *man as so turned in on himself that he uses not only physical but even spiritual goods for his own purposes and in all things seeks only himself. This curvedness is now natural for us, a natural wickedness and a natural sinfulness.* (LECTURES ON ROMANS, LW 25, 345)

A person who sees the world only in terms of their own horizons and their own interests is a perfect example of a sinner. For Luther all human beings are sinners, as it is in their natures to care first for themselves. People do not classify themselves as sinners or acknowledge their self-centred way of life as sinful. This suggests that sin is a theological rather than a moral category. Yet God takes the initiative and comes close to us, and exposes human selfishness as an inappropriate way of life. It is through the devotion of God to us that our selfishness is revealed, because we do not devote ourselves totally and unconditionally to other people or to God.

Martin Luther, like Augustine (see Richard Price's book in the 'Fount Christian Thinkers' series on *Augustine* published by HarperCollins in 1996), strongly emphasized human sin. According to Luther, sin is not only a deficiency or shortcoming of a human being or of human nature in general, rather, sin is the explanation for human beings being totally centred on themselves rather than being centred outward. Luther considered human beings to be totally corrupt, to be utterly sinful and to be unable to do any good by their own efforts. This view has led to some seeing Luther as being pessimistic about human nature, with some biographers trying to find psychological reasons in Luther's character to explain this pessimism. However, Luther is not a pessimist. The question should rather be to ask exactly what it is that Luther is pessimistic about and what he means by sin.

For Luther sin is mainly defined as a lack of trust and confidence in God. He uses the concept of sin to give a theological understanding of human beings, which cannot be identified with a wholly pessimistic anthropology. Sin results in humans being unable to relate to and devote themselves to God. Luther says:

> *In all that he does or leaves undone, he rather seeks his own advantage and his own way. He seeks his own honour, rather than God's and that of his neighbour. Therefore, all his works, all his words, all his thoughts, all his life are evil and not godly.* (TREATISE ON GOOD WORKS (1520), LW 44, 72–73)

Human nature

> *... sets for itself no object but itself toward which it is borne and toward which it is directed; it sees, seeks, and works only toward itself in all matters, and it passes by all other things and even God Himself ... as if it did not see them, and is directed only toward itself ... Nature ... sets itself in the place of all other things, even in the place of God, and seeks only those things which are its own and not the things of God. Therefore it is its own first and greatest idol.* (LECTURES ON ROMANS, LW 25, 346)

In this respect even God and faith may be misused, if one follows God's will with selfish motives. People misuse their relation to God, in only relating to God when they hope God might be useful for their own interests and purposes. In this case piety and spirituality are degraded to a mere means to an end, rather than being followed for their own sake. Luther uses the same argument for explaining the morality of a sinner. A person who acts morally may be sinful, if in their moral activities the person is only attempting to satisfy their own interests and purposes, and is not in the first instance interested in the good of fellow human beings alone. Following this general approach Luther notices three characteristics of sin: a sinner is characterized by self-love (*amor sui*), by the desire for security by becoming owner of as many worldly goods as possible (*concupiscentia*), and by an arrogant, haughty self-complacency (*superbia*).

But these are not the only descriptions of sin. We find texts where Luther calls sin the offence against the Ten Commandments. This might occur in two ways: first, if a human being does not fulfil all the commandments; and second – and this is the core of sin – if a human being offends against the first commandment. Human beings are in particular danger of offending against the first commandment in the moral and religious life ('I am the Lord your God ... You shall have no other gods before me'), when they fail to trust and hope in God alone.

For Luther sin is one of the main characteristics of human existence in so far as no human being is able to guarantee permanent trust in God. Sins, therefore, are not only occasional trespasses against the law and will of God in thought, word and deed, but they represent the permanent tendency to trust not in God but in themselves. In one of his sermons Luther concludes: 'Our deficiency does not lie in our works but in our nature' (LW 52, 151). The whole nature of man is characterized by sin. There is nothing else in us but sin: self-love, arrogant self-complacency, and selfish desires go to the very root of what it is to be human.

In piety and morality, for Luther, there lies the danger of the deepest sin, because in trying to be seriously pious and to be seriously moral people are in the deepest sense related only to themselves, and therefore live as if they do not need God in their lives. Luther understood this as being the normal state of human beings but in no way saw this as devaluing humanity. It is the nature of human beings to be related only to themselves, but by indulging in or accepting this nature they are denying their own abilities and possibilities. It is part of the sinful nature of being human that people overestimate themselves. What is more, they do not have the power to change this situation by their own efforts. Luther makes this point when he talks of an enslaved and unfree will of human beings. The will of all humanity is in the last sense related only to humanity itself. Human beings always want – despite their concrete visible activities – to place themselves at the centre and to be concerned for their own welfare. They want to satisfy their own self-love, their own desires and their own complacency.

Some have held the view that people could give up their selfishness by constant practice of love, devotion, humility and chastity. But for Luther it would be a huge self-deception for a person to assume that, by the regular practice of these virtues, he or she will change from being a sinner to becoming holy. On the contrary, this kind of understanding of human salvation is another subtle expression of the hopeless captivity of human beings in sin. Luther is here in opposition to Thomas Aquinas and Aristotle (384–322 BC):

> *Aquinas and Aristotle are wrong when they say that by exercise one becomes virtuous. Like a harpist who becomes a harpist by constant practice, those fools think one can gain the virtues of love, chastity and humility by exercise. It is not true.* (WA 10/3, 92, 19–93, 1)

Human beings can neither set aside their sin nor can they diminish it by exercise of their own will power. Sin is a part of being human and this cannot be separated from human personality. With these ideas as his foundation, Luther argues for a radical position: human beings *are* sinners and they cannot flee this feature of their lives, and as a result of it they are enslaved. Luther radically demythologizes human beings, and their attempts to be something better, nobler and higher are exposed as being self-delusions and illusory.

Nevertheless, at times people do sense that their selfishness and self-centredness is problematic and painful. This happens when they become aware of being trapped in themselves and unable to change and forsake their way of living, thus remaining the same person as before. They are and remain the people they have become. However, they long for liberation from themselves, they long for salvation, for a *new* life, which they cannot gain for themselves because they are trapped. For Luther human beings, especially Christians, are always in this state of tension, feeling trapped by their nature, which dominates their past, and by their selfishness, but at the same time being drawn away from themselves into the future, into freedom, into a new life. They are drawn to other people and to God. This fundamental tension shows that although human beings are sinners, they can develop an awareness of their sin, even an awareness of being completely in the grip of sin.

Justification

Is there any rescue or hope for people who are in such a desperate situation? And where could help and rescue come from? In this situation the righteousness of God becomes important. Normally we would consider it just that people who relate solely to themselves should be left to their own devices. Such people should look to themselves for a way out of their captivity and hopelessness, but by doing this they would merely lead themselves even deeper into their despair.

This is where Luther introduces the righteousness of God. God does not abandon such a person. Because God is love, God is in the first instance interested in a passionate and joyful relationship with each individual, and thinks beyond punishing people for their sins. Righteousness is a concept of relation and refers to the relations of life. God wants the best possible life for each person, and this will come through a relationship between individuals and God. The loving will of God wants each person, as a beloved child of God, to be in relationship with God. It is here that true justice is expressed. It is a justice that human beings have not deserved, but which comes as a free gift from God. Each human being will be judged just by God provided he or she trusts and believes in God's love. People become righteous when, in faith, they turn wholeheartedly to God.

The personal response of faith by each individual is crucial for this message to become effective, because *each individual human being* is at stake when we talk about the righteousness of God. The righteousness of God refers to our lives and to our ongoing relationships. It is not a truth which can be valid and can exist without our involvement. For this reason, it is necessary that each individual should listen, believe and accept God's righteousness if God's justification is to become a reality. Luther's point is not that a person should begin to improve his or her life *in order to* become worthy of God's love and justice – the whole point about God's love is that it is unconditional.

This understanding of God's righteousness and the justification of the godless person is a good example of Luther's rejection of the prevailing theological tradition of his time, and his reinterpretation of key biblical texts. For Luther 'all words take on a new meaning in Christ' (WA 39/2, 94,17f.), because all the words we use in our talk of God have their meaning from their reference to the gracious and loving devotion of God to human beings. Because *God* has come to all people, all can be judged and made righteous and just by God, despite being godless and sinful.

Aristotle said, 'If we act justly, we become just' (NIKOMACHIAN ETHICS 1103 b 1f.). Luther disagreed with this: before God people are not just and righteous by virtue of their conduct. This would mean that, by their own efforts, they could make themselves worthy to stand before God's holiness and righteousness. Rather, it is God's love that overcomes human sin and enables every individual to stand before God – nothing can stand in the way of God's love, except an individual's refusal to have faith and to accept this love.

Reforming Christianity

The Reformation began with a dispute regarding the understanding of penance and the practice of indulgences in the Church. This provides the best illustration of Luther's understanding of Christian faith.

Luther opened up the issue with ninety-five theses, which he sent on 31 October 1517 to Archbishop Albert of Mainz, and others. He may well have nailed them on to the door of the Castle Church at Wittenberg as well. Prior to this Luther had discussed the problem in academic circles, where his criticisms were even sharper. At stake in the dispute was not merely the practice of indulgences – these were only the visible signs of a more fundamental problem. The real issue was the extent to which Christian faith is directly based on the New Testament.

According to theological understanding in the Middle Ages, a distinction was made between, on the one hand, the permanent, eternal condemnation of a person to hell and, on the other, punishment after death in purgatory for all the sins committed in one's lifetime. The idea was that punishment in purgatory would lead to purification prior to entering eternal life. Eternal damnation could normally be avoided by baptism, in which one became a child of God, but this was not sufficient to secure eternal life. *Original sin*, which since Adam's fall was an essential characteristic of human existence, could not prevent the achievement of future eternal bliss by the baptized, but it still retained its power and had not been totally nullified. Original sin was still effective and ever present. The *actual sins* of human beings could not be overlooked, but had to be confessed and punished by God in order to restore goodness to the sinners. This took place in purgatory which cleansed and punished the sinner for his or her sins. Through their suffering in purgatory, human beings were prepared for an eternal blessed life in the presence of God.

Through penance in this life people could try to avoid punishment in purgatory and could serve a part of their punishment here. Penance was the central doctrine by which human beings were justified and by which people related to God. Through penance people could take on some punishment for their sins and cleanse their lives in order to restore their goodness and to secure eternal life. The Church claimed to know the appropriate penance for each sin, and each believer told the priest, in confession, details of the sin he or she had committed. The Church claimed the power to be able to forgive sins, to restore people to a right relation with God, and to secure their eternal life. The Church was the holder of the 'office of keys' (the keys to open or close paradise), which were conferred upon the Church by Christ (Matthew 16:19). This office of keys had the power of liberating people from their captivity by forgiving them their sins and opening paradise for them. One way to do penance for sin was to buy a letter of indulgence.

Indulgences were a means used by the Church to enable people to escape some of the punishment for their sins which would otherwise have occurred in purgatory after death. To secure indulgences, people, beside certain spiritual penances, had to pay sums of money which would secure their release from punishment in purgatory. This gave rise to the well-known rhyme:

As soon as the coin in the coffer rings,
The soul from purgatory springs.

The attractions to a person of paying substantial sums to the Church to secure release from punishment in purgatory were very great, and the Church derived a very considerable income from the sale of indulgences.

Initially Luther did not reject the idea of purgatory as a place of punishment and cleansing after death, but finally he came to reject the whole idea. From 1530 on he accepted only the alternatives of heaven and hell. Prior to this, in 1517, it was the practice of indulgences which represented the central focus for his attack. Indulgences were used not only to save souls, but also to satisfy the enormous financial needs of the Church.

Luther knew only part of the financial and political background to the practice of indulgences in Germany. Pope Leo X had granted Albert of Brandenburg, who was in desperate need of money, the privilege of dispensing indulgences in his territories. Albert, who was then Bishop of Magdeburg and Halberstadt, was successful in obtaining the archbishopric of Mainz as well, which made him both the spiritual and also the political primate of Germany. For this irregularity of holding three bishoprics at once he had to pay high fines both to the Pope and to the Emperor. He was forced to take out a huge loan from Fugger's bank, and soon needed even more money to pay the interest. Pope Leo X arranged with Albert that half of the returns from indulgences, in addition to the fine Albert had already paid, should go to him to help meet the cost of building the new church of St Peter's in Rome. Albert was allowed to use the remaining half to reimburse his bankers.

However, it was not this financial and political background which provoked Luther's primary criticism but the spiritual and theological problems to which it gave rise. Luther saw the disastrous effects – both materially and psychologically – of the practice of indulgences in his pastoral work amongst ordinary people. His concern was, as he wrote to Albert in the covering letter to his ninety-five theses: 'that the people may learn the Gospel and the love of Christ' (WA Br 1, No. 48, 40–41).

At the heart of Luther's view in his ninety-five theses was his radical new understanding of penance, which derives solely from the New Testament. In his first thesis he wrote:

> When our Lord and Master Jesus Christ said, 'Repent' [Matthew 4:17], he willed the entire life of believers to be one of repentance.'
> (LW 31, 25)

The emphasis lies on 'the entire life' of the individual, which means that penance cannot be practised merely once or even occasionally. Repentance

> ... cannot be understood as referring to the sacrament of penance, that is, confession and satisfaction, as administered by the clergy.
> (THESES 2, LW 31, 25)

One cannot delegate one's own relation to God to the mediation of priests between human beings and God. Luther has a new understanding of penance, which he now uses in the sense of repentance. For Luther this sense is shown in Mark's gospel 1:15, in which, in its Latin version, Jesus was talking about penance. However in the original Greek text Jesus was saying 'Repent and believe!' The word for repentance in the original Greek New Testament literally means 'change your mind'. This shift in meaning enabled Luther to give the doctrine of penance a new definition. It is only through a change of mind and a turn to God – not through doing penance – that people can clarify their relation to God, have their goodness restored and thus secure eternal life.

Luther considered that the Church's use of indulgences separated apparent penance from genuine faith and trust in God. Penance became an autonomous instrument of the Church. If the practice of the Church dispensing indulgences were to be accepted, Luther maintained that a person no longer had the possibility of a direct relationship with God. In his thirty-sixth thesis he wrote:

Any truly repentant Christian has a right to full remission of penalty and guilt, without the need for letters of indulgence. (LW 31, 28)

Anyone who has repented of his or her sins and deeply regrets having turned away from God has, Luther considered, already turned back to God by the very act of repentance and regret. This action alone is sufficient for God to forgive all.

As set out earlier (p. 7), in 1520 Luther wrote a diplomatic letter to Pope Leo X trying to come to a peaceful reconciliation with him and to avoid excommunication. With this letter he sent one of his most important essays, *The Freedom of a Christian*, calling it 'a small book if you regard its size. Unless I am mistaken, however, it contains the whole of Christian life in a brief form, provided you grasp its meaning' (LW 31, 343). In that essay Luther wrote about faith:

When, however, God sees that we consider him truthful and by faith of our heart pay him the great honour which is due him, he does us that great honour of considering us truthful and righteous for the sake of our faith. Faith works truth and righteousness by giving God what belongs to him. Therefore in turn God glorifies our righteousness.
(LW 31, 351)

Luther rejected the official Church's claim that she administers the merits of Christ and the saints like some sort of treasure, which she can distribute to believers and, by doing so, can compensate for their sins:

Nor are they [viz. the indulgences] the merits of Christ and the saints, for, even without the Pope, the latter always work grace for the inner man, and the cross, death, and hell for the outer man. (LW 31, 30)

Rather 'the true treasure of the Church is the most holy Gospel of the glory and grace of God' (LW 31, 31). It is the Gospel which promises the godless and sinful human being the forgiveness of sins. The Gospel is a treasure which is 'naturally most odious, for it makes the first to be last' (LW 31, 31).

The significance of Luther's theses was that he not only criticized the misuse of indulgences, but also questioned the whole theological basis on which this practice was founded. Luther was surprised at the vehement nature of the counter-attack from the Church, and was particularly saddened that the Church charged him with heresy rather than taking up the theological issues he had raised. He quickly came to realize the dangers of holding his own position, because heretics were not only threatened by the Church, but the civil authorities were faithful servants of the ecclesiastical judiciary who would punish the heretic. Luther's opponents compared him with the Czech Jan Hus (1369–1415), who was burnt in 1415 for heresy. When in 1520 Luther was declared a heretic by Pope Leo X, he was threatened with the same fate as Jan Hus.

Luther reacted immediately to the attack on him, and repeatedly specified his own understanding of penance and faith. In his *Explanations of the Ninety-Five Theses or Explanations of the Disputation concerning the value of Indulgences* (1518), Luther came to the conclusion that:

> *The Church needs a reformation which is not the work of one man, namely the Pope, or of many men, namely the Cardinals ... but it is the work of the whole world, indeed it is the work of God alone. However, only God who has created time knows the time for this reformation. In the meantime we cannot deny such manifest wrongs. The power of the keys is abused and enslaved to greed and ambition.* (LW 31, 250)

Luther now called for more rigorous limitations to papal power. He also formulated his ideas of faith more clearly:

We are justified by faith, and by faith also we receive peace, not by works, penance, or confessions. (LW 31, 105)

This does not mean, however, that Luther rejected the need for the Pope or for priests – indeed he praised them both. His attitude to the Pope and priests is a good example of Holy Scripture being the exclusive basis for Luther's theological thinking. According to the New Testament, Jesus said to St Peter:

I will give you the keys of the kingdom of heaven, and whatever you bind on earth shall be bound in heaven, and whatever you loose on earth shall be loosed in heaven. (MATTHEW 16:19)

Luther accepted that the keys of heaven were conferred upon Peter, and with that upon the Church. But Luther restricted his understanding of the range of the office of keys by his interpretation of Matthew 16:19, which says: 'whatever you loose *on earth* ...', which means that the office of keys does not extend to heaven, and the Church cannot loose people in purgatory – yet this is what was promised by the letters of indulgence. The Church's power is confined to this world – and her power of keys is necessary to liberate and redeem people and to save and heal their lives.

The process of liberation and salvation of individuals was described by Luther in his explanation to thesis 7:

When God begins to justify a man, he first of all condemns him; he whom he wishes to raise up, he destroys. (LW 31, 99)

It is characteristic of Luther's theology that the negative side of the relationship with God, that is, the remoteness of God and the consciousness of oneself as being lost, is understood as being caused by God. It is God who leads people into the despair which is found when one becomes locked into a relationship with oneself. In

Luther's first hymn 'Dear Christians, let us now Rejoice' (1523) he sets out the position:

> *I fell but deeper for my strife,*
> *there was no good in all my life,*
> *for sin had all possessed me.* (LW 53, 219)

Luther says with Samuel, the prophet:

> *The Lord kills and makes alive, he leads to hell and leads out again.*
> (1 SAMUEL 2:6)

God leads people to hell, that is, into a situation which is characterized by total ungodliness and in which people have to exist merely related to themselves. However, God does not lead people to hell and with that into the despair about their own lost and lonely existence in order to leave them there, but to lead them out again into true life.

> *Here ... God works a strange work in order that he may work his own work. This is true contrition of heart and humility of spirit, the sacrifice most pleasing to God.* (LW 31, 99)

People who come to despair and rely entirely on themselves cannot perceive anything of a merciful and justifying God, but instead have the impression of their own damnation being near. If they relate their situation to God, they will feel that their despair is due to God's wrath. However, for Luther it is in the very experience of losing oneself before God, that the grace of God is already present. This negative experience of one's own life is actually caused by God's grace and mercy. Luther considered that it is a requirement for real devotion to God that human beings first have to see themselves as locked into a relationship with themselves, and thereby to become conscious of being lost. This requirement is necessary in order for the individual to come to be able to turn their eyes away from themselves. Through despair, they learn to expect everything from God.

The Church comes into the process of healing, liberation and salvation through the priest:

When the priest sees such humility and anguish, he shall, with complete confidence in the power given him to show compassion, loose the penitent and declare him loosed, and thereby give peace to his conscience. (LW 31, 100)

Luther considered that Jesus Christ gave the priestly office great importance, yet the effectiveness of the grace of God does not come from the priestly or ecclesiastical action, but from God. The grace of God is hidden: 'The remission of guilt takes place through the infusion of grace before the remission by the priest' (LW 31, 101). Because the grace of God is hidden, human beings are not conscious of the graciousness and loving devotion of God, even though it has already been given. Because grace is invisible:

... as a general rule we are not sure of the remission of guilt, except through the judgement of the priest ... Moreover, as long as we are uncertain, there is no remission, since there is not yet remission for us. (LW 31, 101)

The priest is important in the whole process of salvation, but is clearly secondary to the gracious divine action which results in the remission of sin. Luther rejects the view 'that God does not remit guilt unless there is a prior remission by the priest' (LW 31, 98), and in so doing challenges the theological position of the priest in the process of salvation. This is one of Luther's central arguments against the traditional definition of the priest, and against the position of the Pope's claimed authority as the 'bearer of the keys'.

Luther's criticism of the Pope developed further, and came to a peak in 1520 when, in an essay 'On the Papacy in Rome', he claimed that the papacy was not founded by Christ. Instead he claimed that Christ had not given the keys of heaven to St Peter alone but to the whole Christian community – from which follows the idea of the priesthood of all believers.

A false understanding of the grace of God and of the Christian faith is one in which:

> *people learn to trust in the delusion that it is possible to have their sins cancelled by their contritions and satisfactions.* (LW 31, 103)

For Luther it is this understanding that gives rise to the belief in justification by works, that is, the attempt to enter into a relationship with God through one's own efforts. Any such religious efforts are expressions of total sin.

In 1518 – while Luther was still an Augustinian monk – the chapter of the German Augustinians met in Heidelberg. Luther was invited to discuss his new approach to theology with them. At that time many Augustinian monks were sympathetic to Luther's ideas, for he was well known and highly respected. Most of them disliked the polemic attacks against Luther by church officials, and wanted to show him their sympathy by providing the opportunity for a theological discussion of his ideas. In the *Heidelberg Disputation* Luther claimed:

> *The person who believes that he can obtain grace by doing what is in him adds sin to sin so that he becomes doubly guilty.* (LW 31, 50)

Penance and actions intended to obtain divine grace and God's remission of sins are not the starting point of faith, but are the results of the grace of God. As a consequence of the experience of God revealing one's misery, an individual may turn their life once again towards God and God's will. Repentance represents the turn to a new way of living life in harmony with God. This mission will not end on earth as long as one lives. Therefore the whole life of a Christian should be repentance, because it is characterized by the task of relating one's life to the loving God by constant critical self-correction.

Luther's doctrine of justification by faith does not imply that people can gain salvation without any effort. His approach is full of the dynamism of the experience of the grace of God. God does everything for his beloved people, and we can relate to God only when we let God do everything for us, and when we expect and hope for everything we need from God. We can do nothing for our own salvation other than to trust totally in God's love and righteousness. Faith should, therefore, be a joyous experience. It is because of the experience of faith that a person becomes eager to make efforts towards a new life. This creates the desire to bring one's life into correspondence with God's will.

To Luther, it is obvious that a loving relationship with God can only be achieved by each individual, and that this relationship has radical consequences for each person's own life, just as love has direct consequences for the lives of lovers. The starting point, however, for the love relationship between God and human beings is God's unconditional love, and this is what Luther means by grace. Because individuals become aware of God's love, they wish to improve their lives to please their partner and their lover – God.

Luther conceived God not as the highest principle or first cause. For Luther, God, the creator of the world and of all life, was above all a personal God. Therefore Luther claimed he could talk with God in the same way as with other people, and he stressed in his writings this personal quality of the relationship to God. It is part of this relationship that the word of God, contained in the Bible, is given to us.

The Source of Truth: The Word of God

Luther's own description of his 'tower experience' showed that he gained his insights from the study of the Bible and his persistent struggle to make its meaning plain. He is, however, in no way a biblical fundamentalist. He claims that the Bible can be the source and norm for human knowledge of God, but that this does not mean that the biblical texts are literally dictated by God to their authors. God speaks to human beings through the words of the Bible and, when this happens, the texts become the word of God. Every sermon is an opportunity for the word of God to be made known, and this may happen in other situations in life as well. God is present in the world through God's word – and it is this subject that interests Luther as a theologian.

In describing Luther's doctrine of the word of God it is necessary to go through three stages:

To clarify Luther's understanding of the Bible and its relation to the word of God;

To consider how Luther relates reason to the Bible; and

To discuss what God actually has to say to people in the law and the Gospel.

The Bible

At the time Luther was writing, the new printing technology invented by Johann Gutenberg (1400–1467), using movable, metal letters, had become widespread, and with it a new stage in human history began, facilitated by ease of communication. Before this invention people communicated mostly by word of mouth, but the new printing methods were used to spread Luther's ideas. The main benefit to Luther of the new printing methods was that the Bible could now be read by lay people, and through this believers could free themselves from the theologians and priests who had previously been the only mediators of God's word.

In 1516 the leading scholar of his time, Erasmus of Rotterdam, had edited the first Greek edition of the New Testament, called *Novum instrumentum*, and this greatly assisted Luther in his task. Erasmus was a humanist (for further explanations of the term 'humanist', which has a different meaning from that used today, see chapter 2 of Anne Murphy's book on *Thomas More* in the 'Fount Christian Thinkers' series), who wanted to reform the Church and renew Christianity, particularly in the light of the Sermon on the Mount (Matthew 5–7). The central motto of the humanist movement was '*ad fontes*' – that is, 'back to the original sources of human experience and knowledge'. These sources were the classical Greek and Latin texts as well as the original Greek and Hebrew texts of the Bible. Humanists like Erasmus were convinced that Christianity could be renewed only by returning to its roots. Luther shared this conviction. When in 1518 the humanist Philipp Melanchthon (1497–1560) arrived in Wittenberg as the new professor of Greek, Luther quickly got in touch with him. Melanchthon, although only twenty-one when he came to Wittenberg, already enjoyed a European reputation as a learned humanist. He had no commitment to Luther on his arrival, but soon converted to Luther's position, because he agreed with Luther's interpretation of the apostle Paul. Luther and Melanchthon became close friends, and Melanchthon became, after Luther, the most important leader of the Reformation.

Luther was following the humanist's 'back to the roots' motto when he first translated the New Testament from the original Greek into German in 1521. Later, he, with other scholars like his friend Melanchthon, translated the Old Testament from Hebrew into German. This was difficult because, at the time, there was no single uniform German language. It was Luther who, with his translation of the Bible, created the German language as it is used today. It is interesting to note, however, that he thought that the preaching or telling of the word of God was better done orally than in writing. For Luther the Gospel was fundamentally an oral message and was best transmitted through sermons:

> *Christ did not write his doctrine himself ... but transmitted it orally, and also commanded that it should be orally continued giving no command that it should be written.* (LW 52, 205)

> *So it is not at all in keeping with the New Testament to write books on Christian doctrine. Rather in all places there should be fine, goodly, learned, spiritual, diligent preachers without books, who extract the living word from the old Scripture and unceasingly inculcate it into the people, just as the apostles did. For before they wrote, they first of all preached to the people by word of mouth and converted them ... However, the need to write books was a serious decline and a lack of the Spirit which necessity forced upon us ... For when heretics, false teachers, and all manner of errors arose in the place of pious preachers ... then every last thing that could and needed to be done, had to be attempted ... So they began to write in order to lead the flock of Christ as much as possible by Scripture into Scripture. They wanted to ensure that the sheep could feed themselves and hence protect themselves against the wolves, if their shepherds failed to feed them or were in danger of becoming wolves too.* (LW 52, 206)

The picture of the sheep which become their own shepherds shows the emancipatory effect of Luther's translation. But Luther did not simply identify the Bible with the word of God. He distinguished between the Bible as a book which represents the Holy Scripture of the Christian Church, and the word of God which represents those parts of the Bible used to address people directly, for example in sermons or in pastoral care. Of course there is a close connection:

> No book may comfort except the Holy Scripture ... because it contains the word of God. (WA 10, 75,3–7)

Luther did not understand the biblical texts as being the absolute truth, but in each case when he read texts of the Bible questioned whether they proclaimed Christ crucified and risen from the dead for the salvation of all people, as well as the doctrine of justification by faith alone. This he regarded as the Bible's own internal measure of truth, which makes it possible to criticize the biblical texts. Luther claims that Christ is the only content of Scripture: 'Without doubt the whole Scripture is orientated to Christ alone' (WA 10/2, 73, 15). With this as the criterion for judging the truth of biblical texts, Luther radically criticizes whole books of the Bible. In his judgement, the Letter of James, the Letter to the Hebrews and the book of the Revelation to John do not belong amongst the main books of the New Testament, because these texts are not orientated to Christ alone. Nevertheless, because of his respect for tradition and its selection of the biblical canon, Luther did not eliminate those Scriptures from his German Bible. He did, however, alter the sequence of the Scriptures in the New Testament, and put those three texts at the end of the Bible.

For Luther, Holy Scripture was the only source and norm for any knowledge of God. Having said this, he used the texts critically and without accepting them blindly. However, the text was not judged against external criteria but by the context of the Bible as a whole. Luther claimed:

Christ is the Lord, not the servant, the Lord of the Sabbath, of law and of all things. The Scriptures must be understood in favour of Christ, not against him. For that reason they must either refer to him or must not be held to be true Scriptures. (LW 34, 112)

Luther further developed his understanding of Scripture in discussion with the traditional Catholic understanding, with the anabaptist movement which became especially strong in 1525, and in his reply to Erasmus of Rotterdam, in *The Bondage of the Will* (to which we will return later, see p. 43).

The discussions were about the authority of Scripture and who guarantees its truth. Early in his disputes with the authorities of the Church, Luther had used the authority of Scripture against some of her doctrines and practices. The Church's official claim was that the Church, which had combined the different biblical texts to create the canon of the New Testament, is the guarantor of the authority of Scripture. Luther, however, did not agree to this subordination of Scripture to the Church and her tradition. Instead he maintained the principle that Scripture was self-authenticating: Scripture has and needs no guarantor other than itself. By this Luther did not mean that the Bible itself was inspired by God simply because it says so (for instance, the second letter of St Paul to Timothy (3:16) says: 'All Scripture is inspired by God'). Such a circular argument was far too weak. Luther rather held a realist position: the authority of Holy Scripture is wholly founded on its contents which refer to Jesus Christ and the divine process of human salvation. Therefore the authority of Scripture *depends on the truth of its central contents*, which are about the relation of God to human beings – nobody and nothing else could give Scripture authority, not even an institution like the Church. Here again we see Luther's stress on truth. The Bible is not true simply because it says so – what makes the Bible true is that it truthfully records God's work of salvation.

Therefore the authority of Scripture and its binding nature upon those who believe in it depends not on the fact that the

Church as a community of people has selected and combined the biblical books together to form the Christian canon – rather church authority depends on the truth of Scripture.

There follows an obvious consequence from this position. The true meaning of the biblical texts is to be found in their reference to the loving and just God and God's gracious relation to human beings, which for Luther is the same as the referring to Jesus Christ. All former and present interpretations of the biblical texts have to be evaluated in this light. Luther sums up this position by saying that Scripture interprets itself. Scripture is:

> *totally certain ... quite easy to understand, completely revealed, its own interpreter.* (WA 7, 97, 23)

> *Therefore Scripture is its own light. It is splendid when Scripture interprets itself.* (WA 10/3, 238, 10)

This principle is used by Luther against the traditional position which held that the teaching office of the Church, guided by the Holy Spirit, has the authority and competence to give a true interpretation of Scripture.

Luther also opposed the understanding of Scripture put forward by the new anabaptist movements. To explain this we first have to consider their origins. As a result of Luther's reforming thoughts some of his followers developed even more radical ideas. In 1521–1522 Luther had to be kept hidden in the Wartburg because he was threatened with death after his excommunication, and could not return to Wittenberg. Some of his friends and followers introduced radical changes in the parish of Wittenberg.

One of these, Andrew Carlstadt (1480–1541), was one of the inspirational figures for the 'radical wing' of the Reformation. In 1522 Carlstadt and others introduced reforms such as the marriage of priests and the rejection of divine orders. They also destroyed all paintings in the churches and abolished church music, because the divine Spirit was considered able to dispense with all external aids, whether of art or music. Luther did not agree with all of those reforms. In particular, he himself loved church music and thought it had an important place in worship, to which he contributed many hymns of his own composition.

Another prominent figure of the 'radical wing' of the Reformation was Thomas Müntzer. Ordinary people expected that, with the coming of the Reformation, their conditions of life would now improve. 'Prophets' like Müntzer preached the end of the world. In 1525 he proclaimed that the kingdom of God was at hand, and he fomented a rebellion of peasants in Saxony. In fact, all over Germany the peasants rebelled, but their rebellions were crushed by the armies of the princes. Müntzer himself was caught and beheaded.

Luther's role in those conflicts in 1525 was very ambiguous, and on the whole it is a part of his life which does him no credit. Although Carlstadt and Müntzer, and the peasants as well, had been inspired by Luther's ideas, for Luther they were far too radical and they threatened the success of the Reformation. He therefore first acquiesced in the banishment of his former friend, Carlstadt, from Saxony. Carlstadt departed, claiming in the same words that Luther had used after the Diet of Worms that he had been condemned 'unheard and unconvicted' and that he had been expelled by his former colleague. Carlstadt went to the south of Germany, where he gained support for his ideas and was given a teaching post, first in Zürich and then in Basle.

In addition, Luther actively assisted the German princes to put down the peasants and the radical Christians who sided with them. In 1525 he wrote two essays, 'Against the Heavenly Prophets' and 'Against the Robbing and Murdering Hordes', which were the starting signal for the princes and their armies to crush the peasants and radical Christians. This they did with great bloodshed and they appealed to Luther's writings for justification.

Because of these actions, many ordinary people were no longer enthusiastic about Luther and his reforming ideas. However,

Luther's support for the princes had pragmatic benefits as he gained the support of many of them to reform the Church in their countries in accordance with his ideas.

The 'radical wing' of the Reformation was termed an anabaptist movement because they rejected infant baptism and considered that each adult had to be baptized again. They stressed the inward and spiritual side of Christian life, and the Holy Spirit was set in opposition to the letter of Scripture. Being possessed by the Holy Spirit was made the necessary qualification for church member-ship. Within their religious communities leadership fell to the spirit-filled, be they clergy or lay. Quite often the result was the abolition of a professional ministry. Müntzer clearly expressed this concentration on the divine spirit:

> *God does disclose himself in the inner word in the abyss of the soul. The man who has not received the living witness of God really knows nothing about God, though he may have swallowed a hundred thousand Bibles. God comes in dreams to his beloved as he did to the patriarchs, prophets, and apostles ... God pours out his Spirit upon all flesh, and now the Spirit reveals to the elect a mighty and irresistible reformation to come.* (QUOTED IN R. H. BAINTON, *HERE I STAND* 204)

Anabaptists claimed that a true interpretation of the biblical texts needed a special spiritual talent, which is a gift from God to par-ticular people. Luther did not ignore the significance of the Holy Spirit for the interpretation of Scripture, but he considered that the spirit in which people are able to give a true interpretation of the Bible has to be the spirit of Scripture itself.

For Luther the Catholics and the anabaptists were both 'enthu-siasts', because in their interpretations they subjugated Scripture under external rules. It is for this reason that Luther was suspi-cious of an allegorical, pictorial interpretation of the biblical texts, and instead emphasized the view that they should be interpreted in a simple, literal sense. Luther assumes this to be possible in most cases, because he considers the Bible to be clear in itself, and its stories have simple meanings which follow from their essential content, which is Jesus Christ.

In 1525, the same year in which Luther was involved in conflicts with the anabaptists and the peasants, he wrote an extensive essay *The Bondage of the Will*, answering a substantial critique of his theological ideas by Erasmus which had been published a year before. Erasmus was a moderate Catholic and, as we have seen, a humanist, but was also a critic of the Church and saw its great abuse being in the externalization of religion. Erasmus was the most famous scholar of his time, and was urged by prominent persons, for example King Henry VIII of England, to declare his position concerning Luther. He did this in a tract entitled *The Freedom of the Will*, in which he did not oppose Luther's position on the papacy and indulgences etc., but Luther's anthropology. The tract went 'to the heart of the problem', as Luther recognized, and it took him over a year to answer it. A fundamental part of Luther's *The Bondage of the Will* is about the understanding of Scripture, and it is here that Luther introduced a new distinction between an external and an internal clarity of Scripture.

> *To put it briefly, there are two kinds of clarity in Scripture, just as there are also two kinds of obscurity: one external and pertaining to the ministry of the Word, the other located in the understanding of the heart. If you speak of internal clarity, no man perceives one iota of what is in the Scriptures unless he has the Spirit of God. All men have a darkened heart, so that even if they can recite everything in Scripture ... yet they apprehend and truly understand nothing of it ... For the Spirit is required for the understanding of Scripture ... If, on the other hand, you speak of the external clarity, nothing at all is left obscure or ambiguous.* (LW 33, 28)

Erasmus had claimed that Scripture contains obscure parts which make it necessary to have their interpretation decided by the church authorities. Against that position Luther argued that Scripture is clear in itself, and therefore it is not necessary for the church authorities to give an authoritative interpretation. In rejecting the need for the authority of the Church, Luther defended the freedom and rationality of the individual Christian far more than did Erasmus.

Human Reason

In the light of the high significance ascribed to Scripture both for human knowledge of God and for the salvific relation of God to human beings, the question has to be raised of how Luther judged human reason and how he saw the relationship between reason and the Bible.

Luther's view of human reason is both positive and negative. His negative view is based on the conflict between Scripture and reason. Reason is part of the whole human person who, as a sinner, wants to exist and act by him- or herself. Scripture competes with reason, because being external to human beings it wants to say something to them which demands their acknowledgement and response. It is in this sense that, in 1528, Luther explained the third article of the apostolic creed in his *Small Catechism*:

> *I believe that I cannot by my own understanding or effort believe in Jesus Christ my Lord or come to him.* (WHAT DOES THIS MEAN? 120)

Sinners, as rational beings, want to develop knowledge and convictions by themselves and do not want to have them imposed. At this point Luther began his criticism of reason, which in its self-relatedness and its absolute will to self-determination does not want to hear about its own good from somebody else, and does not want to acknowledge such an external good. Luther vehemently decried such reason. In one of his strongest attacks, Luther described reason as 'the best whore the devil has' (WA 51, 126, 9f.). The post-Enlightenment view of the second half of the nineteenth and of the twentieth century was to return to Luther's position and to use his polemics and critique of human reason to challenge the Enlightenment, which had given first priority to reason. In this sense Luther lays down a challenge to Kantian ways of thinking which see reason as supreme. Søren Kierkegaard followed in Luther's footsteps in this respect (see the *Kierkegaard* volume in the 'Fount Christian Thinkers' series by Peter Vardy).

The Lutheran theological tradition continued this kind of criticism and condemnation of reason, but Luther's positive attitude towards reason was overlooked. A good example can be found in his disputation 'Concerning Man' in 1536, in which he put forward a strong case in favour of reason. Reason, he says, is a gift from God. Again in his *Small Catechism*, in the explanation to the first article of the apostolic creed, Luther says:

> *I believe that God has created me and all other creatures, and has given me, and preserves for me, body and soul, eyes, ears, and all my limbs, my reason and all my senses.* (WHAT DOES THIS MEAN? 114)

With God's gift of reason, human beings are able to realize their task of dominion over creation (Genesis 1:28). Culture, art and science, medicine and law are created and preserved by reason. Reason is:

> *the inventor and mentor of all the arts, medicines, laws and of whatever wisdom, power, virtue, and glory men possess in this life.*
> (THE DISPUTATION CONCERNING MAN, LW 34, 137)

All these achievements of reason should not be ignored but, on the contrary, should be highly respected and praised. Luther welcomed all the new activity in the sciences of his time. Those tasks awarded majesty to reason and showed its divine origin:

> *And it is certainly true that reason is the most important and the highest ranking among all things and, in comparison with other things in this life, the best and something divine.* (LW 34, 137)

It is true that the tasks given to reason are strictly related to this earthly life, but reason should develop and order the earthly life of man. Reason 'is a sun and a kind of god appointed to administer these things in this life' (LW 34, 137). In this area reason is the court of last appeal. Reason has the competence to decide the best arrangements for economics and politics. Theology and Scripture, on the other hand, do not produce political or economic doctrines, but they respect reason's ability to handle earthly affairs.

It is important to note that Luther did not consider the competence of reason to have been lost as a result of Adam's fall. Godless people are able, with their reason, which was given to them by God, to organize and develop all earthly affairs well:

> *Nor did God after the fall of Adam take away this majesty of reason, but rather confirmed it.* (LW 34, 137)

Reason has lost its way, because after Adam's fall, it no longer recognizes its own majesty and dignity. Reason has become independent from its source (God) and now claims to be able to take responsibility *for the whole* of a person's life. Thus reason has chosen to go beyond its own limitations and possibilities.

For Luther, reason's rebellion against God has at least two results. The first is that reason becomes high-handed: human beings praise themselves because of what they see reason as having achieved. These achievements are no longer understood as stemming from God, but as being due solely to human ability. The second result is that human beings who live without God misuse reason. Reason is no longer set in the context of the task God has given to mankind, but is used simply to look after individual human interests. Reason's rebellion shows that it is blind to the truth, that it is corrupt, and that it is in itself not able to see the truth about itself. It is true that reason in a certain sense has the ability to know God – especially to know the *existence* of God – but reason is so strongly related to earthly affairs, that it is not possible for it truly to come to know God. Moreover, to reason the word of God and faith in God seem to be a closed book.

Reason therefore needs faith to see itself in its proper context, and it needs to be put into a true relationship with God. If this happens reason becomes an excellent and invaluable tool of faith, for example in being used to interpret biblical texts.

For Luther, the perversion and misuse of reason was obvious in people's attempts to get to know God on their own. People who do not want to orientate their lives to God have to be responsible for their own lives, and they use reason to develop and justify their own ideas of what is good and what is evil. Necessarily this produces a moralistic and self-righteous attitude in life. Reason not only tries to develop and justify its own standard of what a good life is, but also attempts to control its realization as well. Therefore reason will always find arguments to justify a person's living on their own terms. Normally, reason will cling to its own ideas of what is good and what is evil, and thereby will judge its own life as good. This is self-righteousness and for Luther this is the greatest sin. Such a person is solely related to him- or herself and thereby radically ignores and avoids God.

Not everyone is on the right path merely because they are 'religious'. God may well be completely ignored and a human idea of religion substituted. Luther emphasized knowing God truly, and not merely as a principle to satisfy moral and self-righteous inclinations. He believed that many people understood God merely as a moral legislator, and for this reason urgently needed a better understanding of God's word. Luther therefore distinguished two ways in which God speaks to people: by commandments ('You shall ...') and by promises – or in Luther's terminology: God speaks to people in the way of the law and in the way of the Gospel.

Law and Gospel

Luther considered himself to be following St Paul in his distinction between the law and the Gospel. This distinction expresses a fundamental twofold experience with the word of God:

> *There are two things, which are presented to us in the word of God: either the wrath of God or the grace of God, sin or righteousness, death or life, hell or heaven.* (WA 39/1, 361, 4–6)

Luther did not want to separate the word of God into two parts or bring them into opposition. Nor did he wish to divide the biblical texts into two parts: the texts of the law and texts of the Gospel. For Luther, the distinction between law and Gospel represents different ways of seeing God's relationship to human beings. Luther sees God as speaking to people in two ways: on the one hand, demanding from them and commanding them, and on the other, making promises to them. These will now be looked at in turn.

THE DIVINE LAW

Luther distinguished at least two different uses of the divine law. First, God's word as law convicts people of their sin, and secondly, God's commandments are concerned with the proper ordering of human life, i.e. in framing rules which help to regulate and govern human society. The first function of the divine law Luther called its theological use, the second he called the political use of the law of God.

The first use of the divine law refers to the experience of God's holiness and justice which sets the standards for human life and opens the way for it to become holy and just. In the Old Testament the prophet Isaiah (6:5) describes his experience of the holiness of God, which Luther himself had experienced in 1507 when he first said the mass. Isaiah cried when he entered the Temple of God:

Woe is me! For I am lost ... for my eyes have seen the King, the Lord of hosts!

In the presence of God, everyone, even a prophet, experiences their own life as being unholy and worthless – a life that has to end and pass away.

God's holiness sets such a high standard for people that they feel unable to fulfil it. God's word as law therefore brings about in a person a realization that their present life does not meet the demands of the true, divine life. The law of God shows people that they stand convicted as sinners. In this sense the law of God does not lead directly to righteousness but exposes human sin, and with this uncovering of sin enables people to see themselves in their true state.

The commandments of God also serve a political purpose in that they help to order human life. God, as part of his creative activity, resists tendencies to chaos. There is, however, a difference between the ten commandments and, for example, the ordering of some procedures and rituals in the temple in Jerusalem. Thus Luther assumes that firstly there is the law of God, which was expressly revealed to Moses, and which is a general law not only for Jews but for all people – this divine law is written into the heart of human beings. Secondly there is in the biblical texts the Jewish law, which is valid only for the ordering of the life of the Jewish people.

The law of God, which God has written into the heart of human beings, is known by all people (compare Romans 2:14–15), and therefore it is older than the ten commandments of Moses. Luther considers that human beings know by nature that one has to worship God and love one's neighbour. This living law in the heart of human beings is identical with the law given by Moses and with the ethical commandments of the New Testament (especially Matthew 7:12: 'So whatever you wish that men would do to you, do so to them; for this is the law and the prophets').

Therefore there is one law which runs through all ages, is known to all men, is written in the hearts of people, and leaves no one from beginning to end with an excuse, although for the Jews ceremonies were added and the other nations had their own laws, which were not binding upon the whole world, but only this one, which the Holy Spirit dictates unceasingly in the hearts of all. (LECTURES ON GALATIANS (1519), LW 27, 355).

By this law human conscience is defined. The law, which is written in the heart of human beings by nature, utters itself in their conscience. In his or her conscience a person knows implicitly the conditions that must be fulfilled for life to be worthy. Thus conscience is a divine voice in the midst of human life, but it is God as a legislator and a severe judge who speaks in conscience. In conscience a person is inexorably confronted by the demands of God and is accused and judged according to the measure of the divine law – and if this was all there was then the end would be desperation and death. Luther lived his own life based on conscience as the final and only judge, for example in his conduct before the Diet of Worms in 1521 (see p. 8). Luther has rendered the freedom of conscience a great service in the history of mankind. Like Thomas More (1477–1535), Luther made a stand on conscience, in the consciousness that before God he could not act otherwise (see in this series the book of Anne Murphy on *Thomas More*, pp. 56, 73–88). But it is God as the author of the divine law who speaks in conscience, and therefore conscience is part of the law to which human beings are subject. Conscience expresses the high dignity of the individual, but at the same time it expresses the fact that humans are not free. It is through failure to live up to one's conscience that one becomes aware of the need for God's grace.

But what are the demands of the law God has written in human hearts? Surely God not only makes demands on people by accusing and convicting them of sin, but has introduced rules – for example the ten commandments – to lay down the principles for an ordered life? For Luther, one of the functions of the political use of the divine law is to restrain crime in our sinful world, which is possessed by the devil, and by that to secure public peace. Commandments like 'You shall not kill', 'You shall not commit adultery' or 'You shall not steal' (Exodus 20:13–15) are examples of that. Other functions of the political use of the divine law are to arrange education and also, and most importantly, to make possible the preaching of the Gospel. Luther considered that God installs authorities and institutions, which have to transfer those fundamental laws into daily life and into political order. These institutions and authorities are the governments in the cities and countries, the civil law and especially the parents and teachers, because it is in the education of young people that foundations for the future are laid. With the help of these institutions and authorities, humans are able to fulfil the fundamental requirements of God for a peaceful and just order in society, because the alternative would be violence and chaos. It is of great importance for Luther that God has supplied a positive and beneficial order for human life in our fallen and sinful world. It is the will of God that people should live peacefully and in harmony with their neighbours. Reason, conscience and the law in human hearts are given by God, their creator, as the conditions necessary for an ordered, just and peaceful society.

On a critical note, it has to be said that there is a tendency for Luther to approve unquestioningly the existing political structures. He seems to consider that provided there is law and order and the word of God can be preached without restrictions, then the political situation should be accepted by Christians. Today we might consider that this is not an adequate specification of a good political system.

It is essential for Luther that people are confronted with both the demands of God in their lives and with the threat of despair. Confrontation with God's law makes it obvious to individuals that they are incapable of coming into a right relationship with God by their own efforts. Only when people come to realize the inadequacy of these efforts, will they then be ready to receive the Gospel. Only when an individual comes to despair and realizes that he or she cannot rely on their own strength does God then give them everything that they themselves could not produce by their own efforts; that is life in its fullness, as proclaimed in the Gospel.

THE GOSPEL

In the Gospel God addresses human beings as a gracious and kind God. The Gospel should not be seen as some sort of concession by God to people who cannot live up to the law, in the sense that God might say: 'My dear child, you do not manage to fulfil my law, but I forgive your failure and shall accept and love you as you are.' This would be a false understanding of Luther's position. When offering forgiveness, justice and love in the Gospel, God not only accepts the situation of people as they are, he also wants to change this for the good. The Gospel does not legitimate the present situation of life. God's aim in the Gospel and in the law are the same.

Here the second part of Scripture comes to our aid, namely, the promises of God which declare the glory of God, saying, 'If you wish to fulfil the law and not covet, as the law demands, come, believe in Christ in whom grace, righteousness, peace, liberty, and all things are promised you. If you believe, you shall have all things; if you do not believe, you shall lack all things. (THE FREEDOM OF A CHRISTIAN, LW 31, 348–49)

The objectives of the divine law and the Gospel are for good things such as justice, peace and freedom, which are important for the whole of a person's life. But the Gospel not only formulates these aims, it already includes the realization of them, because they are realized in God. Once a person believes and trusts in God's promise then he or she will have everything God has promised, because in faith he or she takes part in the divine life. The Gospel therefore requires a response of faith, and it is faith alone that is needed to achieve the objectives. It is Luther's claim, that in believing the Gospel the believers *have* the 'spiritual' goods of peace, justice and freedom because they are made just, free, peaceful etc., by God.

$$\boxed{5}$$

Faith

Faith is the only way in which a person can respond to and honour God:

> *So when the soul firmly trusts God's promises, it regards him as truthful and righteous. Nothing more excellent than this can be ascribed to God. The very highest worship of God is this, that we ascribe to him truthfulness, righteousness, and whatever else should be ascribed to one who is trusted. When this is done, the soul consents to God's will. Then it hallows God's name and allows itself to be treated according to God's good pleasure for, clinging to God's promises, it does not doubt that the One who is true, just, and wise will do, dispose, and provide all things well . . . On the other hand, what greater rebellion against God, what greater wickedness, what greater contempt of God is there than not believing his promise? For what is this but to make God a liar or to doubt that he is truthful? — that is, to ascribe truthfulness to oneself but lying and vanity to God?*
> (THE FREEDOM OF A CHRISTIAN, LW 31, 350)

It is only through their faith in God that people can respond to and honour God. In their faith and their trust in God people let God be their god. For Luther this is the only way to fulfil the first of the ten commandments, which says: 'I am the Lord your God. You shall have no other gods before me' (Exodus 20:2–3). Therefore Luther wrote in the explanation of the first commandment in his *Large Catechism* in 1529:

If your faith and trust are right, then your God is the true God. On the other hand, if your trust is false and wrong, then you have not the true God. For these two belong together, faith and God. That to which your heart clings and entrusts itself is, I say, really your God. (WHAT DOES THIS MEAN? 57)

Faith is a matter of the heart of a person. Luther knows this subjective approach can be misleading, because people can have trust in something other than God and make that to be their god. True faith, therefore, involves the single-minded search for something really trustworthy, and this can only be found in God. In a lecture in 1535 on St Paul's letter to the Galatians, Luther set out the significance of true faith in the life of a believer. Interpreting Galatians 3:6 ('Thus Abraham believed God, and it was reckoned to him as righteousness') he says:

Faith is something omnipotent, and ... its power is inestimable and infinite; for it attributes glory to God, which is the highest thing that can be attributed to Him. To attribute glory to God is to believe in Him, to regard Him as truthful, wise, righteous, merciful, and almighty, in short, to acknowledge Him as the Author and Donor of every good. Reason does not do this, but faith does. It consummates the Deity; and, if I may put it this way, it is the creator of the Deity, not in the substance of God but in us. (LW 26, 227)

It is only through faith that the truth of God becomes vivid and real in people. One of the most rigorous modern critics of religion, the German philosopher Ludwig Feuerbach (1804–1872), saw in Luther's writing ('faith is the creator of the Deity') justification for his claim that God is a human projection. However, this was not Luther's position – he was a philosophic realist who believed that God created and sustains the universe. God does not exist because people believe in, speak to or talk about God. However, God only becomes a reality in human beings if they have faith. Attempts in theology and philosophy to think about God as the ultimate principle of all being, as the ultimate value, or as the first cause etc., do not satisfy Luther, as they do not incorporate a personal relationship of the believer to God. God cannot be thought about only as one more fact. Through faith, God has to become a living reality for people.

Faith comes about by each person being addressed by God's word in his or her heart. For Luther faith is a matter of the heart, that is, a matter for the individual, and he often exemplified that personal dimension of faith by pointing to a person's death. In a sermon in 1522 he said:

> *The summons of death comes to us all, and no one can die for another. Everyone must fight his own battle with death by himself, alone. We can shout into another's ear, but every one must himself be prepared for the time of death, for I will not be with you then, nor you with me. Therefore every one must himself know and be armed with the chief things which concern a Christian.* (LW 51, 70)

A believer cannot trust another or any authority, not even the Church and its representatives, when it comes to faith. He or she cannot say, 'If they believe it, it must be right.' Such a belief will not endure when faced by death. Only a personal faith will be creative, life-changing and liberating. But what are the characteristics of such a new life in faith, and what is in the very centre of Christian faith? Faith consists in placing Jesus Christ at the centre of one's life. To be a Christian is to belong to Christ.

Jesus Christ and Salvation

Luther was not satisfied with the mere theological formulation that Jesus was fully God and fully man although, of course, he accepted this. Faith goes beyond words, and it is the personal relationship to God and Jesus Christ which is of fundamental importance. Luther gives central place to the credal affirmation: 'I believe, that Jesus Christ ... is *my* Lord.' Luther did not totally reject the metaphysical definitions of Jesus Christ which were developed from concepts in Platonic and Aristotelian thought, and which have been part of the Christian confession of faith since the fifth century. However, a doctrine such as the two natures of Christ seems to define Jesus Christ without taking into account the benefits brought to each individual. Luther subordinates such definitions to the basic assertion which set Jesus Christ into relation with the person who believes, thus:

> *I believe, that Jesus Christ – true God, Son of the Father from eternity, and true man, born of the Virgin Mary – is my Lord.* (WHAT DOES THIS MEAN? 117)

For Luther, to seek Jesus Christ is to seek for God. In this he follows John's gospel, where Jesus is recorded as saying: 'He who has seen me has seen the Father' (John 14:9). Thus Luther says that looking at Jesus Christ we look:

> ... *into the depth of the Father's heart, indeed, into the groundless and*
> *eternal kindness and love of God, which God offers to us continually,*
> *from all eternity.* (WA 20, 229, 13–15)

According to Luther the believer develops his or her knowledge of God by climbing steadily up from knowledge of Christ. The starting point of the ladder to God is the human being Jesus of Nazareth who is, for Luther, not simply a religious or moral ideal, but is truly human. Knowledge of God starts with knowledge of Jesus. After contemplating the suffering of Jesus Christ it is necessary to:

> ... *pass beyond that and see his friendly heart and how his heart beats*
> *with such love for you that it impels him to bear with pain your*
> *conscience and your sin. Then your heart will be filled with love for*
> *him, and the confidence of your faith will be strengthened. Now*
> *continue and rise beyond Christ's heart to God's heart and you will*
> *see that Christ would not have shown this love for you if God in his*
> *eternal love had not wanted this, for Christ's love for you is due to his*
> *obedience to God. Thus you will find the divine and kind paternal*
> *heart, and, as Christ says, you will be drawn to the Father through*
> *him. Then you will understand the words of Christ, 'For God so*
> *loved the world that he gave his only Son, etc.' We know God aright*
> *when we grasp him not in his might or wisdom (for then he proves*
> *terrifying), but in his kindness and love. Then faith and confidence are*
> *able to exist, and then man is truly born anew in God.* (A MEDITATION
> ON CHRIST'S PASSION (1519), LW 42, 13)

Reflection on Jesus Christ provides insight into God's will. This basic principle of God's will is God's love for human beings and the world. Luther himself, however, challenges this concept and renders it problematic in some of his most impressive writings, for example, in *The Bondage of the Will* written in 1525, in answer to the critique of his theology in *The Freedom of the Will* by Erasmus.

One passage in Luther's *The Bondage of the Will* discusses the problem of predestination – why some people accept the grace of God and others reject it. If everything happens by God's will then why does God elect some people for salvation and exclude others? Luther, however, retreats behind mystery and says about 'that hidden and awful will of God whereby he ordains by his own counsel which and what sort of persons he wills to be recipients and partakers of his preached and offered mercy ...'

> *... this will is not to be inquired into, but reverently adored, as by far the most awe-inspiring secret of the Divine Majesty, reserved for himself alone and forbidden to us.* (LW 33, 139)

Here we are confronted with one of the greatest problems in Luther's theology. His doctrine of God seems to become paradoxical if not almost contradictory, because he claims, as we have seen, that humans can know the divine will through Christ. It is hardly surprising that many theologians criticized Luther on this point. However, to do him justice we have to consider his position a bit further. The problem of predestination was raised by Erasmus: the problem is that if it is (as Luther claims) God's will which decides whether some accept and others despise God's offered grace, then a person is not free either to accept or reject this grace. Erasmus claimed, against Luther, that human beings are free either to accept or reject God and salvation, and that this decision is not determined by God. Human beings are free to accept or reject grace and to do everything necessary for a person's salvation through God. Luther's position gives rise to the question that Erasmus raises:

> *Does the good Lord deplore the death of his people, which he himself works in them?* (LW 33, 139)

To Luther, raising this question seems to be superficial and academic. As an alternative he proposes a certain hiddenness of God and from this follows:

> ... that we have to argue in one way about God or the will of God as preached, revealed, offered, and worshipped, and in another way about God as he is not preached, not revealed, not offered, not worshipped. To the extent, therefore, that God hides himself and wills to be unknown to us, it is no business of ours. For here the saying truly applies, 'Things above us are no business of ours'. (LW 33, 139)

Luther criticizes Erasmus for not distinguishing 'between God preached and God hidden, that is, between the Word of God and God himself' (LW 33, 140) as, Luther claims, Erasmus wants a consistent theological conception without paradoxes and intellectual problems. But for Luther much of life was full of paradoxes and problems which could not be solved. Thus Luther believed on the one hand that God's saving will was declared in God's word, but on the other hand he maintained that not all events are according to God's declared will. As an example, on the one hand God says 'I desire not the death of a sinner' (Ezekiel 18:23), but on the other hand it seems that God wills that certain people should reject his offer of grace and eternal life.

Does God thus cause people to be condemned? Luther's fellow reformer Jean Calvin in Geneva would have agreed that this is the case, because he thought that God not only elects who shall be saved, but also decides who shall be condemned. Luther rejected the latter position. However, he also rejected the view that it is up to human beings to decide whether or not to believe in God and whether or not to accept salvation. Luther believed that human reason cannot enable people to grasp and understand everything which happens in the course of their life. They cannot understand all the influences on them. In particular they cannot understand those hidden things which go beyond human understanding. For

Luther those 'things above' are hidden in God, who is above human understanding. That is God 'hidden in his majesty', who 'neither deplores nor takes away death, but works life, death, and all in all. For there he has not bound himself by his word, but has kept himself free over all things' (LW 33, 140).

Critics of Luther, such as the Swiss theologian Karl Barth (1886–1968), have pointed out that Luther's distinction between a revealed God and a hidden God brings him close to believing in two Gods, even though he did not intend this. Luther was a theologian who himself was in the midst of the conflicts and paradoxes of life – he recognized these conflicts but did not wish to dissolve them. The problem of the mysterious and hidden God remains a central problem for the whole of Luther's theology. But Luther's advice to believers shows the tendency he followed at least in spirituality:

It is our business ... to pay attention to the word and leave that inscrutable will alone, for we must be guided by the word and not by that inscrutable will. (LW 33, 140)

This advice amounts to a call to have faith in Jesus Christ, who is God's self-revelation, and not to be concerned about an inability to comprehend divine mysteries or even be frightened by God who is hidden from human understanding. In saying this, Luther follows the view of his teacher and counsellor Johann von Staupitz, who had comforted him when his faith was placed on trial because of the possibility that God might not have elected him for heaven. In 1531 Luther reported about that: 'When I complained about such spiritual assaults to my good Staupitz, he replied,"I don't understand this; I know nothing about it" ' (LW 54, 133). Instead Staupitz advised him to cling to Jesus Christ alone. For Luther it is in Jesus Christ that we get to know God, and all efforts to know God through reason are doomed to failure. Luther criticized any philosophy that asserted its independence of God – but he used philosophy to clarify God's relations with human beings. Philosophy and human reason can never be self-sufficient because then reason is put first and the individual no longer listens to God. Philosophy's mistake is to start at the wrong point. Holy Scripture, by contrast:

> ... begins very cautiously and leads us to Christ like to a man and after that to a Lord over all creatures, after that to a God. Thus I come in easily and learn to know God. But philosophy and those people who are full of the wisdom of this world wanted to start from above; but then they have become fools. One has to start from below and then come up. (WA 10, 297, 5–10)

The points we have discussed so far in respect to Luther's understanding of Jesus Christ – our complete knowledge of God in Jesus Christ and the relation of Jesus Christ to the individual – are important for Luther to show that a living relationship with God is possible. Luther did not want to pin God down to orders and structures which human reason can conceive, but to acknowledge God's freedom.

In Jesus Christ God does not meet humanity in general, but concrete individuals. But what happens when Jesus Christ meets a person? What changes occur when a person encounters Christ? To talk about this is to talk of the salvation of a person through Jesus Christ.

To describe the uniting of Jesus Christ and an individual Luther made use of an image from St Paul's letter to the Ephesians (Ephesians 5:31–32). Luther writes in 1520 in *The Freedom of a Christian*, that faith:

> ... unites the soul with Christ as a bride is united with her bridegroom. By this mystery ... Christ and the soul become one flesh. And if they are one flesh and there is between them a true marriage ... it follows that everything they have they hold in common, the good as well as

the evil. Accordingly the soul can boast of and glory in whatever Christ has as though it were its own, and whatever the soul has Christ claims as his own ... Christ is full of grace, life, and salvation. The soul is full of sin, death, and damnation. Now let faith come between them and sin, death, and damnation will be Christ's, while grace, life, and salvation will be the soul's ... Here we have a most pleasing vision not only of communion but of a blessed struggle and victory and salvation and redemption. Christ is God and man in one person. He has neither sinned nor died, and is not condemned, and he cannot sin, die, or be condemned ... By the wedding ring of faith he shares in the sins, death, and pains of hell which are his bride's. As a matter of fact, he makes them his own and acts as if they were his own and as if he himself had sinned; he suffered, died, and descended into hell that he might overcome them all ... His righteousness is greater than the sins of all men, his life stronger than death, his salvation more invincible than hell. Thus the believing soul by means of the pledge of its faith is free in Christ, its bridegroom, free from all sins, secure against death and hell, and is endowed with the eternal righteousness, life, and salvation of Christ its bridegroom ... Here this rich and divine bridegroom, Christ, marries this poor, wicked harlot, redeems her from all her evil, and adorns her with all his goodness. Her sins cannot now destroy her, since they are laid upon Christ and swallowed up by him. And she has that righteousness in Christ, her husband, of which she may boast as of her own and which she can confidently display alongside her sins in the face of death and hell and say, 'If I have sinned, yet my Christ, in whom I believe, has not sinned, and all his is mine and all mine is his.' (LW 31, 351–352)

In this scene Luther pictures salvation. He describes a person becoming free from the past and, in being united with Jesus Christ, becoming a new and free person. The whole marriage of Jesus Christ and the human soul is a glorious and saving event, because Jesus Christ has never sinned nor will ever sin. The evil and sin of a human being cannot change Jesus Christ, but instead sin is engulfed by Christ's righteousness, which overpowers the sins of all. For believers it is essential that they put their whole trust in the promise that Jesus Christ totally overcomes sin, and gives humans a share in his glory, righteousness and freedom. This saving and renewing of humans can only take place if they have become united with God. In this encounter a person participates in the divine glory, righteousness and freedom.

The Priesthood of All Believers
and the Christian Church

The most important consequence of Luther's understanding of people's salvation through Christ was the doctrine of the priesthood of all believers. Luther abolished the distinction between priests and laity, and opened to all people the special relationship which previously existed only between the priest and God. According to Luther, every person may exercise the priestly office by relating directly to God.

Traditional religious opinion holds that a priest is a person who appears before God on behalf of others so that they may gain forgiveness and further divine blessings. In Christianity the priestly office was originally restricted to Jesus Christ, who by his death on the cross was the sacrifice which, once and for all, reconciled God with all people, and who, as the son of God, now appears before him and intercedes for mankind. The traditional priestly office was gradually introduced into the Christian Church as well, but restricted to the priests as an especially selected part of the Christian community. The priests were understood as representing Christ's mediating office here on earth. Luther rejected this idea and saw all believers as priests, because in faith they take part not only in the dignity of Christ but in his tasks and offices as well.

According to Luther, Jesus Christ has the offices of both priest and king. As king, Jesus rules all earthly affairs, and as priest he mediates between human beings and God. In both offices Jesus cares completely for people: for their earthly, bodily and spiritual well-being. But Jesus Christ is not a ruler and mediator remote from those for whom he is caring. He is the God who has come to all people and has devoted himself to them, and Jesus therefore shares with his believers all his goods and all his tasks, including his kingly and his priestly office.

In their faith believers become co-operators with the work and task of Jesus Christ: they become priests and kings. As priests they have the authority to forgive sins in the name of God, to spread the message of the grace of God and to invite people to the Lord's Supper. It is the duty of every Christian to perform priestly tasks and to mediate between human beings and God. That is the purpose of prayer and intercession for others. This new understanding of priesthood is an emancipation of people, because now the priestly office is no longer restricted to a special group of church members, but is open to all. Each person who appears before God in prayer and who intercedes for others is a priest.

To be a priest is to have spiritual power. To appear as a priest before God, asking God for help and interceding for others is not like an appeal to the benevolence of an emperor. According to Luther it is the other way round: in praying to God, in asking and interceding for others, one has power over God.

> *Who can comprehend the lofty dignity of the Christian? By virtue of his royal power he rules over all things, death, life, and sin, and through his priestly glory has power over God because God does the things which he asks and desires, as it is written, 'He will fulfil the desire of those who fear him; he also will hear their cry and save them'.* (THE FREEDOM OF A CHRISTIAN, LW 31, 357)

This is a challenging position, because it can be held that for human beings to have 'power over God' is impossible. To avoid the problematic word 'over' some prefer to translate the Latin text as 'omnipotent with God'. For Luther this challenging position follows on from taking seriously God's own words, as Jesus promised that God would do all the things which we ask for and desire. To have 'power over God' or be 'omnipotent with God' therefore relates to the power of the Christian in prayer.

Luther's position is not that in prayer God is at the believer's disposal. It is characteristic of petitionary prayer that God's freedom is respected when believers ask for anything. When we ask someone for something, we show trust in them, that they will do and grant what we have asked. Similarly it is through trust and confidence in God that Luther talks of humans having power over God or being omnipotent with God in prayer. If we turn to God in total trust and faith then God will not deny our requests and prayers. In Luther's time this was a controversial idea. For Luther this omnipotence of believers in prayer was not dependent on the social, moral or religious status of people, but on the principle that everyone, including scoundrels, could have this power by turning to God in total trust and faith. With this interpretation of the priesthood of all believers, the traditional role of the priest is dramatically reduced, and God is directly accessible through the prayers of each person. The love of God is focused on each single individual, and no institution and no person can act for someone else in this relationship. Never before had the individual been taken so seriously and given such high dignity, and this is a legacy which Luther left to the Western world. This heritage has to be defended again and again against many political and religious developments, in which the importance and value of community is placed above that of individuals. This applies within the Christian Church as well, if there is a tendency to give priority to the community or the church as a group over the individual. The best that a church can do, according to Luther, is to help individuals develop their own relationships with God.

Why, then, did Luther consider that an institutional church and a professional ministry were still important? For Luther, their main purpose was to be an instrument for bringing about successful relationships between individuals and God. However, there are other aspects of his doctrine of the church. He spent much time developing a new, Protestant understanding of the Christian Church, and he had a great deal to do with the new organization of the life of the church. Luther had significant new understandings of the ministry of the church, the need to reform the liturgy of Christian worship, his new understanding of the eucharist, his writing of the two *Catechisms* for the education of believers in Christian doctrine, as well as his ideas about the unity of the Christian Church. In this book, however, there is no space to consider these important aspects of his teaching. But it is significant briefly to review Luther's appraisal of the relationship between the different Christian churches, as this is important today in the field of ecumenical dialogue.

In his doctrine of the church Luther distinguished between the one universal, invisible Church of Jesus Christ and the many visible churches, namely the different organizations and confessions like the Protestant, Roman Catholic and Orthodox churches. For Luther those organizations, which might operate worldwide or only locally or regionally, are mainly justified in their function as a means for nurturing individual Christian faith and life and for further spreading the Gospel. Beyond their differences there is a unity of the churches which is founded in God, and is expressed in worship, in the preaching of the word of God and in the main sacraments. In Christian worship and in the giving of the sacraments (sacraments here being baptism and the Lord's Supper) the invisible community of all believers is present. Luther was convinced that the Christian Church is everywhere on earth where the Gospel of Jesus Christ is preached and the sacraments are administered. People are not united as the Christian Church because of their membership of an institutional church but because of their common faith and common trust in God. It is this community which finds its expression in every act of Christian worship, being a reality where people celebrate in worship, where the Gospel of Jesus Christ is preached and where the sacraments are received.

If the true community of all Christians, which is manifest in public Christian worship, is questioned, then the unity of the Christian churches really is in danger. This happens, for example, by one church excluding from the eucharist Christians who are members of other churches. Bread and wine as the body and blood of Jesus Christ have to be administered to everyone who comes forward for them. By excluding certain believers from the eucharist, a church's own existence should be questioned because it is failing to fulfil the message of the gospels. Such a church fails to be the Church of Jesus Christ, because in behaving in such a manner, a human-made law is made to dominate the Gospel of the saving grace of God.

8

The Christian Life

Luther's understanding of the priesthood of all believers gives rise to his very positive understanding of the Christian as one who participates in the dignity of Jesus Christ. The first characteristic of such a Christian life is **freedom**, the second is **love**. In *The Freedom of a Christian* Luther summed this up in a famous phrase:

> *A Christian is a perfectly free lord of all, subject to none.*
> *A Christian is a perfectly dutiful servant of all, subject to all.*
> (LW 31, 344)

Freedom

Freedom is the central feature of a Christian. Through faith in God people can gain freedom. Without such faith and trust human beings, in Luther's understanding, are not free, because they are captive within themselves. Through God coming into a loving relationship with each individual they gain freedom from earthly constraints. Luther himself gave a good example of his understanding of Christian freedom when he refused to withdraw his theological convictions before the German Diet in the city of Worms in 1521. Obligated only to the word of God, Luther was free to withstand all authorities and their threats. But this individual independence is not the only consequence of a Christian's freedom. A Christian also becomes free from his or her own desires and the covetous drive to possess as many earthly goods as possible.

However Christian freedom relates to the things of this world – the Christian is not free in relation to God. Christians are bound to God and their earthly freedom comes precisely from their bondage to God. As we have seen, Luther rejected the position of Erasmus that it is up to each individual's free will to accept or to reject God's offered grace. Luther, following Augustine, instead claims that human beings owe their salvation entirely to God. Human beings are totally corrupted, because they are totally bound to their own individual interests and abilities, and therefore do not think that they need God and God's salvation in their lives. It follows from this that people make themselves captive and lose their freedom – they have to be liberated from their self-imposed chains, and this can only be done by God.

If people are bound to the word of God and trust in it, they then become free in respect to everything and everybody on earth. However, Christian freedom is not a once-and-for-all affair – Luther considered it to be under continuous threat. This freedom is challenged every day because human nature still has the tendency to put individual interests, desires and covetousness first in life, and therefore there is an in-built tendency to un-freedom, to becoming bound once more by the chains of sin.

In defining a Christian as 'a perfectly free lord of all' and 'a perfectly dutiful servant of all' Luther follows St Paul, who in his first letter to the Corinthians claims: 'For though I am free from all men, I have made myself a slave to all' (1 Corinthians 9:19). For Luther, as for Paul, it was no contradiction to understand Christians as being free and independent, yet at the same time as binding themselves to others and serving them. This follows because, Luther considered, freedom means in particular to be free from themselves: free people are not bound to themselves but may step back from themselves. People who believe in God, and who therefore share in the fullness of the divine life, are free because they have to do nothing for themselves. Everything essential for life has already been done for them by God. Because they are free, Christians are able to begin something new, for example to initiate new relationships or restore old ones by forgiveness and reconciliation. Christians as free people share in the divine creativity. Only a free person is able to give true love, that is free love: a love which does not insist on its own way, but seeks the best interests of others. Freedom and love are like a couple or the two sides of the same coin. We now turn to that other side of the coin – to Luther's understanding of love and the Christian's responsibility for the common life.

Love and Responsibility

The basis of Luther's ethics is his doctrine of the two realms. According to one version of this doctrine (which is not identical with Luther's view), God rules over a heavenly and an earthly realm according to principles, rules and laws which are specific for each of those two realms. In the heavenly realm the principle of the Gospel is valid: this realm is ruled by divine grace. In the earthly realm, with our concrete human conditions of life, God rules by law and through human reason. Therefore as regards the best ordering of all affairs in society and between individuals Christians cannot contribute their insights about the grace of God.

This version of Luther's 'two realms' doctrine is too simple an account of his thought. His ethics are not based on a strict separation of a heavenly and an earthly realm. When in 1520 Luther wrote *To the Christian Nobility of the German Nation Concerning the Reform of the Christian Estate* (LW 44, 115–217) this was intended to convince the German princes of the need for a reformation of the Church. In it, he appealed to Christians in government to take responsibility for the progress of the Reformation and for a good common order. With regard to the actions of individual Christians it is undoubtedly true that these should be motivated and called forth by their faith. In *The Freedom of a Christian* we read:

I will therefore give myself as a Christ to my neighbour, just as Christ offered himself to me. I will do nothing in this life except what I see is necessary, profitable, and salutary for my neighbour, since through faith I have an abundance of all good things in Christ. Behold, from faith flows forth love and joy in the Lord, and from love a joyful, willing, and free mind that serves one's neighbour willingly and takes no account of gratitude or ingratitude, of praise or blame, of gain or loss ... Hence, as our heavenly Father has in Christ freely come to our aid, we also ought freely to help our neighbour through our body and its works, and each one should become as it were a Christ to the other that we may be Christs to one another and Christ may be the same in all, that is, that we may be truly Christians. (LW 31, 367–68)

If good works, deeds and actions for our fellow humans are not done freely, willingly and spontaneously, then love is missing. It is the essence of love to concentrate wholly on the other person, on the beloved and not on oneself. An act of love is characterized by forgetting oneself and having only the other person in mind. Luther wants to emphasize this essence of love, and the true essence of faith as well, when he distinguishes between faith in God and good human works and actions. Luther claims that if we do something good, it should be done for others. The good we do should not be intended to bring praise for ourselves or to give our own life some kind of meaning. If we do something good to other people we should look on ourselves as people of no account. It is a misuse of love when help to others is intended to serve self-interest – for example, by bringing praise to ourselves or salving our own consciences. A good action must be wholly selfless.

Luther's doctrine of justification by faith alone, without good works, can be seen to challenge each individual to ask whether we genuinely live only for the good of others by showing non-preferential love or whether our real motive for our supposedly good actions is pride in our own self-righteousness. Luther wishes each person to probe the motives for his or her own actions – he praises love that does not seek the good of the one who loves but which genuinely seeks the good of the other person alone, even though this may be costly. Luther's emphasis on genuine, true and unconditional love presents a real challenge for every person, because most people, he feels, fail to act in the unselfish manner which genuine love demands.

The challenge to conform truly to such a demand to love remains throughout the life of each individual, and all Christians constantly fail to live up to it. It is for this reason that the grace of God is needed throughout the whole of an individual's life. Again and again each person has to put their trust in God, who is devoted unconditionally to them. Luther considers that Christians are expected to transfer their experience of receiving the saving love of God into their daily lives. For him, faith is not simply a private matter – it has to be lived out in the day-to-day activities of life.

Luther dealt with many practical questions. He wrote on the problems of private and public life, for example on public education, on economic problems, on legal questions and on general political problems. Two examples of Luther's ethics, which well illustrate the doctrine of two realms, are worthy of examination here; firstly Luther's understanding of vocation, and secondly his approach to sexuality and marriage.

Vocation

Luther rejected the idea that priests and monks have a 'higher' or more holy occupation than those who undertake 'worldly' jobs. In his writing *On Monastic Vows* (1521) he rejects the high spiritual status accorded to monks as being the only group called. He quotes 1 Corinthians 7:20: 'Every one should remain in the state to which he was called', and argues that normal working people are undertaking tasks which are approved by

God and good in themselves. For Luther, a 'calling' does not mean to be called out of the world but to be called into service in the world where one is needed. All work, however, should be undertaken as a work of love and to honour and serve God, recognizing the contribution one is making to other people. The office of the priest is, essentially, no different from that of the road sweeper, for both are undertaking worthwhile and important tasks in the service of God and society at large. Whether or not a person does a job well can be judged by reason and by worldly standards of measurement. What it means to work successfully and well will depend on the chosen career or calling, but success in this task is to be measured by ordinary, human means and not by appeal to theological or spiritual principles. Having said this, there is a spiritual dimension to all work since it is undertaken in the service of God and out of love for one's neighbour. As Luther said in a sermon:

> *If everyone serves his neighbour, then the world would be full of worship.* (WA 36, 340, 12–13)

A high standard of education is important to equip young people for lives of service. In Luther's time, there was a strict class system, and Luther did not really challenge this. However, because of his stress on individual responsibility he considered that education for all was vital, and he argued that, through education, all walks of life might be open to young people. There are here, therefore, at least the seeds of a more egalitarian approach to society, although Luther did not develop them further. In 'A Sermon on Keeping Children in School' (1530) Luther said that the task of education was 'to take beggars and make them into lords'. He went on to say:

> *It is not God's will that only those who are born kings, princes, lords, and nobles should exercise rule and lordship. He wills to have his*

beggars among them also, lest they think it is nobility of birth rather than God alone who makes lords and rulers. (LW 46, 250)

Luther believed that all children should be educated, and called for grants to be given by governments and churches to make this possible. The objective was to produce future generations who would live lives of service to God and their neighbour.

Sexuality and Marriage

Luther rejected the idea that priests should have to remain celibate. His early remarks on sex and marriage were made against the background of his knowledge of the problems which many monks and priests had with celibate life. Luther considered sexuality to be part of human nature and to have been created by God, and therefore rejected the heritage of the Middle Ages, which had seen all sexual activity as tainted and as an aspect of the base part of human beings, to be undertaken solely as a duty for the purpose of procreation (cf. *The Puzzle of Sex*, Peter Vardy, Harper-Collins, 1997). For Luther the love of a man and a woman can be contrasted with false love and with natural love – married love can be the greatest and purest of all loves, and there was no reason why a priest should not be married, nor would marriage detract from the exercise of the priestly office. In 'A Sermon on the Estate of Marriage' (1519) Luther writes:

False love is that which seeks its own, as a man loves money, posses-sions, honour, and women taken outside marriage and against God's command. Natural love is that between father and child, brother and sister, friend and relative, and similar relationships. But over and above all these is married love, that is, a bride's love, which glows like a fire and desires nothing but the husband. She says, 'It is you I want, not what is yours: I want neither your silver nor your gold; I want neither. I want only you. I want you in your entirety, or not at all.' All

other kinds of love seek something other than the loved one: this kind
wants only to have the beloved's own self completely. If Adam had not
fallen, the love of bride and groom would have been the loveliest thing.
(LW 44, 9)

However, Adam did fall and with him all human beings. This
means that even 'married love' is no longer flawless:

... now this love is not pure either, for admittedly a married partner
desires to have the other, yet each seeks to satisfy his desire with the
other, and it is this desire which corrupts this kind of love. Therefore,
the married state is now no longer pure and free from sin. (LW 44, 9)

Luther followed Augustine and considered that because of the
Fall, physical desire had become such a strong force that it challenged the will of human beings. It was such a strong force that it
was impossible for human beings to remain virginal and chaste
without the special grace of God. In an essay on 'The Estate
of Marriage' (1522), Luther, following Matthew 19:12, defined
three categories of people, who possibly could remain without a
spouse:

There are eunuchs, who have been so from birth, and there are
eunuchs who have been made eunuchs by men, and there are eunuchs
who have made themselves eunuchs for the sake of the kingdom of
heaven. (LW 45, 18)

In Luther's time, the third category was particularly significant, as
many young men and women went into a monastery or were sent
there by their families even though they had normal sexual
desires. Luther considered that such persons who are naturally
inclined towards marriage by nature but who nevertheless volun-
tarily remain celibate, 'are rare, not one in a thousand, for they
are a special miracle of God'. He goes on to say:

No one should venture on such a life unless he be especially called by God ... or unless he finds God's grace to be so powerful within him that the divine injunction, 'Be fruitful and multiply', has no place in him.
(LW 45, 21)

Luther's comments had dramatic consequences. Many monks and nuns felt free to accept that they had not been called to celibacy but instead to normal married life – they had been called, in other words, to follow the divine injunction to 'Be fruitful and multiply'. Hundreds left their monasteries. Luther writes:

No vow of any youth or maiden is valid before God, except that of a person in one of the three categories which God alone has himself excepted. Therefore, priests, monks, and nuns are duty-bound to forsake their vows whenever they find that God's ordinance to produce seed and to multiply is powerful and strong within them. They have no power by any authority, law, command, or vow to hinder this which God has created within them. If they do hinder it, however, you may be sure that they will not remain pure but inevitably besmirch themselves with secret sins or fornication. For they are simply incapable of resisting the word and ordinance of God within them. (LW 45, 19)

If people are not especially called to celibacy, it is normal for them to follow their sexual inclination and interest. Luther saw that many priests and monks could not resist their natural instincts, and therefore broke their vows in secret and thus fell deeper into sin. It was better for them, he considered, to marry, because marriage then 'may be likened to a hospital for incurables which prevents inmates from falling into graver sin' (A SERMON ON THE ESTATE OF MARRIAGE, LW 44, 9).

In that sense marriage is partly a kind of emergency measure to prevent people from perverting their sexuality. For Luther, only within marriage can sex not lead people away from God or even destroy a person and his or her relations with others. However, this is not the whole story as marriage was also ordained and blessed by God before the Fall. God intended marriage so that the world could be populated and also so that men and women should enjoy their love of each other.

To Luther, marriage is not a sacrament: it is not a means by which people are saved and take part in divine life. Marriage, however, is an institution which is blessed by God. The effect of this teaching was that the new Protestant churches that followed Luther abandoned to the state their jurisdiction over the legal side of the marriage. A couple first had to get married in a civil ceremony and then would receive the blessing in church. Marriage is a worldly affair, and as part of the natural order of the world has to follow the jurisdiction of the state.

Marriage is a good example of the doctrine of the two realms. It is part of the natural order of the world and therefore has to be organized according to the principles of nature and of reason. People do not need to get married in order to find salvation – marriage is merely one answer to the question of how human life should be lived and does not contribute to an understanding of a human individual's relationship to God. However, the kingdom of this world, of nature, of which marriage forms part, is nevertheless still ruled by God. Although all matters within the natural realm are organized by human beings using their reason, this realm is still created and blessed by God. Marriage is part of the order of nature and is ordained by God for the good of human beings. It may not be a part of the way to God, but it is still an important institution and a means of helping people find the form of life most adequate to the needs and desires of their nature.

After being married himself in 1525 Luther's statements about marriage and family life changed in tone. Before his own marriage he emphasized the natural instincts of people in sexuality and marriage, but afterwards he laid more stress on the different aspects of a marriage and the role of his wife, Katherine. Luther did not marry Katherine because he had fallen in love. In a letter of June 1525 he gives some reasons for his marriage. He writes:

The rumour is true that I was suddenly married to Katherine; [I did this] to silence the evil mouths which are so used to complaining about me. For I still hope to live for a little while. In addition, I also did not want to reject this unique [opportunity to obey] my father's wish for progeny, which he so often expressed. At the same time, I also wanted to confirm what I have taught by practising it ... God has willed and brought about this step. For I feel neither passionate love nor burning for my spouse, but I cherish her. (LW 49, 117)

For Luther, merely to be in love was an inadequate basis for marriage. In table talk in the winter of 1542–1543 Luther said:

We hate the things that are present and we love those that are absent ... This is the weakness of our nature ... It's easy enough to get a wife, but to love her with constancy is difficult ... Accordingly if a man intends to take a wife, let him be serious about it and pray to God, 'Dear Lord God ... bestow upon me a good, pious girl with whom I may spend all my life, whom I hold dear, and who loves me.' There is more to it than a union of the flesh. There must be harmony with respect to patterns of life and ways of thinking. (LW 54, 444)

Luther himself was susceptible to the beauty of other women. Even a few days before his death, while he was away from home staying at Eisleben, he wrote to his wife, probably partly to needle her:

Thank God now I am well, except for the fact that beautiful women tempt me so much that I neither care nor worry about becoming unchaste. (LW 50, 291)

When such temptations occurred Luther considered it important to remember that it was God who had given the existing husband or wife. However, Luther also recognized that if a couple were to remain faithful it was necessary for their sexual needs to be satisfied – marriage had to fulfil two functions: the one is to have and to educate children, and the second is that the two people living together should share everything. Sexual intercourse is not only intended for procreation but is a natural part and expression of the love of a couple. In that he criticizes the view of St Paul, when he writes in his essay on 'The Estate of Marriage' (1522):

> *Although Christian married folk should not permit themselves to be governed by their bodies in the passion of lust, as Paul writes to the Thessalonians (1 Thessalonians 4:5), nevertheless each one must examine himself so that by his abstention he does not expose himself to the danger of fornication and other sins.* (LW 45, 36)

In saying this, Luther was accepting and emphasizing the idea of sex as a duty, with both parties under a moral obligation to provide physical access to the other. Refusal of sexual intercourse could, it was traditionally held, lead to sin, and Luther accepted this view.

Luther had a traditional understanding of married life. The man was head of the family and represented it to the outside world. However, his concept of family life is open to accommodate different social circumstances. Katherine not only had responsibility for running the house but for the finances of the family as well, whilst her husband concentrated on his tasks at university and in the wider public arena. Both partners were responsible for the education of children, and, indeed, Luther's own children often played in his study whilst he was working.

9

The Concept of Theology

At the end of this survey of central ideas in Martin Luther's thought, it is important to consider his understanding of the role of theology. Theology, Luther considered, is characterized especially by its content and its subject. For him:

> *The proper subject of theology is man guilty of sin and condemned, and God the Justifier and Saviour of man the sinner. Whatever is asked or discussed in theology outside this subject, is error and poison.*
> (LW 12, 311)

For Luther theology is always concerned with knowledge of God and of human beings in the specific sense which is given in the biblical texts. The subject of theology is not simply God, but the relation between guilty and condemned human beings and the God who justifies and saves. Anything else may have limited interest but it is not part of theology. As an example, consideration of God alone without taking notice of God's relation to people; or a consideration of human beings without their relationship to God would not be theology in Luther's eyes. The mutual relationship between the divine and the human is of paramount importance. Luther considers Jesus Christ to be a proper subject for theological study, because in Jesus Christ sinful and condemned human beings and the justifying and saving God come together. It is through knowledge of Jesus Christ, especially of the *crucified* Jesus Christ, that we get to know that specific quality of the relation of

human beings and God. According to Luther, the true understanding of Jesus Christ is found not in the incarnation, but in the
crucifixion. On the cross the true relation of God and human
beings becomes visible, and it is there that we can arrive at true
knowledge of God and of ourselves.

In 1518 in the Heidelberg disputation and subsequently,
especially in his work on the interpretation of the psalms in 1519–
1521, Luther used the concept of a *theologia crucis* (a theology of
the cross), which he had derived from monastic spirituality:

> *That person does not deserve to be called a theologian who looks upon
> the invisible things of God as though they were clearly perceptible in
> those things which have actually happened. He deserves to be called a
> theologian, however, who comprehends the visible and manifest
> things of God seen through suffering and the cross ... A theology of
> the cross calls the thing what it actually is.* (THE HEIDELBERG DISPU-
> TATION, LW 31, 40)

The possibility is set out by St Paul in Romans 1:20, that:

> *... ever since the creation of the world God's invisible nature, namely,
> his eternal power and deity, has been clearly perceived in the things
> that have been made.*

Luther relates this to paradise and the time before Adam's fall. For
people here on earth after Adam's fall, all that they can know is
that God exists – they can have, using their own natural abilities,
no knowledge of the essence of God. They cannot, therefore, know
whether God is kind or frightening, loving or terrifying. For Luther
this is true for all theological attempts to deduce knowledge of God
from his creation by using reason alone. This was the approach
taken by Philosophical Theology which sought to arrive not
only at God's existence but also at basic knowledge about God's
attributes using reason alone. Luther terms all such attempts a

theology of glory, and claims that people are trying to use reason and their own abilities to grasp the majesty of God. They will necessarily fail in this task – they may see the products of the glory of God but not God himself.

The alternative approach to theology Luther sees as a theology of the cross, which concentrates on the death of the Son of God. Luther wants to understand the crucifixion of the Son of God and what this event reveals about God. In this event God's glory and majesty is hidden under what appears to be exactly the opposite: the living and creative God is hidden in the death of Jesus Christ.

Luther's theology takes seriously both the positive and the negative side of the human experience of life. Luther knew from his own experience – for example, the early death of two of his children – that life is not always successful and happy, and that the activity of a good, merciful, kind, just and loving God is by no means obvious. If one attempts to know God from God's works or by way of rational argument from earthly phenomena, then it is far from obvious that one will arrive at the Christian understanding of God. Any being recognized by such methods could as well be the devil as God. Luther is far too down-to-earth to ignore the negative sides of life in formulating his theology. He is clear that the world contains beauty and glory but also ugliness, cruelty and suffering. In the death of Jesus Christ, the creative and loving God has taken part in the darker side of human experience of a life ending in pain, despair and death. God, therefore, is not revealed through God's works in God's mighty power but rather is revealed in weakness.

Just as God's presence is hidden on the cross, so God is hidden in the human experience of suffering and evil. Luther's theology accepts the bitter side of life and does not attempt to explain it away. However, his refusal to attempt to overcome the tension between the frequent sadness, loneliness, pain and hurt which characterize so much of the human experience of life, and Christian talk of a loving and merciful God, leads to further theological problems. Luther can, in fact, be characterized as working with two concepts of God – the God of revelation and the idea of a hidden and undisclosed God. Luther recognizes this tension but refuses to compromise either of the two views in order to overcome it. Throughout his life Luther was uncompromisingly honest in his thinking, and he would neither sacrifice any part of the truth of Holy Scripture nor reduce his recognition of the bleakness of the concrete experience of human life. Rather he accepted difficulties and paradoxes. He would have accepted much of the writings of Søren Kierkegaard, a Danish Lutheran and probably the greatest philosopher of the nineteenth century, who wrote on paradoxes:

> *However one should not think slightingly of the paradoxical; for the paradox is the source of the thinker's passion, and the thinker without a paradox is like a lover without feeling; a paltry mediocrity ... The supreme passion of all thought is the attempt to discover something that thought cannot think ...* (PHILOSOPHIC FRAGMENTS, TRANSLATED BY DAVID SWENSON, PRINCETON UNIVERSITY PRESS, 46)

For Kierkegaard, Jesus Christ as true God and true Man was 'the Absolute Paradox', and Luther's thought was rooted in paradoxes. However, he did not see the revealed God and the hidden God as contradicting each other. Rather they were held in tension: they might appear to be contradictory but in fact were not. Luther thought in terms of the unity of God, which is the reason why the death of the Son of God is central to his theology.

In Luther's understanding, God, the creator and preserver of life, is hidden in the suffering and dying Jesus. This means for him that God is not absent but present in the cruelty of the crucifixion, which opposes everything for which God stands. The same is true for all the suffering and evil people experience: human beings are not left to their own devices, they are not alone in their suffering – God is present in these and God is also hidden. For Luther it would have been terrifying to assume that there are parts of life where God is not present, as this would have meant the abandonment of those parts of human existence to the devil. Luther preferred to accept and live with the very real and unresolved problem of exactly *how* God is present in death and suffering, rather than to believe that God was absent from them and had abandoned these areas of life. In Luther's view, evil will not have the final word. As Alister E. McGrath (*Luther's Theology of the Cross*) has pointed out, Luther's theology of the hidden presence and of the hidden work of God in the world is a theology of hope for all those who despair over suffering.

It is due to Luther taking seriously the negative experience of life, in which God is not seen as the creator and preserver of life, that he rejects the idea of any theology based on the glory of God. Instead he focuses on a theology of the cross. A positive theology of glory which starts by praising God the creator and his creative majesty would also result in praising human beings, as well as their rational and moral characteristics. This implies a generally positive understanding of human beings which Luther rejected. Luther's refusal to see human beings in a positive light is due to his view that this represents a subtle version of the idea that human beings can be justified by their works rather than by their faith and trust in God. Luther's alternative aims not only to arrive at a true understanding of God but also of human beings. Above all he wishes to guard against the human propensity to overestimate themselves and their own abilities. The way to God does not, for Luther, represent a religious ascent of the individual through the practice of good works and gradually growing intellectual awareness of God. Instead it is characterized by a receptiveness to God and God's word. A person can become open to God not through personal religious efforts and practices but in coming to see their own worthlessness and helplessness and the extent of their reliance on God's goodness and love. Concentration on the Cross of Christ was not a theological invention of Luther's own, it has been present throughout Christian history. Luther's theology is distinctive, however, in that, starting from the Cross, he does not lead people away from worldly affairs but takes them even deeper into all the uncertainty and contingency of the reality of human life.

Luther did not consider theology to be a theoretical but a practical discipline, because its knowledge is not about God and God's activities unrelated to human life. He rather considers God in relationship to human beings. Practical knowledge of theology has to be combined with a kind of passivity, in which people can be still and yet attentive to hear and receive God and his word – and to do nothing more. Passivity is not the same as showing no interest, but means only to dispense with our own activities for the sake of an ever higher concentration and attention to God. Doing theology means investing one's own life in the enterprise – one cannot do theology as a detached observer. Because of this, a personal risk is always involved: the risk of involving one's own personal life in the search for truth and understanding about human beings in relation to God. If one is unwilling to embark on this quest, one will not be able to do theology as Luther envisaged it. Theology, therefore, is quite the opposite from a boring, irrelevant subject concerned with dusty texts and ancient ideas and doctrines – it is rather to do with understanding God and human beings in their relation to each other.

Theology will always continue and develop as long as the story of God's relationship with human beings continues. It is an ongoing exploration process. Theology arises out of a lived faith which is tested time and again. In Luther's understanding it is essential that an individual's faith should be challenged if he or she is to be a theologian. In the introduction to *The Freedom of a Christian* Luther writes about Christian faith:

> It is impossible to write well about it or to understand what has been written about it unless one has at one time or another experienced the courage which faith gives a man when trials oppress him. (LW 31, 343)

For Luther no one can be a theologian who is not related existentially to God, and whose faith has not been tested by the fact that his or her faith does not appear to correspond to his or her experiences in the world. When a person, in a concrete situation, finds themselves unable to trust in the Gospel and promises of God, Luther considers this to be a trial of their faith and their relation to God. The same happens when God's love and grace remain hidden for people in their concrete experiences of life. Then God may be experienced as distant from a person or even as rejecting that person. But for Luther such trials of faith are necessary on the journey of faith, and will continue throughout one's whole life, and doubts and uncertainties are bound to occur. The only way out of trial is to turn to God, to argue with and complain to God, and to remind God of the promises given in God's word. In particular, a glance at Jesus Christ in his fear of death in Gethsemane (Mark 14:32–42), which was the great trial of the Son of God, will help a person not to lapse into despair. In Luther's understanding, trials are part of a living relationship with God, which cause people to argue with God and through this to intensify their relation to God.

Epilogue: Luther's Death

Martin Luther died on 18 February 1546 at the age of sixty-two. On 16 February he wrote the last of his extant written statements. In this, the last line reads:

We are beggars. That is true. (LW 54, 476)

This was the end of a short paragraph, which deals with the understanding of Scripture. Compared with the plenty which Holy Scripture contains, Luther considered that human beings are like beggars who may nevertheless hope to receive a portion of the fullness of life which Scripture speaks about.

In January 1546 Luther travelled to the small town of Eisleben for negotiations with the Counts of Mansfeld, to help them settle some problems in their family and in the organization of the town. He already had a presentiment of death. However, as he frequently did, he talked about the possibility of his own death with humour. On the journey he was accompanied by his three sons and his friend Justus Jonas. When they crossed the River Saale, which was dangerous because of high water, he said to Justus Jonas how enjoyable it would be for the devil if he, his sons and Jonas were to be drowned. However, he was only humorous about his own death – when others were dying he showed deep compassion and grief. He wept for a whole day following the death of a friend, and when his eight-month-old daughter Elisabeth died on 3 August 1528 he wrote in a letter:

My baby daughter, little Elisabeth, has passed away. It is amazing
what a sick, almost woman-like heart she has left to me, so much has
grief for her overcome me. Never before would I have believed that a
father's heart could have such tender feelings for his child. Do pray to
the Lord for me. (LW 49, 203)

Despite all grief and even temptations to his faith through the
death of others, Luther believed that Jesus Christ once and for all
had broken the power of death. In a song he wrote:

That was a right wondrous strife
When Death in Life's grip wallowed:
Off victorious came Life,
Death he has quite upswallowed ...
Thus Death is become a laughter.
(*HYMN, 'DEATH HELD OUR LORD IN PRISON', LW 53, 257*)

Because of his belief in God having defeated death, Luther could
react to it with humour and with laughter though also with
anger. He knew its reality amidst human life, but he believed that
the Gospel of Jesus Christ had enabled Christians to say:

In the midst of death we are in Life's embraces.

Even in the hour of his own death he believed he was held in the
embrace of the God of life. On 17 February his health fluctuated.
Before supper he complained about pains in the chest, which
faded when hot towels were applied. At supper he ate and drank
well; his conversation was as usual a mixture of humour and seriousness. After his evening prayer Luther slept first on a sofa. He
awoke at a quarter past ten to go to bed. At one in the morning he
awoke, stood up and complained about a strong pain in the chest,
which presumably was caused by a heart attack. Doctors were
called, but Luther knew his end had come. He thanked God, and in

his fear comforted himself with words taken from the gospel of John and the psalms, particularly Psalm 68:20, 'To God, the Lord, belongs escape from death'. Then he prayed three times very quickly: 'Father, into thy hands I commit my spirit; thou hast redeemed me, O Lord, faithful God' (Luke 23:46 and Psalm 31:5). Thereafter he remained silent, and at a quarter to three in the morning, died.

Elector John Frederick of Sachsen insisted that Luther's remains were buried in Wittenberg. On 22 February interment took place near the pulpit of the Castle Church, where Luther's earthly remains have rested throughout the centuries.

Luther's ideas live on in the churches and the people he has inspired. It was Luther's unconditional commitment to the truth of the word of God which caused the Reformation. This commitment to truth should be at the centre of the life of all Christian churches, and this is the main heritage he has left to the world.

Suggested Further Reading

Luther's writings

Beside the large American edition of Luther's work with more than 50 volumes (see Abbreviations), there are smaller editions, which give a selection of his writings.

Brokering, H.F, (ed.), *Luther's Prayers*, Fortress Press, 1994.

Dillenberger, John (ed.), *Martin Luther, Selections from his Writings*, Doubleday, 1961.

Lull, Timothy F. (ed.), *Martin Luther's, Basic Theological Writings*, Fortress Press, 1989.

Pederson, Ph.E. (ed.), *What Does This Mean? Luther's Catechisms Today*, Augsburg Publishing House, 1979.

Porter, J. M. (ed.), *Martin Luther, Selected Political Writings*, University Press of America, 1988.

Rupp, E. B. and Drewery, B. (eds.), *Martin Luther*, Edward Arnold, London, 1970 (an anthology of Luther).

Russell, W. R. (ed.), *The Schmalkald Articles: Luther's Theological Testament*, Fortress Press, 1995.

Basic Luther. Four of His Fundamental Works, Templegate Publishers, 1994.

Martin Luther, The Bondage of the Will, James Clarke & Co., Cambridge, 1957 (and Revell Fleming, 1990).

Martin Luther, Table Talk, Fount, 1995. (A selection of recollections, by friends and family, of things Luther said informally. An easily

accessible and personal account of the German Reformation.)
Martin Luther, Three Treatises, Fortress Press, 1970. (Includes three of Luther's main writings of 1520: *To the Christian Nobility of the German Nation; The Babylonian Captivity of the Church; The Freedom of a Christian*.)

Writings about Luther's life and theology

Althaus, Paul, *The Theology of Martin Luther*, Fortress Press, 1966.
Atkinson, James, *Martin Luther and the Birth of Protestantism*, 1982.
Bainton, Roland H., *Here I Stand. A Life of Martin Luther*, Abingdon Press, 1978 (new edition: Lion Publishing, 1994).
Jüngel, Eberhard, *The Freedom of a Christian. Luther's Significance for Contemporary Theology*, Augsburg Publishing House, 1988.
Kittelson, James M., *Luther the Reformer*, Augsburg Publishing House, 1987.
Lindsay, Thomas Martin, *Martin Luther*, Christian Focus Publications, 1996.
Lohse, Bernhard, *Martin Luther. An Introduction to his Life and Work*, T. & T. Clark, Edinburgh, 1987.
McGrath, Alister E., *Luther's Theology of the Cross. Martin Luther's Theological Breakthrough*, Blackwell, Oxford, 1990.
Mullett, Michael A., *Luther*, Routledge, 1994.
Oberman, Heiko A., *Luther. Man between God and the Devil*, Fontana Press, 1993.
Rupp, Gordon, *Luther and Erasmus*, Westminster Press, 1978.
Smith, Preserved, *The Life and Letters of Martin Luther*, Hodder & Stoughton, London, 1993.

Books on the age of the Reformation

erman, Heiko A., *Dawn of the Reformation. Essays in Late edieval and Early Reformation Thought*, T. & T. Clark, burgh, 1992.

Ozment, Steven E., *The Age of Reform (1250–1550). An Intellectual and Religious History of Late Medieval and Reformation Europe*, Yale University Press, 1981.

Ozment, Steven E., *Protestants. The Birth of a Revolution*, Fontana Press, 1993.

Randell, Keith, *Luther and the German Reformation. 1517–55*, Hodder & Stoughton, 1989. (This was planned with the A-level student specifically in mind.)